SUSTAINABLE AND RESPONSIBLE TOURISM

SUSTAINABLE AND RESPONSIBLE TOURISM
Trends, Practices and Cases

Edited by
PARIKSHAT SINGH MANHAS
Associate Professor
The Business School and School of Hospitality and Tourism Management
University of Jammu
Jammu & Kashmir

PHI Learning Private Limited
New Delhi-110001
2012

₹ 350.00

SUSTAINABLE AND RESPONSIBLE TOURISM: Trends, Practices and Cases
Edited by Parikshat Singh Manhas

ISBN-978-81-203-4564-5

Published by Asoke K. Ghosh, PHI Learning Private Limited, M-97, Connaught Circus, New Delhi-110001 and Printed by Rajkamal Electric Press, Plot No. 2, Phase IV, HSIDC, Kundli-131028, Sonepat, Haryana.

To
My Grandparents
Dr. Janki Nath Manhas
&
Smt. Durga Devi

CONTENTS

Foreword *xvii*

Preface *xix*

List of Contributors *xxv*

Section I
SUSTAINABLE AND RESPONSIBLE TOURISM

Chapter 1 REGIONAL DEVELOPMENT AND SUSTAINABILITY: Cultural Tourism in the Southern Region of Jallsco **3–25**

—José G. Vargas-Hernández

1.1 Abstract *3*
1.2 Introduction *3*
1.3 Theoretical Background and Literature Review *6*
1.4 Methods *9*
1.5 Determination of The Demand of Cultural Tourism *9*
  1.5.1 Mexican Tourism in the Hierarchy of the Countries of the World in the Year 2004 *9*
  1.5.2 Economic Impact of Tourism Sector in Mexico *11*
  1.5.3 Growth *12*
1.6 Profile of Tourists with Cultural Statement *13*
1.7 Motivations and Satisfaction of Cultural Tourists *13*
1.8 Market Potential *14*
1.9 Details of the Offer of Tourist Destinations—Cultural *14*
1.10 Operations of Cultural Tourism's Business *15*
  1.10.1 Cultural Tourism Sectors *15*
1.11 SWOT Corporate Analysis *16*
1.12 Design of Cultural Tours Circuits in Southern Jalisco *17*
  1.12.1 Cultural Tourism Circuit "Footsteps in the Land of Great Artists ..." *17*

1.12.2 Cultural Tourism Circuit "at the Feast Eternal" *18*
1.12.3 Cultural Tours "Townships on The Lake's Rivera" *19*
1.12.4 Cultural Tours *20*

1.13 Business Development Strategies of Cultural Tourism *20*
1.14 Conclusion and Recommendations *21*

References *23*

Chapter 2 THE APPLICATION OF SUSTAINABLE TOURISM INDICATORS IN THE DEVELOPMENT OF TAMAN RIMBA TELOK BAHANG, PENANG, MALAYSIA **26–41**

—JABIL MAPJABIL AND AZIZAN MARZUKI

2.1 Abstract *26*
2.2 Introduction *27*
2.3 Literature Review on Sustainable Tourism and Amenity Forests *28*
2.4 Sustainable Tourism Concept and Indicators *31*
2.5 Development of Amenity Forests in Penang *33*
2.6 Research Methodology *35*

2.6.1 Research Sample *35*
2.6.2 Research Design *36*
2.6.3 Instrument *37*

2.7 Research Findings and Discussion *36*
2.8 Conclusion *40*

References *40*

Chapter 3 RURAL TOURISM DEVELOPMENT: Constraints and Potential with Special Reference to Agri-Tourism (A Case Study on Cashew Agri-Tourism Destination—Rajendrapattinam Village in Vriddachalam Taluk of Cuddalore District, Tamil Nadu) **42–53**

—A. BALAMURUGAN, R. KANNAN AND S.K. NAGARAJAN

3.1 Abstract *42*
3.2 Introduction *43*

3.2.1 The Indian Agriculture and Tourism Industry Scenario *43*
3.2.2 Domestic Tourism Growth *43*
3.2.3 Tourism Potential in Tamil Nadu *43*

3.3 Objectives of the Study *44*
3.4 Research Methodology *44*
3.5 Components of Rural Tourism *44*

3.5.1 Defining Agri-Tourism *45*
3.5.2 Advantages of Agri-Tourism *45*
3.5.3 Scope of Agri-Tourism *45*
3.5.4 Basic Principles of Agri-Tourism *46*

3.5.5 Three Important Factors, Which Contribute to the Success of Agri-Tourism as Service *46*
3.5.6 Some Important Factors *46*
3.5.7 Objectives of the Agriculture Development Trust *48*
3.5.8 Formation of Agri-Tourism Development Corporation *49*
3.5.9 TNAU's Role in Agri-Tourism *49*
3.5.10 Attractions *50*

3.6 Discussions *50*
3.7 Suggestions and Recommendations *51*
3.8 Conclusion *52*

References *52*

Chapter 4 CHANGING EXPECTATIONS OF TRADITIONAL PILGRIMS: An Analysis of Expectations and Motivations of Tourists Visiting Badri-Kedar Tourism Zone **54–68**

—S.K. GUPTA AND VIJAY PRAKASH BHATT

4.1 Abstract *54*
4.2 Introduction *55*

4.2.1 The Study Area *55*
4.2.2 Tourism Resources of the Area *56*

4.3 Objective *58*
4.4 Review of Literature *58*
4.5 Research Methodology *58*
4.6 Result and Discussion *59*
4.7 Travel Related Information *59*
4.8 Expectations of Tourists While Choosing the Study Area as a Destination *60*
4.9 Motivations of Tourists Visiting the Study Area *61*
4.10 Conclusion *63*

References *64*
ANNEXURES *66*

Chapter 5 A COMPARATIVE ANALYSIS OF MWALUGHANJE ELEPHANT SANCTUARY AND RUKINGA WILDLIFE SANCTUARY IN KENYA **69–84**

—MARGARET WACHU GICHUHI

5.1 Abstract *69*
5.2 Introduction *70*

5.2.1 Mwalughanje Elephant Sanctuary *70*
5.2.2 Rukinga Wildlife Sanctuary *72*

5.3 Literature Review *74*
5.4 Materials and Methods *77*
5.5 Discussions *83*
5.6 Conclusion and Recommendations *83*

References *84*

Chapter 6 ENVIRONMENTAL PRACTICES IN A MEDIUM SIZE HOTEL: A Case Study Approach **85–107**

—Sharleen Howison and Dagmar Cronaner

6.1 Abstract *85*
6.2 Introduction *86*
6.2.1 Background *86*
6.2.2 Literature Review *86*
6.2.3 Challenges of Sustainable Practice *86*
6.2.4 Impact on the Environment *87*
6.2.5 Implementation of Innovative Environmentally Friendly Strategies *87*
6.2.6 Environmental Practices in Hotels *88*
6.2.7 Environmental Customer Awareness *90*
6.2.8 Corporate Social Responsibility *90*
6.3 Methodology *91*
6.3.1 Case Study Approach *91*
6.3.2 Interviews *92*
6.3.3 Questionnaires *92*
6.3.4 Documentation *92*
6.3.5 Observation *93*
6.4 Analysis *93*
6.4.1 Interviews *93*
6.4.2 Questionnaires *94*
6.4.3 Documentation *97*
6.4.4 Internal Information on Sustainability *97*
6.4.5 Environmental Plan *97*
6.4.6 Environmental Tick List *98*
6.4.7 Qualmark Rating *99*
6.4.8 The Newspaper Handling *99*
6.4.9 Information for Customers *99*
6.4.10 Suppliers *99*
6.4.11 Observation *100*
6.5 Discussion *102*
6.5.1 The Education of Guests *102*
6.5.2 The Communication to Staff *103*
6.5.3 Staff Training *103*
6.5.4 The Customer and Staff's Attitude Towards Sustainable Development *104*
6.5.5 Study Limitations *105*
6.6 Conclusion and Recommendations *105*
6.6.1 Recommendations *105*
References *106*

Chapter 7 **PLANNING CONSIDERATIONS FOR TOURISM IN THE MINHO-LIME REGION (Northwest Portugal)** **108–123**

—PAULA CRISTINA REMOALDO, J. CADIMA RIBEIRO, LAURENTINA CRUZ VAREIRO AND MÉCIA CUNHA MOTA

7.1 Abstract *108*
7.2 Introduction *109*
7.2.1 Territorial Tourism Resources and Cultural Tourism *110*
7.3 Methodology *111*
7.4 Evaluation of the Tourism Strategies Followed in the Minho-Lima Region *114*
7.4.1 Tourism Resources and Stated Preferences *114*
7.4.2 Results Obtained from the Interviews *116*
7.4.3 Resources Available *116*
7.4.4 Tourism and Local and Regional Development *118*
7.4.5 Territorial Promotional Organization of Tourism *118*
7.4.6 The National Strategic Tourism Plan *119*
7.5 Conclusion *120*
References *121*

Section II
COMMUNITY DEVELOPMENT BY TOURISM

Chapter 8 **DEVELOPMENT OF A STANDARD MEASUREMENT SCALE TO MEASURE COMMUNITY ATTITUDE TOWARDS IMPACTS OF TOURISM IN MALAYSIA** **127–153**

— NURHAZANI MOHD. SHARIFF, NOR ASYIKIN MOHD. NOR, JASMINE ZEA RAZIAH RADHA RASHID RADHA AND HASNI HASNAH CHE ISMAIL

8.1 Abstract *127*
8.2 Introduction *128*
8.3 Problem Statement *128*
8.4 Malaysia as a Tourist Destination *129*
8.5 Literature Review *129*
8.6 Methodology *132*
8.7 Results of Data Analysis *133*
8.7.1 Respondents' Characteristics *133*
8.7.2 Items Generation *133*
8.7.3 Expert Survey *134*
8.7.4 Scale Purification *134*
8.7.5 Scale Verification *134*
8.8 Discussion of Findings *137*
8.9 Implications and Contributions *142*

8.10 Limitations and Recommendations for Future Study *143*
8.11 Conclusion *143*

References *144*
APPENDICES *148*

Chapter 9 COMMUNITY-BASED ECOTOURISM AND SUSTAINABLE DEVELOPMENT SUPPORTED BY CASE STUDY: Kumaon Himalayas (Lake District of Uttarakhand) **154–168**

—BIPIN CHANDRA PANT

9.1 Abstract *154*
9.2 Introduction *155*
9.3 Objectives *156*
9.4 Methodology *156*

9.4.1 Green Tourism Concerns *156*

9.5 Problems *160*
9.6 Solutions *160*
9.7 Further Suggestions *161*
9.8 Recommendations *164*
9.9 Conclusion *165*

References *166*
Websites *167*

Section III
CASE STUDIES AND PRACTICES ON TOURISM TRENDS

Chapter 10 TOURIST'S USE OF PUBLIC TRANSPORT INFORMATION: A Case Study in Penang Island **171–179**

—NG KOK MENG

10.1 Abstract *171*
10.2 Introduction *171*
10.3 Literature Review *172*

10.3.1 Penang as an International Destination *172*
10.3.2 Information Resources for Visitor in Penang Island *173*
10.3.3 Significance of Information in Public Transport Service *173*
10.3.4 Visitors' Use of Public Transport Information *174*

10.4 Methodology *174*
10.5 Findings *175*
10.6 Conclusion *178*
10.7 Recommendations for Penang's Government and Local Authority *178*

References *179*

Chapter 11 REBUILDING DESTINATION FUNCTIONALITY: A Strategic Framework Towards Crisis Communication **180–196**

—PARIKSHAT SINGH MANHAS AND ZUBAIR AHMAD DADA

11.1 Abstract *180*
11.2 Introduction *181*
11.2.1 An Epistemological Approach towards Tourism Crisis Management *181*
11.3 Review of Literature *187*
11.4 Discussion *188*
11.4.1 Framework for Crisis Management—A Case Study of Jammu and Kashmir *188*
11.4.2 The Crisis Management Taskforce *190*
11.4.3 The Crisis Management Manual *191*
11.4.4 Collaborating with Law Enforcement Agencies *192*
11.5 Summary and Conclusion *192*
References *194*

Chapter 12 TRUST IN THE ONLINE HOTEL BOOKING DECISION **197–208**

—PAULINE RATNASINGAM AND KULDEEP KUMAR

12.1 Abstract *197*
12.2 Introduction *197*
12.2.1 Three Parts of the Online Booking Decision Making *199*
12.2.2 Entities in the Trusting Relationship *199*
12.2.3 Trust in the Hotel Industry *200*
12.2.4 Types of Trust *201*
12.3 Conclusion *206*
References *207*

Chapter 13 ENDOGENOUS PROJECT ON RURAL TOURISM: A Case Study of Kalamkari **209–219**

—P. SIVA SANKARA REDDY

13.1 Abstract *209*
13.2 Introduction *210*
13.3 Concept of Rural Tourism *212*
13.3.1 Enhancement of Artisan Skills *213*
13.4 Creation of Tourism Infrastructure *214*
13.5 Awareness of Local Community *214*
13.5.1 Direct Revenue and Employment Generation *215*
13.5.2 Contribution of the Local Community *216*
13.5.3 Impediments in Implementation *217*
13.6 Conclusion *218*
References *218*

Chapter 14 CAUSALITY BETWEEN TOURISM AND EDUCATION **220–226**

—G.S. PREMA KUMARA AND RIYAZ AHMAD

14.1 Abstract *220*
14.2 Introduction *221*
14.3 Literature Review *221*
14.4 Methodology *222*

14.4.1 Trend Analysis *222*
14.4.2 Causality Analysis *224*
14.4.3 Impact of Tourism on Education *224*

14.5 Conclusion *225*

References *225*

Chapter 15 GREENING THE MARIKINA CITY: Cycling as an Alternative Transportation **227–239**

—JOY SHEELAH BARAERO-ERA AND EVANGELINE E. TIMBANG

15.1 Introduction *227*
15.2 Background of the Study *228*
15.3 Statement of the Problem *228*
15.4 Review of Related Literature and Studies *229*

15.4.1 Tourism and Sustainability *229*
15.4.2 Tourism Policy *229*
15.4.3 Tourism and Transportation *230*
15.4.4 Cycling as an Alternative Transportation *230*

15.5 Conceptual Framework *232*
15.6 Findings of the Study *233*

15.6.1 Destination's Vision *233*
15.6.2 Ensuring Good Access between and among Different Areas of the City *234*
15.6.3 Defining Space *234*
15.6.4 Making Memorable Spaces *234*
15.6.5 Marikina Bikeways Programme *234*
15.6.6 Changing Mindset *234*
15.6.7 Bikeways Facilities *235*
15.6.8 Education and Promotion Campaign *235*
15.6.9 Kapihan *235*
15.6.10 Bike to School Programme *236*
15.6.11 Bicycle Safety Education Classes *236*

15.7 Low Cost Factor *236*

15.7.1 Bike Loan Programme (Bicycle Loan Project, City Ordinance 92 Series of 2004) *236*
15.7.2 Recognition *237*

15.8 Summary and Conclusion *237*
15.9 Recommendation and Future Direction *238*

References *238*
Websites *239*

Chapter 16 THE STUDY OF RELATIONSHIP BETWEEN CLIMATE AND ANNUAL TOURISM TRENDS CONDITION: Case of Tabriz, Iran **240–251**

—BANAFSHEH M. FARAHANI AND JAFAR MOSIVAND

16.1 Abstract *240*
16.2 Introduction *241*
16.2.1 Importance of Climate in Tourism *241*
16.2.2 Tourism Climate Index (TCI) *243*
16.3 Case Study *244*
16.4 Methodology *245*
16.4.1 TCI Index *246*
16.5 Analysis and Result *247*
16.7 Conclusion and Recommendation *249*

References *249*

INDEX *253–255*

FOREWORD

Tourism has become one of the major sectors of our economy as it makes a major contribution to our Gross National Domestic Product (GDP). Not only it employs a large number of skilled, semi-skilled and non-skilled human resources, both directly and indirectly, but also plays a very important role in bridging the social and political divides. But over the last many years, tourism has been proving to be a nuisance for the environmental and ecological balance as it has had a negative impact on the environment. Generally, in lieu of our short-term financial gains, we tend to forget the long-term environmental implications—it's a simple fact that tourism will continue to flourish as long as we are sensitive to our environment. Therefore, for tourism to be sustainable in the long run, we have to be both ecologically and culturally sensitive because the local environment and the local culture are the two main pillars of our tourism industry. In simple words, immediate financial gains from tourism should not blind us to our responsibilities towards our environment and ecology.

In the long run, the most important thing that would matter more than anything else for tourism is gojng to be one key word: *sustainability*. Sustainability in tourism, according to the UNEP, "refers to the environmental, economic, and socio-cultural aspects of tourism development, and a suitable balance amongst these three dimensions to guarantee its long-term sustainability. Thus, sustainable tourism should:

1. Make optimal use of environmental resources that constitute a key element in tourism development, maintaining essential ecological processes and helping to conserve natural heritage and biodiversity.
2. Respect the socio-cultural authenticity of host communities, conserve their built and living cultural heritage and traditional values, and contribute to inter-culmral understanding and tolerance.
3. Ensure viable, long-term economic operations, providing socio-economic benefits to all stakeholders that are fairly distributed, including stable employment and income-earning opportunities and social services to host communities, and contributing to poverty alleviation."

In a nutshell, *Sustainable* tourism and *Responsive* tourism aim three things: *environmental integrity, social justice and maximization of local economic benefits.*

But for this to happen, we all have a duty to ensure that fragile environments are preserved for future generations as Gandhiji had said long time back that the gracious earth can only afford our need, not greed. And so, we should strive to undertake sustainable practices in everything we do—making little contributions leading to big changes. Starting at home, one ought to, lead by example. We should also try to encourage such responsibility among other fellow beings by getting them involved with the community in environment enhancing. The concern and the will to get involved by those who travel to any destination is a must to make a difference to the places we visit.

Not only this, we should fully assess our tourism infrastructure from a community and environmental perspective: All the tourism properties we put up should have full commitment to improve the environment and/or to work with local communities thereby making tourism more sustainable.

Can there be any better way to protect our important natural and cultural wonders than to create an impression on today's children? We have to strive for special children programmes that sensitize our younger generation towards the fragility of the environment; and, hence, they are accordingly groomed to instil a sense of social obligation towards environmental protection. We can also make extensive use of the information technology not only to awaken the communities and tourists about the responsive part of tourism but also for sharing information (both positive and negative) from different spectrums of the global society—eventually leading to a web of communication resulting in a sort of codifying universally acceptable/applicable moral codes for sustainable tourism.

This book covers discussions on the above mentioned concepts of sustainable and responsible tourism practices. Furthermore, it also helps and contributes in guiding newer directions by widening the horizons of tourism sustainability and responsible practices.

I personally appreciate the efforts of the editor for bringing out this resource in the form of an edited book which provides vibrant insights in one of the most important and relevant topics of this era: sustainability and responsible tourism practice. The academicians and thinkers also deserve the appreciation for their research contributions which further helps in widening the existing literature on tourism in general and sustainable and responsible tourism practices in particular.

NAWANG RIGZIN JORA
Hon'ble Cabinet Minister
Tourism & Culture
Government of Jammu & Kashmir
India

PREFACE

This book is divided into three sections based on major thematic areas related to the practical approaches and case studies, which will ultimately enhance the existing set of knowledge. This book contains the information which is empirically proved and conceptually viable and hence will provide new insights to academicians as well as to the practicing managers in the tourism and hospitality industry across the globe.

Chapter 1 aims to propose a normative model to determine the potential of cultural tourism in the municipalities that comprise the region 6 of the State of Jalisco, territorially delimited in the South of Jalisco, Mexico. Furthermore, the author discusses the motivations and satisfactions of cultural tourists to establish the potential market in accordance with the characteristics of the target market. According to him, any operation of cultural tourism companies should make the strategic diagnosis and perform SWOT analysis for strategic planning of cultural tourism enterprises. He proposes developmental strategies of promoting cultural tourism in the region of Southern Jalisco, Mexico. In this chapter, the main focus is on normative model of cultural tourism which shows an impact on the spatial framework, addresses the sustainability of cultural tourism on cultural sites and attractions. He proposes strategies for economic development of the communities which can help in creating employment and improving living standards of the people. This analysis may kickstart further research about cultural and heritage tourism development, marketing and promotion in Southern Jalisco.

Chapter 2 discusses the practical aspects of sustainable tourism. According to the authors, sustainable indicators are used to measure the changes, identify the processes involved and prepare the framework for the target procedure and performance observation. These indicators provide the method to draw the development chart towards the importance of achieving a balanced style of development in social, economic and environmental fields as the main objective in the sustainable development of a country. Development of a good tourism product and destination could attract more tourists from in and out of the country. It could also generate revenue not only for the government but also for the local people, either directly or indirectly. However, if sustainable tourism is not managed carefully, selectively and thoroughly, it could cause lot more trouble than gaining profit. Therefore, this tourism product needs to be developed comprehensively and effectively in line with the government's goal to introduce Malaysia as a sustainable tourism destination in the world's eyes. Therefore, planning, development and management of a tourism product need consideration from various aspects starting from the policy formulation, strategy, tourism programme development which covers marketing, activity organizing and maintenance, and so on. Besides that, integrating thoughts and opinions is very much needed to implement sustainable tourism development because it should not involve only government institutions but also the support from the professional groups, public sector, nature based organizations and the public.

Chapter 3 dwells on constraints and potential of rural tourism. The rural tourism concept is well accepted all over the world and people travel not only to see places of interest, but also for the opportunity to interact with the locals and to an extent even get introduced to their culture. Tamil Nadu has significant tourist potential and it promotes tourism agrresively and it is advocated by the tourism agencies to get away from the mindset of looking only at the foreign tourist. As the earning power of the young, specifically the software professionals and urban city dwellers, are on the rise, one should also target and cater to the needs of this segment of tourist. According to the authors, it may be worthwhile looking into setting up of the Centre for Rural Tourism (CRT) next to the existing cultural and other tourist centre spots; this will facilitate the people who are visiting places like Chidambaram to do other activities in the village like milking the cow, etc. We can also tie up with organizations like Dakhinchitra with CRT. These should be run as a franchise with the local villager owning the capital investment and managing the day-to-day operations and the tourist operator/hotel chain managing to ensure safe and quality tourism experieinces.

The study area of Chapter 4 is Devbhoomi, Uttarakhand, known for its majestic natural beauty, mighty rivers, lofty mountains, valleys of flowers, rich plethora of floral and faunal wealth, colourful traditions, hearty hospitality of its inhabitants and world famous pilgrim centres like Haridwar, Rishikesh, Badrinath, Kedarnath, Hemkund, etc. These have been quenching the curiosity of pilgrims, wanderers and nature lovers and satisfying their needs for self-actualization, finding peace and salvation for years. With the rapid pace of technological advancements in the field of communication and infrastructural facilities in the region along with significant changes in demographic factors such as level of education, income, lifestyles and availability of leisure among the people of tourist generating areas, the motivations of the traditional pilgrims visiting the region have shifted from traditional pilgrimage to pilgrimage cum holiday making and also their expectation about the availability of activities and supporting facilities in the destination areas. The present chapter is an attempt to analyze the changing pattern of motivations and expectations of the tourists visiting Badrinath and Kedarnath tourist zone in the Garhwal Region of Uttarakhand. The chapter further discloses that expectations of the tourists/pilgrims have also significantly increased about the availability of variety of quality accommodation, nature and wildlife, public utility services and local culture and tradition. Further, a significant shift has been found in importance of various motivational factors determining the visit of tourists visiting this area. The chapter explores that natural beauty is the most important motivational factor, followed by holiday/sightseeing, pilgrimage and adventure.

This study given in Chapter 5, was carried out at the Mwalughanje Elephant Sanctuary, which was set up to create a corridor for movement of animals from Shimba Hills National Reserve (Kenya) to a nearby forested area. It is a community conservancy set up to involve the community in managing and appreciating wildlife resources to help reduce human-wildlife conflict. There is a tented camp, cultural centre where women weave baskets, brand T-shirts and make paper using elephant dung. The objectives of the chapter were to assess ecological linkages, climate change and interactions between human activities, i.e. farming, livestock keeping, tourism and the parks, analyze the socio-economic benefits that may accrue from sustainable management of resources and to identify measures for conflict resolution. Data collection was carried out using interviews and questionnaires. The population size for Mwalughanje was 28 respondents and the entire population was used as a sample. The Rukinga Sanctuary had a total population of 41 respondents who were all used for the purposeful data collection. The variables explored in this study are type of resources, resource conflicts, type of conflict, stakeholder communication, diminishing resources, community welfare, conservancy benefits, best land use, conservation of resources, knowledge of managing resources. The results indicated that the increase of human population and the resultant diminishing natural resources have led to human-wildlife conflict. However, the members of Mwalughanje Conservancy appreciated the wildlife resources more since they benefitted from eco-tourism and they are more committed to the conservancy since they own it. The chapter concludes that we need to involve the communities in issues of wildlife conservation and management, sustainable resource utilization and eco-tourism.

The purpose of Chapter 6 was to identify the factors which are important in achieving long-term sustainability in a medium sized New Zealand hotel. The hotel industry is increasingly under pressure to meet the growing demand for the so-called "green" products and services. As customers are becoming more aware of the importance of preserving the environment for future generations, it is also important to know that the concept of sustainable business practice is a crucial component in the management of hotel businesses today. This chapter provides us with some common issues, which can have an effect on the intention to achieve long-term sustainability. There are three main themes identified within this chapter, viz. the education of the guests, the communication between management and staff, and the customer and staff's attitude towards sustainable development.

Chapter 7 focuses on administering the territories to preserve their natural, historical and ethnographical resources while simultaneously using them to increase revenue and employment. In order to efficiently promote the products and services available and attract tourists, decision makers, private and public, need to know and incorporate tourists' preferences in their marketing strategies. In this chapter, the authors illustrate the use of stated preferences as an instrument to identify national and foreign tourists' preferences regarding the products and services that the touristic destination of the Minho-Lima region (Northwest Portugal) should offer. The chapter concludes that the resources to which the tourists' attribute more importance were oceanic beaches and national parks or protected landscape.

Chapter 8 presents a study conducted in Malaysia with the intention to develop a standard measurement scale to measure the community attitude towards tourism impacts named as MACTIAS. The procedures of developing MACTIAS involved five stages including the generation of the item pool, testing for content validity and scale purification using a pre-test sample. The results indicated that seven factors were derived but only three factors were confirmed. The next stage involved scale verification using Malaysian community as the main respondents. The study confirms MACTIAS as a valid and reliable scale which can be used to measure the community attitudes in other tourism destinations.

From an economy based on transit trade and subsistence agriculture, there has been a shift towards tourism in recent times. This shift has been due to the tradition of eco-tourism to the higher reaches and also due to promotion by the state by developing infrastructure and providing incentives. Chapter 9 is divided into four parts including the policies of the colonial state and the events leading to the destruction of forests, large-scale exploitation of Himalayan forests, the growth of ecotourism as a direct outcome of the process of deforestation and as resulting from the need of society to conserve and yet to earn a livelihood is discussed.

Chapter 10 is based on the role of transportation. This chapter presents results of a study of overseas' visitors' use of public transport in Penang Island. Investigation of visitor use and perceptions of public transport information revealed that visitors had a greater requirement for information, particularly in the case of certain information items. In addition, some issues have been highlighted due to the overall experience in the island. The chapter concludes that the availability, accuracy and reliability of public transport information are essentially important in providing exceptional value to tourist experience. As the quality of public transport information in Penang Island is largely out of the public transport authority control, there is a dire need for greater cooperation amongst the state government, local authority as well as other information providers in order to ensure the accessibility of reliable public transport information for the foreign visitors.

The purpose of Chapter 11 is to review the literature on destination crisis communication as a result of crisis events and to discern mechanisms by which crisis communications can be co-conspirators in crisis recovery. Crises and disasters are inevitable and affect the hospitality and tourism industry with disproportionate frequency. In the midst of the considerable economic impact these business generate, when disaster strikes, we may be able to leverage crisis communication strategies to simultaneously enhance speedier disaster recovery and build stronger customer relationships. This study argues that tourist destinations—particularly those prone to politically induced violence—should induct crisis communication planning into their overall sustainable development and marketing/management strategies to protect and remodel their image of wellbeing/attractiveness, to re-establish confidence in prospective visitors of the security of the area, to restore the area's functionality/attractiveness, and to support local travel and tourism industry members in their economic recovery. The discussion and, therefore, the conclusion deliberates on having a crisis management framework in place, institutionalizing a tourism crisis management task-force, building a crisis management manual, and collaborating with law enforcement agencies. The chapter concludes that there is a need to focus on greater research and understanding which is required in the field of crisis communication and theory to help improve the understanding of such incidents. This understanding will hopefully aid in the development of suitable crisis communication models for managers to implement which can be varied depending on the scale and type of crisis or disasters encountered. The cost of developing a crisis management strategy would be far less than the cost of not having one and a key aspect to any crisis strategy is crisis communication.

Chapter 12 examines trust in the online hotel booking decision. The authors have identified two entities in the trust dyad. The first is the trusted party, the hotel whose role is that of a vendor and service provider and the second is the trusting party, the customer or traveller who could be a potential guest staying at the hotel. The chapter addresses both the first or initial (pre-stay) booking decision and the subsequent repeat online booking decisions. They have identified the impact of three types of trust, namely competence, predictability and goodwill trust based on the customer's initial and subsequent booking decisions and factors that facilitate and are likely to change and impact the customer's online booking decision over time. They have developed a conceptual model to illustrate the impact of the customer's trust in the hotel and how it impacts their online hotel booking decision. In this chapter, the authors discuss the impact of the customer's trust in the hotel and how it influences their online hotel booking decisions. The conceptual model of customer's trust in the online hotel booking decision developed in this study, illustrates the impact of three types of customer's trust on their online hotel booking decisions.

Chapter 13 talks about local culture and craft based tourism for sustainable livelihoods and integrated rural development. The aim of the chapter is to study the Kalamkari industry and how the endogenous project helps in the improvement of the social and economic well-being of artisan households through the development of rural tourism. The chapter concludes with the assumption that in order to make the scheme more meaningful, it is very important that the sustenance issues be discussed with the community before the start of the project and software programmes should precede the hardware activities at least six months before and also aggressive marketing of the destinations be taken up with the local and international tour operators.

In Chapter 14, an attempt has been made to analyze the causality between tourism and education. For empirical estimation and analysis, numbers of tourist arrival and literacy rate have been considered as proxy to tourism and education, respectively. It has been found from the analysis that there is an increase in tourist arrivals on the one side and, on the other side, the literacy rate has also increased. The findings reveal that increase in the number of tourist arrivals has resulted in increase in the literacy rate of all three divisions or regions of the study area. The chapter concludes that there is a dire need of development of tourism infrastructure in order to attract more number of visitors and thereby develop the education system in general and increase the enrolment in particular. To summarize, tourism is one of the important determinants of education and it also leads to human development.

Chapter 15 mainly focuses on government and industry policy and concludes that these policies should not only focus on developing tourism for its economic (monetary) benefits but also towards creating and effectively implementing socio-cultural and environmental regulatory frameworks that will both maintain and sustain the tourism industry in the long run and will in turn benefit not only the tourists but also the local/host communities. In this chapter, the community based green tourism oriented ACCESS programme of the city government for greater and much improved citywide mobility and accessibility has been discussed. According to the authors, heavy investments have been made in green initiatives like the introduction of bikeways and other new policies and programmes and these investments are returned over the long term in the form of healthier communities to work and live. This chapter concludes that with the local and global recognitions received, the Biking programme success is not only worth sustaining but also replicating. The sustainability of the Biking project remained to be one of the greatest challenges to the government and the community of the city of Marikina taking into consideration the new administration both at the national and local levels.

Chapter 16 focuses on tourism role and finds that it plays an important economical role for many countries. Different tourists of various profiles, travel to different destinations every day. There are a number of attributes which influence their decision making to travel to the destination in certain time and for specific purpose. Climate and weather are one of the most important attributes which affect tourists' decision making. The importance of climate in tourism cannot be ingored and lots of studies have been done by different perspective in this area. This chapter tries to find the influence of climate on annual tourism trends condition in the city of Tabriz, Iran, which has different climatic conditions throughout the year. The study assessed the climatic condition for tourism by using Tourism Climatic Index (TCI). Moreover, the result of this chapter shows that Tabriz has a variety of climate through the year. This climate distinctiveness of cities like Tabriz can attract un-similar tourists in different months by dissimilar weather.

PARIKSHAT SINGH MANHAS

LIST OF CONTRIBUTORS

A. Balamurugan is Assistant Professor in the Department of Hotel and Catering Management, Sathyabama University. His areas of interest include new product development, entrepreneurship for agriculture.

Azizan Marzuki (PhD) is Senior Lecturer at the School of Housing Building and Planning, Universiti Sains Malaysia and Adjunct Research Associate at the Faculty of Education, Humanities and Law, Flinders University, South Australia. His research interests include tourism planning, urban and regional planning, and public participation in tourism.

Banafsheh M. Farahani is doing PhD in Tourism Business and Marketing in Universiti Sains Malaysia. She has published several papers in the area of tourist behaviour, tourism environmental issues, climate change, peace and tourism, photography and tourism.

Bipin Chandra Pant (PhD) is Assistant Professor, Tourism and Hospitality, Amity University, Noida, India. He has more than 10 years of teaching experience.

Dagmar Cronauer is currently completing a Master of Tourism. Her interests in tourism are focused on environmental issues.

Evangeline E. Timbang is a hospitality management educator for the last 34 years at the University of Santo Tomas, Manila, Philippines. She has served as the former President of the Council of Hotel and Restaurant Educators of the Philippines (COHREP) and at present the Vice President of the Asia Pacific Federation of the Council of Hotel, Restaurant and Institution in Education (APac CHRIE). Timbang is also engaged in various training and consultancy works on food service operations and effective customer relations with the Philippine Department of Tourism as a Master Trainer.

G.S. Premakumara (PhD) is Assistant Professor of Economics at University of Mysore. His research interests include human development and infrastructure and the teaching of econometrics, research methods and data analysis and theoretical economics. He has published numerous articles in both human development and infrastructure.

Hasni Hasnah Che Ismail is Lecturer in School of Tourism, Hospitality and Environmental Management, College of Law, Government and International Studies Universiti Utara Malaysia.

Jabil Mapjabil (PhD) is a Senior Lecturer for Geography Section at the School of Humanities, Universiti Sains Malaysia. His research interests include tourism (ecotourism, sport tourism, dive tourism and homestay) and geography.

Jafar Mosivand has done her MSc degree in Geography and Urban Planning from Tarbiat Moallem University in Tehran.

Jasmine Zea Raziah Radha Rashid Radha is Lecturer, School of Tourism, Hospitality and Environmental Management, College of Law, Government and International Studies, Universiti Utara, Malaysia.

José Cadima Ribeiro (Leiria, Portugal) is full Professor of Regional Economics in the Department of Economics of the School of Economics and Management, University of Minho, Portugal.

José G. Vargas-Hernández is a member of the National System of Researchers of Mexico and a Research Professor at University Centre for Economic and Managerial Sciences, University of Guadalajara.

Joy Sheelah Baraero-Era, a graduate of Bachelor in Science in Tourism and MA in Art Studies, is presently doing her Ph.D. in Philippine Studies at the University of the Philippines-Diliman. She has been also an active officer of the Union of Filipino Tourism Educators (UFTE) since 2005 and has held various positions such as Secretary, Vice President-External and now Board Adviser to its student organization; the Union of Filipino Tourism Students (UFTS). An Accreditor for the Bachelor of Science in Hotel and Restaurant Management (BSHRM) and Bachelor of Science in Travel/Tourism programs of the Philippine Association of Colleges and Universities Commission on Accreditation (PACUCOA), she is currently the Dean for Travel and Tourism in the School of Hospitality Management of Treston International College located in Bonifacio Global City, Taguig, Metro Manila Philippines.

Kuldeep Kumar (PhD) is Professor in Florida International University, Miami, USA. He is also associated with other global universities like City University of Hong Kong, Hong Kong, China and Chair of Global Process Sourcing, University of Twente, The Netherlands. He is also Co-director of GDW Foundation, Bangalore, India.

Laurentina Cruz Vareiro (Barcelos, Portugal), is Associate Professor of Economics in the School of Management, Polytechnic Institute of Cávado and Ave, Portugal. She has authored or co-authored several papers and her research interests include regional, rural and urban economics, tourism economics, rural and cultural tourism.

Margaret Wachu Gichuhi is a Research Fellow/Lecturer in Environmental Resource Management and a Lead Expert and Consultant in Environmental Impact Assessment and Audit at Jomo Kenyatta University of Agriculture and Technology; Institute for Energy and Environmental Technology (IEET).

Mécia Cunha Mota (Ponte de Lima, Portugal) is Assistant Professor of Tourism in the School of Management, Polytechnic Institute of Cávado and Ave, Portugal. She has co-authored several papers dealing with regional development, cultural tourism and urban questions.

Ng Kok Meng is Lecturer in the School of Hospitality, Tourism and Culinary Arts at KDU College, Penang. His main research interests are in sustainable tourism, especially in green hospitality, cultural and heritage tourism, consumer behaviour and research methods (particularly mixed methods research).

Nor Asyikin Mohd Nor (PhD) is Senior Lecturer, School of Tourism, Hospitality and Environmental Management, College of Law, Government and International Studies, Universiti Utara, Malaysia.

Nurhazani Mohd Shariff (PhD) is Associate Professor and her areas of interest are human resource and tourism community.

Parikshat Singh Manhas (PhD) is Associate Professor, The Business School & School of Hospitality and Tourism Management, University of Jammu is also a Visiting Professor, K. Zhubanov State University of Aktobe, Aktobe, Republic of Kazakhstan and Graduate School of Business, ESAN University, Lima, Peru. He is Editorial Board Member of the *Journal of Management and Sustainability* as well as *Journal of Hospitality and Tourism Education* (*JHTE*) and *Journal of Hospitality and Tourism Cases* (*JHTC*). He is Director of Research for the Asia Pacific Council on Hotel, Restaurant, and Institutional Education (APacCHRIE).

Paula Cristina Remoaldo (Braga, Portugal) is Associate Professor of Human Geography in the Department of Geography of the Social Sciences Institute, University of Minho, Portugal. She has published several papers dealing with health or cultural tourism issues.

Pauline Ratnasingam (PhD) is Associate Professor of MIS, School of Accountancy and Computer Information Systems Department at the University of Central Missouri (UCM). Her research interests include trust in B2B e-commerce, trust in IT innovation, tourism, and business risk management.

P. Siva Sankara Reddy (PhD) has twenty years of teaching experience in the field of History and Tourism. He has published 5 books and 16 research papers pertaining to tourism at national and international fora. He was a recipient of Best Teacher Award and Best Tourism Writer by the Government of Andhra Pradesh. His areas of interest are sustainable tourism and Medical Tourism. He has introduced tourism courses at undergraduate and postgraduate levels in the state of Andhra Pradesh.

R. Kannan (PhD) is Associate Professor and Head, Department of Hotel Management and Catering Science, Madurai Kamaraj University, Madurai.

Riyaz Ahmad is a Research Scholar in DOS in Economics and Cooperation, University of Mysore, Mysore, Karnataka.

Sharleen Howison (PhD) is Principal Lecturer in the School of Applied Business, at Otago Polytechnic Dunedin, New Zealand. Her research interests lay in the tourism area around topics such as environment, events, cruise industry and human resource issues. She is a member of the New Zealand Institute of Travel and Tourism and also the New Zealand Tourism Industry Association.

S.K. Gupta (PhD) is Associate Professor, Centre for Mountain Tourism and Hospitality Studies, H.N.B.G. University, Srinagar (Uttarakhand), India.

S.K. Nagarajan (PhD) is Assistant Professor, Department of Business Administration, Annamalai University. His areas of interest include new product development, branding, software development, entrepreneurship, and project management.

Vijay Prakash Bhatt is a Research Scholar, CMTHS, HNB Garhwal University, Srinagar (Garhwal), India.

Zubair Ahmad Dada is a Research Scholar in School of Hospitality and Tourism Management (SHTM), University of Jammu, Jammu, India.

SECTION I

SUSTAINABLE AND RESPONSIBLE TOURISM

CHAPTER

1

REGIONAL DEVELOPMENT AND SUSTAINABILITY
Cultural Tourism in the Southern Region of Jalisco

—José G. Vargas-Hernández

1.1 ABSTRACT

This study aims to propose a normative model to determine the potential of cultural tourism in the municipalities that comprise the region 6 of the State of Jalisco, territorially delimited in the South of Jalisco. First of all, an anlaysis is conducted to determine the demand for cultural tourism to draw the cultural tourist profile under the assumptions that the tourists, motivated by culture tend to travel longer distances than other tourists. The study discussed the motivations and satisfactions of cultural tourists to establish the potential market in accordance with the characteristics of the target market in the Southern region of Jalisco. Any operation of cultural tourism companies should make the strategic diagnosis. This explains the use of SWOT analysis as a tool for strategic planning of cultural tourism enterprises. Finally, we propose development strategies for cultural tourism in the region of Southern Jalisco.

Keywords: regional development, tourism companies, Southern Jalisco, cultural tourism

1.2 INTRODUCTION

There is an increasing awareness of culture, arts, festivals, heritage sites (natural and cultural), and folklore. Cultural diversity is the base of cultural and heritage tourism. Cultural tourism has been at the centre of the tourism industry in Europe and now other countries are also taking steps to develop their own activities (Nzama, Magi and Ngcobo, 2005). Cultural tourism is a tourism product by itself and can make significant contributions to the regional economic development. Development implies the design, marketing and promotion of new cultural and heritage tourism products and activities while creating a safe and user-friendly atmosphere for visitors and local communities.

Despite that the Southern region of the State of Jalisco in México is considered one of the most culturally rich in manifestations and expressions. In Latin American literature, painting, etc., cultural tourism is almost non-existent. Local communities tend not to be actively interested in cultural tourism related issues and do not understand what the benefits could be. Besides, there is absence of reliable data on cultural tourism for the Southern region of Jalisco.

Cultural tourism is neither common nor universal. It may not be considered as part of the core interests of an organization, government or community, but they appreciate and understand the consequences and possibilities of tourism (Jamieson, 1998). There is also scarce data and information on practice of cultural tourism activities. Social dynamic changes occurring in the Southern Region of Jalisco make it difficult to obtain useful information to be used a reliable input for the design, implementation and effectiveness of cultural tourism policies.

The objective of this study is to address the lack of cultural tourism activities and infrastructure in the Southern Region of Jalisco. One of the aims of this exploratory study is to collect inputs on whether the Southern Region of Jalisco can be transformed into a cultural tourism destination. The concept of cultural tourism can be formulated after understanding the cultural activities offered by a community and considered as an asset to the regional economic development. Cultural tourism is an option to create employment, to improve the quality of life and to eradicate poverty.

As a marketing strategy, cultural tourism is one of the latest buzzwords to attract visitors to cultural sites. Cultural tourism destinations offering cultural products and services linked by geography, townships, folklore, history, celebrations, art experiences and performance can be marketed to local and foreign visitors. Cultural tourism in the Southern Region of Jalisco can offer potential benefits to the regional economic development and to visitors as well, because it has got the resources. The approach involving all stakeholders must be inclusive and participative to ensure sustainable, holistic and efficient cultural tourism ventures.

The term 'cultural tourism' is heavily influenced by professional approaches to be referred more as a concept than as a particular set of objects, articles or products. The World Tourism Organization (WTO) defines tourism as comprising the activities of persons travelling to and staying in places outside their usual environment for not more than one consecutive year for leisure, business and other purposes (WTO, 2000:4). Cultural tourism is defined as the movements of persons for essentially cultural motivations, which includes study tours, performing arts, cultural tours, travel to festivals, visits to historic sites and monuments, folklore and pilgrimages (WTO, 1985).

The concept of cultural tourism encompasses a wide range of views embracing a full range of human expressions and manifestations that visitors to experience the heritages, arts, lifestyles, etc. from people living in cultural destinations. Heritage tourism is usually considered to be cultural tourism. Heritage tourism refers to tourists visiting places of traditional, historical and cultural significance with the aim of learning, paying respect to recreational purposes (Nzama et al., 2005).

The term 'cultural tourism' encompasses historical sites, arts and craft fairs and festivals, museums of all kinds, the performing arts and the visual arts and other heritage sites which tourists enjoy to visit in pursuit of cultural experiences (Tighe, 1985). Heritage tourism, as a synonymous of cultural tourism, is an experiential tourism related to visiting preferred landscape, historic sites, buildings or monuments and seeking an encounter, involvement and stimulation with nature or feeling part of the history of a place (Hall and Zeppel, 1990).

A cultural tourist is a person who stays more than 40 kilometres away from home for at least one night and has attended a cultural venue, which will include visiting an art gallery, museum, library, music concert, opera and a cinema (Australian Bureau of Statistics, 1997). Hall (1998) defines cultural tourism as tourism that focuses on the culture of a destination, the lifestyle, heritage, arts industries and leisure pursuits of the local population.

Cultural tourism is related to the cultural aspects that include the customs and traditions of people, their heritage, history and way of life. The International Council of Monuments and Sites (ICOMOS) defines cultural tourism as "a name that means many things to many people and herein lies its strength and its weakness" (McKercher and Cros, 2002:24). Cultural tourism theory is only beginning to debate issues of gender specialization (Aitchson, 2003).

Cultural tourism refers to travel that is directed towards providing opportunities and access to visitors to experiencing the arts and crafts, museums, heritage, festivals, music, dance, theatres, literature, historic sites and buildings, landscapes, neighbourhoods and special character of local communities. Cultural tourism relates to the temporary short-term movement of people to cultural destinations outside the place of residence and work, and where their activities at these destinations or facilities cater for their recreation needs (Keyser, 2002). Cultural tourism associates the word "tourist and cultural attraction" with the tangible and intangible cultural heritage. Cultural tourism is the attendance by inbound visitors to one or more cultural attractions such as festivals, fairs, museums, art galleries, history buildings and craft workshops (Bureau of Tourism Research, 2004).

Ivanovic (2008) and Cooper et al. (2008) maintain that the greatest motivator for travel is to understand culture and heritage, both emerging as contributing to economic development. Ivanovic (2008) argues that cultural and heritage tourism is a recent development in the tourism activities, and with ecotourism are emerging as the predominant forms of tourism and replacing sun-lust mass tourism. Cultural attractions and events play a key role in cultural tourism and hospitality destinations to entice visitors (George, 2001). Cultural tourism is travelling to experience and to participate in vanishing lifestyles that lie within human memory (Goeldner and Ritchie, 2009).

The aim of cultural tourism policy is to influence and attract visitors (Williams and Shaw, 1991:263). Tourists with special interest in culture belong to the segment of 'cultural tourism', i.e. size and value are directly attributable to the country's cultural values that encourage tourists to take a trip. Tourists with occasional interest in culture belong to other tourism segments (CESTUR). A special programme of incentives for tourism related to culture or values must recognize contributions that tourism can have for culture and vice versa, to capitalize on the positive and generate synergies for the development of both sectors.

Within the designing and developing process, cultural tourism may take many forms. Sharma (2004) adds to the cultural resources debate advocating the economic benefits of developing programmes, resources and facilities for the benefit of local communities, creating a balance between economic imperatives and positive and negative impacts.

Cultural tourism activities may have an economic impact on regional development by creating employment and improving the standards of life. Hanekom and Thornhill (1983:110) describe the activities of cultural tourism as consisting of phenomena such as formulation of policy making, planning and organizing the structure, methods and procedures, recruiting, training, developing and motivating personnel, budgeting and financing operations. The philosophical principles of the tourism discipline must be reconsidered to re-evaluate the fundamentals of cultural tourism.

Cultural and heritage tourism can be considered as a dynamic activity developed through physical experiences, searching and celebrating what is unique and beautiful, represented by our own values and attributes which are worthy to preserve and to inherit to descendents in such a way that communities can be proud of them.

1.3 THEORETICAL BACKGROUND AND LITERATURE REVIEW

Theory building and development is needed in order to use it as a foundation for an explanation and understanding of the normative model on cultural tourism for the Region of Southern Jalisco. The theory for cultural tourism has been developed to explain, analyze, evaluate and predict the related phenomena (Moulin, 1989, 1990). However, a theoretical framework for cultural tourism to sustain the practice and activities requires availability of data on infrastructure, resources and skills.

Easton (1965) developed a normative model of cultural tourism emphasizing the external environments serving as the inputs that may influence the goal achievement, such as the political, economic, socio-cultural, legal, environmental, educational, health, statutory policies, demographics and technological environment, although the numbers and types of possible environments may be unlimited (Ferreira, 1996:403). Each environment requires the adaptation of the conversion mechanism (Easton, 1965:131–132; Ferreira, 1996:403).

After the goal is achieved, the inputs formed by the original external environment generate new needs to be satisfied by achieving a new goal (Easton, 1965:128–129; Ferreira, 1996:404; Cloete and Wissink, 2000:39). An opposing argument underlies conserving and protecting the integrity of the cultural tourism resources, by monitoring overcrowding, overuse of the resource and environmental pollution (McDonald, 1999).

Cultural and heritage tourism brings significant economic benefits and development to cultural and heritage sites, townships and communities. An empirical research conducted by Besculides, Lee and McCormick (2002), using a benefits-based approach to examine the perceptions of cultural tourism by Hispanic and non-Hispanic residents, showed that Hispanics felt strongly that living along a cultural tourism byway provides cultural benefits and has greater concern for its management.

The philosophical approach to cultural tourism of the stakeholders, providers and policy makers shapes the values and norms of the normative model oriented to develop effective policy around cultural tourism. Local communities developing and promoting cultural and heritage tourism may need as a frame of reference an effective implementation of local and national policies. Cultural and heritage tourism products and services development and promotion require planning and implementing on the basis of policies. Philosophical principles of cultural tourism are required to sustain the design and implementation of a normative model aimed to promote regional economic development policies. The literature on cultural tourism policy is relevant in developing a normative framework. There is a need to develop a policy framework for cultural heritage tourism.

The cultural tourism theory, 'Creative cities' recommends investing in cultural and heritage goods. Ximba (2009) analyzed and examined the "variables and principles such as understanding of cultural tourism, development and conservation of culture, provision cultural facilities, participation in cultural tourism, application of tourism policies and practices, and the benefits of cultural and heritage tourism." Cultural tourism is based on the participation in deep cultural experiences, whether intellectual, psychological, aesthetic and emotional (Russo, and van der Borg, 2002) and as specialized cultural tourism focuses on a small number of geographic sites, townships, cultural unities and entities.

The normative model enables to arrange data and information on cultural tourism activities in such a way that they can provide the bases to develop a theoretical framework for cultural tourism. Normative theory is concerned with phenomena and questions regarding the role assumed by government and in general, the public sector (Hanekom and Thornhill, 1983:71).

A normative model of sustainable cultural tourism developed by Ismail (2008) proposes a normative input-output model, with an implementation mechanism to ensure sustainable cultural tourism facilitating initiatives for regional development by creating employment and poverty alleviation. The approach of sustainable cultural and heritage tourism development is aimed to improve the environment by meeting the needs of the present communities without compromising the ability of future generations to meet their own needs (WCED, 1987:8). Sustainable cultural and heritage tourism development requires the best-practices (Magi and Nzama, 2002) to meet the needs of present guest visitors and host local communities while protecting and fostering enhanced opportunities for future generations.

A sustainable cultural tourism contributes to community development if the tourism stakeholders and business are efficient, fair and environmentally oriented. MacDonald and Lee (2003) examined the cultural rural tourism on a framework considering the roles of culture in community-base partnerships. Their findings suggest that culture in rural tourism development is a valuable resource and community-based partnerships may be very effective.

Cultural tourism enhances the identity and esteem of the local community. It provides the opportunity for greater understanding and communication between people of diverse backgrounds (Lubbe, 2003). Sustainable cultural and heritage tourism development is based on the assumption that resources and facilities are finite, limited, some are not renewable, experience degradation and exhaustion, cannot continue to grow to meet the needs of the mass tourism and a growing population (SARDC, 1994).

The practice of cultural and heritage tourism sustainable development is the requirement to share the benefits on a permanent basis between the visitors and the residents of local communities. To overcome some problems associated with cultural tourism development and these include to take advantage of all the opportunities, know-how, financial support, community co-participation, etc. to maximize the benefits. Community participation in cultural and heritage tourism development should become a practice as the core of a people-centred approach to incorporate them in the decision making process on the development of cultural and heritage resources and in sharing all the benefits (Magi and Nzama, 2008).

Participants in cultural tourism activities expect to get enjoyment, satisfaction or fulfillment from the experience (Shivers, 1981). McKercher and Du Cros (2003) test a cultural tourism typology represented by five benefit-based segments tested against a variety of trip, demographic, motivational, preferred activity, awareness, cultural distance and activity variables. They found differences between the groups and suggested that the model presented may be effective in segmenting the cultural tourism market.

Co-participation in decision-making, ownership and benefits of all stakeholders involved in sustainable cultural and heritage tourism is the core of the encounter, experience and enjoyment of resources and opportunities available to the tourist or leisure seeker (Torkildsen, 2007).

Cultural and heritage tourism may be a tool to preserve the culture of host communities. The sustainable cultural and heritage tourist policies must focus and regulate activities and best-practices oriented to the restoration, enhancement and conservation of resources for both present and continuing future use and enjoyment by visitors and local people (Keyser, 2002). The level of maintenance, conservation and preservation of resources is related to the level of cultural tourism infrastructure and facilities.

The research undertook an in-depth literature search to extract a set of normative criteria for cultural tourism and conducted an empirical qualitative survey. From the results of this research, finally a normative model of cultural tourism was designed. The aim of the normative model for sustainable cultural tourism is to facilitate the analysis, design and formulation of cultural tourism policy initiatives. Cultural tourism theory based on normative criteria focuses on formulation, design and implementation of cultural tourism policies. The external political environment influences the governmental tourism policy which, in turn, may have an impact on the development of a normative model for cultural tourism. Cultural tourism theory based on normative criteria is necessary for the formulation of cultural tourism policies oriented towards the improvement of regional economic development.

The aim of any cultural tourism policy oriented to the regional development is to influence and attract visitors (Williams and Shaw 1991:263–264) through the generation of demand and the provision of tourism services. Richards (1996) conducted international research on cultural tourism demand and supply and found a rapid increase in both the production and consumption of cultural heritage tourism attractions.

The normative criteria incorporated in the model may be the framework of reference of the external macro environment which in turn may influence the social cultural tourism policy. Social cultural tourism factors which influence the external environment can be determined by implementing an appraisal system which benefits all the stakeholders. The implementation of the normative framework for cultural tourism is dependent on the commitment of tourism stakeholders, government agencies, communities, etc. to play their corresponding roles.

Thus, the stakeholders in cultural tourism, communities, government agencies, municipal governments, etc. have the responsibility to implement initiatives to develop infrastructure, cultural facilities, cultural tourism attractions, accommodation facilities, etc. The normative model is appropriate to describe, explain and analyze the activities of cultural tourism in order to design, develop, promote and implement policies oriented towards creating employment and improving quality of life. A normative model of cultural tourism can be useful to develop strategies and formulate policies to frame the execution of some relevant proposals, recommendations and projects. A normative model for cultural tourism on the Southern Jalisco, flexible and dynamic as a tool, assists in providing the methodological criteria and procedures, policies and strategies to promote regional economic development.

1.4 METHODS

Research on a normative framework for cultural tourism is deemed necessary to address the current dysfunctional economic development of the Southern Region of Jalisco. A systems approach can be used for the purpose of analyzing and developing a normative framework for cultural tourism (Bayat and Meyer, 1994:83–10). The aim of the normative model for cultural tourism is to analyze the strengths, weaknesses, threats and opportunities in all factors such as infrastructure, facilities, skills and, above all, the design and implementation of cultural tourism policies on the Southern Jalisco.

The normative model is designed as a tool for changing the current situations, policies and strategies into a more dynamic, functional and flexible proposal for regional economic development. The use of a normative model for cultural tourism requires qualitative and quantitative methods of analysis to conduct research. An analysis of the macro external environment includes the micro-environment, macro-environment and marketing environment, representing external forces influencing the decision making processes and goal achievement such as economic, social, political, public policies, demographic, legal, technological, etc.

The micro-internal environment of a normative framework for developing, promoting and sustaining cultural tourism influences suppliers, distribution channels, customers, competitors, community values, local politics, legal requirements, etc. The guiding principles and policies developed by federal and local governments may be the core criteria for designing and developing the normative framework of reference for cultural tourism on the Southern Jalisco.

The goal of the normative model for cultural tourism is to attain effective and efficient criteria and performed to design, develop, maintain, promote and enhance the development of cultural tourism. The feedback mechanism of the normative model senses any possible deficiency and deviation of the ongoing outputs coming from the de-normative model of cultural tourism in relation to the macro- and micro-environmental variables and factors.

1.5 DETERMINATION OF THE DEMAND OF CULTURAL TOURISM

1.5.1 Mexican Tourism in the Hierarchy of the Countries of the World in the Year 2004

When you start the twenty-first century, tourism is the most important factor for economic development and the cornerstone for the development of services with a value estimated at

476,000 million. It is, therefore, a powerful tool to promote the development of villages in terms of leverage.

Mexico ranks eighth among the main recipients of international tourism after France, Spain, United States, Italy, China, UK and Austria (see Table 1.2).

Table 1.1 Mexico's tourism related information

Mexico	*2014*			*2004*		
	Growth			***Growth***		
	Relative	*Absolute*	*Growth*	*Relative*	*Absolute*	***Growth***
Personal travel and tourism	17	130	133	16	137	**124**
Business travel	14	–	131	12	–	**39**
Public expenditure	12	58	168	11	62	**145**
Equity investments	11	93	2	7	94	**3**
Visitor exports	16	113	9	12	115	**15**
Other exports	11	15	27	9	15	**19**
Travel and tourism demand	12	–	34	10	–	**13**
Tourism and travel industry	14	108	91	11	103	**68**
Tourism economy	11	99	52	10	70	**14**
Tourism industry employment	22	115	89	19	110	**68**
Tourism economy employment	14	75	42	8	52	**4**

1. 2004 real growth adjusted for inflation.
2. 2005–2014 annualized real growth adjusted for inflation.

Total 174 countries and 13 regions (largest/highest/The biggest one is number one, the smallest/most under/the worst is number 13 is hierarchy aggregate region.

Source: World Travel and Tourism Council, Mexico travel and tourism merging ahead.

A study by the World Travel and Tourism Council (WTTC) based on eight indicators of Tourist Competitiveness Monitor (Financial Infosel, 2004) and applied to 212 countries, puts Mexico on 70th position. The eight indicators are prices, human tourism, infrastructure, environment, technology, tourist opening, social resources and human resources. The price index considers "the costs that consumers pay for hotel products and services ... taxes on purchases of goods and service utilization." The human tourism index takes into account "the people's participation in tourism activities."

Table 1.2 Place of Mexico from 212 countries

Index	*Place of Mexico from 212 countries*
Tourist opening	54
Prices	66
Human resources	70
Technology	71
Social resources	72
Human tourism	89
Environment	92

1.5.2 Economic Impact of Tourism Sector in Mexico

According to the latest official information available from the Government of Mexico (Bulletin Quarterly Tourism), the number of international tourists to Mexico in 2003 showed growth rates marginally below that recorded during the previous year, representing a significant reduction for the indicator in 2003. The consideration of the total international tourists in 2003 (more border placement) reveals a contraction (–5.1%), resulting from the collapse of border tourists, going from 9.8 million tourists in 2002 to 8.3 million tourists in 2003, a reduction of 15%. The country received 18.7 million international tourists, down by 5.1% over 2002.

The main reason for the negative balance in the number of tourists was due to increased immigration enforcement at the border with the United States, caused by exogenous factors such as recent conflicts in the Middle East and the severe acute respiratory syndrome. Although there was a lower number of international tourists compared with 2002, the inflow of hard currency received in 2003 allowed to record historical figures as the result achieved in 2003 was the highest level seen in the last four years. Tourists coming for treatment generate more foreign exchange for our country, so no border tourism presented a positive change that led to the outflow of hard currency to grow, by increasing the total expenditure of international visitors to Mexico, resulting in a significant increase in the surplus of passengers.

The segment of tourists in hospital ended the year 2003 with 10.4 million, 4.8% higher than the levels presented in 2002. Spending increased from 8.858 at 2002–9457000 dollars, a level which represents an increase of 6.8%. Within this segment, the placement tourism contributed 70% of the total deposits, 23% were in the hikers and the remaining 6% is recorded border tourists (Tourism Quarterly Bulletin). The cruise segment recorded an increase in currency in 2003 to 35.9 over the previous year. There was also a reduction in the flow of tourists and visitors. Transborder international outside Mexico than in 2003 accumulated a 18.6% drop. The total expenditure incurred by Mexicans abroad showed a surplus in the tourism balance of $ 3.204 million for 2003, 14.5% more than in 2002. In 2003 recorded 47.9 million tourist arrivals at national hotel rooms, which means an increase of 1.3% compared to the previous year.

In 2003, domestic tourism increased the average stay of tourists at night overnight or 8.2%, highlighting especially in beach destinations, while the fate of cities recorded lower occupancy rates. The interior and large cities, respectively, showed a contraction of 2.8 and 1.5 percentage points compared with the levels recorded in 2002, while the border cities showed a good performance by recording an average occupancy of 60.2%, which is 6.3% higher than the previous year.

In 2004, it is expected that travel and tourism would generate in Mexico 8.40.200 million pesos equivalent to US $ 73.3 billion in economic activity (total demand). The direct impact of this industry includes:

- 681,354 jobs, representing 2.4% of the total
- 186,800 million Mexican pesos equivalent to US $ 16.3 billion gross domestic product, equivalent to 2.7% of the total

However, because tourism touches all the sectors of the economy, its real impact is greater. The economy of this sector directly and indirectly represents:

- 2,865.740 jobs representing 10.0% of the total
- 643,200 million pesos of gross domestic product, equivalent to 9.4% of the total
- 299,900 million Mexican pesos equivalent to US $ 26.2 billion of exports, goods or services and 13.8% of total exports
- 168,300 million Mexican pesos equivalent to 14.7% billion of capital investments or 10.7% of total investments
- 40,300 million pesos equivalent to US $ 35.5 billion of government expenditure or 5.1% of participation

1.5.3 Growth

For 2004, tourism projects in Mexico:

- Real growth of 11.1% of the total demand
- 9.3% of the domestic product of the tourism industry sector, 186,800 million Mexican pesos equivalent to US $ 16.3 billion gross domestic product for the industry directly, and 10.7%, 643.2 thousand million pesos of gross domestic product, equivalent to 9.4% of the total

For the economy of tourism in general (direct and indirect costs):

- 8% in employment in the tourism industry with direct impact only, or 681.354 jobs, and 9.9% or 2.86574 million jobs in the tourism economy in general, direct and indirect impact

In the next ten years, tourism in Mexico is expected to reach an annualized real growth:

- 7.1% of total tourism demand for lograr 2,340 equivalent to 000 million (US $ 167.4 bn) in 2014
- 55 of total domestic product of the tourism sector up to 422,900 million pesos equivalent to US $ 124.6 billion to the economy of tourism in general
- 3.1 in employment in the tourism sector to reach 921,832 work directly in industry and 5.8% to 5.02955 million jobs in the tourism economy in general for the year 2014
- 7.9% in exports of visitors rising to 382,300 million pesos, equivalent to 27.3 billion dollars for the year 2014
- 9.9% in terms of capital investment to increase to 604,700 million pesos, equivalent to 43. $ 2 trillion in 2014
- 2.3 in terms of increased public expenditure to reach 70.6 thousand million pesos equivalent to $ 5 billion in 2014

In Mexico, cultural tourism figures have not been determined accurately. Only the National Institute of Anthropology and History (NIAH) estimated to have captured in the spaces under their custody 16.4 million visitors in 2002. The domestic visitors accounted for about four-fifths, with a total of 13.2 million and international one-fifth with 3.2 million. However, among domestic visitors do not distinguish between tourists and residents of cities where sites are located.

Culture is in sixth place as the main motivation for domestic tourism and the fourth for international tourism. It is estimated that in Mexico, tourism especially motivated by culture accounts for 5.5% of domestic passengers and 3% for international. Almost 70 million tourists with activities related to culture in Mexico. The cost per trip of tourism demand is related to culture the national average, by increasing their daily intake based on their activities around the cultural heritage and their stay is greater than that of other segments.

1.6 PROFILE OF TOURISTS WITH CULTURAL STATEMENT

Tourists especially motivated by culture tend to travel longer distances than most tourists. To carry out a cultural incursion, personal investment is needed by the tourist, who expresses greater interest in learning and engages in the life of the place visited, which requires more time than a scenic trip, the more visited is the culture of others, more curious results on the tourists. Main activities which are related to tangible heritage are very popular among tourists especially motivated by culture, representing 48% of all tourism activities conducted by national and international 63%. The intangible elements by their very nature are, more difficult to identify although its influence is manifested in a general sense of impregnating the culture visited tourist.

In the case of activities from tangible and intangible heritage, the archaeological sites (27%) are a favourite place of international tourists especially motivated by culture. As for the intangible heritage, tourists prefer to see the traditions and customs of the communities (9%). For its part, Mexicans prefer to attend activities related to intangible assets (52%) among its outstanding regional cuisine tasting (13%). The tangible heritage related activity preferred by Mexican tourists is the observation of architectural monuments (18%). This relates to the interest, rather than didactic aesthetic appreciation of most cultural travellers.

1.7 MOTIVATIONS AND SATISFACTION OF CULTURAL TOURISTS

For both domestic and international tourists, the attributes relating to architecture and living culture are key motivators. The place of these factors between nationals and foreigners is reversed, with the themes related to culture for international tourists and those related to tangible assets for national tourists. The tourist interested in culture is also seeking money, climate, landscape and activities that can meet the members of the following group.

Mexican cultural tourists are sensitive to the cost-benefit purpose, value destinations around the variety and quality of activities offered, is willing to spend on experiences, but not in services that do not provide clear differences with respect to others who have an interesting style. The economic cost factors, emotional and physical are crucial. The relationship between them and their benefits must be proportionate. A cultural tourist destination which provides cultural activities featuring comfort and additional options for leisure and entertainment is more likely to attract tourists or occasional specialized than other destinations. Considered cultural tourists in general are scarce pleasant and attractive cultural offerings for children and adolescents and that failure to appreciate the teaching culture.

1.8 MARKET POTENTIAL

Surveys to estimate and characterize the current volume of demand for cultural tourism in the domestic market indicate that only 5.5% of domestic tourists are considered especially motivated by culture and 35.7% with casual interest. Globally, 37% of the tourists engage in some cultural activity during their trip and the annual growth rate will be 15% from 2000.

Mexico is currently involved with the tourists, –554.233 1.8% of the market they represent the sending countries, USA, Canada, Germany, France, Spain and England, which means there is a huge potential for market penetration, as long as the market develops and there is adequate supply. Mexico is already involved with 8.4% market share amounting to 7.2 million tourists. tourists with a casual interest in culture represent a total of 84.9 million tourists who travel abroad, i.e. 35% of the total. Mexico is already involved with 8.4% market share amounting to 7.2 million tourists.

1.9 DETAILS OF THE OFFER OF TOURIST DESTINATIONS—CULTURAL

The size and competitiveness of the tourist and cultural offer cannot be assessed from the cultural resources in isolation but in relation to geographic locations, and in which the various elements that make it feasible for your visit converge.

The criteria used for selecting the destination locations are:

(a) The role they play in the tourism system.
(b) The main features that have cultural heritage.
(c) The terms of infrastructure and services for tourist use.
(d) Details of the local population.

These become the most apparent difference between domestic and foreign perceptions. Some examples of the wide diversity of cultural tourism resources can be mentioned:

- Cities and towns with secular architecture, historical values and particular environments.
- Groups with techniques of production and exchange themselves, usages and customs, chronicles, legends, rituals, festivities, gastronomy, etc.
- Archaeological sites that are open to the public (INAH).
- Landmarks of historical value of the XVI to XIX (CONACULTA).
- Historical and artistic objects and objects of everyday use, exhibited in museums registered by the INAH, Houses of Culture, Private Museums, State, Municipality and Community.
- Events and festivals, theatrical events, concerts, cinema, dance, etc.
- In terms of infrastructure and services, tourists interested in culture can use the facility for other tourist segments, for example:

- Food and beverage establishments, travel agencies, tour guides and car rental.
- Highways that connect major cities and highways that connect small towns and airports, three of which are international.

1.10 OPERATIONS OF CULTURAL TOURISM'S BUSINESS

In cultural tourism are companies from various sectors of production. In addition to the tourism and cultural sector, significantly involved companies and institutions involved in urban development and the service sector in general and support areas.

1.10.1 Cultural Tourism Sectors

Cultural tourism agencies include public, private and social. This diversity of factors makes the administration has a greater complexity than other fields of tourism.

In specific areas of tourism and culture whose presence turns excel is very important in those places where the activity takes place:

- Hotels
- Tour operators
- Museums
- Craft stores
- Restaurants
- Tourists guides
- Cultural sites managed by the INAH

Within the relations of the actors in the system, the basic structure of marketing generates harmonious relations between private actors in the tourism sector. In addition to these key players, cultural tourism has other players such as:

- Municipal authorities, state and federal
- Bodies promoters culture
- Administration agencies of sites and monuments
- Non-governmental organizations
- Universities, schools and institutes
- Business of entertainment
- Carriers
- Tourists guides
- Travel agencies
- Independent travel promoters
- Associations and clubs

1.11 SWOT CORPORATE ANALYSIS

Table 1.3 SWOT corporate analysis

Internal/External	**Strength**	**Weakness**
	Emergence of companies in the process of modernization that value culture	Predominance of firms with conventional approaches to culture and tourism and lack of adequate supply
Opportunities Recognition of culture as the value of differentiation and identity and its importance for the competitiveness of the company	Companies and products competitive heritage value and participate in strengthening cultures local	Simulated development and use of conventional spaces property in tourism
Threats Short-term business vision and prominence of big business (mass model) as a paradigm	Creating enclaves business without local benefits regional	The use of heritage limited to entertainment. Competition price, and loss of profitability businesses and destinations

In general, the business outlook is favourable for the development of cultural tourism and it requires better use of cultural resources to strengthen the identity of the destinations and the country as there are more strengths than weaknesses. Need greater certainty about the path to take to seize the assets and improve the participation of cultural tourism companies. There is willingness to undertake the necessary improvements to enhance the development of these communities and tourism enterprises.

Recognized six areas for action in proposing a series of strategic guidance and tactical approaches that will strengthen and enhance the relationship of tourism activities in their cultural side are as follows:

1. Revaluation of the relationship between culture and tourism
2. Systematization of planning and control instruments
3. Organizational strengthening
4. Optimization of cultural heritage management
5. Enriching the cultural tourism offer
6. Rethinking the promotion and marketing

1.12 DESIGN OF CULTURAL TOURS CIRCUITS IN SOUTHERN JALISCO

1.12.1 Cultural Tourism Circuit "Footsteps in the Land of Great Artists ..."

Municipalities that comprise the cultural tour:

(a) Zapotlán the Great
(b) Sayula
(c) San Gabriel
(d) Tolimán
(e) Vadillo Zapotitlan

Cultural scene

FIRST DAY

1. **City Tour:** Historic Centre of Painting and Sculpture Guzman City Hall, illustrious men Columnario Zapotlán the Great House where he was born, Juan José Arreola Lazaro Cardenas street, Mendoza Portal architecture, temple architecture and sculpture of the Tabernacle, painting, sculpture and architecture of the Third Order temple and former convent, painting, architecture and sculpture of the cathedral, market Paulino Navarro, Portales, birthplace of painter José Clemente Orozco, architecture Town Hall, Palace of the cob architecture, snack restaurant above the Portal Hidalgo, backyards overlooking the Portal Hidalgo. (Estimated time: 4 hours). From 12 to 23 October, you can visit the Fair with all its traditions and customs, which culminates with the floats or litter.

Suggested meal in some of the excellent restaurants of Ciudad Guzmán.

2. **Sayula Tour:** Legend of the poem of the soul Sayula and location of the main places referred to, Downtown and portals Sayula, visit the Centre of the Immaculate Conception Parish and a former convent, visit the Museum and Casa de la Cultura Juan Rulfo, visit the house of Handicrafts, cutlery shop visit of Ojeda, Juan Rulfo birthplace, architecture and paintings of the Santuario de Guadalupe and a former Franciscan convent. The carnival was staged on Shrove Tuesday to end on Ash Wednesday. (Estimated time: 4 hours)

Suggested dinner with typical food and sleep in Sayula in La Casa de los Patios.

SECOND DAY

Typical breakfast is suggested Sayula.

3. **Travel in San Gabriel:** On the way to San Gabriel Sayula suggested references to places mentioned in the works of Juan Rulfo: Apango, Apulco, etc.; Apango visit.

View of Llano Grande, Puerto Los colimotes view, visit the Historic Centre of San Gabriel, paintings and sculptures of Trujillo Enrrique the Lord of Mercy Amula, visit the house where Juan Rulfo, visit house where Jose Mojica, priest, composer and singer, a visit to the stones with petroglyphs Telcampana visit, visit to the former estate of Juan Rulfo Apulco where he lived most of his childhood, can be visited if it coincides in time, the Feasts of the Lord is Amula held from 11 to 19 January each year, the feasts of the Lord of Mercy. (Estimated time: 6 hours)

For lunch and dinner is suggested typical local food and stay overnight in San Gabriel.

THIRD DAY

4. **Tour of Toliman, and Vadillo Zapotitlan:** It is suggested breakfast at Toliman.

Visit the Cerro Encantado and Petacal, Crescent View, visit the Museum in Toliman, visit the Wall of the Temple of the Assumption. If you match 6 to August 15, you can join the feast of Our Lady of the Assumption, to appreciate their dances and traditions. Typical meal is suggested.

Visit the Historical Centre of Zapotitlan Vadillo presentation is suggested poems and legends that abound in the folklore of this place, as the Cerro Chino, if it coincides in time can participate in the Feast of the Virgin of Guadalupe from 1 to January 15 and the feasts of Mary Magdalene on 22 July, the religious feast day image borne in procession through the streets ornate people, parade floats, music and dance.

Return to Cd Guzman, and cultural tourism circuit ends.

1.12.2 Cultural Tourism Circuit "at the Feast Eternal"

Municipalities comprising the tour:

(a) Tonila
(b) Tuxpan
(c) Zapotiltic

Cultural scene

Tour the city of Tonila: Breakfast and visit to the Ex Hacienda La Esperanza, visit Tonila Parish Temple is a replica colonial style carved stone used for construction, has seen Swiss watch among the few of its kind, Temple San Marcos, modernist baroque and Byzantine motifs. If it is agreed at the time, you can participate in religious festivals in the honour of the Virgin of Guadalupe celebrated from 3 to 12 December in the municipal and San Marcos. (Estimated time: 3 hours)

Tour the city of Tuxpan: Visit the Historic Centre of Tuxpan, Atrial view of the Cross dating from the sixteenth century and visit the parish church, Indian House visit, shows typical food of Tuxpan (The Cuaxala) Celebration Indian wedding where the groom dressed in beautiful and intricate costumes, dance performances and Paixtles Chayacates Indians, in the afternoon visit to the Museum Melquiades Rubalcaba. If it matches on dates, visitors can participate in the Regional Competition that takes place Rattles 23 to May 31 and coincides with the festivities of the Lord of Forgiveness. (Estimated time: 4 hours)

Tour the city of Zapotiltic: Visit the Historic Center of Zapotiltic, visit the Temple of the former estate of Huescalapa. If the dates coincide with the celebrations of the Lord of Forgiveness in the first two weeks of May, visitors can participate.

1.12.3 Cultural Tours "Townships on the Lake's Rivera"

Municipalities comprising the tour:

(a) Gómez Farías
(b) Atoyac
(c) Teocuitatlán
(d) Techaluta
(e) Amacueca

Cultural scene

Farias Township: Visit the Historic Centre of San Sebastian, visit the Artisan House (tule crafts), participation in workshops. Visitors can participate if they coincide with the festival of Candlemas on February 2, the Feast of St. Andrew from 20 to 30 November and the festivities of Our Lady of Refuge on July 4. (Estimated time: 1 hour)

Atoyac Municipality: Visit the Historical Centre and view the paintings of Painting. Box-Painted by Antonio Zamarripa Castellón in 1968. Craft Site visits belts, participation in craft workshops. If it matches on dates, visitors can witness the Health Festival on Friday of Lent and Carnival, which takes place in the month of February. (Estimated time: 1 hour)

City of Corona Teocuitatlán: Visit to the Ex Hacienda San José de Gracia and the Indian Pantheon. Are recommended to present the legends about these two scenarios. Visit the historic centre of Teocuitatlán, visit to places of crafts and antiques collector blankets, if we agree the dates when you visit the site, you can witness the festivities of the Virgin of Guadalupe from 1 to 12 December. (Estimated time: 3 hours).

Suggested meal in a restaurant Teocuitatlán.

Techaluta Township: Municipal Palace Tour 1878 coincides in time if visitors can witness and participate in the most important celebrations in the town that bullfighting are held from 9 to 16 September; religious holidays in the honour of St. Sebastian Martyr taking place from 11 to 20 January, and the Pitaya Annual Fair every May for approximately 8 to 15. (Estimated time: 1 hour)

Amacueca Township: Visit the Historic Centre of Amacueca, visit the ruins of the Franciscan monastery, XVII century building facade with twisted columns and gilded altarpiece. Visit to the Holy Name of Jesus, carved wooden sculpture of the sixteenth century. If we agree on the dates, you can participate in bullfights on the third Sunday of January, the celebrations of the Holy Name of Jesus on January 8 and carnival that takes place in the month of February.

1.12.4 Cultural Tours

Municipalities comprising the tour:

(a) Torres Zacoalco
(b) Atemajac de Brizuela
(c) Tapalpa cultural scene

Zacoalco Tower: Visit the Historic Centre of Zacoalco Torres, visit equipales craft centres, participation in craft workshops, representing Indian wedding. If there is agreement on dates, visitors can witness the Feast of the Virgin of Guadalupe on January 12, the Lord of Health on August 6, and the feasts of St. Francis of Assisi on October 14. (Estimated time: 3 hours)

Atemajac de Brizuela: Visit the Historic Centre of Brown Atemajac. If there is coincidence of dates, visitors can participate in the festivities of Our Lady of the Defense from 6 to 9 September, the pilgrimage of the Virgen de la Defense 7 and October 8 and the festivities of St. Bartholomew on 24 August. It is suggested to eat at this place the typical food, lamb to the shepherd with punch and sweet fruit preserves.

Tapalpa: Visit the Historic Centre of Tapalpa, typical of mountain people, visit the Chapel of the Soledad, visit the Casa de la Cultura (Parish of San Antonio de Tapalpa) Juanacatlán Temple and Temple of Our Lady of Mercy, visit the paper mache crafts, visit the Hostal de la Casona del Manzano, visit the Water House, a visit to the Chapel of the Immaculate Conception, visit the Chapel of Solitude.

1.13 BUSINESS DEVELOPMENT STRATEGIES OF CULTURAL TOURISM

1. Improve the coordination of the various factors involved in the activity for development programs, marketing, participation in the conservation and enhancement of cultural heritage in the areas: intersectional and interdisciplinary.
2. Improve mechanisms for training of human resources.
3. Facilitate the development of small and medium companies and grocery services to strengthen the system as a whole.
4. Strengthen the bond of action of the companies with conservation and enhancement of cultural heritage.
5. Encourage companies to provide information to tourists on cultural activities that exist in the destination, and to establish awareness programmes for the care of heritage and respect for local customs.
6. Promoting and using cultural tourism to differentiate the existing tourist facility, opening new market opportunities.
7. Diversify mechanisms to promote and market segments with an interest in culture.
8. Harnessing the elements of cultural identification of each region to increase differentiation of Mexican companies in domestic and international markets.
9. Promote use of sustainable technology (alternative energy, recycling, etc.).

1.14 CONCLUSION AND RECOMMENDATIONS

The Southern Region of Jalisco has the potential elements and resources, identified as opportunities and strengths, to be developed and promoted as a cultural tourism destination. This paper identifies that there is a need for a theoretical framework to design a normative model of sustainable cultural tourism policy in the Southern Region of the state of Jalisco, México. Cultural tourism stakeholders and suppliers in the Southern Jalisco can benefit from the implementation of a normative model to promote regional economic development through the creation of employment and poverty alleviation.

A normative model for cultural tourism requires active participation from the tourist stakeholders, businesses, government agencies and the community, from the inception phase until the implementation of a programme for developing the potential as a cultural tourism destination. The design and implementation of cultural and heritage tourism programmes must promote, preserve and enhance the communities' cultures, folklore, arts, artifacts, etc. Active participation of all cultural tourism stakeholders, governmental agencies and local communities in decision making process not only legitimates the activities but provides experience and grounding to design and implement the strategies to pursue the effectiveness of cultural tourism policies (Blench, 1999) and promote responsible and sustainable cultural tourism.

The normative model establishes a set of normative criteria as an approach to achieve functional cultural tourism in the Southern Jalisco. Variables identified in the normative model as weaknesses, strengths, opportunities and threats can assist tourism stakeholders, government agencies, business and the community as a whole, in designing and developing cultural tourism products and services and offerings for national and international tourists participating in the cultural market. Any development or promotion of a cultural tourism product needs to be well designed and implemented on the basis of the existing cultural tourism policies. A permanent approach on the practice of sustainable cultural and heritage development is a requirement to spill over the benefits to the local communities.

Cultural tourism brings the best benefits to the development of local community after an effective implementation of cultural tourism policies. The effectiveness of cultural tourism policies must be assessed. Local communities must attempt to manage cultural tourism resources whilst linking them to the development and economic growth.

Local and municipal government plays an important role with respect to cultural tourism for the Region of Southern Jalisco. Besides, the planning, development, promotion, marketing and implementation of these products and services can sustain cultural tourism as an economic activity that can improve the standards of living for people on the Southern Jalisco.

The design and development of a normative model is concomitant to a set of recommendations for the implementation of cultural tourism in the Southern Jalisco. A cultural tourism must offer intrinsic value for tourism consumption while adding value to local cultural tourism resources. Cultural tourism must offer to fulfil the expectations of tourists with memorable experiences. Cultural tourism on the Southern Jalisco can be a development tool for creating better conditions of employment, opportunities for economic development and improvement of the standards of life for the people living in the communities. The recommendations here offered are only an attempt to change the current dysfunctional situation into an efficient system of cultural tourism management based on a normative model.

The development of cultural tourism requires cultural heritage attractions in order to achieve the objectives, and preservation of the tangible and intangible cultural heritage. The scope of cultural tourism for the Southern Jalisco may include ethnic tourism and historical tourism, comprising the observation, participation and sharing cultural expressions and lifestyles, dance and music performance, religious ceremonies, visual arts exhibitions, visiting monuments, sites and buildings, etc. Cultural tourism initiatives may succeed in consolidating the ethnographic 'gaze' if it designs and develops tour routes involving living and interactive experiences in real life in the townships and cultural houses or centres.

Cultural tourism in the Southern Jalisco can be an opportunity for the local communities to market and promote overseas experience-periods holidays to share and assimilate cultural values and life experiences taking advantage of the weather conditions and the beautiful natural landscape. The design of cultural tourism routes is necessary supported by the necessary to improve the infrastructure. To facilitate promotion and marketing of cultural tourism on the Southern Jalisco, easy access to a tourism information management system is required.

Local tourism information centres at the municipalities play an important role in spreading, guiding and providing assistance to visitors, rendering products and services alive and meaningful, and sharing responsibilities with tour and guide operators. Also, the roles that play communities, owners of facilities, etc. are vital on these matters. With respect to development, maintenance, promotion and marketing of cultural tourism in the Region Southern Jalisco, it is an imperative to design, formulate and implement a public policy-making process.

This paper on cultural tourism addresses the critical shortages of resources, infrastructure and skills amongst tourism stakeholders, business, practitioners, communities, etc. and offers some strategies as recommendations to improve the regional market with new cultural products and services. A differentiation between cultural tourism resources development and cultural production is essential for the design and implementation of cultural tourism strategies.

The implementation of a normative model leads to the development of cultural tourism infrastructure, develops entrepreneurial skills of the community, creates opportunities to attract foreign investors and funding agencies, helps design and implement marketing and promotional strategies, etc. all of which can contribute to the regional economic development of Southern Jalisco.

Fostering cultural tourism in the Southern Jalisco has a positive impact on developing infrastructure, offering diversified products and services in the cultural tourism market, creation of employment, development of entrepreneurial skills of the community, improvement of living conditions, etc. But most importantly, the normative model of cultural tourism has an impact on the spatial framework to address the sustainability of cultural tourism on cultural sites and attractions and economic development for the communities creating employment and improving the standards of life for the people.

This analysis may be the starting point for further research about cultural and heritage tourism development, marketing and promotion in the Region of Southern Jalisco.

REFERENCES

Aitchson, C. (2003). *Gender and Leisure: Social and Cultural Perspectives*. London: Routledge.

Australian Bureau of Statistics (1997). *Domestic Cultural Tourism in Australia,* www.dcita.gov.au.

Bayat, M.S. and Meyer, I. (Eds.) (1994). *Public Administration: Concepts, Theory and Practice.* Halfway House: Southern.

Besculides, A., Lee, M.E. and McCormick, P.J. (2002). "Resident's perceptions of cultural benefits of tourism", *Annals of Tourism Research* (2002), Vol. 29, No. 2, pp. 303–319.

Blench, B.D. (1999). *Sustainable Development in Africa*. London: Overseas Development Institute.

Bureau of Tourism Research (2004). *Economic Impact of Cultural Tourists in Australia.* http://www.culturaldata.gov.au/__data/assets/pdf_file/58358/Economic_Impact_of_Cultural_Tourists_in_Australia.pdf. [06 November 2007].

Bywater, M. (1993). *The Market for Cultural Tourism in Europe*, EIU N. 6.

CESTU (2002). *El turismo cultural en México*. Centro de estudios de la Secretaría de Turismo.

Cloete, F. and Wissink, H. (Eds.) (2000). *Improving Public Policy,* Pretoria: Van Schaik.

Cooper, C., Fletcher, J., Fyall, A., Gilbert, D. and Shepherd, R. (2008). *Tourism: Principles and Practice*. New York: Prentice Hall.

Easton, D. (1965). *A Framework for Political Analysis*. London: Prentice-Hall Inc.

Encarnación, S. (2008). *Los Famosos Equipales de Zacoalco*. Colección Espejo Diario.

FACUN (2010). *Tras las huellas de Juan Rulfo*. Capturado de http://www.papelesdeviaje.com/facundo46.htm

Ferreira, I.W. (1996). A normative model for managing orientation procedures for effective and efficient public personnel management in post-apartheid South Africa (Unpublished dissertation presented for the doctor administrationis degree at the University of Durban Westville (now University of KwaZuklu Natal).

George, R. (2001). *Marketing South African Tourism and Hospitality*. Cape Town: Oxford University Press.

González Castolo, F. (2010). *Danza de la Conquista de Hernán Cortés*. H. Ayuntamiento de Cd. Guzman, Jalisco.

_____ (2010). *Leyenda de la diosa Tzaputlatena*. H. Ayuntamiento de Cd. Guzman, Jalisco.

_____ (2010). *Leyenda Tzapotleca (La Laguna de Zapotlán)*. H. Ayuntamiento de Cd. Guzman, Jalisco.

_____ (2010). *Leyenda tzapotleca II (Las Piedras del Sochule o de "Los Compadres")*. H. Ayuntamiento de Cd. Guzman, Jalisco.

_____ (2010). *Una Feria originada de una Fiesta Patronal*. H. Ayuntamiento de Cd. Guzman, Jalisco.

Goeldner, C.R. and Ritchie, J.R.B. (2009). *Tourism: Principles, Practices, Philosophies*. New Jersey: John Wiley & Sons.

Hall, C.M. (1998). *Introduction to Tourism: Development, Dimension and Issues*. Sydney: Addison-Wesley & Longman.

Hall, C.M. and Zeppel, H. (1990). "Cultural and Heritage Tourism: The new grand tour?" *Historic Environment*, Vol. 7, No. 3–4, pp. 86–98.

Hanekom, S.X. and Thornhill, C. (1983). *Public Administration in Contemporary Socie—A South African Perspective*. Southern Book Publishers.

Ismail, Reedwaan (2008). "Development of a normative model for cultural tourism on the Cape Flats", CPUT Theses and Dissertations.

Ivanovic, M. (2008). *Cultural Tourism.* Cape Town, South Africa. Juta & Co.

Jamieson, W. (1998). "Cultural Heritage Tourism Planning and Development: Defining the Field and Its Challenges", *APT Bulletin*, Vol. 29, No. 3/4, Thirtieth-Anniversary Issue, pp. 65–67.

Keyser, H. (2002). *Tourism Development.* Cape Town: University Press Publishers.

Lara, J. (2010). *La cocina jaliscience, tradición que permanece viva en la memoria y en los paladares.*

Lubbe, B. (2003). *Tourism Distribution: Managing the Travel Intermediary*. Cape Town: Juta & Co.

Magi, L.M. and Nzama, A.T. (2008). "Interplay of Nature and Heritage for Communities Around the Ukhahlamba-Drakensberg World Heritage Park", *Journal of Tourism and Hospitality.* Vol. 6, No. 2, pp. 13–30.

McDonald, G. (1999). *Unpacking Cultural Tourism.* Vancouver: Simon Fraser University Press.

MacDonald, R. and Lee, J. (April 2003) "Cultural rural tourism: Evidence from Canada", *Annals of Tourism Research*, Vol. 30, No. 2, April 2003, pp. 307–322.

McKercher, B. and Du Cros, H. (January–February, 2003). "Testing a cultural tourism typology", *International Journal of Tourism Research*, Vol. 5, Issue 1, pp. 45–58.

McKercher, B. and Cros, H. (2002). *Cultural Tourism: The Partnership Between Tourism and Cultural Heritage Management.* New York: The Haworth Hospitality Press.

Moulin, C. (1990). "Cultural Tourism Theory". *Planning for Cultural Tourism*, Walter Jamieson (Ed.), Calgary: University of Calgary, pp. 43–61.

_____ (1989). "Cultural Tourism Theory". Paper presented at the Planning for Cultural Tourism Symposium, The University of Calgary, Alberta (Canada).

Nzama, A.T., Magi, L.M. and Ngcobo, N.R. (2005). *Workbook-I Tourism Workbook for Educators: 2004 Curriculum Statement.* Unpublished Tourism Workshop Educational Materials. Centre for Recreation and Tourism, UZ. and Tourism KwaZulu-Natal.

Ornelas, Mendoza y Valdivia, N.A. (1962). *Crónica de la Provincia de Santiago de Xalisco* (1719–1722). IJAH. Guadalajara. 1962. Páginas 142, 143 y 144.

Presidencia Municipal de Tonila. (2010). *Plan de desarrollo Municipal del municipio de Tonila Jalisco* 2004-200.

Richards, G. (1996). "Production and consumption of European cultural tourism". *Annals of Tourism Research,* Vol. 23, No. 2, pp. 261–283.

Russo, A.P. and J. van der Borg (2002). "Planning Considerations for Cultural Tourism: A Case Study of Four European Cities." *Tourism Management*, Vol. 23, No. 6, pp. 631–637.

SARDC [Southern African Research and Documentation Centre] (1994). *State of the Environment in Southern Africa.* Johannesburg: The Penrose Press.

Sharma, K. (2004). *Tourism and Socio-Cultural Development*. New Delhi: Sarup & Sons.

Shivers, J.S. (1981). *Leisure and Recreation Concept: A Critical Analysis*. Boston: Allyn & Bacon.

Spillane, B Brian A. (1997). "Zacoalco de Torres, Tierra de equipales". *México desconocido,* No. 240/febrero 1997.

Tighe, A.J. (1985). "Cultural tourism in the USA." *Tourism Management*, Vol. 6, No. 4, pp. 234–251.

Torkildsen, G. (2007). *Leisure and Recreation Management.* London. E. & F.N. Spon.

Villaseñor, Bordes, R. (1989). "Yendo a ver dos hospitales". *Suplemento Cultural del Informador.* 18 de Junio de 1989, pp. 13 and 14.

WCED [World Commission on Environment Development] (1987). *Our Common Future*. Oxford: Oxford Publishers.

Williams, M.A. and Shaw, G. (1991). Tourism policies in a changing economic environment. In *Tourism and economic development, Western European experiences.* London: Belhaven Press.

World Tourism Organization (WTO) (2000). *Definitions Concerning Tourists Statistics*. Madrid: WTO.

_____ (1985). *The state's role in protecting and promoting culture as a factor of tourism development and the proper use and exploitation of the national culture of heritage of sites and monuments for tourism.* Madrid: World Tourism Organization.

Ximba, E.Z. (2009). *Cultural and heritage tourism development and promotion in the Ndwedwe municipal area: perceived policy and practice.* Dissertation submitted to the Faculty of Arts. Department of Recreation and Tourism at the University of Zululand.

CHAPTER

2

THE APPLICATION OF SUSTAINABLE TOURISM INDICATORS IN THE DEVELOPMENT OF TAMAN RIMBA TELOK BAHANG, PENANG, MALAYSIA

—JABIL MAPJABIL AND AZIZAN MARZUKI

2.1 ABSTRACT

Sustainable indicators are used to measure the changes, identify the processes involved and prepare the framework for the target procedure and performance observation. These indicators provide the method to draw the development chart towards the importance of achieving a balanced style of development in social, economic and environmental fields as the main objective in the sustainable development of a country. Some of the sustainable tourism indicators used in determining the development of a tourism destination are site preservation according to the index in the International Union for the Conservation of Nature and Natural Resource (IUCN), social impact and the contribution to the local economy. The forest park of Telok Bahang is an amenity forest which was founded in 1974 and covers an area as large as 32 hectares out of the total 873 hectares of the forest reserve area in Telok Bahang. The amenity forest caters to various types of facilities such as jungle trekking activities, recreational sports, camping sites and a forest museum. The research method used in this study was the collection of primary data by using questionnaire forms. The purpose of implementing this method was to be able to obtain information directly from any of the selected respondents. The research sample consisted of 141 respondents, who were visitors to the park. The development of a sustainable amenity forest could only be realized if there is high awareness and commitment among those who are involved, which include the policy makers, policy enforcers and the people themselves. The development plan, which includes the economic, social and environmental aspects, has to be integrated harmoniously and those who are involved have to play an important role in the process of deciding the policy and making decisions related to the development of sustainable tourism in amenity forests in this country.

KEYWORDS: sustainable indicators, amenity forest, sustainable tourism

2.2 INTRODUCTION

Tourism is one of the largest industries and economic sectors which have grown extremely rapid all over the world. It has given many positive as well as negative effects to human life and the environment (United Nations World Tourism Organization, 2004). The National Ecotourism Plan of Malaysia (PEPNM), which was introduced by the Ministry of Culture, Arts and Tourism in 1997, was established based on the existing 426 ecotourism locations and on those which had the potential to be developed, which included 11 diagnostic factors, 14 types of attractions and 20 various types of activities. This is a golden opportunity for Malaysia considering that Malaysia is rich with her natural resources which could be a major tourist attraction to this country (Daud, 2003). Sustainable tourism is one the components of the sustainable development focused by Malaysia. In the Ninth Malaysian Plan (RMK-9), as much as RM 1.8 billion was allocated to the tourism sector to improve its infrastructure, provide tourism facilities and also develop more innovative tourism products and services (Hassan and Che Leh, 2007).

Malaysia has many places of interest and specialties which could be developed into world famous tourist destinations. The country's main asset is her unique culture, people from various backgrounds and religions as well as historical places and also her beautiful and interesting natural environment. This comprises waterfalls, exotic islands, jungle parks, caves and hill stations (Osman and Suhana, 2007). Nevertheless, a continuous increase in the number of tourists has created pressure onto the destinations, particularly on the nature based ones (Deng et al., 2002). Therefore, a sustainable tourism concept is an important policy towards the development of a perpetual and everlasting tourism industry (Mohamed, 2008). According to UNWTO (2004), sustainable tourism is a continuous process which requires observation, prevention and collective action whenever needed. Besides this, sustainable tourism is important in maintaining the satisfaction and also ensuring a memorable experience for tourists, increasing their awareness about sustainability as well as to promote sustainable tourism among them.

2.3 LITERATURE REVIEW ON SUSTAINABLE TOURISM AND AMENITY FORESTS

Sustainable tourism is now receiving more international attention since many bad outcomes had been associated with this sector following the increase in mass tourism in the 1960s. This had created much criticism and debate in the tourism industry until the sustainable tourism phenomenon was developed, which is also known for its concept of greenery and softness. Sustainable tourism has been developed as a result of the idea of sustainable development. Until the early 1990s, the efforts to develop sustainable tourism had not been actively carried out. However, the importance of tourism had been officially acknowledged and became an important issue within global politics in the aspect of nature through the Convention on Biological Diversity and in the *Agenda 21* Plan. The development of sustainable tourism is part of a strategy which aims to fulfil the needs of today's generation without neglecting the ability of the next generation to fulfil their needs (World Commission on Environment and Development, 1987). This means there is quality control on the ecological environment, stability and social justice, besides economic development to fulfil the future needs. The implications of the concept towards the future needs are huge. Since the development of sustainable tourism was introduced, tourism activities have moved to a more positive stage. This sector has started to receive more attention on the ability of nature to accommodate increasing tourists and visitors while not only focusing on physical development (Mohamed, 2008). Sustainable tourism is seen from various aspects such as natural, social and also economic perspective. Sustainable tourism is associated with types of tourism that are sensitive towards ecological systems and local people's culture by minimizing the negative effects on nature, besides contributing to the preservation of nature and giving job opportunities to the local community (Wells, 1997).

Hardy et al. (2010) observed the concept and position of tourism within the topic of sustainable tourism. Research about sustainable tourism had now been done in the strategic frame of tourism documentation. However, most previous studies on sustainable tourism rarely argue on how history could affect tourism conceptualities. Therefore, the purpose of this study is to observe the development in the concept of sustainable tourism and how it is applied today. In this study, models which combined sustainable development into new tourism approaches were also looked into. In the tourism industry, from the operators to the government agencies, a lot of habits in sustainable tourism have been modified and carried out. However, whether they contribute to changes which are significant or otherwise, could still be argued and this leads to various opinions which state that changes should be brought about by looking into history to fix the existing inherent problems instead of building more tourism development aspects which are sustainable. Focusing on environmental and economic issues, this research had identified the concept and operation of development within sustainable tourism.

The concept of sustainable tourism is a basic and crucial element towards the everlasting development of the tourism industry. Continuous increase in the number of tourists, either local or foreign, has increased the pressure on tourist destinations especially on those which are nature based (Wearing and Neil, 1999). Therefore, an integrated approach taking into account the ability of the place to accommodate the number of tourists and visitors is very important. This concept had introduced aspects such as nurturing and preserving nature and also the involvement of people in the development of the tourism industry.

Sustainable tourism is a type of tourism which integrates all the successful resources either existing aspects or those that could be formed into interesting tourism products. There are four categories identified as successful resources, which are:

1. Natural successful resources: beaches, river, mountains, lakes, hills, caves, seas and jungles
2. Heritage successful resources: monuments, buildings, culture, way of life
3. Agricultural successful resources: paddy fields, orchards, plantation, livestock, fishery
4. Man-made successful resources: theme parks, stages, stadiums

As the importance of the development of sustainable tourism is very critical, the initiators for the development have been established to determine the course of planning in facilitating achievement of the aims of sustainable tourism development. There are four main routes for the places or destinations as a means of enabling sustainable tourism development (Table 2.1).

Wild (1994) explained sustainable tourism as tourism that prepares economic opportunities and also maintains the quality of nature so that it is not polluted. This tourism concept is also based on the desire and aspirations of the local people. Therefore, the local people's cultural elements and customs must become part of the marketed tourism product. Economic benefits that are gained from the tourism activities happening around the residential area of the local people have to be accepted and enjoyed by them (Dulude, 2002). The sustainable concept is being introduced into and used more and more with the concept of tourism development lately. Some of the types of tourism have always been associated with the sustainable concept such as natural tourism, home stay, green tourism and also ecotourism in amenity forests.

In Malaysia, there have been some previous studies on sustainable tourism carried out by a few experts and researchers. Hassan and Che Leh (2007) have conducted research on sustainable tourism elements in FELDA Gugusan Trolak, which has a few existing tourism products such as the River Klah Hot Water Park and the Trolak Orchard. This research also suggested a few steps to achieve development in sustainable farming tourism in the efforts to diversify the national tourism concept and also to help improve the standard of living of the FELDA settlers, their family and the future generation of the settlers. Some of the studies found that there are less than 10 elements of successful resources places which have the potential as a multi concept tourism product such as educational tourism, ecological tourism, country-side tourism, plantation tourism, industrial tourism, and so on. However, a few steps to improve things like infrastructure facilities, development of the tourism package as well as marketing and promotion of the tourism product were suggested so that profit could be increased, distributed and enjoyed together with the local community, besides helping to increase their standard of living.

Amenity forest is an area in the jungle within a Reserved Forest that could be used for resting, conducting research and educational activities and also to preserve flora and fauna

Table 2.1 Four main routes for sustainable tourism (Destination)

Perspective	*Details*
1. *Economic sustainability*—current and long-term profit	• Using international standardization and guides for training and certification • Diversify activities and tourism products • Preparing assistance for training, development and product marketing • Promoting alertness towards ethics and environment • Giving incentives for businesses that use sustainable concept-Building the relationship chain at all levels of business
2. *Ecological sustainability*—maintaining the importance of ecological process, resources and biodiversity	• Determining a code of habit/practice for tourism at all levels • Determining and guiding operation, evaluation and impact control • Framing the development policies and strategies so that they are in line with the concept • Making sure the design, planning, development and operations of facilities incorporate the principles and concept of sustainable development • Making sure the development of sensitive areas incorporate appropriate management and planning • Control and carry out research on actual tourism impacts • Determining and promoting the behaviour of responsible tourism
3. *Cultural sustainability*—adjusting to the original cultural and community values and strengthening local identity	• Encouraging tourism with original community assistance and input • Making sure training programmes and education help and control heritage and natural resources • Preserving the various cultures • Respect the right of the land and for the traditions practiced • Taking care of nature, the locals and their culture as well as traditional knowledge • Giving an accurate and precise picture of the existing cultures • Encouraging the use of traditional skills • Educating tourists about responsible and acceptable behaviour
4. *Local sustainability*—profitable to the local people and increases their income	• Maintaining local control on tourism development • Providing quality occupations for the locals • Encouraging fair division from the gained profit • Preparing financial incentives for the local entrepreneurs to join the tourism sector • Improving the capacity of local energy sources

Source: Modified from Mckercher (2003).

(Mohamad et al., 2006). This place has a special attraction in the form of in-situ elements and could be used positively. The natural or man-made resources as well as the ecosystems and ecology found in this place are one of the important sources of recreational and tourism activities and has the potential to be developed as a sustainable tourism product for that place. In Malaysia, the amenity forest is a type of forest which has been categorized by the Forestry Department in the process of silviculture management. Besides this forest, there are eight types of other forests that have been classified as original forests, after work forest, chosen forest, farm forest, virgin reserved forest, community forest, city forest, and forest research plots. In 1967, the Forestry Department commercialized the amenity forest concept.

Amenity forest is part of the tourism based on ecology which could create awareness to the people about the importance of nurturing and preserving forests. This is because throughout the ages, the original forest has been playing various types of important roles such as balancing the temperature, water reserve area, controlling erosion and floods, reducing air velocity and so on (Ayob, 2006). In Malaysia, the creation of the amenity forest started with the introduction of five areas of amenity forest in Peninsular Malaysia under the First Malaysian Plan (1966–1970) (Jalil, 1983). Recreation is one of the elements in the strategy of forestry which leads to the management of reserved forests in Malaysia. The existence of recreational forests will give economically beneficial values through the presence of the visiting tourists and users (National Ecotourism Plan, 1997).

The purpose of creating recreational forests is to fulfil all or parts of the following:

1. Prepare resting facilities in the forests for picnics, swimming, lookout places, flora parks, resting huts and beautiful natural scenery for all age groups.
2. Create awareness in the society on the importance of making the authenticity of nature, particularly the preserved forest maintained for their wellbeing.
3. To give support and chance to explore the jungle area while enjoying the beauty through the trails done in the forest. Facilities such as mountain climbing, camping in the forest and other adventure based activities could be introduced.
4. Increase places of tropical forest ecological research for learning purposes and scientific knowledge, especially for the younger generation and for students.
5. Maintaining the forest area to function as a natural balancer and "green lung" to the other development around it.

2.4 SUSTAINABLE TOURISM CONCEPT AND INDICATORS

In nature's context, tourism needs to be developed sustainably, not only because of its positive effects but also negative impacts, depending on the way the management of the development is planned, monitored and controlled. Tourism development and management which is inappropriate and does not follow fixed procedure will cause destruction of habitat and landscape, destroy natural sources, and finally, the pollution of nature becomes more serious, especially the problem of unmanaged waste disposal (Gouva, 2004). Therefore, the sustainable tourism approach for every tourism planning is extremely important because if this source is destroyed, then the tourist destination will no longer attract visitors and the place will become isolated (Ioannides, 1995; Godfrey, 1998). To make this concept real, indicators of the sustainable level have to be drawn and be used as a measurement tool towards the selected criteria. According to Sani (2001), an indicator is a measurement for a criterion. It is used for two purposes which are to quantify information in explaining the research outcome in detail and summarizing information about a complex situation so that it is easier to understand. Sustainable indicators are to measure changes, identify the involved processes and prepare the framework for the target procedure and performance observation (Crabtree & Bayfield, 1998). These indicators prepare a method to chart the development towards goal importance in achieving a form of balanced development in the aspects of social, economic and nature as the main objective in the sustainable development of a country. Table 2.2 shows the main indicators in sustainable tourism according to Dymond (1997).

Table 2.2 Main indicators of sustainable tourism

Indicator	*Measurement details*	*Field of indicator*
1. Site preservation	Site preservation category according to International Union for the Conservation of Nature and Natural Resources (IUCN) index	Ecology
2. Pressure	Total amount of tourists to the location (annual and monthly)	Ecology
3. Intensive usage	Intensive usage during the highest period (total visitors per hectare)	Ecology
4. Management of waste	Percentage of waste sent to the disposal site (extra indicators such as water supply could be used)	Ecology
5. Critical ecosystem	Number of unique species, extinct and soon to be extinct species in that area	Ecology
6. Social impact	Ratio of total tourists to local people (during peak seasons and subsequent seasons)	Social
7. Local people's satisfaction	Satisfaction level expressed by the local people (using questionnaire census)	Economy
8. Development control	Using environment reference procedure or formal control towards development of the site and the density	Planning
9. Planning process	Using territorial planning plan which had been planned for areas of tourism planning	Planning
10. Customer satisfaction (tourism)	Satisfactory level that is expressed by tourists (using questionnaire census)	Economy
11. Contribution to the local economy	Total economic contribution gained from the tourism sector	Economy

Source: Dymond (1997)

2.5 DEVELOPMENT OF AMENITY FORESTS IN PENANG

Amenity forest is a forest specified to be developed as an open to public resort area for resting, picnics, camping purposes, and so on. The development of amenity forests in the reserved forest area tallies with the National Forestry Policy 1978 and the National Forestry Act 1984 to create a place which is adequate and appropriate for recreational, ecotourism and educational purposes for the society to understand forest functions and its importance. In Malaysia, the establishment of the amenity forest was introduced under the First Malaysian Plan (1966–1970) with five amenity forests in Peninsular Malaysia. Amenity forest is one of the ecological based tourism categories which could create awareness in the society on the importance of nurturing and preserving the forest. For ages, the original forest has played many important roles from balancing the temperature, water reserve area, controlling erosion and floods, reducing wind speed to many other functions (Ayob, 2006).

In line with the requirements of the National Forestry Policy, every state is required to carry out efforts to develop and preserve forest through silviculture acts which are effective and efficient. A few programmes have been planned towards this aim and one of them is society foresting. This programme is one of the department's efforts to involve the public in the endeavours to maintain the forest areas for recreational and educational purposes. Some of the activities carried out are forest villages, urban forests and amenity forests. Amenity forests in Penang have long been established and have continued to grow rapidly due to the increasing requests from the visitors and tourists. There are three amenity forests in this state, namely *Hutan Lipur Bukit Mertajam, Hutan Lipur Bukit Panchor* and *Taman Rimba Telok Bahang.*

1. **Taman Rimba Telok Bahang**

Rimba Rekreasi Telok Bahang is situated in the Forest Reserve area of Telok Bahang, which is located 24 km from the city of Georgetown, Penang via the main trunk road to Teluk Bahang. It is also known as *Hutan Lipur Telok Bahang.* This amenity forest is part of a virgin reserve forest which has various types of flora and fauna. Visitors can enjoy the beauty of the plants through a readymade trail. *Taman Rimba Telok Bahang* is one of the locations from the 111 amenity forests in Peninsular Malaysia. This park was founded in 1974 and covers an area of 32 hectares from the total 873 hectares of the *Hutan Simpan Kekal Telok Bahang*. However, the real acreage that has been used for recreational purposes comprises two sections as large as 117 hectares. The establishment of the amenity forest in the reserved forest area tallies with the National Forestry Policy 1978 (Amendment 1992), which is to maintain sufficient areas for recreation, ecotourism as well as for awareness in society on aspects of forestry. Various types of activities could be carried out here such as resting, picnic and swimming. Besides that, some of the facilities such as playgrounds, camping sites and resting huts have also been built. In addition to these, there is a pond which has a collection of freshwater fishes in the amenity forest. Various facilities have been provided to carry out the recreational activities such as jungle trekking, camping, resting, swimming, and so on. Facilities such as an Annex Hall and Forestry Museum have also been established for the visitors to know the development and usage of the forest towards human life.

PHOTO 2.1 ***Taman Rimba Telok Bahang.***

2. **Taman Rimba Bukit Mertajam**

The *Taman Rimba Bukit Mertajam* has an area of 37 hectares with the highest point of 545 metres above sea level. The location of this popular recreational spot still has various tree species and original plants such as the Meranti Seraya (*Shorea curtisll*). Some of its main attractions are the rivers, the waterfalls, camping sites and chalet facilities. For extreme sports adventurers, mountain climbing could be done in two different ways, either through the use of jeeps or walking through the trail. The challenging climb involves a journey as long as 3.5 km from the base and it takes more than 1 hour for an intermediate climber to reach the third station. Along the climb, the visitors could enjoy the various bird species, exotic insects and the beauty of the scenery from the top. Drinks are provided in the third station by volunteers for the public.

PHOTO 2.2 ***Taman Rimba Bukit Mertajam.***

3. **Taman Negeri Bukit Panchor**

Taman Negeri Bukit Panchor, which is located in the Bukit Panchor Forest Reserve in the district of southern Seberang Perai, Penang has become a recreational place for the local people. The park with an area of 8 hectares has a camping facility along the exquisite River

Buaya. This facility could accommodate as much 200 participants at one time and it was a favourite location for many campers. It is also complete with basic facilities for family or group activities. The Wetland Park offers swamp exploration, which is rich with untouched flora and fauna. During the holiday season, the park is full of visitors who love the peaceful environment and to be surrounded by nature. This park also offers challenging exploration activities through its caves and along the river. The main attraction here is the *Gua Kelawar,* which has a huge population of bats. The group activities here require high physical endurance. The collection of the flora and fauna is still well preserved in this park and could be made into reference sources and valuable educational notes for the visitors and tourists.

PHOTO 2.3 ***Taman Negeri Bukit Panchor.***

2.6 RESEARCH METHODOLOGY

Research on the community perspective on the application of sustainable development in the amenity forest has been carried out on the visitors who visited the *Taman Rimba Telok Bahang.*

2.6.1 Research Sample

For this research, as many as 141 respondents comprising local people, domestic and foreign tourists have been chosen as the study sample (Table 2.3). The respondents were chosen randomly to ensure an accurate and fair result. According to Neill (2003), a random sample means that every one unit within the entire sample has an equal chance to be chosen. By choosing randomly from the sample, the probability theory says that the sample could be more probable to be representing the whole population. According to this method, respondents are not chosen based on any criterion, but every visitor and person in the research conducted has an equal probability to be chosen to become a respondent. In research that requires surveys and observation, the sampling methodology is often used. This is because of the cost factors and the constraints involved in collecting information from all the population, organization or other types of bodies focused in the research (Veal, 2006).

Table 2.3 Respondent demographic profile

Characteristics	*Criteria*	*Number*	*Percentage*
Respondent category	Local residents	102	72.3
	Daily visitors	19	13.5
	Domestic tourist	20	14.2
	Foreign tourist	0	0.0
Sex	Male	57	40.4
	Female	84	59.6
Age	20 years and below	20	14.2
	21–30 years	64	45.4
	31–40 years	40	28.4
	41–50 years	13	9.2
	50 years and above	4	2.8
Race	Malay	117	83.0
	Chinese	15	10.6
	Indian	6	4.3
	Others	3	2.1
Status	Single	77	54.6
	Married	64	45.5
Education	University/College/Matriculation	62	44.0
	Secondary level (Form 1–6)	71	50.4
	Primary level (Year 1–6)	8	5.7
	No formal education	0	0.0
Occupation	Government sector	32	22.7
	Private sector	17	12.1
	Self employed	17	12.1
	Business	15	10.6
	Retired	1	0.7
	Housewife	9	6.4
	Students	50	35.5
	Others	0	0.0

2.6.2 Research Design

This research uses the inductive approach that is specific to a particular topic and is not generalizing, and where decisions are taken from specific facts rather than general ones. In this matter, the research which is done is in the form of case study and involves utilizing methodology and interpreting a phenomenon to gain profound and detailed information about an occurred act or process. Research in the inductive form starts with an observation and carries on with analyzing and finally ends with making an explanation about the research (Veal, 2006). Next, it will be transformed into the deductive form through data analysis with the help of the SPSS (Statistical Package for the Social Sciences) software to analyze and gain a statistical formula in order to save time in terms of research handling.

2.6.3 Instrument

A research instrument is the tool used while conducting a research in an area. In this research, a few tools and methods were used to gain data and information from the respondents, namely: (a) Questionnaire forms; (b) Interview; (c) Snowball; (d) Observation; (e) Photo and (f) Statistical Package for Social Science (SPSS) software.

2.7 RESEARCH FINDINGS AND DISCUSSION

Table 2.3 shows that the majority of respondents are from the local people, as much as 72.3%. More female respondents were interviewed than males, where there were 84 females and 57 males. Most of the respondents were Malays (83%) and in the age range of 21 till 30 years old (45.4%). Next, the majority of the respondents were single, representing 54.6%. The research found that the education levels of most respondents were of an intermediate level, where they were more than 50%. More students were interviewed than those who are working, comprising more than 30% (50 people) from the 141 respondents involved in this research.

The existence of waterfalls and river is the main attraction, which motivates respondents to visit to the *Taman Rimba Bahang* comprising more than 40 people followed by the attraction from the forest reserve as much as 26.95% of the respondents (Table 2.4). The amenity forest provides places for swimming and picnics. It is shown clearly that nature could attract more tourists than man-made attractions such as forestry museum and hiking tracts which only registered 5.67% (8 people) respectively. Environment and human are two components of nature components which interact and communicate with each other. A sustainable development approach must be implemented so that the rights or the interests of the current and the next generation are not neglected. An ideal environment could fulfil all the requirements and needs of human life.

Table 2.4 Main tourist attraction in *Taman Rimba Telok Bahang*

Attraction attributes	*Number*	*Percentage*
1. Waterfall/river	41	29.08
2. Forest reserve	38	26.95
3. Interesting places and environments	31	21.99
4. Hiking activity	8	5.67
5. Visiting forestry museum	8	5.67
6. No answer	15	10.64
Total	**141**	**100.0**

According to Table 2.5, there are a few indicators which can become the measurement for the development of sustainable tourism in the research area. An indicator or measurement indicator of the development of sustainable tourism becomes an important fundamental element to the theoretical framework for the development of eco-friendly tourism activities

Table 2.5 Sustainable tourism development indicators in *Taman Rimba Telok Bahang*

Attributes of indicators	*Yes*	*%*	*No*	*%*
1. The park is well maintained (*caring for the site*)	95	67.5	46	32.5
2. There is pressure of rapid development beside the park (*pressure*)	100	70.9	41	29.1
3. There is development in the parks (*intensive development*)	100	70.9	41	29.1
4. The waste disposal is managed systematically in the park (*waste disposal management*)	92	71.6	49	28.4
5. The ecosystem/environment is suffering from critical destruction (*critical ecosystem)*	83	58.9	58	41.1
6. The park gives benefit to the people around it (*resident satisfaction*)	116	82.3	25	17.7
7. The visitors are satisfied with the conditions and the facilities in the park (*visitors satisfaction*)	60	42.2	81	57.8
8. The park contributes to the economy as a whole	104	73.4	37	26.6
9. The development of the park is well planned and very systematic	106	75.2	35	24.8
10. The development of the park is under control (*development control*)	109	77	32	23
11. The park could contribute to negative social effects	91	64.5	50	35.5

especially in the rural areas (Hassan and Che Leh, 2010). Majority of the respondents agree that the park could give benefit to the people around it, the development of the park is under control and the development of the park is planned nicely and systematically, making up as much as 75% of the respondents. From the perspective of the caring for the site, development pressure, intensive development, waste disposal management and the contribution to the economy on the whole is considered as intermediate, comprising as much as 65%. The research finds that the respondents do not quite agree on the satisfaction level of the visitors, critical ecosystems, and that the park encourages negative social effects with each element represented by less than 65% of the respondents.

Table 2.6 shows the level of satisfaction of the respondents to the environment and the facilities in the *Taman Rimba Telok Bahang* according to gender. There is a mean value between 3.42 to 4.05, which shows the respondents of both genders saying that the park is in the moderate (level 3) and satisfactory (level 4) levels based on their observation and experience. Both genders have a similarity in one aspect, that is, giving the highest satisfactory mark with the highest mean value to the location of the park which is as much as 3.91 (1.84) for males and a mean value of 4.05 (1.005) for female respondents. This value shows that the location of the park is satisfactory. However, a difference could be seen in the lowest mean value of men who have chosen the complaint facilities and information to the visitors with the lowest mean value of 3.65 (0.876) whereas, the female respondents chose the food court with a mean value of 3.42 (0.984). Therefore, it could be seen clearly that there is a similarity and difference for the gender variable in determining the satisfactory level while visiting the *Taman Rimba Telok Bahang*. The research also supports Mathieson and Wall's (1992) findings which say that a clear location and knowledge about the destination, facilities and services provided will encourage the visitors to visit the destination again. Choosing a tourism destination requires consideration of a few factors such as distance of the location, time to stay in the destination, travel time, cost of journey and so on.

Table 2.6 Satisfactory level of the respondents towards the environment and facilities in *Taman Rimba Telok Bahang*

Gender	*Male*								*Female*							
Item	1	2	3	4	5	Mean	SD	R	1	2	3	4	5	Mean	SD	R
1. Park's location	1	9	9	13	25	3.91	1.184	1	0	5	25	15	39	4.05	1.005	1
2. Cleanliness of the park's environment	0	6	12	23	16	3.86	0.953	6	0	10	30	25	19	3.63	0.967	6
3. Facilities provided (on the whole)	2	2	18	20	15	3.77	1.000	9	0	6	38	24	16	3.60	0.880	7
4. Complaint facilities and information for the visitors	0	2	29	13	13	3.65	0.876	11	0	2	45	23	14	3.58	0.795	8
5. Sign board/ location map facilities in the park	0	5	11	26	15	3.89	0.900	3	2	3	27	36	16	3.73	0.896	4
6. Educational facilities	1	1	21	22	12	3.75	0.872	10	3	5	34	26	16	3.56	0.986	9
7. Rubbish bin facilities	0	2	17	27	11	3.82	0.782	8	4	6	30	29	15	3.45	1.023	11
8. Toilet facilities	0	1	19	21	16	3.91	0.830	2	6	7	30	21	20	3.50	1.156	10
9. Food/drink stalls	1	0	17	26	13	3.88	0.825	5	3	10	31	29	11	3.42	0.984	12
10. The effort to preserve various types of flora species (*plants, tress etc.*)	0	3	16	25	13	3.84	0.841	7	0	5	24	36	19	3.82	0.853	2
11. The effort to preserve various types of fauna species (*animals, fishes etc.*)	3	0	12	29	13	3.86	0.953	6	1	7	28	29	19	3.69	0.957	5
12. Park management system (*on the whole*)	0	1	19	22	15	3.89	0.817	4	0	7	22	40	15	3.75	0.848	3

2.8 CONCLUSION

The development of a good tourism product and destination could attract more tourists from in and out of the country. It could also generate the economy not only for the government but also for the local people either directly or indirectly. Many people think that sustainable tourism could balance the development of tourism with the preservation of nature. However, if sustainable tourism is not managed carefully, selectively and thoroughly, it could cause a lot more trouble than gaining profit. Therefore, this tourism product needs to be developed comprehensively and effectively in line with the government's goal to introduce Malaysia as a sustainable tourism destination in the world's eyes. Therefore, planning, development and management of a tourism product need consideration from various angles starting from policy formulation, strategy, tourism programme development which covers marketing, activity organizing, maintenance, and so on. Besides that, integrating thoughts and opinions is very much needed to implement sustainable tourism development because it should not involve only government institutions but also the support from the professional groups, public sector, nature based organizations and the public.

REFERENCES

Ayob, W. (2006). Pengurusan hutan rekreasi Sungai Tekala, Hulu Langat, Selangor (*The Management of Sungai Tekala Forest Reserve, Kuala Langat, Selangor*). In H. Ismail, T.P. Rokiah and J.A. Ibrahim (Eds.). Pengurusan Persekitaran dan Pelancongan di Malaysia: Konsepsi dan Kajian (*Research on Tourism and Environment Management in Malaysia*). Sintok: Universiti Utara Malaysia. 124 –140.

Crabtree, R. and Bayfield, N. (1998). Developing sustainability indicators for mountain ecosystems: A study of the Cairngorms, Scotland. *Journal of Environmental Management*, 52(1), 1–14.

Deng, J., King, B. and Bauer, T. (2002). Evaluating natural attractions for tourism. *Annals of Tourism Research,* 29(2), 422– 438.

Daud, M. (2003). *Masa Hadapan Industri Pelancongan Negara* (*The Future of the National Tourism Industry*). [Online]. Accessed: 1 April 2011. Available from World Wide Web: (http: //mohamadsofee.blogspot.).

Dulude, J. (2002). 'Trouble in Paradise: Critics say lack of protection endangers Costa Rica's famed nature preserves'. *The San Francisco Chronicle*, December 28.

Dymond, S.J. (1997). Indicators of sustainable tourism in New Zealand: A local government perspective. *Journal of Sustainable Tourism*, 5(4), 279–293.

Godfrey, K.B. (1998). Attitudes towards 'sustainable tourism' in the UK: A view from local government. *Tourism Management*, 19(3), 213–224.

Gouvea, R. (2004). Doing business in Brazil: A strategic approach. *Thunderbird International Business Review*, 46(20), 43–52.

Hardy, A., R.J.S. and Pearson, L. (2010). An overview of the concept and its position in relation to conceptualizations tourism. *Journal of Sustainable Tourism*, 10(6), 475–496.

Hassan, F. and Che Leh, F. (2007). Pembangunan Pelancongan Lestari di Felda Gugusan Trolak: Satu Analisis (*An analysis on sustainable tourism development in Felda Gugusan Trolak*). In the Proceeding of the *Seminar Kebangsaan Geografi-Dunia Tanpa Sempadan.* 8–9 September 2007. Universiti Pendidikan Sultan Idris, Malaysia.

Ioannides, D. (1995). A flawed implementation of sustainable tourism: The experience of Akamas, Cyprus. *Tourism Management*, 16(8), 583–592.

Jalil, M.S. (1983). Discussion session. *Outdoor Recreation in Malaysia.* Serdang, Selangor, Malaysia, Discussion Session: Faculty of Forestry, University Pertanian Malaysia.

Mathieson, A. and Wall, G. (1992). *Tourism: Economic, physical and social impacts.* London: Longman.

McKercher, B. (2003). Sustainable tourism development: Guiding principles for planning and management. *National Seminar on Sustainable Tourism Development, Bishkek, Kyrgystan*, November 5–9.

Mohamed, B. (2008). *Pelancongan Lestari (Sustainable Tourism).* Kuala Lumpur: Dewan Bahasa dan Pustaka.

Mohamad, M.K., Yunus, N. and Hassan, C.H. (2006). Pelancongan dan alam semula jadi: Satu tinjauan terhadap peranan hutan lipur sebagai produk rekreasi dan pelancongan berasaskan alam semula jadi di negeri Kedah *(Tourism and nature: An overview of waterfalls' role as recreation and tourism product in the State of Kedah).* In H. Ismail, T.P. Rokiah and J.A. Ibrahim (Eds.). *Pengurusan Persekitaran dan Pelancongan di Malaysia: Konsepsi dan Kajian.* Sintok *(Research on Tourism and Environment Management in Malaysia)*: Universiti Utara Malaysia. 70–76.

National Ecotourism Plan (1996). *Ministry of Culture, Art and Tourism.* Federal Government of Malaysia.

Neill, J. (2003). *Random Sample.* [Online]. Accessed: 24 April 2011. Available from World Wide Web: Http://wilderdom.com/Oecourse/PROFLIT/JamesNeill.htm.

Osman, F. and Suhaina, S. (2007). Malaysia bukan destinasi pilihan. In *Isu-isu Kenegaraan Malaysia (Malaysia is not a popular destination: National Issues*). Kuala Lumpur: Dewan Bahasa dan Pustaka.

Sani, S. (2001). *Public lecture: Developing urban sustainability indicators for Malaysia.* No. 3. Bangi: Universiti Kebangsaan Malaysia.

UNWTO (2004). *Sustainable Tourism: Definition* [Online]. Accessed: 1 October 2010. Available from World Wide Web: http://www.unep.fr/scp/tourism/sustain/.

Veal, A.J. (2006). *Research Methods for Leisure and Tourism: A Practical Guide.* Harlow, England: Prentice Hall.

Wearing, S. and Neil, J. (1999). *Ecotourism: Impacts, Potentials and Possibilities*, Butterworth Heinemann: Oxford, UK.

Wells, M.P. (1997). *Economic perspectives on nature tourism, conservation and development.* Environment Department Paper No. 55. Pollution and Environmental Economics Division. Washington, DC: World Bank.

Wild, C. (1994). Issues in Ecotourism. In *Progress in Tourism, Recreation, and Hospitality Management* (Vol. 6), C.P. Cooper and A. Lockwood (Eds.), Chichester: Wiley, pp. 12–21.

World Commission on Environment and Development (1987). *Our Common Future.* Oxford: Oxford University Press.

CHAPTER

3

RURAL TOURISM DEVELOPMENT Constraints and Potential with Special Reference to Agri-Tourism

(A Case Study on Cashew Agri-Tourism Destination—Rajendrapattinam Village in Vridddachalam Taluk of Cuddalore District, Tamil Nadu)

—A. BALAMURUGAN, R. KANNAN AND S.K. NAGARAJAN

3.1 ABSTRACT

The concept of rural tourism is well accepted all over the world. People from all over the world travel far and wide not only to see places of interest, but also for the opportunity to interact with the locals and to an extent even get introduced to their culture. Tamil Nadu has significant tourist potential.

As we in Tamil Nadu promote tourism, we should get away from the mindset of looking only at the foreign tourist. As the earning power of the young, specifically the software professionals and urban city dwellers, are on the rise, we should also target to cater to their needs. It may be worthwhile looking into setting up this Centre for Rural Tourism (CRT) next to the existing cultural and other tourist centre spots; this will facilitate the people who are visiting places like Chidambaram to do other activities in the village like milking the cow, etc. We can also tie up with organizations like Dakhinchitra model with CRT. These initiatives should be run as a franchise, with the local villager owning the capital investment and managing the day-to-day operations while the Tourist operator/Hotel Chain managing safety and hygiene and ensuring that adequate quality is maintained.

3.2 INTRODUCTION

Global economic restructuring has created a climate in which many local economies have to adjust in order to maintain or enhance their socio-economic viability. Economic and social forces operating at the global level are determining both the nature and form of the rural landscape and how we value and use it. These changes, coupled with new ideas and approaches to leisure and recreation time, are encouraging tourism development in rural areas at an ever increasing pace.

Rural tourism development in the areas not traditionally considered tourism destinations per se occurs incrementally, either as a result of entrepreneurs developing businesses that attract visitors or as a result of visitors discovering the area and thereby generating a demand for tourism related activities to which local entrepreneurs respond. The development of tourism in a rural area is not simply a matter of matching tourist demands with local product supply but a matter of evaluating local suitability and acceptability.

3.2.1 The Indian Agriculture and Tourism Industry Scenario

India is known as "Land of villages". More than 77 crore farmers live in 5.5 lakhs of village (2007). Agriculture contributed about 18.5% of the national income (2008–2009) as compared to a high 50% in 1950. Eighty-five per cent of the population of India still depends on agriculture. Hence, agriculture is not mere business, but is still the "True Culture of India".

3.2.2 Domestic Tourism Growth

India has achieved great prosperity in tourism as a product. India being the home to many leading religions of the world has many important pilgrim sites of different religions scattered throughout the country. Besides, the average Indian is also an avid sightseer. It is also stated that every 30 million additional tourists translate into ₹ 4,300 crores in revenue. It is also stated that farm tourism, if developed along unique indigenous lines, could have a multiplier effect and high revenue capital ratio.

During 2010, the number of domestic tourist visit (FTVs) to the states/UTs was 740 million as compared to 669 million in 2009 and 563 million in 2008 (Ministry of Tourism, Government of India, 2012). The World Travel and Tourism Council has rated India as one of the five fastest growing tourism economies in the world.

3.2.3 Tourism Potential in Tamil Nadu

Tamil Nadu has multifarious tourist attractions—religious centres, spiritual retreats, beaches, hill stations, waterfalls, wildlife, art, culture, architecture, crafts, heritage, monuments, Agri form, etc. which enchant tourists. Tamil Nadu promotes zero-tolerant tourism without any compromise on socio-cultural values and customs. This has resulted in generating quality tourism. The tourists are invariably aesthetic and mature, who appreciate the cultural heritage of the State. Tamil Nadu is now ranked third in attracting both domestic and foreign tourists.

Proactive efforts are being continued to make Tamil Nadu the most preferred destination in India.

3.3 OBJECTIVES OF THE STUDY

With the growing importance of Agri-tourism and the thrust given by the government to promote tourism, this paper:

- Examines the key issues involved in the development of Agri-tourism in India.
- Discusses the challenges faced by Agri-tourism industry.
- Suggests recommendations for the success of this industry.

The Agri-tourism industry being a very vast subject and also considering the several diversities of the Indian sub-continent, it was physically not possible to study the Agri-tourism market for the whole country. Consequently, a study was conducted in Rajendrapattinam village in Vriddhachalam Taluk of Cuddalore District, Tamil Nadu.

3.4 RESEARCH METHODOLOGY

The research methodology involved both the desk research and the field research which was widely used to understand the concept of Agri-tourism and the various aspects that are involved in the successful development of Agri-tourism.

For the field research, a questionnaire was used comprising both open-ended questions and close-ended questions. The sample size used for the study was 100. The sample was selected in a random manner and the respondents were personally interviewed by us. Additionally, discussions were also held with the officials of the district and other taluka levels to understand the government policies, etc. The subject being vast, we have limited the study to the project at Rajendrapattinam village in Vriddhachalam Taluk of Cuddalore.

3.5 COMPONENTS OF RURAL TOURISM

1. **Agri-tourism:** Tourism on the farms enables farmers to diversify their activities while enhancing the value of their products and property. Farm tourism also helps to reconcile farming interests and environmental protection through integrated land management in which farmers continue to play a key role. Tourists who choose farm accommodation rather than other kinds of accommodation facilities look for genuine rural atmosphere where they can share intimacy of the household they live in, learn traditional crafts and skills with their hosts, make friends, which is a quality modern times have almost forgotten and, above all, enjoy home-made food and drinks. Some specific food labels can help consumers establish a local produce and can be used as a selling point to tourists who want to taste home-grown quality food and drink.

2. **Heritage and cultural tourism:** In rural areas, it comes in a wide range of forms, most of which are unique to an individual local and a valuable component of the rural tourism product. Heritage and cultural tourism includes temples, rural buildings but may be extended to local features of interest including war remnants, monuments to famous literary, artistic or scientific people, historic remains, archaeological sites, traditional parkland, etc.
3. **Eco-tourism:** Many tourists visit rural areas for the purpose of bird and animal watching and learning about the local flora and fauna. Rural tourist destination as a product is definitely very fragile in ecological, social and cultural sense. Its development requires very specific approach that could help it remain sustainable in the long term.

3.5.1 Defining Agri-Tourism

Agri-tourism is defined as travel which combines agricultural or rural settings with products of agricultural operations all within a tourism experience. The product can be "experience itself". Agri-tourism can be defined as "a range of activities, services and amenities provided by farmers and rural status of agri-tourism Internationally with specific focus on Asia Agri-tourism in India: Innovative Income generating activity for Enterprising Farmers.

Agriculture is the backbone of the Indian economy. This sector's contribution towards GDP is decreasing and the farmers are finding it difficult to carry the agricultural activities without an additional income. Whereas tourism is termed an instrument for employment generation, poverty alleviation and development, agri-tourism brings in together the declining and booming sectors.

3.5.2 Advantages of Agri-Tourism

1. It brings major primary sector agriculture closer to major service sector tourism expected to create a win-win situation for both the sectors.
2. The tourism sector has the potential to expand.
3. The agriculture sector has the capacity to absorb the expansion in the tourism sector.

3.5.3 Scope of Agri-Tourism

1. **An inexpensive gateway:** The cost of food, accommodation, recreation and travel and tourism is low, widening the scope of tourism.
2. **Curiosity for the urban about farming industry and life style:** Agri-tourism, which involves villages and agriculture, has the capacity to satisfy the curiosity of the urban segment by providing scope for re-discovering the rural life, which is rich in diversity.
3. **Strong family oriented recreational activities:** Through rural games, festivals, food, dress.

4. **Finding solace with nature friendly life style:** Peace and tranquility are in-built in agri-tourism.
5. **Nostalgia for their roots on the farm:** For tourists, it is like returning back to their roots.
6. **Educational value:** Agri-tourism is spreading knowledge about agriculture science where urban students are moving with the pace of technology.

3.5.4 Basic Principles of Agri-Tourism

1. **Have something for visitors to see:** Animals, birds, farms, culture of the village, dress and festivals.
2. **Have something for visitors to do:** Participating in agricultural operations, riding horse, buffalo, cooking and participating in the rural games, i.e. swmming, cricket, etc.
3. **Have something for visitors to buy:** Rural crafts, dress materials, farm gate fresh processed food are a few items.

3.5.5 Three Important Factors, Which Contribute to the Success of Agri-Tourism as Service

Detailed discussions with various knowledgeable persons indicated the following three factors:

1. **Farmer:** In majority of the cases, the farmer is less educated, less exposed and innocent. For him, an outsider as guest is (like god) and is treated wholeheartedly without any commercial motive. He entertains the guest and while entertaining himself in the process, he fills all the service gaps. This makes him a natural businessman.
2. **Village:** The village being located far from the city lacks urban facilities but is rich in natural resources. The investment is the natural resources itself.
3. **Agriculture field:** Each field is unique which adds to the attraction of the urban population. This is the incentive wealth of the rural people.

3.5.6 Some Important Factors

The discussions also revealed that for the success of any agri-tourism venture, the following factors play a major role:

- Connectivity
- Attractions
- Accommodation
- Outdoor recreational activities
- Entertainment programmes

- Meals for tourists
- Safety and security aspects
- Medical facilities
- Risk and liability in case of accidents

Agri-tourism destination: Rajendrapattinam village in Vriddhachalam Taluk of Cuddalore District, Tamil Nadu.

CENTRES OF AICRP ON CASHEW

FIGURE 3.1 Centres of AICRP on cashew.

Formation of the Agricultural Development Trust, Vridhachalam, Cuddalore: Cuddalore district today is considered as the hub of co-operative sugar factories and a place which receives a strong political back up. But that is not all; 40 years back, Vridhachalam was a drought prone area.

CASHEW RESEARCH CENTRES

1–Bapatla (ANGRAU)	8–Jagdalpur (IGKV)
2–Bhubaneswar (OUAT)	9–CRS Anakkayam (KAU)
3–Chintamani (UAS)	10–NARP Spl. Station Kottarakkara (KAU)
4–Jhargram (BCKV)	11–RARS Pilliicode (KAU)
5–Madakkathara (KAU)	12–ARS Ullal (UAS)
6–Vengurle (BSKKV)	13–CRS Kavali (ANGRAU)
7–Vridhachalam (TNAU)	•–NRC Cashew, Puttur

FIGURE 3.2 Cashew research centres.

3.5.7 Objectives of the Agriculture Development Trust

- To popularize and spread the actual demonstration and cultivation of new varieties of crops.
- To test and spread the use of improved seed varieties.

- To improve methods of crop cultivation.
- To develop vocations supplementary to agriculture.
- To undertake various projects of water supply.
- To train the farmers for the vocational projects.
- To undertake afforestation in barren and fallow land.
- To spread the use of cross bred cows.
- To educate and provide facilities to poor, promising and deserving women for earning their livelihood.
- Agricultural research laboratory to guide farmers to build library providing books to update farmer's knowledge.
- To organize seminars, workshop related to agricultural activities.

3.5.8 Formation of Agri-Tourism Development Corporation

TNAU's mission is "To promote agriculture tourism to achieve income, employment and economic stability in rural communities in India. To help boosting a range of activities, services and amenities provided by farmers and rural people to attract urban tourists to their area. Thus providing opportunity to urban people to get back to the rural roots."

3.5.9 TNAU's Role in Agri-Tourism

- Prepare agri-tourism project report and business plan for each applicant agriculture farm.
- Help facilitate the financial support from nationalized banks, institutes and government agencies to build agri and rural tourism facilities and infrastructure like accommodation, sanitation, approach road, etc.
- Conduct agri-tourism business training programme.
- Conduct seminars and conferences on agri-tourism business.
- Provide sales and marketing support.
- Coordinate tours from urban areas to the farms.

The trust decided to experiment agri-tourism concept on a pilot scale on its own 110 acres model farm, Cuddalore District.

Prior to setting up the successful pilot agri and rural tourism project in Tamil Nadu, the analysis of the survey was:

- 35% do not have relatives in village.
- 43% never stayed or visited village.
- 57% never visited dairy farm.

This survey promoted to experiment agri-tourism in the 110 acre model farm of the agriculture development trust.

3.5.10 Attractions

Agri-tourism activities include farm tours; tractor and bullock cart rides; sugar cane, mangoes, and other horticulture farms and by-product farms; bird and animal farms. There are lots of things the visitors or guests can enjoy in this agri-tourism unit/farm.

The total area under cultivation here is of 110 acres, primarily used for agricultural purposes, out of which 65 acres is used for horticultural plantations and cultivation, consisting of various seasonal fruits farms. The added attractions here are the poultry farm, dairy farm, goat farm, and most visited point silk processing unit. The visitors here can also visit the gram panchayat village office and school, village fairs and markets, nearby Jaggery making unit, Emu bird farm, and sugar factory.

3.6 DISCUSSIONS

Based upon a detailed analysis of the case, the following positive outcomes at the Rajendrapattinam village in Vriddhachalam Taluk of Cuddalore District, Tamil Nadu emerged:

1. Lives of the farmers changed considerably with the agri-tourism destination venture.
2. The farmers today have developed themselves into entrepreneurs.
3. They have learned soft skills to handle customer service and to market their product.
4. The entire agri-tourism venture has raised the self-esteem of the farmers.
5. The agri-tourism venture has a positive effect among the community from a drought prone area where the suicide cases were increasing.
6. Today the agri-tourism destination has more than 4,300 tourists from urban cities every year from 2007.
7. Efficient utilization of the existing natural resources.

The study indicated that the critical factors involved in the successful development of the rural tourism industry are:

1. Establishment of a rural environment, especially an Indian rural environment. Many of the tourists wanted to establish their roots in India.
2. The setting of the destination should indicate a rural bias including cultures and artifacts.
3. Hygienic accommodation and catering is a must.
4. It should be connected with the farm accommodation.
5. Attitude of the Central and the State Governments, especially with respect to the seed money required, subsidies required or even tax exemptions. This aspect is very important as can be seen through the tax exemptions, etc. given in Asian countries.

The success or failure of any tourism, in the ultimate analysis, depends on the involvement of the local community and also the deep-rooted networking requirements not only at the local levels but also the state levels. This networking is one of the key issues in making rural tourism sustainable in the long run.

3.7 SUGGESTIONS AND RECOMMENDATIONS

For any agri-tourism venture to be successful, some important pre-conditions need to be fulfilled. These are: complete tourism package can be provided through initiation by the local government bodies of activities such as beautification campaigns, sponsorship of special events that tie in with local tourist attractions and participation of all businesses in the area.

Good community leadership: Successful tourism promotion and development requires good leadership by open-minded and enthusiastic persons from local government, community groups, the business community and non-profit organizations such as chamber of commerce and convention and visitors.

Support and participation of local government: The role of local government is especially important in the following areas: Funding for tourism development and promotion, creating and maintenance of infrastructure necessary for tourism, zoning and maintenance of the community so that it looks clean and appealing to tourists, and educational support for farmers.

Sufficient funds for tourism development: Most of the rural communities depend on public funds that are very often insufficient to cover all the needs of the rural community. Private funds are something that most often cannot be reached since local people do not have sufficient incomes by themselves to invest. Therefore, it is very important to explore other sources of funding and assistance.

Strategic planning: Planning is fundamental for the efficient and effective use of resources and funds, especially in rural areas that have few funds and resources. Good planning for tourism development and promotion can help develop and support local businesses connected to tourism. Planning for tourism development should be integrated into a community's overall economic strategy because of the interdependence of the community and key aspects of tourism development and promotion. Hence, planning for tourism requires the involvement of various stakeholders in the community.

Coordination and cooperation between businessmen and local leadership: For tourism development and planning to work, coordination and cooperation between local government and entrepreneurs is crucial. While the strength of rural communities is their strong personnel networks, coordination and cooperation between local government and the business community does not always occur easily, if at all.

Coordination and cooperation between rural tourism entrepreneurs: Tourism requires different types of businesses to work together because, by its nature, tourism has intertwined relations between different types of business such as shops, accommodation facilities, restaurants and tourist attractions. They may create different types of networks, both formal and informal. Tourism network allows for a standardized, yet high quality, business management, which small enterprises lack. Strategic planning and tactical decisions such as pricing, product differentiation and yield management can be handled much better by a qualified management. A tourism network can substantially improve small tourism business performance by transforming their sporadically scattered products into a one-stop-shop, selling a wide variety of functionally interrelated tourism products.

Information and technical assistance for tourism development and promotion: Different types of information for tourism development and promotion are especially important to agri-tourism development because small communities usually cannot afford to hire experts. To this end, the role of the above explained networks is also of utmost importance.

Widespread community support for tourism: Community support for tourism development and the attitudes and hospitality of local tourism workers are important for successful tourism. It is obvious that management and marketing of tourism often require a community effort because of the nature of tourism; the community as a whole and its image must be marketed, not just one attraction.

3.8 CONCLUSION

The development of agri-tourism in rural areas of Tamil Nadu is still in its nascent stage. Tamil Nadu has perfect opportunities to enhance its agri-tourism offer and it also represents one of the few states which unify different climates, natural characteristics and socio-cultural entities. Though there has not been much initiative by the state government for agri-tourism development, it has been successfully initiated through the farmers' efforts.

For the agri-tourism to succeed, it is imperative that the tourists must have:

1. **Something to see:** Animals, birds, farms, culture of the village, dress and festivals.
2. **Something to do:** Participating in agricultural operations, riding camel and buffalo, cooking and participating in the rural games, i.e. cricket, swimming, etc
3. **Something to buy:** Rural crafts, dress materials, farm gate fresh processed food are a few items.

REFERENCES

Balasubramanian, P.P., Director (DCCD) and Shri Venkatesh N. Hubballi, Deputy Director (Dev.) was released by Shri R.C.A. Jain, Secretary (A&C) on 23.12.03 at New Delhi during National Horticulture Conference. A book titled *Organic Production of Cashew*. The book contains guidelines for organic production of cashewnut.

Balasubramanian, D. (2010). Present status and future prospects of cashewnut processing with special emphasis on 'Farm Level Cashewnut Processing'. In Inter State Horticultural show organized by National Horticultural Board, GOI at Lalbagh, Bangalore during 9–12 October, 2009.

Betters, D.R. (1988). Planning optimal economic strategies for agroforestry systems. *Agroforestry Systems*, 7: 17–31.

Bhat, M.G., National Group Meeting of Scientists of AICRP Cashew, Directorate of Cashewnut and Cocoa Development, Govt. of India, Ministry of Agriculture, Department of Agriculture and Co-operation, Cochin.

Hoekstra, D.A. (1990). Economics of agroforestry. In *Agroforestry Classification and Management*. John Wiley, New York, pp. 425–427.

Mandal, R.C. (1992). *Cashetu Production and Processing Technology*. Agrobotanical Publishers, Bikaner, pp. 4–21.

Ministry of Tourism, Government of India (2012). Domestic Tourism registers an impressive growth during 2010. Domestic and Foreign Tourist Visit Year, 2008–2010, Brief write-up. Retrieved on July 6, 2012 from www.tourism.gov.in/writereaddata/cmspagepicture/file/marketresearch/new/write-up.pdf

Nagaraja, K.V. at Tamil Nadu Agricultural University, Coimbatore. 13–15 November, 2009.

Rawat, J.K. (1989). Economic behaviour of a wood producing firm. *Indian Forester*, 115: 589–695.

Sekar, C., Pillai, O.A., Randhir, O.T. and Kumaravelu, G. (1990). Economic analysis of kapok under Agroforestry conditions of Tamil Nadu, in *Agricultural Situation in India*, pp. 537–540.

Sharma, S.K. and Diwakar, G.D. (1989). Economic evaluation of hortipastoral system of Western Rajasthan. *Indian Journal of Range Management*, 10(2): 119–122.

"Social Entrepreneurship: The Alicia Polak Way", *ICFAI Journal of Entrepreneurship Development*, Vol. IV, No. 2, June 2007.

The Cashew Export Promotion Council of India, Ernakulam South, Cochin.

The Commissioner of Horticulture and Plantation Crops, Govt. of Tamil Nadu, Chepauk, Chennai.

CHAPTER

4

CHANGING EXPECTATIONS OF TRADITIONAL PILGRIMS

An Analysis of Expectations and Motivations of Tourists Visiting Badri-Kedar Tourism Zone

—S.K. GUPTA AND VIJAY PRAKASH BHATT

4.1 ABSTRACT

Devbhoomi, Uttarakhand, known for its majestic natural beauty, mighty rivers, lofty mountains, valleys of flowers, rich plethora of floral and faunal wealth, colourful traditions, hearty hospitality of its inhabitants and world famous pilgrim centres like Haridwar, Rishikesh, Badrinath, Kedarnath, Hemkund, etc. has been quenching the curiosity of pilgrims, wanderers and nature lovers and satisfying their needs for self-actualization, finding peace and salvation. The land of India's two most famous shrines, namely Badrinath and Kedarnath, is not an exception.

With the rapid pace of technological advancements in the field of communication and infrastructural facilities in the region along with significant changes in demographic factors such as level of education, income, lifestyles and availability of leisure among the people of tourist generating areas, the motivations of the traditional pilgrims visiting the region have shifted from traditional pilgrimage to pilgrimage-cum-holiday making and also their expectation about the availability of activities and supporting facilities in the destination areas. The present paper is an attempt to analyze the changing pattern of motivations and expectations of the tourists visiting Badrinath and Kedarnath tourist zone in the Garhwal Region of Uttarakhand.

KEYWORDS: pilgrimage, motivation, expectation, Badrinath and Kedarnath tourist zone.

4.2 INTRODUCTION

Before the middle of the 19th century, a few travellers visited the Himalayas except explorers, traders or pilgrims. This situation changed with the establishment of the British rule in India and the development of the summer resorts. The tremendous growth in mountaineering (and subsequently trekking) tourism dates from the 1950s, stimulated by the conquest of Everest by Sir Edmund Hilary and Sherpa Tenzing in 1953. *TirthaYatra* (pilgrimage) is the earliest form of tourism in Garhwal Himalaya in Uttarakhand, where thousands of pilgrims, since time immemorial, have been attracted to the numerous holy places of the region. Nestling in the hills of the Himalaya is the El-Dora do Garhwal, the land of *rishis*, sages, and *ashrams*, which is also travellers' delight and naturalists' paradise. Encompassing scenic locales along the Himalayan range, Garhwal is redolent with mythology and includes some of the holiest places of Hindu pilgrimage. Since the ancient time, pilgrims in great numbers visited this region due to the location of most sacred places like Badrinath, Kedarnath, Gangotri and Yamunotri and Sikh Gurudwara at Hemkund Lokpal, origin of holy rivers like the Ganga and Yamuna and holy mountains like Nanda Devi, and Gangotri Peak. The natural beauty of the majestic Himalaya, wildlife, peace and tranquillity of the region have attracted people from far and wide. The parks and sanctuaries of Garhwal Himalaya are the rich depository of natural resources, viz. wildlife, forests, meadows, water bodies, mountain peaks and glaciers. Some of the resources are also dotted with important historical and religious sites and the tribal settlements. The driving force to visit this region has been to experience the rich, unique natural and cultural heritage of this region.

Today's visitor is likely to be a special interest traveller although adventure and cultural tourism are major motivations. Visitors to this region are often seeking 'life-enhancing' travel experiences where contact with other cultures is used to gain a sense of personal achievement and satisfaction. Many visitors travel with adventure tour companies and have a constant need for new regions and new tourism products. However, in this region, domestic tourism remains significant and pilgrimage still represents a major motivation.

4.2.1 The Study Area

The study has been focused on Badrinath and Kedarnath shrines and other upcoming nearby destinations like Ukhimath, Chopta-Tungnath,Valley of Flowers and Auli and major halting places like Joshimath, Gaurikund, Rudraprayag, etc. Most of these areas are located in two districts of Uttarakhand (Rudraprayag and Chamoli). These two districts are unique for their dramatic Himalayan land architecture and for their religio-spiritual geography. While the topography is characterized by daunting snow-clad summits, huge glaciers, rugged black mountains, stupendous waterfalls, crystal clear lakes, hot and cold water springs, gurgling tumbling falling foaming rivers, colourful meadows, rich and diverse forest types and fascinating vales and dales, the socio-cultural landscape is all the more fascinating, lively and varied. Perhaps, the serene, soothing and divine ambience dynamically complemented by awesome moods, modes and chores of the nature, all around, may have motivated the pilgrim forefathers to identify these twin districts as 'religio-spiritual sanctuary', and establish a series of shrine resorts all through, so that people have the opportunity to eye the awe-inspiring grandeur of nature while satisfying their religious urge. Consequently, this part of the Himalaya came to be known as *Devbhoomi* and *Tapobhoomi*. Religious significance of the study area is aptly evident from the fact that apart from Badrinath (one of the four Hindu Dhamas) and Kedarnath, Adi Badri, Vridha Badri, Yogdhyan Badri, Bhawishya Badri, Jyotirmatha, Hemkund Sahib (one of the most sacred Sikh Shrines), the Panch Kedars and four of the sacred Prayagas of the state (Rudra Prayag, Karan Prayag, Nand Prayag and Vishnu Prayag) and many other important religious centres are located in this part of the Himalaya. Not only this, there are tremendous opportunities for the tourist interested in adventure, nature and culture.

4.2.2 Tourism Resources of the Area

Religious tourism resources

Apart from the famous shrines of Badrinath, Kedarnath and Hemkund Sahib, there are a large number of religious sites scattered throughout the area. Four Badris (Adi Badri, Vridha Badri, Yogdhyan Badri and Bhawishya Badri), four Kedars (Madmaheshwar, Tungnath, Rudranath and Kalpeshwar), four Prayags (Rudra Prayag, Karan Prayag, Nand Prayag and Vishnu Prayag), Jyotirmath, Ukhimath, Kalimath, Guptkshi, Haryali Devi, Kartikswami, Trijuginarayan, Gopeshwar and Anusuya Devi are some of the religious attractions of the area.

Nature tourism

Nature has blessed the study area with immense natural beauty in the form of its lakes, magnificent views of Himalayan peaks, lush green meadows, mighty rivers, thundering waterfalls, miraculous hot water springs and a rich plethora of flora and fauna. Table 4.1 shows the major nature tourism sites in the area.

Table 4.1 Major nature tourism destinations

S. No.	*Attractions*	*Sites*
1	**Protected areas**	Valley of Flower National Park, Nanda Devi National Park and Kedarnath Wildlife Sanctuary
2	**Lakes**	Deoriatal, Hemkund-lokpal, Satopanth, Gandhi Sarovar, Vasuki Tal, Kagbhushundi Tal, etc.
3	**Meadows**	Auli-Gorson, Chopta-Dogabhita, Panar Bugyal, Rudranath Bugyal, Madmaheshwar Bugyal, etc.
4	**Hot springs**	Badrinath, Tapovan, Gaurikund

Adventure tourism

There are varieties of trekking routes scattered in the study area. Most of these are associated with some cultural/religious significance. Kedarnath–Vasukital, Panchkedar, Mandal–Anusuya Devi, Urgam–Banshinarayan, Tapovan–Bhavishya Badri, Kuari Pass, etc. are a few to name. Apart from trek routes, the meadows like Auli and Dogalbhita provide opportunities for winter sports. SAF Winter Games, 2011 was organized at the Skiing Resort of Auli.

Eco/Rural tourism

Along with its natural beauty, the study area has also been blessed with the unique culture and joyous lifestyle of its inhabitants which makes the rural life worth experiencing. Recognizing this potential, some of the villages have been identified as tourist villages by Uttarakhand Government for ecotourism development such as Triyuginarayan, Narayankoti and Sari. Besides these tourist villages, there are numerous other villages, especially in the vicinity of Nanda Devi Biosphere Reserve having tremendous potential for community-based ecotourism development.

Table 4.2 Tourist arrivals at various selected tourist/pilgrim centres of Uttarakhand (2006–2008)

Name of the tourist centre	Year 2006			Year 2007			Year 2008		
	Indian	*Foreign*	*Total*	*Indian*	*Foreign*	*Total*	*Indian*	*Foreign*	*Total*
Badrinath	695,230	12	695,242	**768,025**	82	**768,107**	1,075,372	211	4,002,281
Joshimath (Ghangariya and Govindghat)	1,047,687	1,214	**104,8901**	1,201,174	832	**1,202,006**	1,279,659	1411	5,782,884
Gopeshwar (Karan Prayag, Nand Prayag, Gwaldam)	231,774	319	**232,093**	283,368	162	**283,530**	389,978	108	1,421,332
Hemkund Sahib	576,626	32	**576,658**	557,066	63	**557,129**	400,410	123	2,668,107
Auli	11,365	311	**11,676**	19,729	319	**20,048**	24,902	561	88,911
Valley of Flower	5,489	455	**5,944**	12,531	308	**12,839**	11,551	511	49,628
Kedarnath	485,464	1,539	**487,003**	555,918	1,505	**557,423**	468,982	1,066	2,558,900
Rudraprayag Distt. (except Kedarnath)	496,220	1,430	497,650	590,136	1,571	591,707	592,368	1,429	2,772,511

Source: Uttarakhand Tourism Development Board (UTDB).

4.3 OBJECTIVE

The objective of the present study is to find out the changing expectations and motivations of tourists visiting Badrinath and Kedarnath tourism zone regarding the attractions, amenities and facilities available in the destination region.

4.4 REVIEW OF LITERATURE

Religious tourism, of which pilgrimage is the most important form, has received little attention from policy makers, development agencies and academicians (Singh, 1994; Cohen, 1992; Rinschede, 1992; Ingold, 2000). Sax (1991), Cohen (1992), Morinis (1992), Hirsch and O'Hanlon (1995) have represented the interrelationship between tourism and pilgrimage on the basis of anthropological approach to it. However, Chattopadhyay (2006) and Dasgupta et al. (2007) have discussed the economic impacts of the pilgrimage tourism. Pilgrimage tourism is the most revenue generating of all forms of tourism as it attracts huge crowds (Chattopadhyay, 2006; Jha, 1985; Mishra, 2000). Tourist expectations are second-order factors based on inter-correlations among several first-order factors (i.e. past experience, external communication, destination image and word-of-mouth communication) (Cathy, 2010). The expectations of tourists are ever changing and this shift in the paradigms can be better understood by studying the factors influencing the cognitive and socio-psychological parameters (Plog, 1972; Butler, 1980; Adler, 1989; Cohen, 1988; Lutz, 1981; Pratkanis, Breckler and Greenwald, 1989; Zajonc, 1980).

Though there is no dearth of the literature on tourist behaviours globally, a very limited work is undertaken to understand the changing expectations and motivations of tourists visiting Badri-Kedar tourism zone in particular. Researchers like Reisinger and Turner (2002a), Tisdell and Wen (1991), Klenosky (2002), Enright and Newton (2005), Plog (2002), and Ryan (2003) have studied various motivational factors including the push and pull-factors. Several studies related to the study area made by researchers like Dabral (1965); Saklani (1987); Thapliyal (2005); Uniyal (1982); Raturi (1980); Vijayram and Baliram, Raturi (1920); Kandari and Gusain (2001); Smythe (1931); Fonia (1998); Chamoli (1993); Kohli (1989); Bagri et al (2005); Gupta (2002), proved vitally important in documenting the prevailing tourism resource potential in the study circuit.

4.5 RESEARCH METHODOLOGY

The study was conducted during the months of May, June and October 2010 at Badrinath and Kedarnath towns. The data has been collected through structured questionnaires by means of convenient sample of 50 tourists at each town. The data has been analyzed using percentage and cross tabulation of various dependent and independent variables in order to achieve the framed objective.

4.6 RESULT AND DISCUSSION

Table 4.3 Demographic profile of sample population

S. No.	*Demographic factor*	*Percentage*
1.	**Gender of the respondent**	
	• Male	75
	• Female	25
2.	**Age of the respondent**	
	• 20–30 years	27
	• 31–40 years	22
	• 41–50 years	20
	• 51–60 years	24
	• Above 60 years	07
3.	**Educational level**	
	• Intermediate	13
	• Graduate	45
	• Postgraduate	23
	• Others	19
4.	**Occupation**	
	• Business	33
	• Service—government or private	40
	• Agriculture	06
	• Student	11
	• Others	10
5.	**Monthly income**	
	• Upto 15,000	11
	• 15,001–30,000	15
	• 30,001–45,000	33
	• 45,001–60,000	32
	• Above 60,000	09

4.7 TRAVEL RELATED INFORMATION

The travel related information of the respondents (Table 4.4) reveals that the majority of the tourists (58%) have visited Badri–Kedar tourism zone for 3 to 7 days, followed by 31% and 11% who have chosen to visit the area for 8–15 days, and more than 15 days, respectively. A further analysis of per person expenditure incurred in the trip shows that the majority (35%) fall under the expenditure group ranging from ₹ 5,000–10,000 followed by ₹ 10,000–15,000 (31%) who have spent 8–15 days in the study area. Recommendation of friends and relatives (46%) was the prime source of information, followed by electronic media (28%). Holiday sightseeing and pilgrimage was the prime purpose of the visit, followed by purely pilgrimage whereas family, friends and relative (33%) was the largest travel group, closely followed by with family (25%).

Table 4.4 Travel related information

S. No.	*Travel related information*	*Percentage*
1.	**Duration of visit**	
	• 3–7 days	58
	• 8–15 days	31
	• More than 15 days	11
2.	**Per person expenditure incurred in this trip**	
	• Below 5,000	4
	• 5,000–10,000	35
	• 10,000–15,000	33
	• 15,000–20,000	21
	• More than 20,000	7
3.	**Source of information which motivated you to visit the area**	
	• Electronic media	28
	• Travel agents and tour operators	11
	• Government tourist office	03
	• Recommendation of friends/relatives	46
	• Other	12
4.	**Purpose of visit**	
	• Pilgrimage	28
	• Holiday, sightseeing and pilgrimage	54
	• Adventure	12
	• Education	06
5.	**Travel group**	
	• Alone	12
	• With spouse	13
	• With family	25
	• With friends	17
	• With family, friends and relatives	33

4.8 EXPECTATIONS OF TOURISTS WHILE CHOOSING THE STUDY AREA AS A DESTINATION

It is a well-known fact that in the past, pilgrimage in the Garhwal region was a very difficult task and not a pleasure activity as there were lack of modern amenities and facilities in and around the destination areas. The expectations of the visitors/pilgrims were also not so high and diverse. But the gradual development of the touristic facilities and infrastructure in the last few decades has brought a significant shift in the expectation of the pilgrims visiting the region. The expectations of the tourists were measured using a five-point Likert scale, where 1 being 'not important at all' to 5 being 'very important'. Table 4.5 reveals the mean values of the answers related to the statement asked to measure the expectation of tourists regarding various aspects.

Table 4.5 Measurement of expectations of tourists

Statement	*N*	*Minimum*	*Maximum*	*Mean*	*Std. Deviation*
Friendliness of the residents	100	1.00	5.00	3.3500	1.24215
Importance of nature and wildlife	100	1.00	5.00	3.6700	1.31852
Availability of cultural sites and activities	100	1.00	5.00	3.1200	1.01782
Availability of recreational facilities	100	1.00	5.00	2.8900	1.23005
Travelling distance to tourist destination	100	1.00	5.00	2.7900	1.22512
Pleasant weather and good climate	100	1.00	5.00	3.7900	1.17461
Availability of adventure activities	100	1.00	5.00	2.9200	1.36093
Importance of local culture and tradition	100	1.00	5.00	3.2700	1.07172
Availability of better accommodation	100	1.00	5.00	3.3300	1.29533
Availability of means of transport to and within the area	100	1.00	5.00	3.4300	1.22479
Condition of roads	100	1.00	5.00	3.2600	1.06002
Quality of public utility services	100	1.00	5.00	3.1200	1.21672
Travelling and accommodation costs	100	1.00	5.00	3.0500	1.17529
Freedom from threat of disease	100	1.00	5.00	2.7700	1.09963
Shopping facilities	100	1.00	5.00	2.8100	1.17804
Importance of religious discourses and ritual	100	1.00	5.00	3.0100	1.12362
Valid N (listwise)	100				

The mean values regarding the importance of friendliness of the residents (mean value 3.35), importance of religious discourses and ritual (mean value 3.01), availability of means of transport to and within the area (mean value 3.43), condition of roads (mean value 3.26), quality of public utility services (mean value 3.12), availability of cultural sites and activities (mean value 3.12) and travelling and accommodation costs (mean value 3.05) suggests that most of the respondents considered it as important. Importance of nature and wildlife (mean value 3.67) was the most important expectation in choosing the study area as a destination. Whereas availability of shopping facilities and freedom from threat of diseases, mean values 2.81 and 2.77 respectively, were the least important expectations while choosing the study area as a destination.

4.9 MOTIVATIONS OF TOURISTS VISITING THE STUDY AREA

Apart from pilgrimage, holiday and sightseeing, adventure, rest and relaxation, health/yoga, natural beauty, enhancement of knowledge, to spend time with the family members, peace and tranquillity and to explore new places have been considered as the major factors motivating the tourists to visit the study area (Table 4.6).

Table 4.6 Motivational factors for the tourists (%)

Motivational factor	*Least important*	*Less important*	*Neutral*	*Important*	*Very important*	*Total*
Pilgrimage	15	32	6	24	23	100
Holiday and sightseeing	13	19	10	31	27	100
Adventure	12	23	23	21	16	100
Rest and relaxation	15	29	17	19	20	100
Health/Yoga	10	46	13	25	06	100
Natural beauty	04	09	05	33	49	100
Enhancement of knowledge	06	21	14	40	19	100
To spend some time with family	06	31	06	44	13	100
Peace and tranquillity	08	16	17	45	14	100
To explore new places	06	11	07	39	37	100

It has been assumed from past studies that, a few decades before, pilgrimage was the most important motivational factor for the tourists visiting Badrinath and Kedarnath tourism zone. Table 4.6 depicts that 47% of the respondents have opted pilgrimage as important and the same percentage have chosen it as not important motivational factor to undertake the journey to the study area. On going through all the points in the scale, it is evident that 32% of all respondents have pointed out that pilgrimage as a less important motivational factor, followed by 24%, 23% and 15% who have chosen pilgrimage as important, very important and least important motivational factor to visit the study area. On going through the cross tabulation of age and pilgrimage (Annexure I) as a motivational factor, it is apparent that the age group of above 60 years have opted pilgrimage as a prime motivational factor whereas the 22.2% respondents within the age group of 20–30 have opted pilgrimage as the least important motivational factor.

The cross tabulation between occupation and pilgrimage (Annexure II) as a motivation to visit the area suggests that among the occupational groups, namely business, service, agriculture and students, the students have given the least priority to pilgrimage as a motivational factor whereas among the occupation level agriculture, 100% of respondents have opted pilgrimage as a very important factor in determining the visit to the study area.

31% and 27% of respondents have opted holiday and sightseeing as an important and very important motivational factor in deciding to visit the area respectively. However, again observing the cross tabulation of age group with holiday and sightseeing (Annexure III) the data reveals that 40.9% and 22.7% of the respondents belonging to the age group of 31–40 have opted holiday and sightseeing as a very important and important motivation to visit the area respectively, constituting the largest group in this category whereas the age group above 60 years found it as a least important (0%) motivational factor.

When considering adventure as a motivational factor to visit the area, 37% and 35% respondents have given the view as important and non-important to the adventure activities as a motivation to undertake the visit. However, 23% of the respondents were neutral about it. The reason for this can be cited in the combination of adventure activity (trekking) along with the pilgrimage in the region. Whereas 44% and 56% of the respondents believed that rest and relaxation and health/yoga respectively is not an important motivational factor in considering the study area as a destination.

In response to the natural beauty as a motivational factor to visit the area, 49% and 33% (total 82%) of the total respondents have considered it as very important and important respectively and 4% and 9% have opted natural beauty as least important and less important whereas merely 5% were neutral about it. The data regarding the natural beauty as motivation reveals that it has emerged as a significant motivational factor in considering the study area as a destination. Similarly, a significant percentage of the respondents has also opted enhancement of knowledge (59%), to spend some time with family (57%), peace and tranquillity (59%) and to explore new places (76%) as important motivational factors in considering the study area as a destination to be visited.

4.10 CONCLUSION

The form of tourism development in a destination is directly related to the nature of tourism consumption in terms of both product demanded and actual behaviour on site. Destination choice is, to a great extent, influenced by the knowledge, image and perceptions tourists have of particular places or experiences. The level of expectations of the potential tourists acts as the deciding factor in making the decision to visit any destination. Motivation is an important determinant of tourist behaviour. At any destination accommodation, catering and other support services constitute the primary tourist services which are vital to tourists. For spiritual and pilgrimage purpose, a large number of people in India desire to visit holy places and different shrines, but still they require various services like comfortable accommodation, transportation, safety, etc. The destination developer must put together an assemblage of facilities so that the tourists not only get the visit but repeatedly visit the same place where they enjoy maximum satisfaction. The study contributes to the existing tourism literature on the expectations and motivations of tourists visiting Badrinath and Kedarnath tourism zone. The current study deals with the demographic profile, travel related information, expectations and motivations of tourists visiting the study area. The demographic profile suggests that against the traditional belief and pattern of higher age group people undertaking the pilgrimage, the area is being visited by almost all age groups of tourist in the present time. Further, the study suggests that a significant shift in the purpose of visit from traditional pilgrimage to the holiday and sightseeing combined with pilgrimage and adventure. Similarly, a significant change in the travel group has also been noticed where most people have preferred to visit the area with their family, friends and relatives. The study further discloses that expectations of the tourists/pilgrims have also been significantly increased about availability of variety of quality accommodation, nature and wildlife, public utility services and local culture and tradition. Further, a significant shift has been found in the importance of various motivational factors determining the visit of tourists visiting this area. The study explores that natural beauty was the most important motivational factor, followed by holiday/sightseeing, pilgrimage and adventure.

REFERENCES

Adler, J. (1989). The Origins of Sightseeing, *Annals of Tourism Research,* 16: 7–29.

Bagri, S.C. and Mishra, J.M. (2005). Mountain Ecotourism in Lata and Tolma Villages of Nanda Devi Biosphere Reserve (NDBR): A study of stakeholders' perception and forecasting future facilities and amenities, *Journal of Tourism*, Vol. VII (2005).

Butler, R.W. (1980). The Concept of the Tourist Area Cycle of Evolution: Implications for Management of Resources, *Canadian Geographer*, 24(1): 5–12.

Cathy, H.C. Hsu, Liping A. Cai and Mimi Li, (August 2010). Expectation, Motivation, and Attitude: A Tourist Behavioral Model, *Journal of Travel Research*, Vol. 49(3) pp. 282–296.

Chamoli, S.P. (1993). *The Great Himalayan—Transverse,* Vikas, New Delhi.

Chattopadhyay, M. (2006). *Religious Tourism: An Introduction*, The ICFAI University Press, Hyderabad.

Cohen, E. (1988). Authenticity and Commoditization in Tourism, *Annals of Tourism Research*. Vol. 15(3): 371–386.

Cohen, E. (1992). Pilgrimage and Tourism: Convergence and Divergence. In Alan Morinis (Ed.), *Sacred Journeys: The Anthropology of Pilgrimage*, Greenwood Press, Westport, CT, pp. 47–61.

Dabral, S.P. (1965). *Uttarakhand Ka Itihas* (in Hindi), Veer Gatha Prakashan, Dogadda Garhwal.

Dasgupta, S., Biswas, Rabiranjan, Mallick and Gautam, K. (2007). Some observations on the cultural tourism at Bishnupur, *Journal of Social Anthropology*, Vol. 4: 65–97.

Enright, Michael J. and James Newton (2005). Determinants of Tourism Destination Competitiveness in Asia Pacific: Comprehensiveness and Universality, *Journal of Travel Research*, 43 (May): 339–350.

Fonia, K.S. (1998). *The Traveler's Guide To Uttrakhand,* Garuda Books, Chamoli, Garhwal.

Gupta, S.K. (2002). *Tourism and Heritage Resources in Garhwal: An Approach to Planning and Management,* Kavery Books, New Delhi.

Hirsch, E. and O'Hanlon, M. (Eds.) (1995). *The Anthropology of Landscape: Perspectives on Place and Space*, Clarendon Press, Oxford.

Ingold, T. (2000). *The Perception of the Environment: Essays in Livelihood, Dwelling and skill,* Routledge, London.

Jha, M. (1985). *Dimensions of Pilgrimage*, Inter India Publication, New Delhi.

Kandari, O.P. and Gusain, O.P. (2001). *Garhwal Himalaya: Nature, Culture and Society,* Trans Media, Srinagar, Garhwal.

Klenosky, David B. (2002). The 'Pull' of Tourism Destinations: A Means-End Investigation, *Journal of Travel Research*, 40 (May): 385–395.

Kohli, M.S. (1989). *Mountaineering in India*, Vikas, New Delhi.

Lutz, R.J. (1981). The Role of Attitudes in the Theory of Marketing. In Kassarjan and Robertson (Eds.), *Perspectives in Consumer Behavior*, Prentice-Hall, Englewood Cliffs NJ, pp. 371–390.

Mishra, L. (2000). *Religious Tourism in India*, Mohit Publications, New Delhi.

Morinis (1992). *Sacred Journeys: The Anthropology of Pilgrimage*, Alan Morinis (Ed.), Greenwood Press, Westport, CT.

Plog (1972). Why Destination Areas Rise and Fall in Popularity, *Cornell Quarterly,* November, 13–16.

Plog, Stanley, C. (2002). The Power of Psychographics and the Concept of Venturesomeness, *Journal of Travel Research*, 40 (February): 244–251.

Pratkanis A., Breckler, S.J. and Greenwald A.G. (1989). *Attitude Structure and Function*, Erlbaum, Hillsdale, NJ.

Raturi, H.K. (1980). *Garhwal Ka Itihas* (in Hindi), Bhagirathi Prakashan, Tehri Garhwal.

Reisinger, Yvette and Lindsay W. Turner (2002a). Cultural Differences between Asian Tourist Markets and Australian Hosts, Part 1, *Journal of Travel Research*, 40 (February): 295–315.

Rinschede, G. (1992). Forms of religious tourism, *Annals of Tourism Research,* 19: 51–67.

Ryan, Chris (2003). *Recreational Tourism—Demand and Impact*, Channel View Publications, Clevedon, Buffalo, Toronto and Sydney.

Saklani, A. (1987). *The History of a Himalayan Princely State: Change, Conflicts and Awakening,* Durga Publishers, Delhi.

Sax, W.S. (1991). *Mountain Goddess: Gender and Politics in a Himalayan Pilgrimage,* Oxford University Press, New York.

Singh, Shalini (1994). *Cultural Tourism and Heritage Management*, Rawat Publication, Jaipur.

Smythe, F.S. (1931). *The Valley of Flowers* (reprint), Natraj Publication, Rajpur Road, Dehradun.

Thapliyal, U.P. (2005). *Uttarakhand Historical and Cultural Perspective*, B.R. Publishing Co., Delhi.

Tisdell, C. and Wen, J. (1991). Foreign tourism as an element in PR China's economic development strategy, *Tourism Management*, 12(1): 55–67.

Uniyal, Dharmanand (1982). *Badri Kedar Ki Aur* (in Hindi), Randheer Book Sales, Haridwar. Raturi Vijayram and Baliram, (1920): *Garhwal Ka Itihas.* Tehri.

Zajonc, R.B. (1980). Feeling and Thinking, Preferences Need no Inferences, *American Psychologist,* 35: 151–175.

ANNEXURE I
Age of Respondent * Pilgrimage Cross Tabulation

			Pilgrimage					
			Least important %	*Less important* %	*Neutral* %	*Important* %	*Very important* %	*Total* %
Age of respondent	20–30 years	Count	6	10	0	9	2	27
		within age of respondent	**22.2**	**37.0**	0	33.3	7.4	100.0
		within pilgrimage	40.0	31.3	0	37.5	8.7	27.0
		of total	6.0	10.0	0	9.0	2.0	27.0
	31–40 years	Count	0	9	6	0	7	22
		within age of respondent	0	40.9	27.3	0	31.8	100.0
		within pilgrimage	0	28.1	100.0	0	30.4	22.0
		of total	0	9.0	6.0	0	7.0	22.0
	41–50 years	Count	0	9	0	10	1	20
		within age of respondent	0	45.0	0	50.0	5.0	100.0
		within pilgrimage	0	28.1	0	41.7	4.3	20.0
		of total	0	9.0	0	10.0	1.0	20.0
	51–60 years	Count	9	4	0	4	7	24
		within age of respondent	37.5	16.7	0	16.7	29.2	100.0
		within pilgrimage	60.0	12.5	0	16.7	30.4	24.0
		of total	9.0	4.0	0	4.0	7.0	24.0
	Above 60 years	Count	0	0	0	1	6	7
		within age of respondent	0	0	0	14.3	85.7	100.0
		within pilgrimage	0	0	0	4.2	26.1	7.0
		of total	0	0	0	1.0	6.0	7.0
Total	Count		15	32	6	24	23	100
		within age of respondent	15.0	32.0	6.0	24.0	23.0	100.0
		within pilgrimage	100.0	100.0	100.0	100.0	100.0	100.0
		of total	15.0	32.0	6.0	24.0	23.0	100.0

ANNEXURE II
Occupation * Pilgrimage Cross Tabulation

			Pilgrimage					
			Least important %	*Less important* %	*Neutral* %	*Important* %	*Very important* %	*Total* %
Occupation	Business	Count	9	9	0	3	12	33
		within occupation	27.3	27.3	0	9.1	36.4	100.0
		within pilgrimage	60.0	28.1	0	12.5	52.2	33.0
		of total	9.0	9.0	0	3.0	12.0	33.0
	Service–government or private	Count	0	20	4	14	2	40
		within occupation	0	50.0	10.0	35.0	5.0	100.0
		within pilgrimage	0	62.5	66.7	58.3	8.7	40.0
		of total	0	20.0	4.0	14.0	2.0	40.0
	Agriculture	Count	0	0	0	0	6	6
		within occupation	0	0	0	0	100.0	100.0
		within pilgrimage	0	0	0	0	26.1	6.0
		of total	0	0	0	0	6.0	6.0
	Student	Count	6	3	0	2	0	11
		within occupation	54.5	27.3	0	18.2	0	100.0
		within pilgrimage	40.0	9.4	0	8.3	0	11.0
		of total	6.0	3.0	0	2.0	0	11.0
	Other	Count	0	0	2	5	3	10
		within occupation	0	0	20.0	50.0	30.0	100.0
		within pilgrimage	0	0	33.3	20.8	13.0	10.0
		of total	0	0	2.0	5.0	3.0	10.0
Total		Count	15	32	6	24	23	100
		within occupation	15.0	32.0	6.0	24.0	23.0	100.0
		within pilgrimage	100.0	100.0	100.0	100.0	100.0	100.0
		of total	15.0	32.0	6.0	24.0	23.0	100.0

ANNEXURE III
Age of Respondent * Holiday and Sightseeing Cross Tabulation

			Holiday and Sightseeing					
			Least important %	*Less important* %	*Neutral* %	*Important* %	*Very important* %	*Total* %
Age of respondent	20–30 years	Count	4	7	7	2	7	27
		within age of respondent	14.8	25.9	25.9	7.4	25.9	100.0
		within holiday and sightseeing	30.8	36.8	70.0	6.5	25.9	27.0
		of total	4.0	7.0	7.0	2.0	7.0	27.0
	31–40 years	Count	4	4	0	5	9	22
		within age of respondent	18.2	18.2	0	22.7	40.9	100.0
		within holiday and sightseeing	30.8	21.1	0	16.1	33.3	22.0
		of total	4.0	4.0	0	5.0	9.0	22.0
	41–50 years	Count	3	1	0	10	6	20
		within age of respondent	15.0	5.0	0	50.0	30.0	100.0
		within holiday and sightseeing	23.1	5.3	0	32.3	22.2	20.0
		of total	3.0	1.0	0	10.0	6.0	20.0
	51–60 years	Count	2	7	0	11	4	24
		within age of respondent	8.3	29.2	0	45.8	16.7	100.0
		within holiday and sightseeing	15.4	36.8	0	35.5	14.8	24.0
		of total	2.0	7.0	0	11.0	4.0	24.0
	Above 60 years	Count	0	0	3	3	1	7
		within age of respondent	0	0	42.9	42.9	14.3	100.0
		within holiday and sightseeing	0	0	30.0	9.7	3.7	7.0
		of total	0	0	3.0	3.0	1.0	7.0
Total		Count	13	19	10	31	27	100
		within age of respondent	13.0	19.0	10.0	31.0	27.0	100.0
		within holiday and sightseeing	100.0	100.0	100.0	100.0	100.0	100.0
		of total	13.0	19.0	10.0	31.0	27.0	100.0

CHAPTER

5

A COMPARATIVE ANALYSIS OF MWALUGHANJE ELEPHANT SANCTUARY AND RUKINGA WILDLIFE SANCTUARY IN KENYA

—MARGARET WACHU GICHUHI

5.1 ABSTRACT

Mwalughanje Elephant Sanctuary was set up to create a corridor for movement of animals from Shimba Hills National Reserve to a nearby forest area. It is a community conservancy set up to involve the community in managing and appreciating wildlife resources to help reduce human-wildlife conflict. There is a tented camp, cultural centre where women weave baskets, brand T-shirts and make paper using elephant dung. Rukinga Wildlife Sanctuary is a private ranch, which is also a migratory corridor between Tsavo East and West National parks. The ranch is used for tourism and it has set up the Taita Discovery Centre, which is used as a laboratory, classrooms and dormitories for education of the locals and as an outreach for students from around the world. The ranch, through its Corporate Social Responsibility (CSR), has benefited the communities through the Kasigau Corridor REDD project, Eco-factory for the production of textiles, greenhouse organic project which supplies seedlings to the community for free, soap factory that produces hand-made soap and the jojoba tree experimental farm for bio-fuel.

The objectives of the research are to assess ecological linkages, climate change and interactions between human activities, i.e. farming, livestock keeping, tourism and the parks, analyze the socio-economic benefits that may accrue from sustainable management of resources and to identify measures for conflict resolution.

Data collection was carried out using interviews and questionnaires. The population size for Mwalughanje was 28 respondents and the entire population was used as a sample. The Rukinga Sanctuary had a total population of 41 respondents who were all used for the purposeful data collection. The following variables were used: type of resources, resource conflicts, type of conflict, stakeholder communication, diminishing resources, community welfare, conservancy benefits, best land use, conservation of resources, and knowledge of managing resources. The Statistical Package for Social Sciences (SPSS) software was used in data analysis.

The results indicated that the increase in human population and the resultant diminishing natural resources have led to human-wildlife conflict. However, the members of Mwalughanje Conservancy appreciated the wildlife resources more since they benefitted from eco-tourism and they are more committed to the conservancy since they own it. On the other hand, Rukinga, Wildlife Sanctuary is using its Corporate Social Responsibility to benefit the neighbouring communities through several projects aimed at encouraging them to engage in sustainable use of resources and to appreciate wildlife resources. In both cases, the respondents indicated that there was a correlation between diminishing resources and the available natural resources which contributed to human-wildlife conflicts, especially through crop destruction and wildlife attacks.

The increased involvement of the communities neighbouring these two conservation areas will lead to the conservation of resources, appreciation of wildlife and increased tourism.

KEYWORDS: conservation areas, conflict, management, carbon credit, redd.

5.2 INTRODUCTION

Sustainable management and use of environmental resources is vital and can only succeed if communities' neighbouring conservation areas are involved in the conservation of resources through consultation and involvement by the park management. This study looks at Mwalughanje Elephant Sanctuary (a community owned conservancy) and Rukinga Wildlife Sanctuary (a private owned conservancy). The analysis will assist in identifying the areas of improvement which could be replicated in other parts of the country.

5.2.1 Mwalughanje Elephant Sanctuary

Mwaluganje elephant sanctuary is located on the South Coast of Mombasa at lat. 4 degrees, 10' 60 south and long. 39 degrees 27' 0 East, Kenya. It is a forested area of approximately 23,736 hectares, comprising Shimba forest, Mkongani West, Mkongani North, and Mwaluganje forest. The sanctuary covers an area of 36 km^2 and is characterized by forests, steep cliffs, rolling hills, bush land with baobabs, streams and water holes and the warm blue Indian Ocean. The beautiful hills roll up to Tsavo National Parks to the west and are marked by striking features like the Golini Cliffs, Kitanze Falls, and Manolo River, which consists of riverine vegetation and meandering rivers.

The sanctuary was established in 1993 specifically to preserve the fragile ecosystem and to help manage and maintain the population of various species inhabiting the area with the main focus being the conservation of elephants. With over 150 elephants living in the sanctuary, and with many other elephants living in the hills, forests and nearby Shimba Hills National Reserve, the area is the most densely populated natural breeding ground for elephants in the world. Mwaluganje is a historical bull area where independent elephant bulls grow in preparation for the demanding life of breeding males. Their families live in the neighbouring Shimba Hills Reserve and Mwaluganje forest and they gather in the Shimba Hills and move into Mwaluganje during the rainy season (December, and March/April). Mwalughanje conservancy was set up to create a corridor for the movement of animals from Shimba Hills National Reserve to a nearby forest area (refer to Photo 5.1).

PHOTO 5.1 Mwalughanje Elephant Sanctuary.

Other attractions in the sanctuary are the warthog, bushbuck, waterbuck, baboons and occasionally the sable antelope during the day time. There are also nocturnal creatures like the bush babies, porcupines, genets, leopards, mongooses, hyenas and honey badgers. The flora has an extraordinary botanical life with a wide variety of different plant species, including many which have their origins in the Jurassic period of 300 million years ago. Examples are the Dinosaur Cycads (*cycas revoluta*) and six other Cycad species (*Eucephalartos hildebrantii*) in Kenya and the Baobab trees (*adansonia digitata).* Mwalughanje hosts two kaya sacred forests where traditional spiritual leaders gather to worship.

The number of human-elephant conflicts was increasing prior to the sanctuary's establishment, as elephants would trample crops and disturb villages. In retaliation, people felt the need to control the elephant population. The resources at stake in the Mwalughanje

Elephant Sanctuary are crops, elephants and human beings (Mumene, 1992). To solve this problem, the sanctuary was set up with the following objectives: To reduce human-elephant conflict within the area, to ensure that community members who gave their farms benefit from the project through ecotourism activities and to conserve and protect wildlife.

The migratory routes range from sea level stands of baobab trees along the coast to moist deciduous forests on the hills and rain forests along the watercourses. Human activities within protected areas such as lodges/hotels have led to removal of vegetation for construction of infrastructure such as buildings and roads. At the same time, vehicle traffic and off-road driving has negatively impacted vegetation. Some local Duruma small-scale farmers were relocated to allow the development of the sanctuary.

The Kenya Wildlife Services (KWS) educated the community on the benefits of wildlife resources and it was taken positively (Litoroh et al., 2001). Land was leased and fenced along the corridor. KWS and Eden Wildlife Trust constructed roads, gates and staff houses. A private investor constructed a tent Camp in the sanctuary, which collects revenue from the tourists on behalf of the community. Every year, the landowners are compensated from the benefits accrued from the sanctuary. The income from a luxury-tented camp is shared among the community members. A fee is payable to the local community for every visitor to the reserve and a fence has been erected to protect man from the elephants and vice versa. There are other activities at the cultural centre such as weaving baskets, making branded items such as T-shirts and the Elephant Dung project that makes paper from the elephant dung.

In conjunction with GEF, small grant programme, there are trials of Jatropha farming. This crop is planted around the perimeter fence to deter elephants from breaking the current fence, prevent domestic animals from going into the sanctuary and as an alternative source of fuel for lighting in homes. Jatropha is planted along the fence as an edge plant so as not to threaten food security.

5.2.2 Rukinga Wildlife Sanctuary

Rukinga Sanctuary is located at lat. 3 degrees S of the equator and long. 38 to 39 degrees east and covers an area of 74,516 acres (30,168.66 ha). It is an ecosystem with incredible species diversity of large mammals and birds. The vast majority of the area falls with Tsavo East and Tsavo West National Parks and forms a corridor of land (the Kasigau Wildlife Corridor) between the two parks. There are estimated to be approximately 35,000 people within 5 kms of the ranch boundary. An investment group eventually purchased the Rukinga ranch to use for tourism—safaris and animal observing. The ranch forms a corridor of land between the two National Parks and as such, almost all of the species present in the National Parks are also present in Rukinga. It forms an important corridor for migration and dispersal of large mammals, and supports a significant concentration of African elephants with as many as 1500 using the corridor either as dispersal and feeding area or to move between the two National Parks seasonally (refer to Photo 5.2).

Climate

The climate in this region of Kenya is semi-arid, with average annual rainfall in the 300–450 mm range. There are no permanent water sources traversing the ranch. Historically,

PHOTO 5.2 Elephants at Rukinga Wildlife Sanctuary.

rains occurred seasonally twice a year, in December and April, known as the grass rains, and the long rains respectively. However, in the past ten years, local climatic conditions appear much more irregular and there have been two periods of extended drought in the last ten years. It receives strong sunshine most days of the year and the coolest month is August while the hottest month is February.

Soils

The dominant soil type within the Project Area is red laterite soil typical of this region of Kenya. There are small bands of soil that occur of black cotton randomly within the ranch area, but account for a tiny and, we believe, insignificant element from the standpoint of the other soils.

There are also areas within the Ranch Boundary where Gneiss Islands or rocky outcrops penetrate the soils to form small rocky hills. These outcrops represent a tiny and insignificant portion of the land.

Geology

This area is dominated geologically by the remnants of the Eastern Arc Mountains, which include the Taita Hills, Mt. Kasigau, to the southern end of the ranch, and lesser hills such as Sagalla, and the Marungu Range that runs North-South to the Western boundary. These hills are home to remnant patches of montane or cloud forest, and to several endemic species of bird and flora.

Current biodiversity

Rukinga Ranch, now known as Rukinga Wildlife Sanctuary, is part of the greater Tsavo ecosystem, a semi-arid area of Dryland Forest interspersed with Savannah Grasslands that spreads north to the Tana River and South into Tanzania. It is an ecosystem with incredible species diversity of large mammals and birds. The vast majority of the area falls within Tsavo East and Tsavo West National Parks (Owen et al., 2002).

Rukinga provides a home and area of relative safety to several key species of interest, including an average population of African elephants (*Loxodonta africana*) estimated between 200 and 300. A few other notable species present on Rukinga are lion (*Panthera leo*), leopard (*Panthera pardus*), cheetah (*Acinonyx jubatus*), serval cat (*Felis serval*), spotted hyena (*Crocuta crocuta*), African hunting dog (*Lycaon pictus*) and about 12 species of ungulates, such as eland (*Taurotragus oryx*), Cape buffalo (*Syncerus caffer*) and the highly endangered Grevy's zebra (*Equus grevyi*). A wide range of other species is included in the area's wildlife population, among them various carnivorous, primates, rodents, reptiles, amphibians, and over 300 avian species. For such a use, it is important to encourage the wildlife, so it became a commercial area devoted to the preservation of wildlife (Wildlife Works Carbon, 2008).

5.3 LITERATURE REVIEW

Tyller et al. (1986), refer to wildlife resources as all undomesticated species of plants and animals on earth. Wildlife species should be conserved and protected since these resources provide direct economic benefits as irreplaceable sources of food, medicines, scientific understanding, fuel, fibres, cooking oils, lubricating oils and waxes, dyes, natural insecticides, building and industrial materials. Many wildlife species provide a never-ending source of beauty, joy and recreational pleasure for humans.

According to Akama (1996), sources of human-wildlife conflict in Kenya include increasing human population, encroachment onto wildlife habitat, wildlife policies and legislation, and land use changes. The causes of conflicts are numerous and include death/injury to man and his livestock, crop damage, competition for space water and forage, destruction of property, water works and fences. Others are transmission of diseases to livestock, denial of subsistence of wildlife resources (meat, trophies), negative environmental impacts of tourism and denial of revenue from tourism.

The KWS, over the last three years, has established modalities for community partnership in wildlife management to help resolve the human-wildlife conflict. PAMU's objective is to work with communities outside protected areas whose land accommodates various wildlife species with a view to protecting human life and property. This could also involve developing early warning systems for the management of problem animals and also coming up with protective barriers (Ngethe 1995).

Community wildlife strategic framework is to enhance efficiency and effectiveness in the implementation of overall KWS goals and strategic approach to wildlife conservation and management in the areas outside National Parks and Reserves. Ideally, effective implementation of community wildlife conservation requires action-oriented strategic framework with defined legislative, administrative and institutional linkages geared towards achieving optimal resource allocation, impact generation and community based programmes sustainability (Kireria, 2000).

Community wildlife management could lead to increased community involvement in the protection of the fauna and flora, create new jobs through increased tourism, and benefit rural households either directly or indirectly through community projects.

The most significant current threat to the Coastal Forests of Eastern Africa Hotspot is the expansion of agriculture. Because the soil is poor and can only support subsistence agriculture, most agricultural development involves short-term shifting cultivation concentrating on food crops such as cassava, maize, banana, pawpaw and coconut. The human population is increasing 2.5–3.5% annually, and the demand for additional farmland increases every year (Conservation International, 2008).

Conservation policies and actions need to be based on realities and those realities include the spatial dimension of conservation areas and how society tolerates temporal change. By spatially simulating landscapes, conflicts can be reduced, but political boundaries between land uses will always give rise to special concerns. If those boundaries are ecologically and politically sound, the conflicts will be much reduced (Salmons, 2000).

Ntiati (1999), states that different conservancies and sanctuaries have some areas of commonality since land has to be set aside for the said purpose. This is often very sensitive and characterized by strong opposition for the fear of losing land. This fear is associated with the history of creation of parks in Kenya where eviction of local landowners and loss of land was the end result. This can be resolved by linking private investors with the local communities. At the same time, understanding the socio-economic activities of the local people is very important. The way forward could be through Enterprise development and management where if wildlife resource has to survive, then it has to be of benefit to the communities that it shares with.

Pimbert et al. (1995) identify six elements that can be incorporated into all conservation activities, i.e. local systems of knowledge and management, local rights to resources, local institutions and social organization, local participation in planning, management and evaluation, and process-oriented and flexible projects. These elements can be supported by appropriate national and international policy frameworks.

Mwanzaga (1998) summarizes the conflicts in Kwale district, Coast province, as human/resource use conflict, and human/wildlife conflict. He recommends mitigation strategies as follows: Creation of awareness to the community and other stakeholders in form of discussion forums and meetings, promotion of alternative land use practices and activities in both marine and inland areas. This is by promoting conservation as a form of land use that can compete with agriculture and livestock. The promotion of private and community conservation sanctuaries for the purpose of ecological tourism, and the use of the traditional control of problem animal involving KWS ranger patrols should be enforced.

Wargute (2006), in reference to Kwale district, states that conservation of wildlife resources will only succeed if the partnership between all the stakeholders such as the government, conservation agencies and local communities is strengthened and incentives for conservation where revenue sharing and socio-economic development is provided. Ecotourism activities should, therefore, be encouraged and developed within the framework of various wildlife conservation and management/associations/forums.

Wargute (2006) summarizes by stating that one of the important goals of the government in the national strategy of Economic Recovery Strategy (ERS) is environmental sustainability, an issue which is also highlighted in the United Nation's initiative of Millennium Development Goals (MDGs) launched in (2002), i.e. goal seven (7). This project looked at wildlife, which falls within this domain, and its utilization and conservation are crucial issues. The data generated in the form of numbers, distribution and trends have either direct impact in conservation and management of wildlife resources and their habitat or indirect contribution to socio-economic development through industry and other related activities.

Toxopeus (1996), states that better understanding of ecosystem functioning is necessary since a certain type of use may be considered as being sustainable for a relatively short time period depending on the socio-economic context, ecosystems may be affected by anthropogenic factors coming from outside the system, and ecosystems face short- and long-term 'natural' changes, imposed both within and outside the system (e.g. climatic changes).

The Conservation Development Paradigm states that there are links between human needs, conservation and economics. The underlying philosophy is that plans to protect species and habitats most often go awry if social dimensions are ignored or local communities are marginalized. The local people must be appropriately empowered before they can start playing the vanguard in development and conservation. This should entail enhancing their competence in terms of knowledge (what to do), skills (how to do it), and attitudes (willingness to do).

The detailed planning of community conservation programme depends on the potential of different areas for tourism or other uses of wildlife. It also depends on the structure and culture of the individual communities (Kamugisha et al., 1997).

In managing human-wildlife conflict, the challenges of conserving wildlife in protected areas should relate to the following:

- Instituting scientifically sound management procedures based on the findings of research and monitoring.
- Improving relationships with protected area adjacent communities.
- Effecting appropriate control over physical and infrastructure development.
- Improving visitor and wildlife security. (KWS–Strategic plan, 2001–2005).

Peasant farmers, cattle herdsmen and land owners in Kenya have suffered heavy losses, thanks to wildlife conservation policies aimed at appeasing the international donor community. Today, wildlife within parks is practically boxed-in by human activities and as the concentration of wildlife in the parks goes up, there emerges increased competition for food resources (Kimega, 2003).

The Kasigau Corridor REDD Project aims to leverage the financial support of the global carbon marketplace to prevent the emission of over 53,000,000 tonnes of CO_2 over the 30-year crediting period of the project by preventing any further deforestation of the project area and the surrounding area (Korchisnky et al., 2008).

Odera (2007), in another article 'An ecosystem Kit for Kenyans', noted, "who has access to environmental resources and who benefits, who bears the cost of environmental depletion and degradation, what is the impact of resource depletion on the economy and livelihoods, and where could we restore ecosystems and create economic opportunities among others."

Stakeholders play important but complementary roles in supporting wildlife conservation and management. The stakeholders among others include: Communities around the parks who are expected to provide security to wildlife and welcome tourists. Where possible, KWS will, through corporate social responsibility initiatives, empower them with specific welfare programmes. The other major stakeholders include the Government, in collaboration with its other security agencies, expects security of tourists and wildlife to be enhanced, conflict between human/wildlife to be reduced and conservation of eco-systems including vital water towers ensured.

An important influencing factor of the cooperation between community and wildlife works is the human/wildlife conflict. The community is willing to cooperate but only when the damage is kept minimal (Rietveld, 2007).

Wildlife will find support if it is seen as part of the common conservation practices of all people, rather than a special interest of a privileged few (Western, 2008).

The other critical stakeholders are private ranchers who are generally required to have their operations guided by the overall wildlife policy and legislation. In addition, the County Councils involved in wildlife conservation and management will continue their collaboration with KWS, especially on security and scientific management of wildlife (KWS, 2008).

5.4 MATERIALS AND METHODS

Quantitative method of data collection and analysis was used to analyze primary data. Primary data using questionnaires and interviews was used to assess the communities' opinions on the use of natural resources. Random and purposeful sampling was used to select respondents in the Mwalughanje and Rukinga conservation areas. The population size of the respondents in Mwalughanje was 28 and Rukinga Wildlife Conservancy had 41 respondents. The Statistical Package for Social Sciences (SPSS) statistical software was used in the analysis of variables using frequencies.

The frequencies of the following variables were compared in the two conservation areas, i.e. Community view on parks, Conservancy benefits, Practiced land use, Disadvantages of living next to the park, Type of conflict, Type of animal, Conflict resolution, Visitor facilities, Community welfare and Diminishing resources.

Mwalughanje Elephant Sanctuary frequencies:

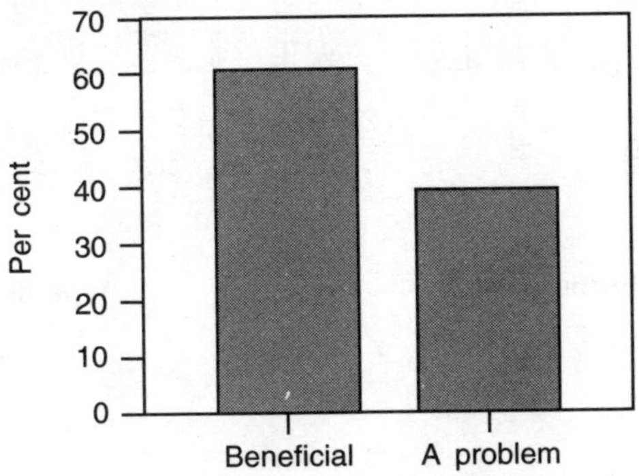

Community view on national parks

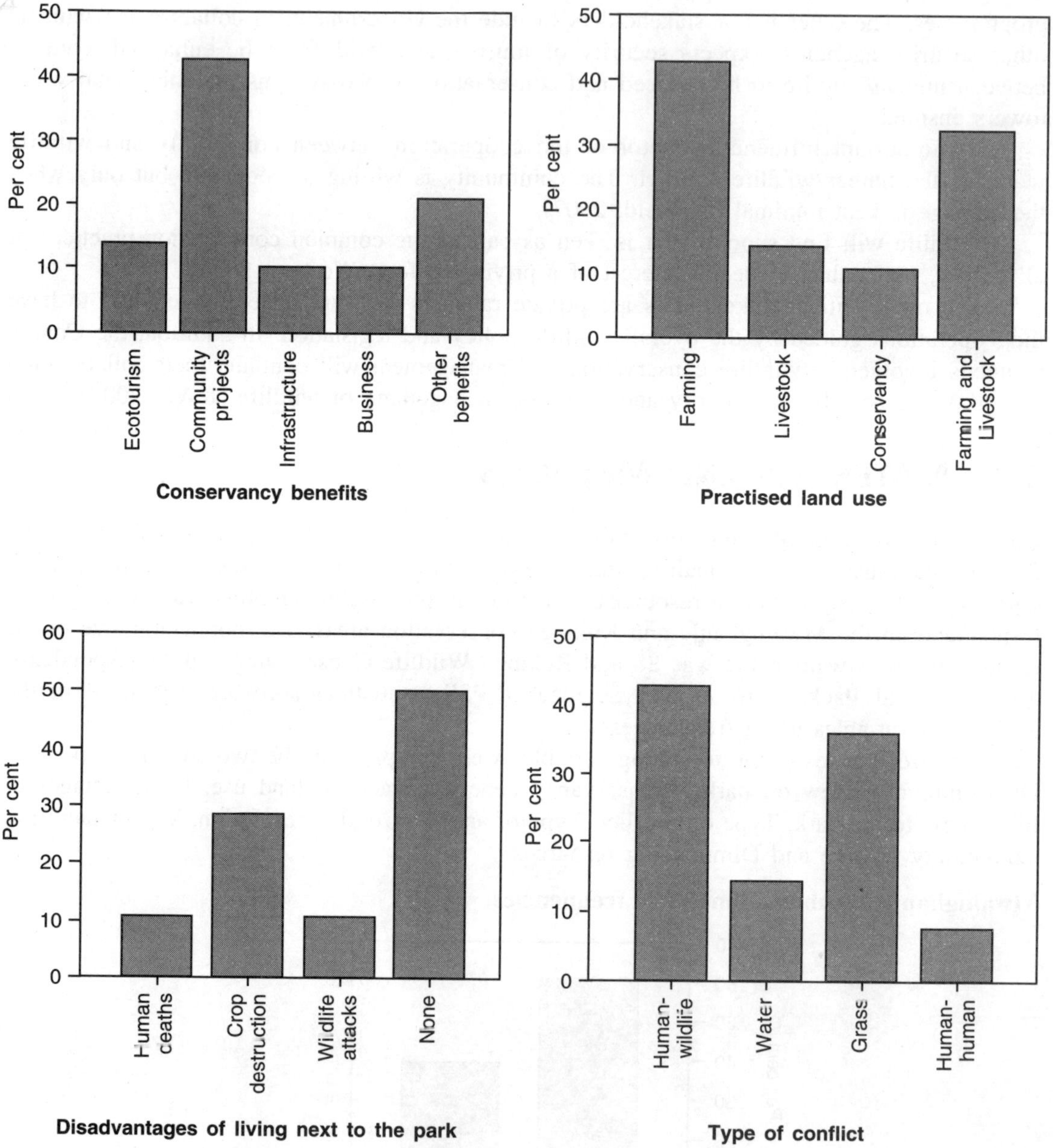

Per cent
Ecotourism
Community projects
Infrastructure
Business
Other benefits
Conservancy benefits
Per cent
Farming
Livestock
Conservancy
Farming and Livestock
Practised land use
Per cent
Human deaths
Crop destruction
Wildlife attacks
None
Disadvantages of living next to the park
Per cent
Human-wildlife
Water
Grass
Human-human
Type of conflict

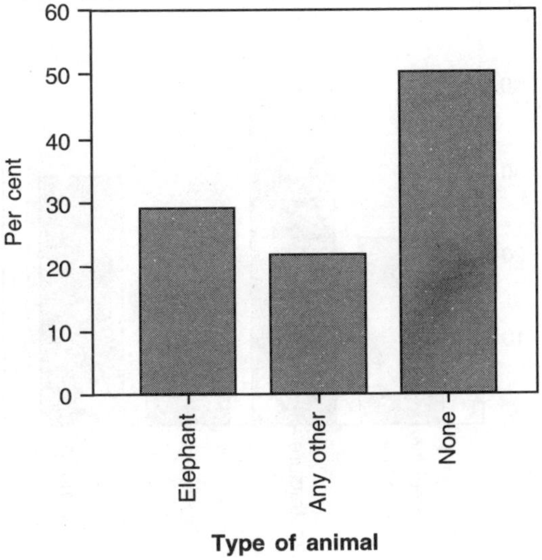
60
50
40
30
20
10
0
Per cent
Elephant
Any other
None
Type of animal

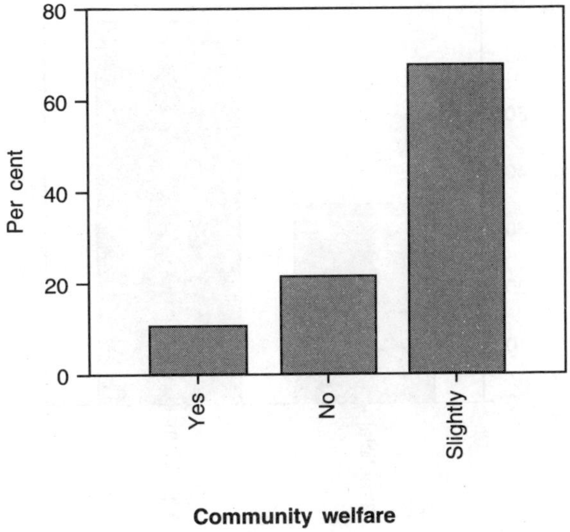
80
60
40
20
0
Per cent
Yes
No
Slightly
Community welfare

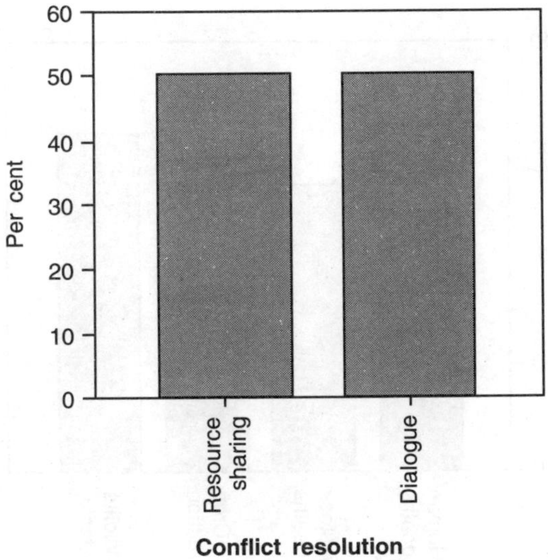
60
50
40
30
20
10
0
Per cent
Resource sharing
Dialogue
Conflict resolution

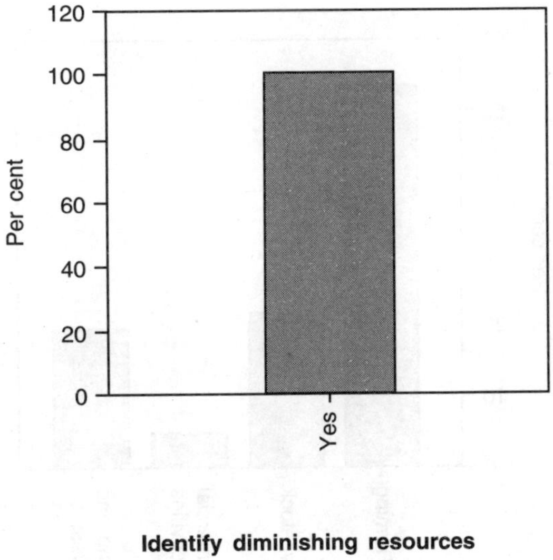
120
100
80
60
40
20
0
Per cent
Yes
Identify diminishing resources

Rukinga Wildlife Conservancy frequencies:

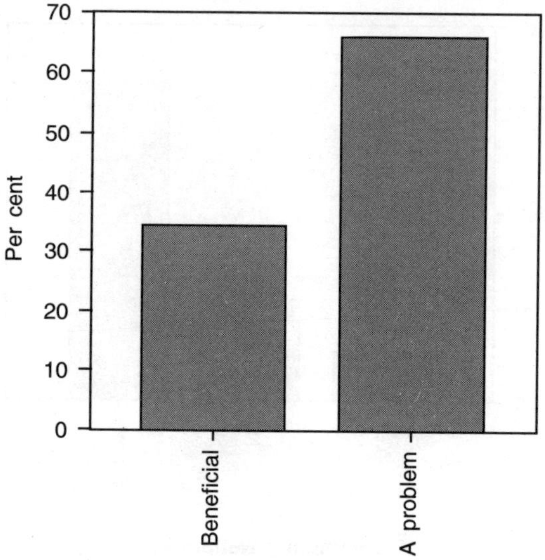

Community view on national parks

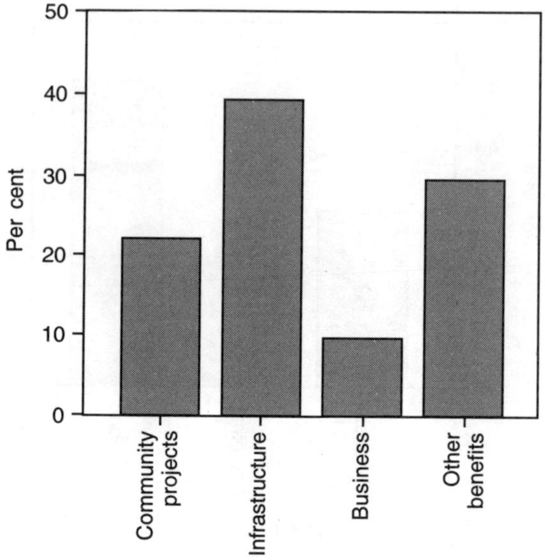

Conservancy benefits

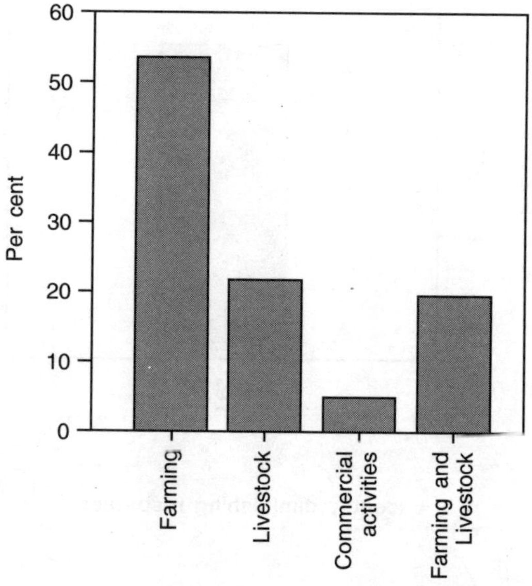

Practised land use

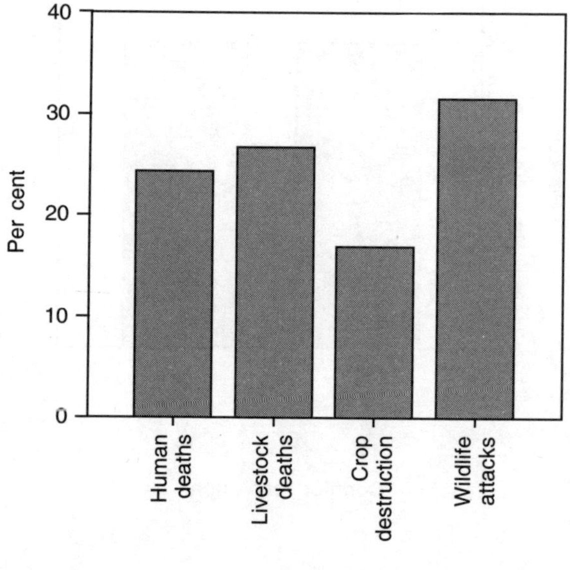

Disadvantages of living next to the park

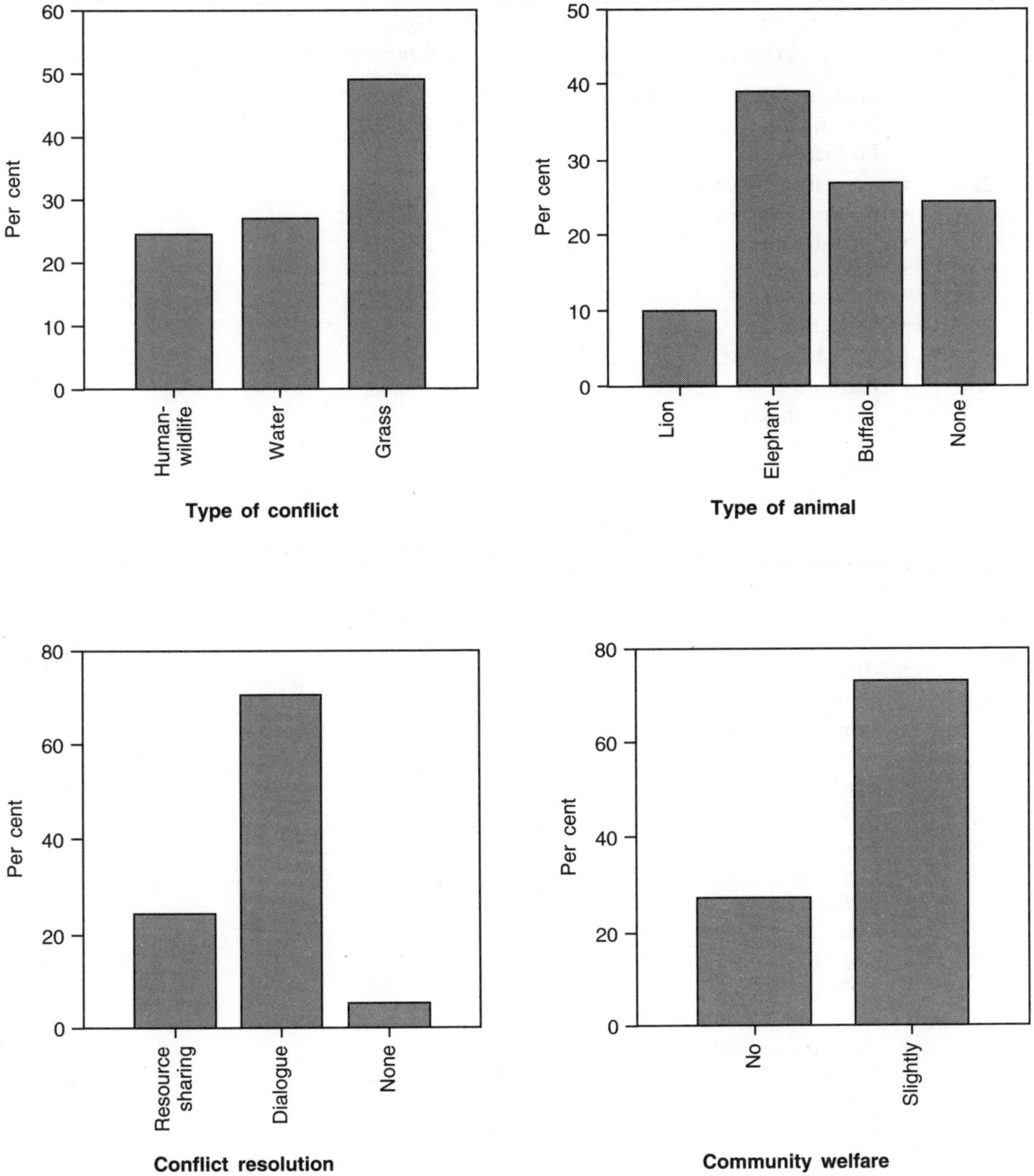
60
50
40
30
20
10
0
Per cent
Human-wildlife
Water
Grass
Type of conflict
50
40
30
20
10
0
Per cent
Lion
Elephant
Buffalo
None
Type of animal
80
60
40
20
0
Per cent
Resource sharing
Dialogue
None
Conflict resolution
80
60
40
20
0
Per cent
No
Slightly
Community welfare

Table 5.1 gives a comparative study of these two conservancies.

Table 5.1 A comparative table of variables in Mwalughanje and Rukinga Conservancies

Sl. No.	*Type of variables in percentages*	*Mwalughanje Elephant Sanctuary (%)*	*Rukinga Wildlife Conservancy (%)*
1.	Community view on parks:		
	• Beneficial	60.7	34.1
	• Problem	39.3	65.9
2.	Conservancy benefits:		
	• Community projects	42.9	22
	• Infrastructure	10.7	39
	• Business	10.7	9.8
	• Ecotourism	14.3	None
	• Other benefits	21.4	29.3
3.	Practiced land use:		
	• Farming	42.9	53.7
	• Livestock keeping	14.3	22
	• Commercial	0	49
	• Farming and livestock keeping	32.1	19.5
	• Conservancy	10.7	0
4.	Disadvantages of living next to the park:		
	• Human deaths	10.7	24.4
	• Livestock deaths	0	26.8
	• Crop destruction	28.6	17.1
	• Wildlife attacks	10.7	31.7
	• Any other	50	
5.	Type of conflict:		
	• Human/Wildlife conflict	42.9	24.4
	• Water conflict	14.3	26.8
	• Grass conflict	35.7	48.8
	• Human/Human conflict	7.1	0
6.	Type of animal:		
	• Elephant	28.6	39
	• Buffalo	0	26.8
	• Lion	0	4
	• Any other	21.4	24.4
	• None	50	0
7.	Conflict resolution:		
	• Resource sharing	50	24.4
	• Dialoque	50	70.7
8.	Community welfare:		
	• Yes	10.7	0
	• Slightly	67.9	73.2
	• None	21.4	26.8
9.	Diminishing resources:		
	• Yes	100	78
	• No	0	22

A comparative analysis of the above variables indicates thus: Community view on national parks/conservation areas in Mwalughanje was that it was beneficial (67.7%) while (34.1%) in Rukinga Conservancy indicated that it was beneficial. This could be the result of the Mwalughanje community owning the conservancy and therefore sharing the eco-tourism income among themselves as compared to Rukinga conservancy, which is a private park and the community may not have direct management of the resources. The variable on Conservancy benefits shows that in Mwalughanje 42.9% benefited from community projects while Rukinga had 22%, infrastructure for Mwalughanje was 10.7% which was quite low compared to Rukinga's 39%, Business for Mwalughanje was 10.7% compared to Rukinga's 9.8% where most people conduct business along Mombasa-Nairobi highway.

Practised land use indicated that farming in Mwalughanje had 42.9% farming while Rukinga had 53.7%, farming and livestock had 32.1% in Mwalughanje and 19.5% in Rukinga. Conservancy in Mwalughanje had 10.7% but none in Rukinga. This could be the result of the former being owned by the community.

Disadvantages of living next to the park indicate that human-wildlife contributed 24.4% human deaths in Rukinga and 10.75% in Mwalughanje since the sanctuary has an electric fence. The community living next to Rukinga is also attacked by wildlife from Tsavo East National Park. Wildlife attacks and crop destruction are quite high in both conservancies.

The type of animal that causes the greatest human-wildlife conflict is the elephant 29%, buffalo 26.8% and lion 45% in Rukinga area, while in Mwalughanje the elephant is the main wild animal that causes conflict (28.6%). Respondents in both study areas indicated that the resources were diminishing with Mwalughanje indicating 100% and Rukinga Community 78%. Conflict resolution through dialogue and resource sharing was agreed upon as the best solution.

5.5 DISCUSSIONS

The analysis of the aforementioned variables in Mwalughanje Elephant Sanctuary and Rukinga Wildlife Sanctuary indicate that both areas mainly suffer from human-wildlife conflicts. This is due to the type of land use practiced such as farming and keeping of livestock, diminishing resources such as grass, forests and water. Access to benefits from the conservation areas and lack of awareness of sustainable use of resources also contribute to conflict over water or land.

5.6 CONCLUSION AND RECOMMENDATIONS

The Mwalughanje Elephant Sanctuary has the goodwill from the community since they own it and benefit directly from ecotourism. On the other hand, Rukinga Wildlife conservancy is privately owned, but through their corporate social responsibility they have started projects to benefit the communities such as the hand-made dish soap, jatropha project and the REDD carbon trading project. These benefits will encourage communities to appreciate and conserve wildlife resources.

There is the need to involve the communities in issues of wildlife conservation and management, sustainable resource utilization and ecotourism.

REFERENCES

Akama, J.J. (1996). *Western Environmental Values and Nature-based Tourism in Kenya; Tourism Management.*

Conservation International (2008).

Kamugisha, J.R., Ogutu, Z.A. and Stahl, M. (1997). *Parks and People—Conservation and Livelihoods at Crossroads*, Technical Report No. 17, Regional Conservation Unit/SIDA.

Kimega, G.M. (Sept. 2003). *Unresolved Human-Wildlife Conflict in Kenya,* Eco-files.

Kireria, A.M. (March 2000). *KWS: Community Wildlife Strategic Framework, 2001–2005, Final Report.*

Korchisnky, M., Freud, J., Cowan. L. and Dodson. R. (December 2008). *The Kasigau Corridor REDD Project Phase II—The Community Ranches*, 2nd ed., KWS-Strategic Plan, 2001–2005.

Litoroh, W.M., Njue, A., Bitok, E. and Omondi, P. (2001). *KWS: Mwalughanje Elephant Sanctuary Joint Management Plan, Shimba Hills Ecosystem.*

Marit, R. (August 2007). *Wildlife Works EPZ.*

Michael, J.S. (2000). *Evaluating Community Conservation in Kenya.* University of Alberta. *Millenium Development Goals* (2002) United Nations.

Mumene, R. (May 1992). *Interactions between People and Wildlife around Shimba Hills National Reserve and Mwalughanje Forest: A KWS Rural Services Design Report.*

Mwanzaga, H. (Oct. 1998). *KWS: Conflict Resolution Plan for Coast Province.*

Nge'the, S. (Feb. 1995). *Problem Animal Management Unit, (PAMU): KWS Draft Policy.*

Ntiati, P. (Sept. 1999). *Community Conservation Program, Annual Report for the European Union (EU)*, African Conservation Centre.

Owen, A. and Dodson, R. (2002). *Wildlife Distribution in Rukinga Sanctuary: A comparison of wildlife numbers since the arrival of wildlife works report.*

Omondi, P., King. J., Bitok, E. and Geddes, C. (2002). *Total Aerial Count of Elephants and Buffalo in the Tsavo; Mkomazi Ecosystem,* KWS-Elephant Programme.

Pimbert, M. and Pretty, J.N. (1995). *Parks, People and Professionals: Putting 'Participation' into Protected Area Management*, UN Research Institute for Social Development, Discussion, Geneva.

Toxopeus, A.G. (1996). *Spatial and Temporal Modelling for Sustainable Managementof Semiarid Rangelands; The Wildlife versus Livestock Issue in the Amboseli Ecosystem, Southern Kenya.*

UNEP, 2009, "Kenya: Atlas of Our Changing Environment." Division of Early Warning and Assessment (DEWA) United Nations Environment Programme, Kenya.

Wargute, P.W. (Jan. 2006). *Numbers and Distribution of Wildlife in Kwale, Kilifi, Malindi and Lamu districts;* Technical Report No. 170, Department of Resource Surveys and Remote Sensing (DRSRS), Ministry of Environment and Natural Resources.

Western. D. et al. (Aug. 2008). *Reconceptualisation of Wildlife Conservation; Toward Resonatable between subsistence and wildlife.*

CHAPTER

6

ENVIRONMENTAL PRACTICES IN A MEDIUM SIZE HOTEL A Case Study Approach

—Sharleen Howison and Dagmar Cronaner

6.1 ABSTRACT

The purpose of this research case study was to identify the factors which are important in achieving long-term sustainability in a medium sized New Zealand hotel. The hotel industry is increasingly under pressure to meet the growing demand for the so-called "green" products and services. As customers are becoming more aware of the importance of preserving the environment for future generations, it is also important to know that the concept of sustainable business practice is a crucial component in the management of hotel business today. The study was conducted adopting interview, survey, observation and documentation gathering methods. Quantitative and qualitative results were analysed from the findings that included three manager interviews and thirteen staff surveys. The findings of the study confirmed that the participants have a solid understanding of how sustainability can be achieved. There was, however, a lack of appropriate communication channels, which did result in a lack of staff education in environmental practice. Moreover, the staff recognized a lack of information on decisions being made and actioned by management. Further to this, the study did support the need for the appointment of a nominated person, who is responsible for the appropriate training, monitoring and evaluation of environmental practices within the hotel. This research could be extended to include the economic impact for hotels that incorporate environmental practices, into their day-to-day operations, as a future research study.

Keywords: environmental practices, hotel, sustainability

6.2 INTRODUCTION

6.2.1 Background

The hotel industry is under pressure to meet the growing demand for sustainable goods and services while working to remedy its impact on the environment, society and the economy. By taking responsibility for its actions, the industry is moving towards its primary goals of formulating mission and vision statements. Before the company can introduce the statements, however, it must thoroughly analyse its current economic, social and environmental impact and its status in the industry and compare them with the main competitors. According to Bader (2005), the continued existence of a hotel is greatly dependant on its environment. Therefore, hoteliers frequently need to develop a sustainable practice plan that will help preserve the natural and cultural habitat and ensure a continual flow of tourists. The hotel is a four-star hotel in New Zealand, with a Silver Qualmark Environmental rating.

6.2.2 Literature Review

Lockyer (2007) said, "Sustainability is becoming an important focus being directly related to the resources available and how those resources are used today and how they will be used in the future" (p. 185). Therefore, the concept of sustainable practice is a crucial component in the management of a business today. Especially the demand for the so-called "green" environment friendly travel suppliers is growing since customers are becoming increasingly aware of environmental concerns in the world. Consequently, the tourism and hospitality industry is part of those businesses that have to be held accountable when it comes to their negative impact on the environment. As stated by Hobson and Essex (2001), "sustainable tourism may represent a threat to the environment by being used as a guise to sell more holidays and open up new destinations rather than contribute to environmental conservation" (p. 135). With the growing demand of "green" accommodation, the hotel industry is coming under pressure to act sustainably but rapidly to keep on track with the tourist's awareness regarding sustainability.

6.2.3 Challenges of Sustainable Practice

Different components in a destination have to contribute to a more environmentally sound management. Andrews, Convery, Flanagan and Ruddy (2002) state that those components are the host community, the tourists and the industry. According to Iwanowski and Rushmore (1994), acting environmentally sensitive makes business sense since it enables businesses to gain more profit and ensures the attention of the public while acting as a "corporate citizen". Brown (1996) makes a similar statement and establishes that cost benefits through operating environment friendly can be achieved. However, "of more concern to the hotelier is the impact of environmental initiatives on the perceived quality and service of the hotel" (Brown, 1996, p. 135). "The major barrier is that hotel managers do not recognize the importance of environmental management to hotel effectiveness and competitiveness" (Penny, 2007, p. 286).

Although many suppliers and business partners of hotels have chosen to deliver environment friendly products, hoteliers often think that using them is less efficient and complicated to implement (Penny, 2007). When it comes to the financial and environmental performance of a hotel, the connection between both has to be more precisely examined. As stated by Sharma and Aragón-Correa (2005), the improved performance and productivity could just be the outcome of improved profitability rather than environmental practices. Furthermore, they argue that it is often not possible to reconstruct if the relationship between financial and environmental performance was sustainable over time. As mentioned by Goodman (2000), companies do not often use sustainable development to achieve a turnaround, but they consider it after they are financially secure to minimize the risk of financial failure.

6.2.4 Impact on the Environment

As mentioned by Hobson and Essex (2001), it is very challenging to monitor the impact of the tourism industry on the environment since "the environmental impacts of tourism are not simply those related to degradation caused by the volume of visitors, but the resource implications resulting from the operation of tourism related businesses, such as transportation pressures and pollution, energy and water consumption, waste generation and purchasing strategies" (Hobson and Essex, 2001, p. 134). Even though the impact of the industry on the environment is difficult to monitor, it is the tourism operator's responsibility to protect those resources for sustainable tourism development.

It is the natural, built and cultural environment that are susceptible to unsustainable practices of hotels. Therefore, practical solutions to reduce the hotel's impact are crucial. Hobson and Essex (2001) realize this and mention, "as with other sectors the translation of theory into practice has been problematic as awareness, understanding, interpretation, interest and implementation within the sector have been highly variable" (p. 134).

6.2.5 Implementation of Innovative Environmentally Friendly Strategies

According to Iwanowski and Rushmore (1994), in their emphasis to create a sustainable business environment, many hotels have started to implement certain strategies, such as solid waste management, energy saving measures or recycling methods to regulate their usage of resources and reduce their impact on the environment. Moreover, the authors support environment friendly measures and state that "consumers are increasingly strident about the responsibility of business to preserve and conserve the environment in which it operates" (p. 35, 1994) and therefore it is easier for hoteliers to implement and promote those measures in order to sell their service successfully. It is also necessary to mention that changing customer behaviour towards the consumption of sustainable products supports a more sustainable role of hotels in the marketplace.

Environmental costs are hard to measure. However, with the help of a few adjustments, some negative impacts on the environment can be minimized. Since the "surveillance of industry's behaviour and impact on the environment will increase", many hotels are forced to "tailor an environmental programme to the needs of their property and the environment in which it operates" (Iwanowski and Rushmore, 1994, p. 34). As stated by Iwanowski and Rushmore (1994), "careful examination of existing systems and operational procedures, especially in the areas of solid waste management, water conservation, and energy management, will reveal an abundance of possible modifications that cost nothing or will pay for themselves in a few years" (p. 34).

One strategy demonstrates a well-organized energy saving system, which starts with a well thought-out energy efficient design of the hotel property (Iwanowski and Rushmore, 1994). Solid waste management constitutes an essential component in achieving a proper management to reduce the operating expenses at the hotel. It "reduces the volume and toxicity of the garbage being sent to the landfill" (Iwanowski and Rushmore, 1994, p. 34). To save money while concurrently reducing the impact on the environment, the hotel manager has to implement a recycling programme. With the help of this programme, staff will be prompted to reuse and refill items, to recycle different materials in separate rubbish bins and they will be encouraged to pass their practice down to the guest. Reusable plastic, packaging with as little material as possible and the reuse of paper make a big difference. It is important that one person is in charge of the correct run of the programme who should also ensure that recycle bins are located on an accessible place and are clearly marked. Clearly visible reminders should advise the guests and all staff of the location of recycle bins (Iwanowski and Rushmore, 1994).

All electronic devices, such as the heater or air-conditioner, should be furnished with advice for the employees and the guests on how to operate them as efficiently as possible. This will save costs and will help the staff and guests to make convenient choices when it comes to energy usage. Replacements of old devices, such as light bulbs, can be seen as an opportunity to choose the most environment friendly and in the long-term cost efficient energy option (Iwanowski and Rushmore, 1994).

An appropriate maintenance routine also needs to be applied to develop a framework for long-term sustainable practice. According to Iwanowski and Rushmore (1994), an accurate analysis of current equipment enables the maintenance staff to measure and document the productivity of certain devices. It provides the opportunity to monitor, which equipment needs to be improved and to identify the departments that need more training in how to maintain sustainable items (Iwanowski and Rushmore, 1994).

A successful business relationship between local suppliers and the hotel should be composed of a mutual understanding of sustainable practice. Having a supportive supplier and business partner makes it easier to work together on environment friendly solutions. Valuable information can come from such a relationship. Maintaining contact with local and national producers of demanded products for the hotel and keeping uptodate with latest sustainable product innovations provides the hotel with useful tips on how to apply new technologies in order to stay sustainable and economical at a long term (Iwanowski and Rushmore, 1994).

6.2.6 Environmental Practices in Hotels

An example of the Macao hotel sector shows that good environmental "intentions are not always translated into actions" (Penny, 2007, p. 293). As stated by Penny (2007), the city Macao in China has been attracting a growing number of tourists over the past decade and the demand for environmental services has grown significantly. A survey with the help of questionnaires was conducted in August 2006 to examine hotel managers' attitude towards environmental management. The findings showed that environmental strategies, such as electricity, water, waste and noise reduction "are directly associated to cost savings or regulatory compliance" (Penny, 2007, p. 293). However, only a few hoteliers actually implemented such programmes and have taken actions in avoiding their negative impact on the environment. "This is evidenced by the fact that only 29.7% of the hotels have a formal environmental policy and only 13.5% of them have designated a team/staff to be in charge of environmental management" (Penny, 2007, p. 293). Hoteliers in Macao are aware of the actions they need to adopt to minimize their impact on the environment. Even though they have good environmental knowledge, they are "not active enough in seeking information about environmental matters" (Penny, 2007, p. 293). Furthermore, many do not negotiate about eco-friendly products and only a few hotels sponsor or donate products (Penny, 2007).

An impressive example of the successful implementation of environmental practices is the Scandic Hotel chain. As stated by Goodman (2000), the Nordic European hotel chain, which was about to collapse in the early 1990s, managed to boost its hotel practices by implementing environmental information systems and employee training programmes as well as developing innovative collaborations with its suppliers. After its crises, partly caused by the recession in Sweden, a new CEO introduced a new leadership philosophy, in which he "made sustainability a key building block of Scandic's new direction" (Goodman, 2000, p. 204). Furthermore, as mentioned by Goodman, the CEO integrated environmental thinking into the company's philosophy by establishing a well-thoughtout staff training programme and assigning responsibility to the staff directly confronted with the customer's expectations. "Interestingly, initial customer demand for heightened environmental awareness came not from Swedish guests but from those who stayed in Scandic's German and Danish hotels and began to ask about the company's waste disposal practices and larger environmental policy" (Goodman, 2000, p. 205). Therefore, the CEO made environmental policy a central component of the hotel chain's business strategy. To communicate new environmental innovations to its employees, the management established environmental training courses and an intranet environmental learning programme. It also became possible for different hotels in the chain to compare their environmental performance on a platform using the intranet. The hotel also installed a completely recyclable and environment friendly soap and shampoo-use system and has been determined to design the guest rooms as environment friendly as possible. This also includes a complete "energy-management and temperature control system that works via TV signals" (Goodman, 2000, p. 210). This enables the front and back office staff to receive feedback from the rooms regarding their temperatures and to comfort rooms with the help of a computer in the office. Scandic has been able to develop valuable co-operations with various suppliers and also accomplished to transfer their environmental ideas to their suppliers. The changes within the company did not only benefit the environment, but also the financial performance, the reputation of the chain in different countries and enabled the company to build marketing partnerships with other hotel chains. "Decentralization of management, especially putting responsibility in the hands of frontline employees, has also contributed to implementing sustainability measures" (Goodman, 2000, p. 214). Scandic's CEO has been determined to not only change the philosophy of an entire hotel chain but also forcing suppliers into environment friendly practices, which in turn emerged as a benefit for their businesses (Goodman, 2000).

6.2.7 Environmental Customer Awareness

It is crucial to know that "the current market demand for environment friendly products pressures firms into innovation in environmental management as a factor of competitiveness" (Sharma and Aragón-Correa, 2005, p. 141). Additionally, environmental awareness of tourism providers and accommodation business is a significant component of the tourist's decision-making process. Tourists are willing to pay more for their vacations if they ascertain that the tourism business is actively involved in the attempt to preserve the destination's environment. Unfortunately, many consumers still have the perception that businesses can hardly ever be trusted when it comes to environmental protection (Iwanowski and Rushmore, 1994). The conception of the business being obsessed of making as much profit as possible alters the overall picture of such organizations. However, Iwanowski and Rushmore also reveal that "a property that institutes eco-friendly practices and communicates those efforts to the general public can gain access to a growing market segment" (1994, p. 34).

Importantly, hotel chains might have better opportunities to market their environmental practices than privately owned hotels since they most likely have a highly organized environmental marketing and management as a backbone (Hobson and Essex, 2001). This will be highly valued by the tourist who demands "green" accommodation as the corporate culture of the hotel chain is able to reflect the appreciation of environmental sensitivity. Moreover, as stated by Hobson and Essex (2001), the impact of environmental practices on the perceived quality of the services for guests is of primary concern for the hotelier. Therefore, the management has to ensure the education of the guests about environmental concerns and of which measures the hotel implements to support long-term sustainability. Manaktola and Jauhari (2007) endorse this approach and apply to Kotler's (1997) approach when they establish that the "customers make product choices based on which combination of product attributes best meets their needs based on dimensions of value, cost, and prior satisfaction" (as cited in Manaktola and Jauhari, 2007, p. 365). Secondary benefits including environmental practice are significant attributes that, alongside basic needs of the guest such as physical satisfaction, determine the appreciation of the stay for the customer.

Another important task for the management is to contribute to the overall appeal of the destination by not only practicing environmentally sensitive but also including the destination as a whole in the marketing of the hotel. This will give the tourist the possibility to associate both as a sustainable collaboration. According to Hobson and Essex (2001), this will also result in the greater appeal of more fluent customers.

6.2.8 Corporate Social Responsibility

Corporate social responsibility (CSR) contributes to the protection of the natural and built environment and has the ability to benefit the local community. Socially responsible behaviour enables the hotel to maintain its reputation as a sustainable business as well as attracting visitors to participate in the support of communal happenings; by donating money for example. CSR is defined by the Business in the Community (BITC) as "the management of company's positive impact on society and the environment through its operations, products or services and through its interaction with key stakeholders, such as employees, customers, investors and suppliers" (as cited in Holcomb, Upchurch and Okumus, 2007, p. 462). That is, businesses have a responsibility towards society and therefore have to carry their success over to their stakeholders, to an extent that they will benefit from the business's performance. Accordingly, Holcomb et al. (2007) discover that the hotel businesses should take part in socially responsible behaviour as an important component of their organizational strategy, which benefits them in the market environment.

According to Lockyer (2007), sustainability has to consider all the stakeholders of the hotel. They have an interest in the hotel's performance and want to benefit from it in the long-term. To achieve this beneficial relationship between each stakeholder and the business, the management has to provide them with certain incentives to lead them into a supportive direction. Hotels can provide potential employment opportunities for locals, for instance. It is crucial that the stakeholders, especially the employees, appreciate the sustainable practices of the hotel in order to sell the offered products and services convincingly. Therefore, good working conditions are crucial, and the various elements of the environment the hotel is operating in have to build a complementary unity (Lockyer, 2007).

Additionally, Lockyer (2007) emphasises that "sustainable management is not about how managers do things to try and make a business more sustainable, it is how the managers view the business and the environment in which the business operates. As management in a hotel think about the day-to-day operations, long-term financial viability and the employees, along with other resources, all of these need to be evaluated in a sustainable way" (Lockyer, 2007, pp. 185, 186).

In conclusion, it can be said that many factors contribute to a successful sustainable performance of a hotel. Being environment friendly includes not only the application of practices benefiting the natural environment but also the support of the local community, the staff and all other stakeholders. Ebner and Baumgartner (2006) establish that businesses in general have to incorporate the sustainability aspect into their business management and should maintain a certain ethical belief, which is supposed to provide a base for the business to start with. A hotel is dependent on its stakeholders and therefore corporate social responsibility has to help in the "company's commitment in protecting the environment or reducing its ecological footprint". Furthermore, the hotel's corporate social responsibility should "focus especially on the corporate engagement realizing its responsibilities as a member of society and meeting the expectations of all stakeholders" (Ebner and Baumgartner, 2006, p. 13).

6.3 METHODOLOGY

6.3.1 Case Study Approach

A case study approach will enable me to determine the factors that are important in achieving long-term sustainable development in a medium sized New Zealand hotel. "A research case study is an empirical inquiry into a social or human problem. It begins with a research question and involves the collection of data to analyze and to answer that research question" (Tharenou, Donohue and Cooper, 2007, p. 73). According to Yin (2009), a case study is able to answer "how" and "why" questions as well as to point the focus on a "contemporary phenomenon with a real-life context" (p. 2, 2009). The concept of triangulation, which is a method of establishing the accuracy of information by comparing three or more types of independent viewpoints on data sources considering the same findings (Yin, 2003), allows for a broader investigation of "historical, attitudinal and behavioural issues" (Yin, 2003, p. 98). This research adopted four different types of evidence gathering methods including; interviews, surveys, observation and documentation. Robson (2003) suggests that multiple methods of evidence collection are a requirement, since a case study approach relies on the collection of data about the situation.

6.3.2 Interviews

Interviews are one of the most important sources of case study information (Yin, 2009) and will be conducted with management staff. Since one of the management's tasks is to implement innovative sustainable practices and to maintain staff's motivation to practice in a sustainable manner, the manager's opinion and viewpoint is highly valuable. The interview should only provide relevant answers, which are specifically focused on the research topic. Posing too many questions would lengthen the interview time and increase the possibility of unnecessary or repeating conclusions.

6.3.3 Questionnaires

The usage of questionnaires is of most value in collaboration with other research methods and adds to a more quantitative approach (Gillham, 2007). In this case study, they will be used to gather data from office and housekeeping staff about their perception of the current sustainable practice of the hotel. The participants will also be asked to evaluate the practices and to make suggestions on the improvement of the contemplated. Open and closed questions will be used to either confirm predetermined questions or gather opinions or judgements (Gillham, 2007). Closed questions are easy to analyze and straightforward, whereas open questions need more attention and should only appear in a small amount to avoid an excessive demand of the respondent.

6.3.4 Documentation

According to Yin (2009), documentation can be reviewed repeatedly, contains exact names, references and details of an event and can cover a long span of time as well as many events and settings. However, appropriate documents may be difficult to find or incomplete. Special attention should be on the critical observation of the documents, since they could reflect a bias of the author (Yin, 2009).

6.3.5 Observation

The observation of the behaviour of staff contributed to a more comprehensive understanding of the everyday activities in the organization. The application of sustainable practices was observed in the housekeeping department. "A major advantage of observation as a technique is directness. You do not ask people about their views, feelings or attitudes; you watch what they do and listen to what they say" (Robson, 2003, p. 191).

6.4 ANALYSIS

6.4.1 Interviews

Three interviews were conducted with management staff of the hotel. Each interview took approximately twenty to thirty minutes and the interviewer asked similar questions. However, they slightly differed depending on the position of the manager. Fifteen to eighteen different questions were asked. Due to the anonymity of the interviewees, they will be referred to as person A, person B and person C in this study. Only key questions and answers will be highlighted.

I. What is an environmentally sensitive hotel?

A: *Use energy efficient light bulbs; general things should be applied, e.g. turning lights off when not in use, use environment friendly packaging, or change suppliers when necessary.*

B: *Recycling, using electricity cards where the lights get switched on when entering the room or the reuse of certain types of water.*

C: *Consider special needs of staff, the individual persons and suppliers when it comes to environment friendly practice.*

II. What instruments do you use to communicate eco-friendly practices to the general public?

A: *New recycle bins and reminders, which advise staff to practice in a sustainable manner, reminders in the guest rooms, offering to use towels several times; logo of the Qualmark rating and mission statement on the website.*

B: *Signs in the two lifts, advising guests of our double stained steeled recycling bin on the fifth floor, information sheet on environmental practices in the books in the rooms, Yellow Eyed Penguin Trust.*

III. How satisfied are you with the staff's participation in the recycling programme?

A: *Great participation of staff, especially the Housekeeping Department is doing well.*

B: *About 6 out of 10 and a lot more improvement is to do but only just started; especially with computers, there is the facility to go forward to a much less paper use.*

C: *A lot more to do, but some staff have good suggestions; the participation is 50/50 at the moment and some take the easy way out.*

IV. How important is the negotiation with suppliers for eco-friendly materials and products? Do you compare their environmental statements with your requirements for environment friendly practice?

A: *The negotiation with suppliers is extremely important and not that difficult. Many potential suppliers make an effort to adjust their environmental policies to the Hotel's to become a supplier. The hotel also has a look at their policies to ensure they are environmentally conscious.*

B: *It is becoming more and more important. The suppliers get asked to provide facts and answers on what products they use. If potential suppliers don't have any environmental statements, they can't work with the Hotel.*

C: *They are becoming aware of the eco-friendly products, now more than a year ago. We don't compare their statements with ours.*

6.4.2 Questionnaires

25 questionnaires were provided and *13 were completed*, that is a return rate of 52%. Key findings from the analysis include the following (see Figures 6.1 to 6.8):

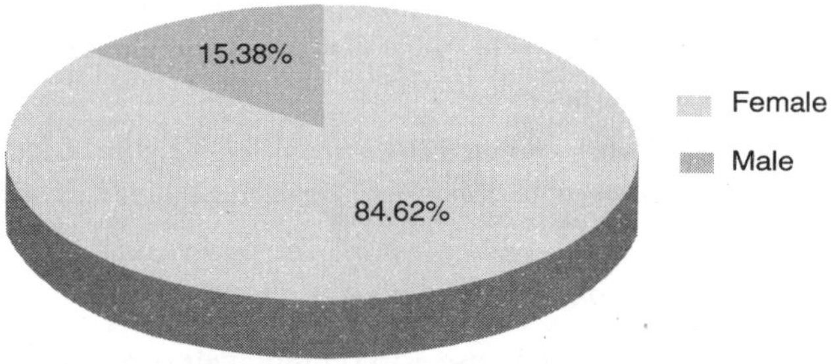

FIGURE 6.1 Gender statistics of participants.

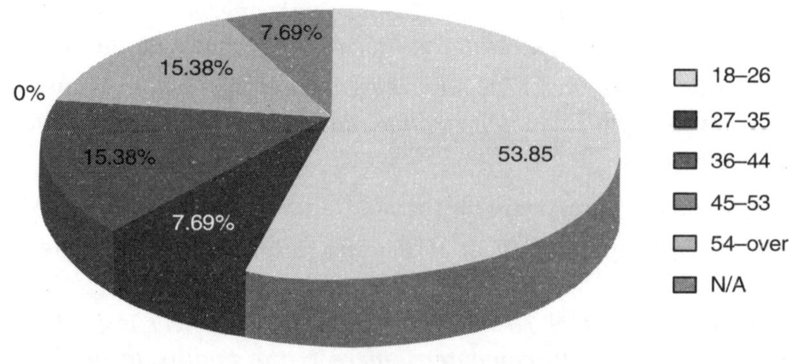

FIGURE 6.2 Age categories of participants.

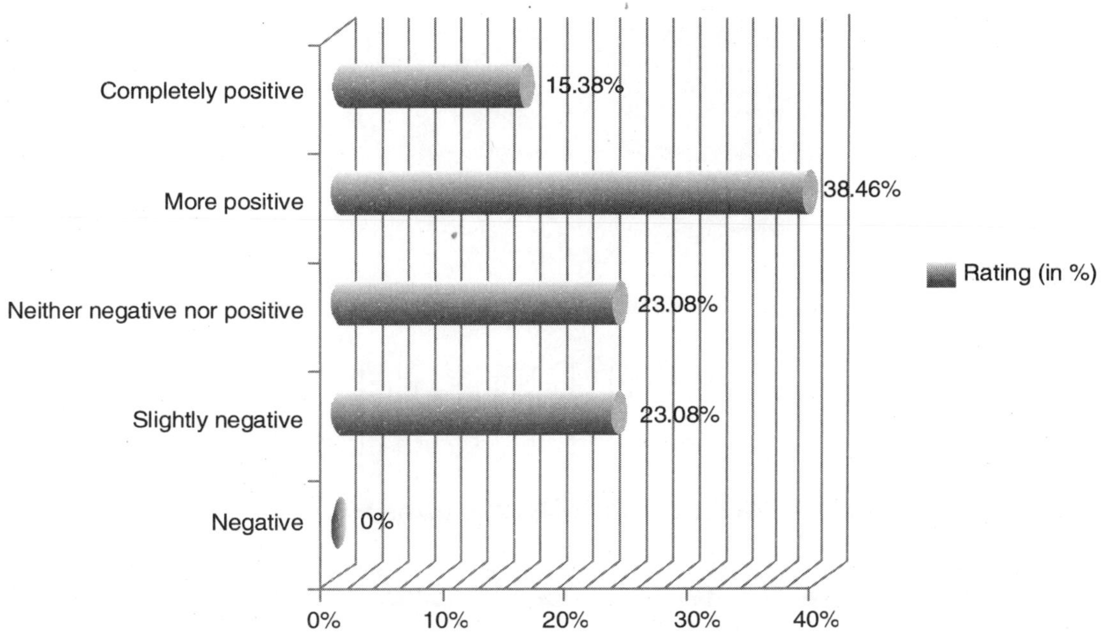

FIGURE 6.3 Rating of the hotel's impact on the environment.

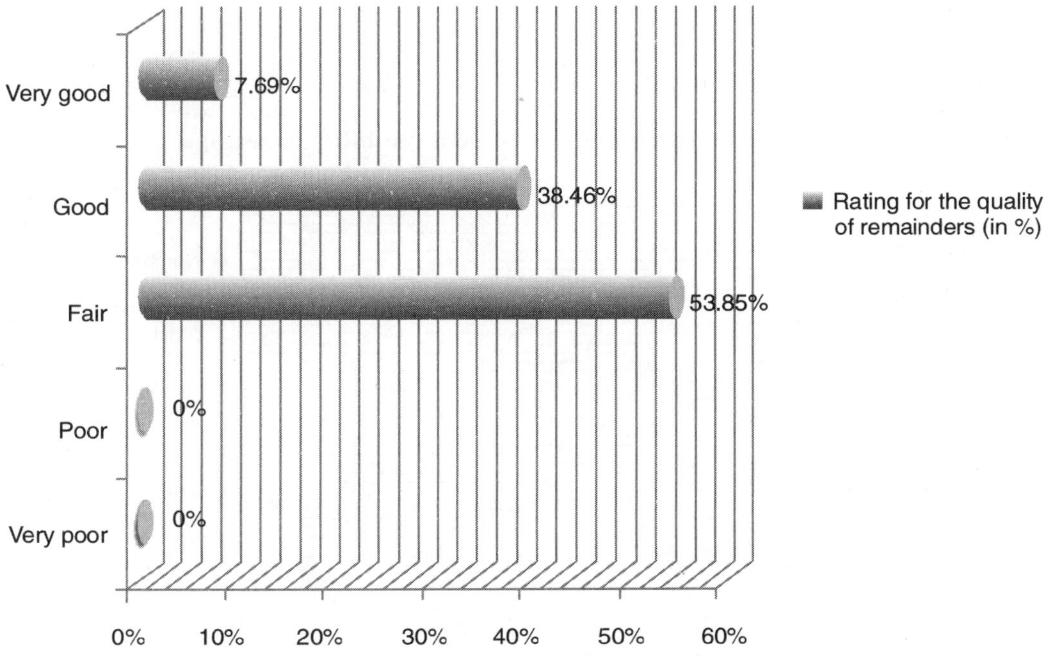

FIGURE 6.4 Rating for the quality of reminders to guests and staff to behave in an environment friendly manner.

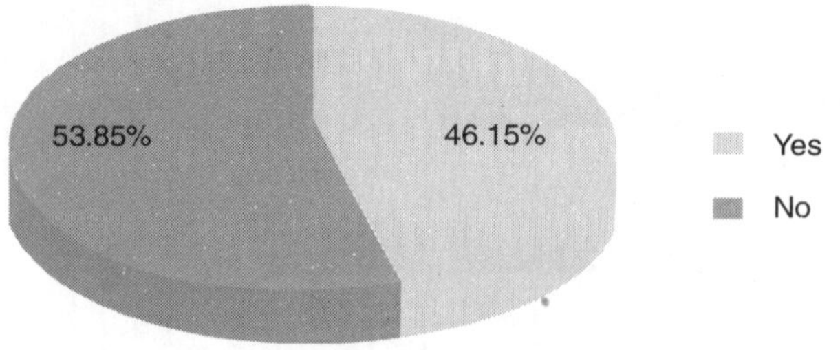

FIGURE 6.5 Statistics on the recycling training.

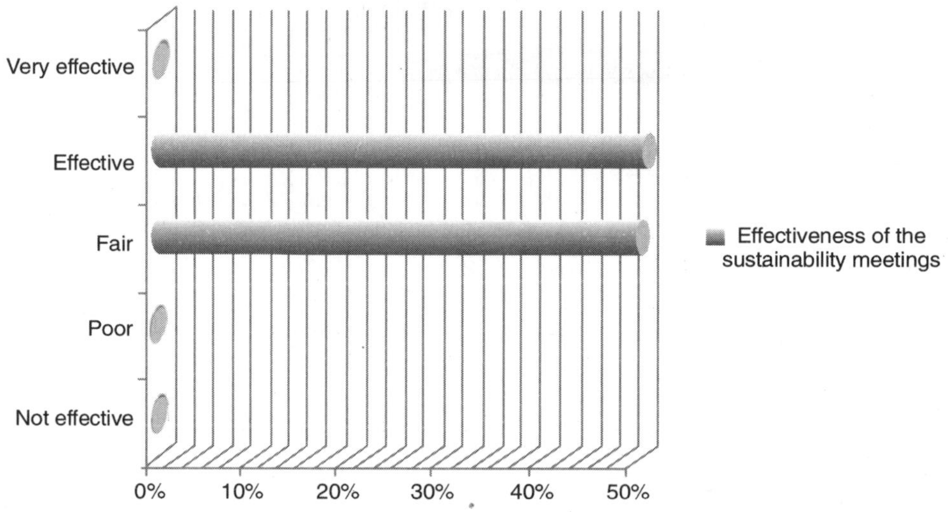

FIGURE 6.6 Effectiveness of sustainability meetings.

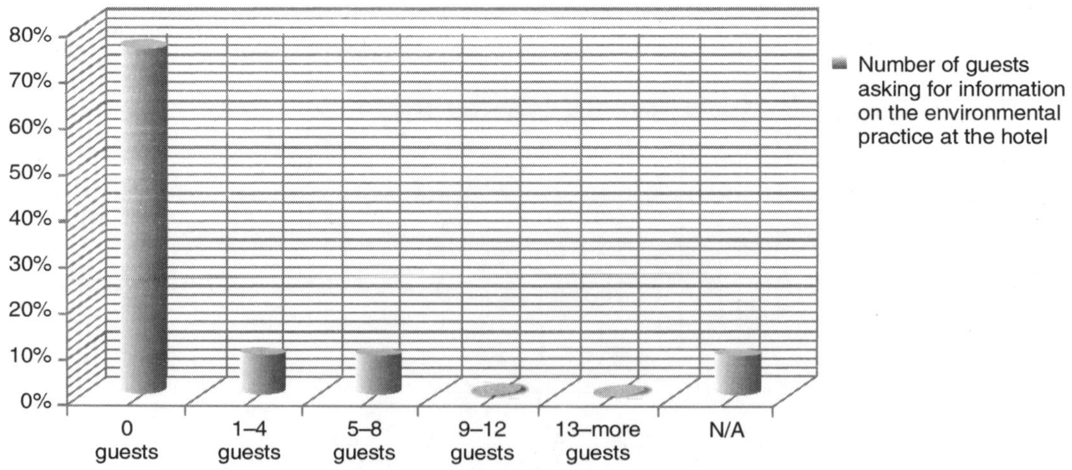

FIGURE 6.7 Number of guests asking for information on environment friendly practice in the hotel.

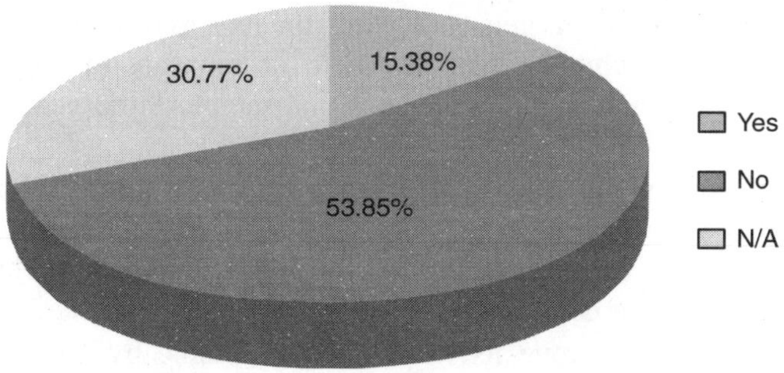

FIGURE 6.8 Are guests willing to pay more for environmentally sensitive supplies?

6.4.3 Documentation

The gathering of suitable documentation on sustainability in the hotel has been a significant component of this study. It helps to understand what has been done to evolve sustainable practice and provides an overview of what could be improved to achieve a higher environmental rating or a greater involvement in social events in the future. Furthermore, it gives an insight into the Intranet technology of the hotel and the information provided in the Intranet. With the help of a documentation checklist, a variety of internal information addressed to staff and external information for customers and for or from suppliers has been found.

6.4.4 Internal Information on Sustainability

The Hotel Intranet contains an Environmental Mission Statement, "our Environmental Journey", which embodies the commitment of the hotel to "be a leader in responsible and sustainable tourism". It expresses the aim to "minimize any detrimental impact on the environment" through the cooperation of the "guests, staff, business partners and the wider community" to achieve long-term sustainability. For example, by turning electronic appliances off, allocating rooms on the lower floors, or using the recycling bins, the staff has the possibility to act responsible and to be involved in the sustainable development process.

6.4.5 Environmental Plan

Areas that required attention in October 2008 (Figure 6.9).

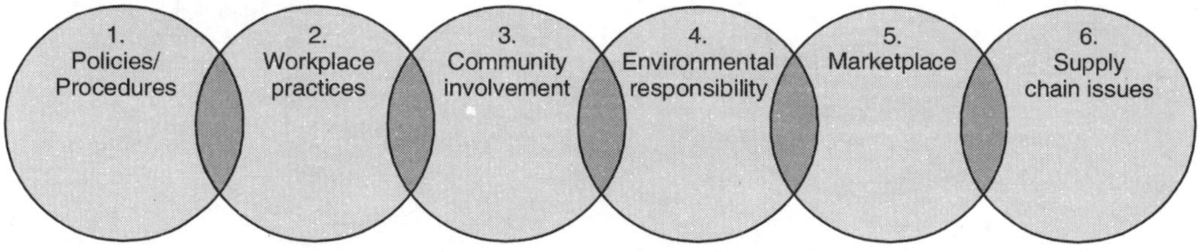

FIGURE 6.9 Topics of the environmental plan.

1. The hotel wants to set targets and work on its environmental performance. This is supposed to be achieved with the help of monthly meetings of a committee, which passes information on to the staff and monitors the goals set in the previous meeting.
2. The management wants to establish an incentive plan for staff, participating in environmental practices.
3. The hotel wants to cooperate with other businesses, such as a Hospice, to achieve a positive effect for the community.
4. The hotel wants to improve its recycling programme by purchasing stainless steel recycle bins and using recycled paper.
5. The hotel wants to include an extra question on guest satisfaction around sustainability into the guest comment forms.
6. The hotel intends to develop a contact list of local organizations, which support sustainable development. They are also required to make sure that minimal packaging is used.

6.4.6 Environmental Tick List

Below is the hotel environmental tick list, which demonstrates what the hotel is doing to practice in a sustainable manner. Figure 6.10 shows the different points which are mentioned in this list.

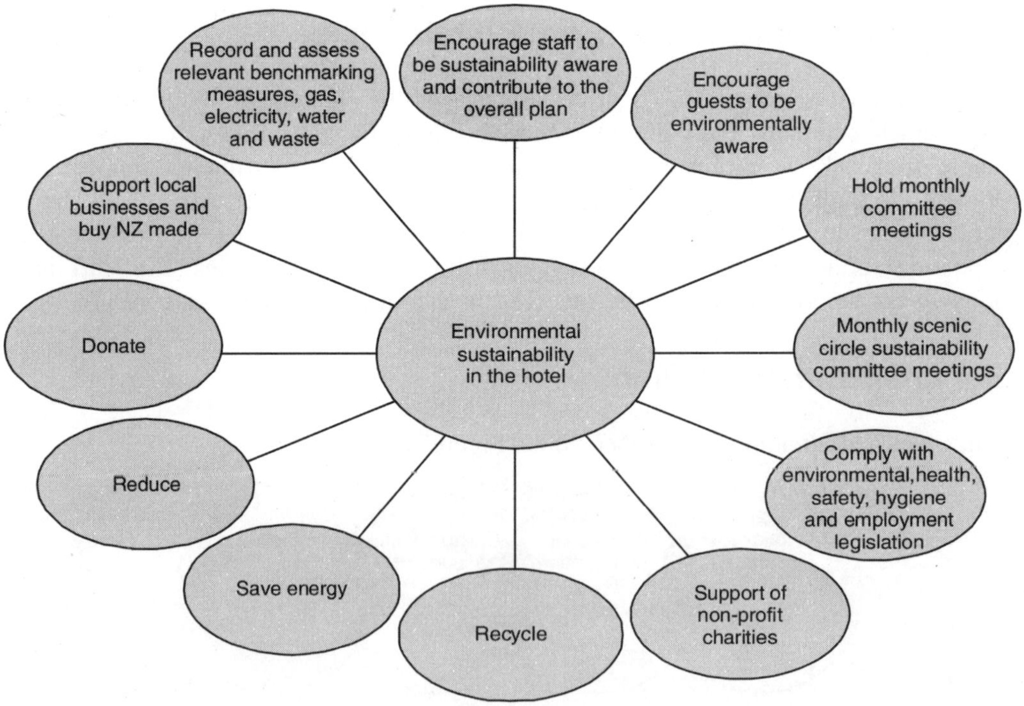

FIGURE 6.10 Topics of the environmental tick list.

6.4.7 Qualmark Rating

The Responsible Tourism Initiatives List provided by Qualmark gives the hotel the opportunity to list all sustainable initiatives actioned in the hotel to give the Qualmark assessor an overview of what has been implemented as well as of what needs to be improved. It demonstrates a very positive tool to measure where the hotel was positioned with its sustainable practice at the time when the list was completed.

6.4.8 The Newspaper Handling

A memo regarding the environment friendly newspaper handling advised the staff that the hotel is changing the "guest newspaper procedure to lessen the impact on the environment" due to the fact that many guests do not necessarily want to have a newspaper in the morning. Therefore, the memo encourages the front office staff to ask each individual guest during check-in if he or she requires a newspaper in the morning. This saves money and contributes to the protection of the environment. Information transferred to staff with the help of a channel like memos is usually very effective.

6.4.9 Information for Customers

Yellow Eyed Penguin Trust: Each guest compendium in the rooms is equipped with an information sheet on the Yellow Eyed Penguin Trust, which is also an invitation for guests to donate money. The hotel supports the organization and provides the guest with information around the danger of extinction of animals in New Zealand, especially the Penguins.

6.4.10 Suppliers

The mission and vision statements of the hotel's suppliers can be found in the Intranet, accessible for each staff member. Figure 6.11 shows some of the main suppliers and the main points of their conformable environmental policies (Table 6.11).

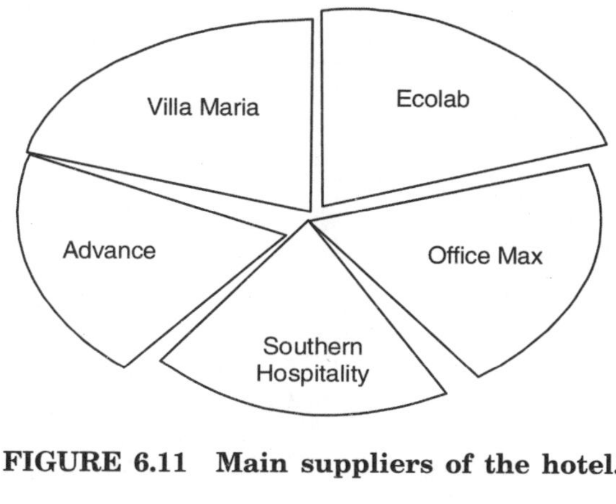

FIGURE 6.11 Main suppliers of the hotel.

Table 6.1 Environmental aim of suppliers

Supplier	*Environmental aim*
Ecolab	Conservation of water and energy; increase of safety and reduce waist; consider the total impact of products, including recycling of products; be socially responsible
Office Max	Reduction or/and prevention of pollution, minimize consumption of resources, communication of environmental principles to staff, staff training
Southern Hospitality	Apply the principles of reuse, reduce and recycle; use of environment friendly logistics
Advance	Development of products that can minimize the impact on the environment; consider all laws and legislation regarding sustainable practice; enhance training skills of employees; investigate and report
Villa Maria	Meet legal requirements for wine production, monitoring and reduce pollution created by the business, conserve non-renewable resources, improve waist management

Even though the environmental mission statements and policies of the suppliers are easy accessible, they are too bulky and it is arguable that every employee reads through this. The quality of the statements is good and the fact that they are provided much appreciated. However, a summary of the main environmental aims of the suppliers would awaken the interest of the staff.

6.4.11 Observation

The observation of three housekeeping teams proved to be very interesting and contributed to a real life point of view. It exemplified the cleaning methods that are being applied every day as well as the recycling, chemical-use and guest amenities handling methods. The researcher functioned as an objective observer and had the advantage of a previous work experience in the housekeeping department of the Hotel. Each team was observed for approximately 30 minutes in three rooms (see Figures 6.12 and 6.13).

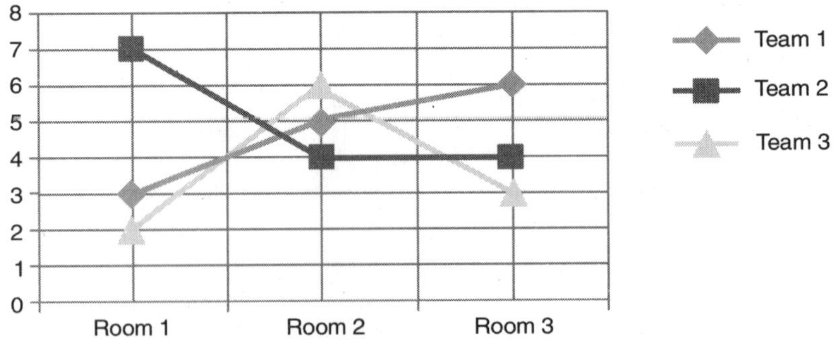

FIGURE 6.12 Rating of the dirtiness of the guest rooms.

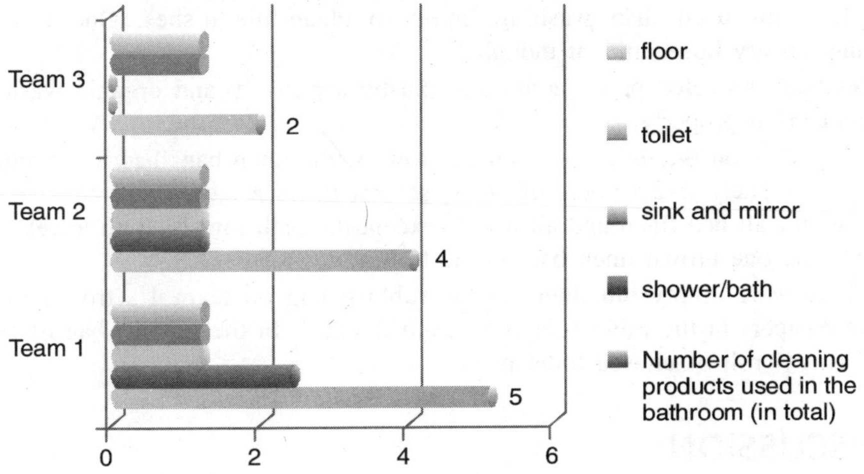

FIGURE 6.13 Cleaning practices of the 3 teams of housekeepers.

1. None of the housekeepers reused the bin liners if only a small amount of rubbish, such as paper or plastic, was in the bin. After throwing the bin bags away, they used new bin bags.
2. Two out of three teams did not turn the lights on (when switched off) when entering the bedroom. All of the teams had to switch the light in the bathroom on though, since it does not have a window.

In the bedrooms:

3. No team used cleaning products in the bedroom.
4. Items such as comment cards, pens and brochures, were only replaced when necessary. This means that nobody threw unused items away.
5. The cloth used to clean the bedroom had not been washed while cleaning the room. After cleaning a room, it had been rinsed and used again.
6. One team turned unnecessary lights, such as desk lights and bed lights off after entering the room. The other two teams switched them off before leaving the room.
7. Two teams used cloths to clean the bedroom and the other team used one handtowel for dusting and another one for cleaning the floor, which got replaced for every room.
8. Tea and coffee had to be replaced in four out of nine rooms, which is a rate of 44.44%.

In the bathrooms:

9. One team did not use the cloth to clean the bathroom, the other two teams washed the cloth to rinse it several times or before cleaning the bathroom.
10. The number of cleaning products being used in the bathroom differed. Team 1 used five products in total, team 2 used four and team 3, two.

11. All teams used dish washing liquid to clean the dishes. One team used an unnecessary huge amount though.
12. No team recycled paper, glass and plastic separately and organic waster was not composted properly.
13. Dependent on the usage of linen and towels, the linen bags had to be replaced after approximately 2–2.5 hours of work, several times a day. There are two blue linen bags for all bed linen and all towels except the bath towels. Bath towels have to go into the one brown linen bag on the trolley.
14. There were empty bin liners in the rubbish bag on team 1's trolley. There were newspapers in the rubbish bags of team 2 and 3. In the rubbish bag of team 2 also was a ¼ roll of unused toilet paper.

6.5 DISCUSSION

The research findings demonstrate some common issues, which can have an effect on the intention to achieve long-term sustainability in the hotel. There are three main themes that occurred within the research findings: *the education of the guests, the communication between management and staff,* and *the customer and staff's attitude towards sustainable development.*

6.5.1 The Education of Guests

According to Hobson and Essex (2001), the potential of customer requirements plays a crucial role in the adoption of sustainable practices. Therefore, the guest needs to be well educated by the hotel company. In turn, the business may retain a better understanding of the customer's needs. The questionnaire results demonstrate that surprisingly ten out of thirteen staff members state that no guest asks them about information on environment friendly practice in the hotel. Therefore, the guest may not be very concerned about sustainable development in the hotel industry, or the advertisement in the hotel and in the media does not call the guest's attention to encourage him or her to gain more knowledge on this topic. It is also possible to suggest that the guest finds the quality of the reminders or the information provided through the media adequate and consequently does not need to encourage staff to give him or her further information. As stated by the International Hotel Environment Initiative (1996), it is crucial to make the customer aware of the schemes and the reasons for the hotel's initiatives. A study by Goodman (2000), exploring the success of Scandic Hotels in Northern Europe, established that the guests began to ask about the company's environmental practices, such as waste disposal, after the implementation of sustainable measures. However, a similar study discovers that "operators suggested that very few guests show any regard for environmental practices carried out in hotels and usually only require a 'clean, comfortable bed' and a 'good breakfast'" (Hobson and Essex, 2001, p. 145). The staff's proposition that guests consider the location, price and service quality as the most important factors in their decision to choose the hotel affirms the authors' findings.

The majority of employees highlighted in the questionnaires that in their opinion guests are not willing to pay more for environment friendly travel supplies. Their denoted reasons are that the price is more important for the guest and that the guests may not be very environmental friendly. It is crucial to notice that the authors' opinion on this statement in the literature differs significantly. As cited in Hobson and Essex (2001), guests may be willing to pay more for environmentally sensitive products and services. In contrast, a study carried out in the United States demonstrates that even though the majority of guests would prefer to be accommodated in an environment friendly hotel, they were not disposed to pay more (Kirk, 1996, as cited in Hobson and Essex, 2001). Moreover, a study conducted by Manaktola and Jauhari (2007) confirms those findings, because despite positive behaviour towards sustainability, customers are not willing to pay more.

6.5.2 The Communication to Staff

It is evident that communication between different parties in the hotel is definitely a huge issue. It becomes apparent by looking at the questionnaire results as well as the interviews. Too many staff members consider the quality of information they receive from the Sustainability Meetings as only fair. Furthermore, the response for the quality of the reminders in the hotel is not adequate, which indicates that the majority may not be satisfied with some decisions being made. Although staff demonstrates a solid knowledge of what could be improved to make the guests more aware of the topic, more than half of the participants did not have any suggestions. This shows that some may not have ideas or they may not want to exert critique on the current practice.

Although the management has the overall feeling that the staff's participation in sustainable practice is good, the majority of staff members stated that they did not undergo training on how to recycle properly or on how to give the guest information on the Qualmark rating. Considering the fact that the Qualmark rating itself is new to all employees in the hotel, there could be more done to communicate the requirements that need to be fulfilled to achieve a high environmental rating as well as the benefits that the rating brings with it to staff.

6.5.3 Staff Training

As discussed earlier, appropriate staff training is crucial. Employees have to be motivated to include the learnt procedures into their daily routine, which is achievable with the help of proper education of the staff. Education starts with the training, which is a key requirement to achieve consistency. The appropriate training of staff is an essential component, which can contribute to a more successful environmental performance. According to Goodman (2000), the ongoing education of staff and the transference of responsibility to "frontline employees" allow them to apply what they learned and therefore to contribute ideas as well as doubts. Despite the statement of the management that the staff receives an appropriate training including topics surrounding sustainability, the majority of the questionnaire participants did not receive information on the environmental policy of the hotel during their training time. This indicates that the two parties have completely different perceptions when it comes to staff training. Furthermore, there was a poor response when the participants were required to explain the hotel's environmental policy in their own words. It is also to note that the ideas of the context of the environmental policy differed.

The findings reveal, especially by looking at the response rate in the questionnaires, that many participants do not seem to be motivated enough to contribute their own ideas to the topic. To motivate staff to contribute to environment friendly development, the management should apply the management method of assigning empowerment to staff (Samson and Daft, 2003). While trying to achieve tasks correctly, the employee may perform more productively and therefore contribute to the company's goal (Samson and Daft, 2003) to evolve environmental sound management.

6.5.4 The Customer and Staff's Attitude Towards Sustainable Development

By looking at the interviews, the management believes that the environmental rating is a good marketing tool, and good intentions are obvious. However, it is important to note that "despite the fact that hoteliers generally recognize that their facilities would influence the natural surroundings and that practicing green would bring economic benefits and boost the hotels' image and competitiveness, this awareness or 'good' intentions are not always translated into actions" (Penny, 2007, p. 293). It is important to create a base, which functions as a platform where staff members are able to exchange experiences. The International Hotels Environmental Initiative (1996) confirms this by stating that hotels should implement an environmental working group in order to achieve a functioning environmental program. Furthermore, the Initiative emphasizes that one person should be appointed, whose task is "to ensure that all employees understand how the policy affects them" (p. 7, 1996). This, in turn, affects the staff training since it includes the education of staff. The hotel has done something similar by setting up the Sustainability Committee, which includes representatives from every department.

The findings demonstrate that "there is a growing understanding that these steps are crucial to ensure long-term business prospects and profitability" (Bader, 2005, p. 76). However, the most essential step towards sustainable development is the individual responsibility of all stakeholders involved. Personal interest in environmental issues functions as a significant motivator to support an environment friendly business concept (Hobson and Essex, 2001). As is evident in the observation, it is the employees' own choice to recycle and separate waste and to use fewer chemicals. It is inevitable to give constructive feedback to staff on their environmental performance. Especially in the housekeeping department, it is important to encourage new cleaning methods, such as using less chemicals and a cloth instead of towels to clean the bathroom. This would minimize the usage of towels and cleaning products and save money. Some staff members seem to have already realized that cleaning as clean as possible does not necessarily require a huge amount of cleaning products. However, it is evident that more has to be done when it comes to waste management, especially when it comes to waste separation on the floors. Many success stories approve that proper waste management saves money (International Hotels Environmental Initiative, 1996). As established in the literature review, Iwanowski and Rushmore (1994) support the statement above and recommend the "careful examination of existing systems and operational procedures, especially in the areas of solid waste management, water conservation, and energy management" (1994, p. 34).

6.5.5 Study Limitations

It is important to note that this study examines which factors contribute to long-term sustainability in a medium sized New Zealand hotel with the focus on environment friendly performance. It does not analyze data of the economic performance of the hotel in particular, which would exceed the scope of this study. It would be interesting for researchers to examine how environmental management affects the financial performance of the hotel in the long-term. Further, research should also include the interrogation of suppliers and the investigation of the role of Corporate Social Responsibility (CSR) when it comes to sustainability in the hotel industry. As discussed in the literature review, CSR has the ability to contribute to the protection of natural and built environment and encourage the interaction with stakeholders (as cited in Holcomb, Upchurch and Okumus, 2007).

6.6 CONCLUSION AND RECOMMENDATIONS

"What has been done so far in the hotel industry, especially by global companies, is a start. But it must be understood that deeper changes are required in the long-term" (Bader, 2005, p. 77). It is to acknowledge that the hotel made a good start towards sustainability and achieved a great award in a relatively short period of time. It implemented the Hotel Environmental Policy, nominated an environmental committee and provided easy accessible information for every employee through the company's Intranet. "The hotel company operating with an environmental policy has shown itself to be more aware of the environmental issue and its importance" (Brown, 1996, p. 22). The hotel shows social responsibility towards eco-tourism ventures, such as the Yellow Eyed Penguin Trust and is conscious of new sustainable innovations. The most relevant benefits for the hotel are the economic (Bader, 2005) and therefore it is inevitable to educate all stakeholders to be able to achieve a good environmental performance that can benefit the hotel in a long-term. With a more elaborate education of staff and customers, the hotel will be able to take advantage of its reparatory work to achieve sustainable development.

6.6.1 Recommendations

Staff training

As discussed earlier, appoint one person who is responsible for staff training and the education of staff about environment friendly behaviour. During the training period, this person should encourage staff to perform environment friendly and show them how to include this practice into their daily routine. It is useful to create a list of what has to be covered during the training, such as passing the key points of the sustainable mission statements of the suppliers on to the trainee, explaining the function of the Qualmark assessments and the basic concept of waste management.

Communication to staff

Collect staff suggestions on environment friendly management on a daily basis and reward staff for their ideas. Incentives motivate staff to act in a sustainable manner.

Education of guests

It is recommended that further research should include the interviews of customers to examine their perception on the quality of information that they receive from the hotel. This will help to establish their attitude towards sustainability more precisely.

Future investigations on this topic should involve the suppliers of the hotel with special emphasis on the improvement of the steady establishment of common environmental goals.

REFERENCES

Andrews, N., Convery, F., Flanagan, S. and Ruddy, J. (Eds.) (2002). *Tourism and the environment: sustainability in tourism development.* Dublin: Dublin Institute of Technology.

Bader, E.E. (2005). Hotels: sustainable hotel business practices. *Journal of Retail and Leisure Property*, 5(1), ABI/INFORM Global, p. 70.

Brown, M. (1996). Environmental policy in the hotel sector: "green" strategy or stratagem? *International Journal of Contemporary Hospitality Management*, 8(3), 18–23.

Ebner, D. and Baumgartner, Dr. R. (2006). The relationship between sustainable development and corporate social responsibility [Electronic Version]. *Corporate Responsibility Research Conference 2006,* 4th–5th September, Dublin.

Gillham, B. (2007). *Developing a questionnaire* (2nd ed.), London, New York: Continuum.

Goodman, A. (May–June 2000). Implementing sustainable service operations at Scandic hotels. *Interfaces,* 30(3), 202–214.

Gray, D.E. (2004). *Doing research in the real world.* London. Thousand Oaks, CA: Sage Publications.

Hobson, S. and Essex, S. (2001). Sustainable tourism: a view from accommodation businesses. *The Service Industries Journal,* 21(4), 133–146.

Holcomb, J.L., Upchurch, R.S. and Okumus, F. (2007). Corporate social responsibility: what are top hotel companies reporting? *International Journal of Contemporary Hospitality Management,* 19(6), 461–475.

International Hotels Environment Initiative (1996). *Environmental management for hotels: The industry guide to best practice.* Oxford, Boston: Butterworth Heinemann.

Iwanowski, K. and Rushmore, C. (1994). Introducing the eco-friendly hotel. *The Cornell H.R.A. Quarterly*, 34–38.

Lockyer, T.L.G. (2007). *The international hotel industry: sustainable management.* New York: Haworth Hospitality and Tourism Press.

Manaktola, K. and Jauhari, V. (2007). Exploring consumer attitude and behaviour towards green practices in the lodging industry in India. *International Journal of Contemporary Hospitality Management,* 19(5), 364–376.

Penny, W.Y. (2007). The use of environmental management as a facilities management tool in the Macao hotel sector. *Facilities,* 25(7/8), 286–295.

Robson, C. (2003). *Real world research: a resource for social scientists and practitioner-researchers.* Oxford, UK: Cambridge, Mass., USA: Blackwell.

Samson, D.A. and Daft, R.L. (2003). *Management.* South Melbourne, Vic.: Thomson.

Sharma, S. and Aragón-Correa, J.A. (Eds.) (2005). *Corporate environmental strategy and competitive advantage.* Cheltenham, UK, Northhampton, MA: Edward Elga.

Tharenou, P., Donohue, R. and Cooper, B. (2007). *Management research methods.* Cambridge [U.K.]; New York: Cambridge University Press.

Yin, R.K. (2003). *Case study research: Design and methods* (3th ed.). Thousand Oaks, CA: Sage Publications.

_____. (2009). *Case study research: Design and methods* (4th ed.). Thousand Oaks, CA: Sage Publications.

CHAPTER

7

PLANNING CONSIDERATIONS FOR TOURISM IN THE MINHO-LIMA REGION (Northwest Portugal)

—PAULA CRISTINA REMOALDO, JOSE CADIMA RIBEIRO,
LAURENTINA CRUZ VAREIRO AND MECIA CUNHA MOTA

7.1 ABSTRACT

In administering their territories, most local municipalities aim to preserve their natural, historical and ethnographical resources while simultaneously using them to increase revenue and employment. In order to efficiently promote the products and services available and attract tourists, decision makers, both private and public, need to know and incorporate tourists' preferences in their marketing strategies.

In this chapter, we illustrate the use of stated preferences as an instrument to identify national and foreign tourists' preferences regarding the products and services that the touristic destination of the Minho-Lima region (Northwest Portugal) should offer. As a starting point, we have taken the three general groups of touristic resources mentioned above as attributes. We take Ponte de Lima, a municipality in this region that has a strong cultural tourism potential, as an example to identify possible future tourism scenarios for this territory.

We believe the previously identified methodology can be a valuable instrument in the identification of the strengths and weaknesses of the selected territory and, thus, support the decision making process behind its future tourist development and marketing strategies.

Keywords: tourism resources, tourism potential, stated preferences, conjoint analysis, cultural tourism, creative tourism.

7.2 INTRODUCTION

Since the 1980s, western economies seem to have entered a phase of "economic coalescence". This phenomenon has greatly contributed to important changes across the world map in economic dynamism and the emergence of new territories, which in turn have driven changes in regional development policies and strategies. At the European Union level, the regional policies implemented tend to focus on reducing regional imbalances by promoting the economic competitiveness of territories, aiming simultaneously to preserve social cohesion. In this new scenario, tourism could play a major role as it is an industry that leads to significant interaction among territories, facilitating important contact between communities. Its development potential, however, remains far from fully explored.

Tourism is commonly presented as an activity that has been following a path of increasing growth due to circumstances arising from: (i) the considerable increase in leisure time which people have access to; (ii) changes in consumption patterns; (iii) the increase of people's mobility; (iv) changes in family structures; (v) greater allocation of vacation time throughout the year; (vi) the spread of the new information technologies, allowing people to more easily access information about places and their attractiveness; (vii) the dissemination of new values of society, and (viii) the internationalization and globalization of economies (Cunha, 1997; Mota, Remoaldo, and Cadima Ribeiro, 2010; Vogeler Ruiz and Hernández Armand, 1997).

In Portugal, tourism is already a major economic activity, with significant growth potential and impacts on wealth and employment. At present, tourism represents 10% of Portuguese GDP and accounts for 10% of the workforce employment (Lopes, 2010).

The small town of Ponte de Lima is one of the oldest in Portugal. It is endowed with a wealth of natural resources, a remarkable architectural and gastronomic heritage, and strong social traditions. Supported by such environmental and patrimonial wealth and traditions, Ponte de Lima has the potential to become a creative city and, thus, to be able to develop new and more attractive tourism products.

Cultural tourism was one of the segments outlined by the National Strategic Tourism Plan (PENT) for development in Portugal in the period 2006–2015. In that context, the Minho-Lima region is thought to have one of the greatest tourism potentials in the whole country, specifically as regards developing a creative cultural dimension.

According to the aims of PENT, of the 10 strategic tourism products predicted for sustainable development, environmental tourism and cultural and landscape touring feature as the main growth products for the Northern region of Portugal and the city of Oporto.

The chapter is structured as follows: in Section 7.2.1, we present an overview of a few tourism concepts, focusing in particular on tourism resources and cultural tourism; in Section 7.3, we set out the methodology used; in Section 7.4, we proceed to an evaluation of the consistency of the tourism strategy followed in the Minho-Lima region based on an analysis of the results from a questionnaire applied to visitors and interviews conducted with local and regional tourism agents; the final section offers a few concluding remarks about possible strategies for achieving a consolidation of the Minho-Lima region as a cultural tourism destination, using Ponte de Lima as an example.

7.2.1 Territorial Tourism Resources and Cultural Tourism

Natural, historical and ethnographical resources are the base sources for the development of territories. This being a fact, any regions and towns aiming to increase revenue and employment should envisage preserving these resources. As resources are invariably scarce, particularly financial and human ones, any planning process implies a selection process and an evaluation of the available alternatives.

The existing tourism resources can provide a starting point for the definition of alternatives, and knowing the tourists' opinion on these resources can provide a more solid basis for selecting strategic alternatives appropriate to their preferences and the characteristics of the territory under analysis.

In recent decades, tourism destinations have been confronted with a new generation of tourists that have shown increasing preference for more diversified tourism products, including cultural ones. This has made cultural tourism a more complex segment of tourism activity (Besculides, Lee and McCormick, 2002; Hu, Horng and Sun, 2009; Pulido Fernández and Sánchez Rivero, 2009; Vareiro, Cadima Ribeiro, Remoaldo and Marques, 2011).

In a comprehensive approach, cultural tourism can be defined as every trip made by individuals to unusual places with the aim of increasing their cultural level, furthering their knowledge of historic facts, interacting with people of a different culture and having access to new knowledge and experiences (Simeon, Buonincontri and Trapani, 2009). In a more restricted sense, cultural tourism can be broadly defined as travelling for cultural and education reasons (Henriques, 2007).

In the context of changing consumer behaviour, tourism destinations can only continue supplying "traditional" cultural tourism if they are willing to accept a loss of customers. An alternative way of dealing with the changes experienced by the tourism markets is to develop new products and concepts, like those associated with creative tourism (Richards, 2009).

The concept of creativity appears to be capable of making a contribution to the changes needed in the traditional strategies followed by cultural tourism destinations and of facilitating the emergence of a more active dimension in the tourist experience.

Creativity is a complex and multidisciplinary concept, and is recognized as being one which is difficult to define (Landry et al., 1996). In general terms, it is the search for different solutions and products to be made available to the general society and to individuals, implying some or all of the following: bringing something new into our life; producing an invention, and using the imagination. That is, it has to do with the capacity to solve unexpected problems or problems that have been identified. Real creativity involves searching by trial and error, originality, breaking rules, being unconventional, building upon future scenarios, and a flexible and lateral way of looking at issues and situations (Landry et al., 1996).

For Florida (2002), the creative class includes scientists, engineers, university teachers, artists, designers and writers, researchers and analysts, and architects, among others. What these different kinds of workers have in common is what he calls a creative "ethos", which is a certain way of working with creativity, singularity, originality and merit.

Richards and Raymond (2000) defined creative tourism as a product which offers tourists the opportunity to develop their own creative potential through an active participation in the tourism experiences made available by the package of resources in the tourism destination they are visiting. For Richards and Wilson (2006), creativity gives value to places and cultural products, makes new products available, and secures the sustainability of the destination. These are just some of the reasons behind the thinking that creative tourism is a good alternative to traditional cultural tourism. In addition, it is well recognized that people travel to visit archaeological and historic places to experience the *atmosphere of those places*, to make contact with places and cities seen as having strong symbolic images (Cadima Ribeiro and Remoaldo, 2011; Riganti, 2009). The featuring of these places can be achieved through the implementation of creative cultural events, such as the 2012 European Cultural Capital in Guimarães, or, in a more restricted sense, through the renewal of certain urban quarters, like that of Bairro dos Couros, in Guimarães (a municipality also located in Northwest Portugal).

The complexity of the tourism market and the increase of segment diversity demands a well-conceived and properly defined strategy, supported by close partnerships with tourism operators, prime community actors and other stakeholders (Besculides, Lee, and Mccormick, 2002; Kuvan and Akan, 2005; Pulido Fernández and Sánchez Rivero, 2009; Vareiro, L., Cadima Ribeiro, J., Remoaldo, P. and Marques, 2011).

7.3 METHODOLOGY

This chapter makes use of the results of a survey applied between May and December 2006, by Vareiro, Cadima Ribeiro, and Pardellas (2009), and of data from interviews with local and regional tourism agents, implemented between April and May 2010, by Mota, Remoaldo, and Cadima Ribeiro (2010). While in the first empirical investigation, the aim was to capture the (declared) preferences of 350 respondents, the second investigation envisaged capturing the views on the tourism phenomenon of 13 agents from representative institutions of Ponte de Lima and from some other territories that were directly or indirectly associated with regional tourism development. Both investigations studied tourism development in the Minho-Lima region, although the second was more specifically focused on the reality of the municipality of Ponte de Lima, one of the municipalities in this region.

In the first study, the empirical approach followed was based on stated preferences, a technique where data is obtained from the choices declared by individuals about hypothetical situations of consumption through a structured questionnaire (Vareiro, Cadima Ribeiro, and Pardellas, 2009). "Because it relies on individual's statements about their preferences or choices, this approach has become known as 'stated preference' (or choice) analysis" (Louvière and Timmermans, 1990, p. 10).

From a range of stated preference techniques developed in recent years, we chose to use Conjoint Analysis techniques in this particular investigation. These techniques are a family of survey-based methodologies for modelling preferences for certain products, where products are described in terms of their attributes or characteristics and the levels that these take (Louviere and Timmermans, 1990; Merino-Castelló, 2003). In Conjoint Analysis, therefore, the choice process is determined by the utilities associated at the product representation levels of a set of attributes.

Following Luce and Tukey (1964), Conjoint Analysis is a methodology that is used to analyze the action or conjoint effect of two or more independent variables on a dependent variable, or to determine the contribution of the independent variables (levels) and their respective values (utilities) for the consumers' preferences for goods or services.

One of the advantages of these techniques over revealed preference methods, and which is of particular interest to our study, is the possibility to control the attribute levels that configure the choice alternatives and the context (questionnaire) through which data are obtained. This makes it possible to evaluate possible former interventions, that is to say, before the questionnaire's application (i.e., through hypothetical attributes and levels). One of the disadvantages, as highlighted by Rodríguez and González (2002), is the effort exerted by each respondent as they move through the choice sequence, making fatigue probable, and resulting in a final loss of quality in their answers.

Besides a revision of the literature, a consultation with experts was held in order to define the particular tourism attributes in the territory to be used in the questionnaire. In this case, the experts consulted were employees from each municipal delegation of Alto Minho's Tourist Board (RTAM); hotels and restaurant owners; public and private agents with connections to tourism, and other researchers working in this area. Based on these consultations, and following the recommendations of Green and Srinivasan (1990), who suggest that a full-profile data collection method should be used in studies with only six or fewer attributes, four attributes were selected. Wittink et al. (1982, cf. Trinidad and Rotondaro, 2004) verified that attributes with larger number of levels have, proportionally, more importance than those with few levels, which suggests that a uniform number of levels should be used among different attributes.

Taking into consideration the before mentioned concerns and recommendations, three attributes were presented with three levels and one as a variable including four levels:

- *Natural resources* (*water*): oceanic beaches, fluvial beaches, and rivers
- *Natural resources* (*land*): national parks or protected landscape, natural recreation and leisure parks, and mountains
- *Ethnographical resources:* handicraft, festivals and gastronomy
- *Historical resources:* archaeological patrimony, religious patrimony, military patrimony and civil patrimony.

According to Louviere and Timmermans (1990), a profile is the designation given in the literature of Conjoint Analysis to each combination of attribute levels. After having defined the attributes and their levels, it was necessary to design these profiles or choice alternatives to be presented to tourists.

As such, it was necessary to determine the number of profiles that respondents were able to handle. It is important to get a certain balance between the maximization of the level of information obtained and the fatigue effect that arises when the questionnaire is too long or complex, or the exercises that the respondent should complete are repetitive (Dellaert, Brazell, and Louviere, 1999; Swait and Adamowicz, 1997).

If we use all the possible profiles (combinations and attribute levels) in a study, it is called a complete factorial design. However, in practice, complete factorial design is rarely used because the number of possible combinations is, usually, impracticable. For example, the factorial design of an experience with x attributes with a levels, and y attributes with b levels includes $a^x b^y$ combinations, the total number of situations required to identify all the effects and interactions. In our case, that meant $3^3 \times 4 = 108$ possible different combinations of levels.

An alternative is to show respondents only a small set of possible combinations, that is, to use fractional factorial designs to construct profiles (Haider, 2002; Louviere and Timmermans, 1990; Louviere, Hensher and Swait, 2000).

In this study, applying the fractional factorial design solution obtained 12 combinations/profiles (Vareiro, Cadima Ribeiro and Pardellas, 2009).

Once the profiles/choice alternatives have been defined, respondents are requested to classify the cards/profiles according to their preference. They could be asked to rank the various alternatives, to rate them or to choose their most preferred.

For the data collection process, a questionnaire was designed and then applied to tourists in several municipalities between May and December of 2006. A total of 350 complete questionnaires were obtained, 74 from foreign tourists and 276 from national tourists (Vareiro, Cadima Ribeiro, and Pardellas, 2009).

In order to formulate the model that is capable of explaining the relationship between the evaluations in the form of preference levels (dependent variable) and the different attribute levels chosen as determinant of the product in question (independent variables), the independent variables must have the dummy code (0, 1). In this way, the presence or absence of a certain level of a specific attribute will be defined by the value 1 or 0 of the correspondent variable dummy in the model. Therefore, the model to estimate is as follows:

$$y_t = \quad + \sum_{i=l}^{I} \sum_{j=l}^{J} \quad {}_{ij} \quad {}_{ij} + e_t$$

where

y_t = evaluation of preference or hierarchy that represents the level of preference associated with profile t expressed by the respondent

α = constant

β_{ij} = coefficient or part-worth utility corresponding to level j of i attribute

χ_{ij} = 1 if level j of i attribute is present in profile t

χ_{ij} = 0 if level j of i attribute is not present in the profile t

e_t = estimate residue.

Besides the estimative for each attribute level, which are referred to as part-worth utilities, we also determined the importance of each attribute.

The analysis of data and the reliability test applied to estimates were accomplished through SPSS Conjoint 15.0.

The technique used to approach the regional and local agents, taken as privileged sources of information, was the semi-structured interview, a qualitative methodological approach to collecting data. This empirical approach was considered rewarding because it would allow for collecting different live experiences and, at the same time, ensure a large degree of flexibility to our communications with the interviewees. Specifically, this approach allowed us to adapt the questions to inquire about the specificities of each of the interviewees, taking into account the different nature of the institutions contacted. Prior to this, we had established a certain number of categories that would give some consistency and uniformity to the various interviews to be implemented. The organizing categories predicted in the 25 questions used were: (i) region and tourism region; (ii) marketing and promotion; (iii) the strategy defined in the aims of the Tourism Strategic National Plan; (iv) working areas where the organizations contacted commonly operated; (v) projects; (vi) partnerships and cooperation between tourism agents; (vii) resources; (viii) planning strategy; (ix) cultural tourism development; (x) cultural tourism potentialities.

One of the criteria used in the selection of the interviewees was to ensure the representation of the main agents directly and indirectly linked to tourism development in the Minho-Lima region and in the Oporto and Northern Portugal tourism promotional area. To this end, a list of the institutions in the target territory was drawn up. The resulting sample included 13 institutional local and regional agents, dispersed geographically by the municipally of Ponte de Lima and Northern Portugal, and ranging from a tourism expert working in the Northern Region Coordination and Development Commission (CCDR-N), the Head of the Tourism Office, the Municipal Tourism Councillor, the Manager of the Nautical Club, two professors (one from polytechnic and the other from a private university), and some technicians from various local museums and from regional and local development associations (e.g., ADRIL and TURIHAB). The Cultural Programme Director of the 2012 Guimarães European Capital of Culture was also interviewed, as Guimarães is a nearby municipality, and as such Ponte de Lima can, we believe, profit from the mega-event that will take place there during 2012.

7.4 EVALUATION OF THE TOURISM STRATEGIES FOLLOWED IN THE MINHO-LIMA REGION

7.4.1 Tourism Resources and Stated Preferences

As regards the first survey and the existing resources of the tourism destination, the results obtained are shown in Table 7.1.

The quality of the adjustment was verified via the calculation of the correlation coefficient among the classifications stated by the tourists that compose the sample and the classifications foreseen for the model, applying the *tau* of Kendall and the Pearson correlation

Table 7.1 Estimates of utilities and importance of the attributes (total of respondents)

Attribute	*Level*	*Utility*	*Relative importance*
Natural resources (water)	Oceanic beaches	1,768	31,790
	Fluvial beaches	–0,407	
	Rivers	–1,361	
Natural resources (land)	Mountains	–0,020	17,205
	National parks or protected landscape	0,057	
	Natural recreation and leisure parks	–0,037	
Ethnographical resources	Festivals	0,191	18,591
	Handicrafts	–0,284	
	Gastronomy	0,093	
Historical resources	Archaeological patrimony	0,938	32,415
	Religious patrimony	–0,649	
	Military patrimony	–0,399	
	Civil patrimony	0,110	
Constant			6,500
Pearson's R			0,996
Kendall's *tau*			0,970

Source: Authors' own survey data.

coefficient methods. Taking into account the values of these indicators (*tau* of Kendall: 0,970; and R of Pearson: 0,996), the quality of the adjustment was confirmed to be high.

From Table 7.1, we could verify that the tourism resources more highly valued by tourists were historical resources, with a score of 32.4%, followed by natural resources (water), with a relative importance conferred on 31.8%. The least valued attribute was natural resources (land), with a score of 17.2%. However, if we combine the natural resources (water and land), these reach a total importance of 49%.

From the previous results (Table 7.1), we can assume that the destination profile that Minho-Lima tourists prefer has the following characteristics:

(i) *Natural resources (water)*: oceanic beaches
(ii) *Historical resources*: archaeological and civil patrimony
(iii) *Ethnographical resources*: festivals and gastronomy
(iv) *Natural resources (land)*: national parks or protected landscape.

The results were also analyzed with regard to the respondents' nationality, and similar percentages of importance of the attributes were obtained. However, some differences associated with the preferred profiles could be observed, since national tourists prefer the National Parks or the Protected Landscapes, while foreign tourists attribute more value to Mountains and, in the case of the Ethnographical Resources, the national tourists attribute greater importance to Gastronomy while foreigners showed a preference for Festivals. Finally, with regard to Natural Resources (water), national as well as foreign tourists prefer Oceanic

Beaches and, as regard Historical Resources, the preference was clearly for Archaeological Patrimony.

7.4.2 Results Obtained from the Interviews

As mentioned, the municipally of Ponte de Lima is integrated in the Minho-Lima region and, in geographical terms, has a central location in the Lima Valley. It covers an area of 320.3 km^2, distributed among 51 parishes.

According to the National Statistical Office data (I.N.E., 2008a), it had 44.618 inhabitants in 2007. According to other data from the same Statistical Office (I.N.E., 2008b), the young people represented 24% of the total population of Ponte de Lima.

The municipality's economic base is weak and undiversified. Nevertheless, it has an important natural and historical patrimony and its main vocation is rural tourism. One of the Portuguese pilgrimage routes to Santiago de Compostela crosses the municipality. The town's historical centre, which is the main tourist attraction, has been undergoing a renovation process in recent years.

In the last fifteen years, Ponte de Lima registered a rise in terms of hotel guests. In 2006, the municipality experienced a total of 27,222 overnight stays for visitors (Mota, Remoaldo, and Cadima Ribeiro, 2010).

The Ponte de Lima free-market is one of the oldest in the country and constitutes an important tourism attraction (Sá et al., 2007). The municipality has one of the few natural protected areas in the country, The Pentieiros Pedagogical Farm, and its small lakes and ecological routes should be considered as strong bases for establishing environmental tourism projects (Sá et al., 2007). The Horse Market and the International Festival of Gardens are other events with major tourism potential that should be considered in the redesign of its tourism strategy.

7.4.3 Resources Available

Taking into account the general tourism features of Ponte de Lima, we felt it relevant to listen to the actors interviewed about the role of cultural tourism in the development of Ponte de Lima and of Northern Portugal, in general.

In terms of resources identified at the cultural level, the municipality and the cultural institutions recognize the historical centre of Ponte de Lima as the main asset. At the natural level, the Protected Area of *Lagoas de Bertiandos* is seen as the most important resource. The AREA Alto Minho (the Alto Minho Environment and Energy Regional Agency) technician also identified the Historical Centre and the Protected Areas (Natural network places) as the main local resources. The protected areas were also referred to by the tourism expert from CCDR-N.

The teachers and researchers interviewed referred to the value of the local gastronomy and the attributes of the residents, and some monuments, such as the *Paço do Curutelo*, at Freixo. They also mentioned the manorhouses, the river, the biodiversity and the Peneda-Gerês National Park (PNPG) as other import resources available.

The representatives from the services sector also made mention to the historical monuments, the small lakes, the ecological routes, the manorhouses, the gastronomy, the traditional festivals, the nautical sports, the Small Food Market and the Horse Market.

The 2012 Guimarães cultural programme director claimed that North Portugal's main resources were the World Heritage Sites, the Historical Centres of the cities and towns, and the immaterial patrimony, that is, the symbolic capital of places, the industrial heritage sites, and the traditional festivals and the rituals preserved. However, the director maintained that the region does not yet know how to sell these products and continues to be inward looking. The following sentence illustrates his main view on the issue:

> What we should be looking into is a mix between what is physical patrimony, immaterial patrimony and contemporaneous production. I think the solution and the success of tourism in the Northern region should be built around this triangle (2012, Guimarães European Capital Culture cultural programme director).

As regards the stage of development of cultural tourism, the representative of the Ponte de Lima municipal council felt that it is experiencing a period of growth, and indicated a few key projects to illustrate his point:

> We are experiencing a period of growth as the *Terceiros* Museum is becoming a cultural attraction (…). We are developing more projects. (…) We are going to have the Earth House, (…) and we will continue promoting all traditional products and the culture of Ponte de Lima (…). (Municipal tourism councillor)

The Head of the IPVC (the Polytechnic Institute of Viana do Castelo) Tourism Studics Programme, commenting on the state of the cultural tourism in the region, claims that this segment is under stagnation. By their turn, the representatives of the Associations interviewed considered that the town is experiencing a growth period. The following statement illustrates their thoughts:

> Tourism must be in constant change (…). They [the tourists] want all that is traditional but with a touch of modernity. And what are we doing to achieve that? Nothing. This year, what will we present that is new? Nothing at all (…). (Head of the IPVC Tourism Studies Programme)

On the other hand, the 2012 Guimarães cultural programme director mentioned that cultural tourism is in an initial phase of development, mainly because the public perception of its economic impacts is quite recent. He claims that it is the cultural dimension that is making people travel to different places. He was the sole respondent that underlined the need to make creative experiences available in those territories that want to have a future as cultural tourism destinations.

The technician from AREA Alto Minho focused her answer on the potentialities that Ponte de Lima possesses, such as the small lakes and the ecological routes, the gastronomic competition and the mountain of Agra. Finally, the teacher and researcher from the private University of Fernando Pessoa called attention to the need to identify precisely the target market. In his words:

> It is necessary to attract a public with an ecologic sensibility and with economic purchasing power. Viana do Castelo [in Northern Portugal] is experiencing a deep crisis in its retail shops. Many are closing. We must put in place a more attractive social environment (…). Each territory must supply a diversified set of tourism products, trying to reach diversified consumers. (Teacher and researcher from Fernando Pessoa University)

The several local associations expressed different points of view about the available resources because, on the one hand, they feel that there are potentialities, but, on the other, they made mention to the existing external obstacles (the economic and financial crisis) and also to the internal ones, namely the low quality of the public transport system in place.

7.4.4 Tourism and Local and Regional Development

All answers obtained agreed about the role the tourism industry should take in the development of the Ponte de Lima municipality and in the Minho-Lima region, as a whole. Many of them told us that tourism is an economic driving force for local and regional development. The statement that follows expresses that idea of tourism as a key industry in local and regional development:

> For us, tourism is a key sector (...). I used to say that Portugal should be the "leisure site" of Europe, because the best that we have is the beauty of the country; in this case, Ponte de Lima is the best that we have. (Municipal tourism councillor)

Another important element caught from the interviews is the residents' role in tourism development:

> Nowadays, and I speak of creative tourism, the emergent tourism tendencies are that the tourist wants to do something, wants experiences, wants emotions and I have defended that here, in the region, we are not taking an important resource into due account (...) the residents (...), because they are part of the touristic experience (...). (Head of the IPVC tourism programme)

The importance of tourism, in terms of companies and jobs created, is mentioned in the next statement:

> That question has a short and obvious answer, which is: it is very important (...), either in terms of companies operating or as regards jobs (...). It is related to its cultural expression, its patrimonial dimension, and the every day practices of the people. Every day, it is becoming more important. (2012 Guimarães European Capital Culture cultural programme director)

7.4.5 Territorial Promotional Organization of Tourism

From the analysis of the interviews, it is also clear that the promotion of tourism is considered to be a very important issue. However, it should be underlined that the opinions about the work done in terms of the promotion of Ponte de Lima and of the region are not convergent. This is related to the difficult role played by the present promotional tourism board, which is supposed to deal with a territory as large and complex as the North of Portugal. The next statement shows us that divergence:

> For me, the question has two sides, because to have the tourism boards that we had before did not make any sense, because territories were all promoting the same thing (...), but (...) the Oporto and Northern Tourism promotional area is too embracing and is composed of realities that are completely different from each other. (...) Anyway, I think the strategy they are following is interesting. (Municipal tourism councillor)

A different opinion is given by the author of the statement that follows, who emphasizes the difficulty of making the institutional promotional model defined operative:

> My opinion is very positive, as, at present, we have only one promotional region. But there is an aspect that should be reviewed, which is: it was made into just one region and then several strategic products were anchored in it (...). In this change, there was one aspect that was not taken into due consideration: the region, and the way it really is (...). It is not homogeneous, it has (...) the different destinations, Minho, Trás-os-Montes, the Douro and Oporto, and to this complex reality not enough attention is paid to the concept of a Northern Region promotional area (...). (Head of ADRIL and TURIHAB associations)

Another opinion also tells us a lot about the difficulties and contradictions of the promotional model put in place:

> (...) at the national level, the idea behind this restructuration seems positive to me, that is, in theory, now we organize ourselves according to thematic territories or products, which is more appropriate in responding to the needs of tourists, while before we were organized by geographic spaces (…). Nevertheless, in real terms, what we have now is only the replication of the previous system. (2012 Guimarães European Capital Culture cultural programme director)

7.4.6 The National Strategic Tourism Plan

In this section, we will address the importance of planning in tourism and the respondents' opinion about the National Strategic Tourism Plan (PENT), that is, the national strategy on tourism from the Ministry of Economy and Innovation that will be in place until 2015. The general opinion collected is that it has a positive role. Meanwhile, there are some people who think that PENT, even if it makes clear the strategic priorities to be followed, does not establish a regional vision and fails to provide the organizational framework able to promote a more efficient performance within each promotional area established. The statement that follows addresses those issues:

> Concerning PENT (…), from my point of view it is a strategic plan, and it provides us with positive signs as it gives us a global insight. It defines the priorities (…). What I think is that it requires a complementary operational approach as regards the different regions. (Tourism expert of CCDR-N, and Coordinator of the Regional Tourism Agenda)

The statements that we present in the following paragraphs show the prevalent concerns about the operationalization of PENT. On the one hand, it is thought that it satisfactorily defines the strategic products but, on the other, it makes clear the existence of a deficit of competences in the aim of the related local structures:

> I think that a strategic document works, above all, to guide, and PENT fulfils that and provides us with a set of orientations that, to me, seem to be enough (…). The insufficiencies (…) emerge when we think about its implementation by the local structures or by the national ones, by the local public authorities or even by the private agents. Even in the private sector, we have a great deficit as regards qualifications (…). (2012 Guimarães European Capital Culture cultural programme director)

A concern expressed by several respondents was the absence in the PENT of certain products, which, in the opinion of one respondent, should be seen as strategic by both the Minho-Lima region and the Northern region promotional area, namely: Golf, ManorHouse Tourism and Rural Tourism. This is clearly expressed in the following statement:

> I think that PENT must be restructured, because it was launched four years ago (…). There are two aspects that must be taken into consideration: one is the Golf product, which must be

> considered as strategic for the Minho region and for the Northern region, as a whole (…). Another one is the ManorHouse Tourism and Rural Tourism, which must also be considered, because those products are now scattered between two other tourism products, Environmental and Touring tourism (Head of ADRIL and TURIHAB associations).

7.5 CONCLUSION

Tourism operators and public decision makers of a certain destination would undoubtedly be interested in knowing the contribution of each of the tourism resources (attributes) available to the success of the tourism destination where they operate or act. Such information can come from the preferences of actual or potential consumers (tourists). In the possession of this knowledge, they can evaluate the consistency of the strategy of use of those resources, as well as to make more informed decisions as regards the promotion of products and services, considering the range of resources the region is endowed with.

To summarize our results obtained from the empirical research on the Minho-Lima case, we have to conclude that the resources to which the tourists attributed more importance were Oceanic Beaches and National Parks or Protected Landscape. From a promotional perspective, because the coastal municipalities that are integrated in our study are not inserted in the Peneda-Gêres National Park, tourists should be made aware that this natural park is located in the region to which the coastal municipalities also belong. In the same way, the municipalities that are inserted in this National Park should call attention to the fact that the coastline is at just *X* km distance, in order to somehow include that resource in their supply offer.

By contrast, in the case of the Religious Patrimony and Handicrafts, it seems that there is a clear need to review the prominence that has been given to them in the promotional materials used, given the small importance that was conferred on them in the answers obtained from the national and foreign tourists. However, taking the perspective that it would be desirable for a tourism destination to have a wide range of products, instead of a narrow one, it seems to make sense that these last resources are taken as complementary.

In the case of Ponte de Lima, tourism is already one of the main sources of income and of job creation in the municipality. Even so, looking at the resources available, one feels that there are potentialities that have not yet been explored. From our point of view, the strengths of Ponte de Lima are: its wealth of cultural and historical built patrimony; its beautiful historical centre; its ethnographic patrimony; its rural and natural attributes; its close proximity to some of the more important towns in the region and in Northern Portugal, such as Viana do Castelo, Braga, Guimarães and Porto, and the border with Galicia (Spain); and, finally, the youth of its population.

The research developed has tried to make it clear that tourism could be an economic driving force for both the Minho-Lima region in general, and Ponte de Lima, as a particular case. Additionally, this study aims to contribute to the establishment of a new discourse in regional tourism strategy. Accordingly, the focal concept should be cultural tourism.

Our study has tried to establish the need to implement a well structured tourism planning and marketing strategy. At the resources level, to speak of better organization means also creating more attractive product packages. Having in mind the potential of Ponte de Lima to become a creative cultural tourism destination, events like the International Gardens

Festival and the Opera Festival should be complemented by other events following the same innovative pattern. The Feiras-Novas festivities and the Vaca das Cordas (the Cow's Rope festival) can, similarly, be capitalized upon as major cultural events.

To conclude from the data collected and the analysis performed, we strongly believe that the Minho-Lima has the potential to turn itself into an attractive cultural tourism destination. In order to achieve that goal, it has a huge challenge to surpass, namely in terms of: (i) developing consistent packages of cultural products; (ii) establishing consistent and long-term cooperation between the regional tourism agents and those of neighbouring places than can help it in the supply of cultural tourism packages able to capture tourist segments motivated by singular social environments and active cultural experiences; and (iii) reaching a more efficient and consensual institutional tourism organization.

REFERENCES

Besculides, A., Lee, M. and McCormick, P. (2002). Residents' perceptions of the cultural benefits of tourism. *Annals of Tourism Research*, 29(2), 303–319.

Cadima Ribeiro, J. and Remoaldo, P.C. (2011). Cultural heritage and tourism development policies—the case of a Portuguese U.N.E.S.C.O. World Heritage City. In M.M.S. Coelho and Á.A. Matias (Eds.), *Economics and Management of Tourism: Tendencies and Recent Developments* (pp. 199–223), Lisbon: Universidade Lusíada Editora, Colecção Manuais.

Cunha, L. (1997). *Economia e política do turismo*. Lisboa: McGraw-Hill.

Dellaert, B., Brazell, J. and Louviere, J. (1999). The Effect of Attribute Variation on Consumer Choice Consistency. *Marketing Letters*, 10(2), 139–147.

Florida, R. (2002). *The Rise of the Creative Class*. New York: The Perseus Books Group.

Green, P. and Srinivasan, V. (1990). Conjoint Analysis in Marketing: New Development with Implications for Research and Practice. *Journal of Marketing*, 54(4), 3–19.

Haider, W. (2002). Stated Preference and Choice Models—A Versatile Alternative to Traditional Recreation Research. In Amberger et al. (Eds.), *Monitoring and Management of Visitor Flows in Recreational and Protected Areas—Conference Proceedings* (pp. 115–121), Vienna.

Henriques, C. (2007). Turismo Cultural e desenvolvimento local: uma relação criativa? In 13° Congresso da APDR—Actas do Congresso (CD-ROM), Ilha Terceira, Açores, 24 pp.

Hu, M., Horng, J. and Sun, Y. (2009). Hospitality teams: knowledge sharing and service innovation performance. *Tourism Management,* 30(1), 41–50.

I.N.E. (2008a). *Estimativas da População Residente de 2007.* Lisboa: Instituto Nacional de Estatística.

I.N.E. (2008b). *Anuário Estatístico da Região Norte de 2007.* Instituto Nacional de Estatística (www.ine.pt).

Kuvan, Y. and Akan, P. (2005). Residents' attitudes toward general and forest-related impacts of tourism: the case of Belek, Antalya. *Tourism Management,* Vol. 26, 691–706.

Landry, C. et al. (1996). *The Creative City in Britain and Germany*. United Kingdom and Germany: Anglo-German Foundation.

Lopes, E. [coord.] (2010). *A constelação do turismo na economia portuguesa*. Mirandela: Edições Jornal Sol.

Louviere, J. and Timmermans, H. (1990). Stated Preference and Choice Models Applied to Recreation Research: A Review. *Leisure Sciences*, Vol. 12, 9–32.

Louviere, J., Hensher, D. and Swait, J. (2000). *Stated Choice Methods—Analysis and Application*, Cambridge: Cambridge University Press.

Luce, R. and Tukey (1964). Simultaneous Conjoint Measurement: a New Type of Fundamental Measurement. *Journal of Mathematical Psychology,* Vol. 1, 1–27.

Merino-Castelló, A. (2003). Eliciting Consumers Preferences Using Stated Preference Discrete Choice Models: Contingent Ranking versus Choice Experiment. *UPF Economics and Business Working Paper No. 705* (http://www.econ.upf.es/docs/papers/downloads/705.pdf).

Mota, M., Remoaldo, P.C. and Cadima Ribeiro, J. (2010). A evolução do turismo cultural e os desafios que se colocam aos pequenos núcleos urbanos: o caso de Ponte de Lima. In *I Congresso Internacional de Turismo da ESG/IPCA–Produtos e Destinos Turísticos de Excelência*–1 e 2 de Outubro de 2010, Barcelos, p. 22.

Pulido Fernández, J. and Sánchez Rivero, M. (2009). Attitudes of the cultural tourism: a latent segmentation approach applied to the case of Andalusia's middle towns initiative. In *Proceedings of the Advances in Tourism Economics 2009 Conference*. Lisbon, April 23–24.

Richards, G. (2009). Tourism development trajectories: From culture to creativity? In *Asia-Pacific Creativity Forum on Culture and Tourism*, Jeju Island, Republic of Korea, 3–5 June.

Richards, G. and Raymond, C. (2000). Creative Tourism. *ATLAS News*, Vol. 23, 16–20.

Richards, G. and Wilson, J. (2006). Developing creativity in tourists experiences: A solution to the serial reproduction of culture? *Tourism Management,* Vol. 27, 1209–1223.

Riganti, P. (2009). Cultural Capital, local identities and ethnic diversity: A study of Amsterdam cultural tourism trends. In *Proceedings of the Advances in Tourism Economics 2009 Conference*, Lisbon, 23–24 April.

Rodríguez, M. and González, C. (2002). Métodos de Preferencias Declaradas y Cambios en la Salud. Análisis de Consistencia Interna. In *V Encuentro de Economía Aplicada*, 6–8 de Junio de 2002, Oviedo.

Sá, A. et al. (2007). *Plano de Acção Sectorial para o Turismo*, Vol. 2, Diagnóstico, Valimar Comunidade Urbana.

Simeon, M.L., Buonincontri, P. and Trapani, D.G. (2009). Importance, features and trends of cultural tourism in Italy: The case Pompeii, Herculaneum and the Archaeological system of Vesuvius. In *Proceedings of the Advances in Tourism Economics 2009 Conference*, Lisbon, 23–24 April.

Swait, J. and Adamowicz, W. (1997). Perceptions versus Objective Measures of Environmental Quality in Combined Revealed and Stated Preference Models of Environmental Valuation. *Journal of Environmental Economics and Management,* 32(1), 65–84.

Trindade, A. and Rotondaro (2004). Modificação da Escala de Classificação por Postos utilizada em Análise Conjunta para aprimorar o modelo obtido por regressão com variáveis *dummy*. In *XXIV Encontro Nacional de Engenharia de Produção*, 3–5 de Novembro de 2004, Florianópolis.

Vareiro, L., Cadima Ribeiro, J. and Pardellas, X. (2009). As preferências dos turistas que visitam o Minho-Lima: uma análise com base nas preferências declaradas. *Revista Portuguesa de Estudos Regionais*, 22, 35-46.

Vareiro, L., Cadima Ribeiro, J., Remoaldo, P. and Marques, V. (2011), Residents' perception of the benefits of cultural tourism: the case of Guimarães. In A. Steinecke and A. Kagermeier (Eds.), *Kultur als Touristischer Standortfaktor–Potenziale–Nutzung–Management* (pp. 187–202). Institute series n°23. University of Paderborn, Germany, Paderborner Geographische Studien zu Tourismusentwicklung und Destinationsmanagement (Paderborn Geographical Studies).

Vogeler, Ruiz and Hernández Armand, E. (1997). *Estructura, y organización del mercado turístico* Madrid: Editorial Centro de Estudios Ramón Areces.

SECTION II

COMMUNITY DEVELOPMENT BY TOURISM

CHAPTER

8

DEVELOPMENT OF A STANDARD MEASUREMENT SCALE TO MEASURE COMMUNITY ATTITUDE TOWARDS IMPACTS OF TOURISM IN MALAYSIA

—NURHAZANI MOHD. SHARIFF, NOR ASYIKIN MOHD. NOR,
JASMINE ZEA RAZIAH RADHA RASHID RADHA AND
HASNI HASNAH CHE ISMAIL

8.1 ABSTRACT

Community plays an important role in determining the success of tourism development. Even though there have been many studies to understand community attitude towards tourism impacts, only a few studies are conducted to develop a standard measurement attitudinal scale which is valid and reliable generally to the country and specifically to the community. The paper presents a study conducted in Malaysia with the intention to develop a standard measurement scale to measure the community attitude towards tourism impacts named as MACTIAS. The scale has followed a procedure suggested by Churchill (1979) and DeVellis (1991) in developing a standard scale. The procedures of developing MACTIAS involved five stages. The first stage in generating the item pool ended with 68 tourism impact items derived from literature and interview session. The second stage involved testing for content validity of the scale. It was measured by a panel of experts in tourism consisting of 10 judges. The results ended with 50 tourism impact items. The third stage completed with scale purification using a pre-test sample. The results indicated seven factors derived but only three factors were confirmed. The next stage involved scale verification using Malaysian community as the main respondents. The results of factor analysis indicated eight factors derived but only seven factors were confirmed. Thus, the items to be further tested were only 49. Finally, the results of the reliability test indicated 13 items had low coefficient alpha value and were eliminated from the scale. The process, therefore, ended with only 36 items to be retained in the scale. The study confirms MACTIAS as a valid and reliable scale which can be used to measure the community attitudes in other tourism destinations.

KEYWORDS: tourism impacts, community attitude, scale development, scale purification, scale verification, factor analysis, reliability test

8.2 INTRODUCTION

Tourism, like many other industries, plays an important and vital role in developing a country's economy. As noted by Ibrahim (2010), tourism is widely perceived as a promising basic industry in Malaysia, particularly in providing local employment opportunities, maximizing tax revenues, and diversifying economic opportunities to rural communities. In addition, several literature have also noted positive outcomes of tourism development to the community such as the contributions to income and standard of living, generation of job opportunities, preservation of the natural environment, promotion of cultural exchange, improvement of public utilities infrastructure, and increment in tax revenues (Akis, Peristianis and Warner, 1996; Belisle and Hoy, 1980; Husbands, 1989; Liu and Var, 1986; Pizam, 1978). However, previous studies on perceived impacts have also highlighted many negative outcomes of tourism development such as high cost of living, overcrowding, prostitution, noise pollution, litter and traffic congestion (Bystrzanowski, 1989; Mathieson and Wall, 1993; Perdue, Long and Allen, 1990; Pizam, 1978; Var, Kendall and Tarakcioglu, 1985).

In order to determine these impacts, numerous studies have focused on the assessment of community attitudes and perceptions (Belisle and Hoy, 1980; Cooke, 1982; Liu and Var, 1986; Liu, Sheldon and Var, 1987; Murphy, 1981; Perdue et al., 1990; Ross, 1992; Sethna and Richmond, 1978). According to Allen, Long, Perdue and Keiselbach (1988), to sustain tourism based economy in local communities, community attitudes and perceptions on impacts of tourism must be continually assessed. In addition, several studies have stressed on the involvement of the community in tourism planning and development (Butler, 1975; Hin, 2010; Ibrahim, 2010; Murphy, 1981; Sheldon and Var, 1984). As for Malaysia, the community's involvement in tourism planning has started to play an important role in order to ensure long-term acceptance and social sustainability of the industry (Din, 1997). A recent study on Langkawi Islands, Malaysia also supports this fact based on the findings that tourism has provided entrepreneurial opportunities to the community (Marzuki, 2011).

8.3 PROBLEM STATEMENT

Even though a large number of perceived impacts have been reported, additional research still needs to be conducted to develop appropriate attitude scales and better measures of perceived tourism impacts (Lankford and Howard, 1994). It is believed that such study should be conducted in Malaysia where tourism is currently expanded at the international level. The Malaysian community consists of different racial backgrounds with different cultures and beliefs. Thus, in order to determine the community's attitudes, it is important to develop a standard measurement tool which is reliable and valid by taking into account the diversity of races in the community. Several studies have been conducted to understand the community's attitudes towards tourism in Malaysia (Ahmad and Jusoh, 2008; Hin, 2010; Ibrahim, 2010; Mapjabil and Din, 2008) but none have studied on the development of a standard measurement scale. A study in Langkawi, however, was considered as a first step to expand the study in a much broader area. Thus, the main objective of the study is to develop a standard measurement scale to examine the community's attitudes towards tourism impacts in Malaysia.

8.4 MALAYSIA AS A TOURIST DESTINATION

Today, the tourism industry in Malaysia is expanding quite rapidly as in any other developing countries. This fact can be seen in terms of the contribution to the gross domestic product (GDP) growth, foreign exchange earner, services account of the balance of payments and, furthermore, to the investment and employment opportunities (Jalis, Zahari, Izzat and Othman, 2009). Marketing Malaysia as an international tourist destination has been given serious attention by Tourism Malaysia, beginning in the early 1970s. Malaysia was formerly marketed as "A Tropical Paradise", but today Malaysia is more famously known as "Malaysia Truly Asia". This new marketing tagline represents Malaysia as a destination of nature as well as culture. In fact, due to the yearly campaign of "Visit Malaysia Year" by Tourism Malaysia, the number of tourist arrivals has reached 23.65 million and tourist receipts of RM 53,394 billion in 2009 (Tourism Malaysia Website, 2010).

Just like many other countries, the tourism industry in Malaysia has also experienced the impacts of the Asian financial crisis and the localized outbreaks of Coxsackie viruses. This, in addition, has decreased the number of tourist arrivals by about 13% in 1997 and 10.6% in 1998. It is a fact that Malaysia is competing with its neighbouring countries such as Singapore and Thailand to be in the top Asian tourism destination brands. Nevertheless, Malaysia has special attributes such as friendly people and exotic cultures which enable it to stand in the competitive market among Asian destinations. Tourism Malaysia is striving to achieve this target by positioning and promoting Malaysia accordingly to the objective stated in the Ninth Malaysia Plan 2006–2010 (Tourism Malaysia, 2006).

8.5 LITERATURE REVIEW

Many studies and literature have supported the positive economic impacts and negative economic impacts due to tourism development in different countries. In fact, several previous studies have showed that the main positive outcome derived from economic impacts of tourism is generating more employment opportunities (Hin, 2010; Ibrahim, 2010; Liu and

Var, 1986; Milman and Pizam, 1988; Ross, 1992). In addition, Mathieson and Wall (1993) found that contribution to foreign exchange is a positive impact due to tourism development of the community. Studies have also noted that attracting more investment and improving development and infrastructure are positive outcomes from the economic impacts of tourism (Belisle and Hoy, 1980; Johnson, Snepenger and Akis, 1994; McCool and Martin, 1994). Furthermore, the impacts of tourism have been found to contribute towards income and improved standard of living. This has been supported by studies from Pizam (1978), King, Pizam and Milman (1993) and Harambopoulos and Pizam (1996).

Other positive economic impacts of tourism have been identified as improvement in the local economy (Ibrahim, 2010; Perdue et al., 1990), increment in tax revenues (Rothman, 1978), enhancement of rural and regional development (Lankford, 1994), improvement of public utilities infrastructure (Sethna and Richmond, 1978) and improvement of transport infrastructure (Belisle and Hoy, 1980). Some economic outcomes have also found to be negative such as increment in prices of goods and services (Akis et al., 1996; Brougham and Butler, 1981; Husbands, 1989; Johnson et al., 1994; Pizam, 1978).

According to Mathieson and Wall (1993), socio-cultural impacts of tourism are more towards the changes in the quality of the community's life. Previously, Singer (1968) referred to it as the changes in culture which consists of traditional ideas and values. The issues of socio-cultural impacts of tourism have appeared to be more problematic in the Malaysian community due to the fact that they are related to values, ethics and religion whilst cultural impacts are more towards artistic and craft (Din, 1997). In addition, several previous studies have noted that prostitution, alcoholism, drug addiction and crime are regarded as negative socio-cultural impacts of tourism development (Haralambopoulos and Pizam, 1996; Rothman, 1978). In fact, studies have also found that creation of a phony folk culture (Akis et al., 1996) and heightened tension among the community (Rothman, 1978) as negative socio-cultural impacts of tourism.

In the case of Malaysia, the environment is considered as something to be preserved and restored. According to Khalifah and Tahir (1997), Malaysia's tropical rainforests are among the oldest and most diverse ecosystems in the world. In addition, the government has also planned to promote and target ecotourism and 'green' environment as an intensive tourism development strategy in the Seventh Malaysia Plan 1996–2000 (Economic Planning Unit, 2011). Wang and Miko (1997) identified tourism's contribution to the degradation of major elements of the natural environment into several aspects, namely water quality, air quality, vegetation (flora), wildlife (fauna) and coastlines/shorelines. In the State of Sarawak, Malaysia, environmental preservation is based on ecotourism which is being demonstrated through the concepts of time-sharing, interval ownership and holiday ownership (Edmonds and Leposky, 2000).

Researches on the community's attitudes towards tourism are seriously conducted due to the fact that the community plays an important role in determining the future development of tourism at the destination (Ahmad and Jusoh, 2008; Akis et al., 1996; Allen et. al., 1988; Ap, 1990; Lankford, 1994; Liu and Var, 1986; Shariff, 2002; Shariff and Tahir, 2003). A study undertaken in Cyprus by Akis et al. (1996) indicated that tourism development in the area that benefits the communities the most, will lead to positive attitude of the communities towards tourism. Meanwhile, Paralimni has less tourism development which is more of an agricultural destination in Cyprus. Kyrenia, on the other hand, represents Cyprus tourism industry with its famously ancient foundation and traditional historic castles.

In line with this, a study by Andereck and Vogt (2000) suggested that there is a relationship between attitudes towards tourism and opinions on tourism development. They studied seven communities in Arizona with the purpose of understanding different communities' needs as to achieve the objectives of tourism development. Previously, Liu and Var (1986) conducted a study among communities in Hawaii State to evaluate their attitudes towards impacts of tourism development. The study found that even though economic impacts in general are not strongly preferred by the communities, they are accepted as positive impacts of tourism development. The communities were also found to be reluctant in putting social and environmental impacts as negative tourism impacts such as stated by the media and literature. Nevertheless, the study supported previous studies on community attitudes which believe that attitude is a vital component in providing valuable inputs for sustainable tourism development.

Besides all the studies being mentioned before, another study was undertaken in Colorado communities which indicate that only those who perceive high impacts of tourism and economic activity will show positive attitude towards the statement in the questionnaire (Allen et al., 1988). Jurowski et al. (1997) conducted a study in Southwest Virginia which included five counties surrounding the Mount Rogers National Recreation Area (NRA). The study adopted a social exchange theory explaining that individuals who economically gain from tourism tend to view the impacts positively and will lead to more support towards tourism. As for Malaysia, Shariff (2002) studied the attitudes of Langkawi communities towards impacts of tourism by developing a new attitudinal measurement scale. The study had taken into account the culture value as a factor, which contributes to different attitudes among other communities throughout the world.

It has been noted that even though there are many studies on attitudes towards impacts of tourism, only a few studies have concentrated on the development of a standard measurement tool to examine the community's attitude. The first tool was developed by Lankford and Howard (1994) and named Tourism Impact Attitude Scale (TIAS). However, it has also been considered that the tool was developed for the purpose of understanding the community's attitude from the Western perspective. The second tool was developed by Ap and Crompton (1998) and consisted of 147 items. The tool involved six steps and ended with a 35-item. Still, the same procedure as suggested by Churchill (1979) has been followed. Besides the two previous tools development, Dalamere (1998) has also developed a tool for measuring attitude, which is known as FSIAS (Festival Social Impact Analysis Scale). The tool has been developed for the purpose of measuring resident attitudes towards the social impacts of community festivals and was tested on the Cloverdale of Edmonton, Alberta, Canada and the Edmonton Folk Music Festival.

Furthermore, a study on the residents of Langkawi (Shariff, 2002) has been adopted as a basic theory towards understanding the Malaysian community's attitudes. In accordance, they represent Malaysian culture, beliefs and values which eventually lead to consistency in the items derived and specific tourism impacts domains constructed. LATIAS (Langkawi Tourism Impact Attitude Scale) has been tested on 145 residents of Langkawi and the results have ended with 13 items and five specific tourism impacts domains. Even though the tool allows for greater understanding of resident attitudes towards tourism, another study to further verify the tool particularly in a similar context is recommended in order to substantiate it.

8.6 METHODOLOGY

The study is exploratory and descriptive in nature with the intention to understand the community's attitudes towards tourism impacts in Malaysia. Basically, it is a study to develop a standard measurement tool to examine the community's attitudes towards tourism impacts. Thus, the study constitutes both qualitative and quantitative methods where several individuals in the tourism area were interviewed and the questionnaire was the main instrumentation distributed to the expert judges and respondents. For the purpose of exploring and understanding tourism impacts, a group of experts in tourism were identified. The tourism experts helped to determine the validity of the measurement tool and were identified throughout Malaysia. Priority is given to the academic scholars and tourism sectors' practitioners/managers due to the fact that they can make better and practical judgment regarding impacts items of tourism development in Malaysia. A total of 15 experts were selected at the beginning of the stage which represented both academic institutions and tourism sectors. However, only ten experts agreed to participate in the study due to several personal constraints.

Since the study only focused on the northern part of Malaysia, the unit of analysis for the study was the residences of Universiti Utara Malaysia (UUM), excluding the students. The main reason for excluding the students is to avoid biases in the answers, particularly regarding the age and knowledge factors. Other groups of people in UUM were considered as a reliable sample due to the fact that they can represent the Malaysian community. In order to determine the sample size of the study, a criterion suggested by Tinsley and Tinsley (1987) on the statistical method of measuring the tool using factor analysis was used. According to them, a minimum of five cases is needed for every item in order to enable the testing of factor analysis. Consequently, the remaining items after the pretest were 50. Thus, the sample size was calculated as 250 respondents. However, to fulfil the objective of the study in developing a standard tool, 350 questionnaires were distributed.

The first stage is the collection of all related literature regarding the topic under study, known as secondary data. The secondary data for the study involved information on tourism impacts and attitudinal measurement studies which were obtained from previous literature. All the tourism impact items were identified and presented in a survey questionnaire. An interview was also undertaken which involved several individuals for the purpose of gaining further information on tourism impact items. In order to gain information directly from specific respondents, primary data collection was used in the study. The study used questionnaire survey as the major source of primary data. Eventually, the tourism experts were contacted through email in November 2010 by the researcher to confirm their participation in the study. They were then asked to answer several questions in the questionnaire emailed to them in December 2010. A pre-test study to confirm the validity and reliability of the questionnaire was conducted in January 2011 which involved 220 residences of UUM. In addition, a survey involving 350 respondents from UUM was undertaken within two months, starting from February 2011 to March 2011.

The data was then analyzed using Statistical Package of Social Sciences (SPSS) Software 2007. Two main techniques of analysis were used to evaluate the items in the questionnaire, namely factor analysis and reliability test. In this study, factor analysis was used to test for tool purification. Meaning, factor analysis helps to identify the underlying constructs in the data and reduced the number of items to a more manageable set. In addition, it is also used to identify which items belong together and measured the same thing. The first stage of factor analysis in this study involved calculating an item-to-item correlation matrix. This was done by using a principal component analysis where the items in the questionnaire are transformed into a new set of items which are not correlated with each other. Consequently, the combinations are known as factors and are accounted for the variance in the whole data. The second stage was to redefine the factors, known as factor rotation. This study used varimax rotation due to the fact that the factors are unrelated to or independent of one another. The items which failed to meet the criterion as suggested by Tinsley and Tinsley (1987), that is, .3 or loaded on more than one factor were eliminated from the questionnaire. This study used reliability test to estimate the degree to which a measurement is free of error. The procedure involved calculating the average inter-correlations among the items measuring concept. A high internal consistency is indicated by alpha value of 1 and above. Thus, item-to-item correlation below .5 was eliminated from the scale.

8.7 RESULTS OF DATA ANALYSIS

8.7.1 Respondents' Characteristics

Three hundred and one questionnaires were completed from 350 respondents approached, representing 86% response rate for the study. The demographic characteristics of respondents are presented in Table 8.1 and are as follows: males constituted 29.2% and females constituted 70.8% of the sample. In terms of the age groups, the highest proportion was represented by the 21–40 years old (96.7%). In addition, most of the respondents were formed by Malays (52.8%) and Chinese (40.5%) whilst Indian and other races both formed 3.3%. The findings also indicated that most of the respondents sampled have stayed more than five years (98.7%). Out of the total respondents, only 11.3% claimed that their occupations were related to the tourism sectors. Furthermore, they also claimed that the highest sector occupied was accommodation (5%), followed by food and beverages (4%), others (3.7%) and travel and services (1%).

8.7.2 Items Generation

The first stage in developing an attitudinal scale for tourism impact involved the generation of items, also known as development of an item pool. The interview session involved eight respondents in tourism area with different backgrounds consisting of three lecturers and two tourism entrepreneurs whilst tourism policy maker, tourism planner, and tour operator each consisted of one presenter. They were interviewed through telephone and were asked to identify and name the items representing tourism impacts in the case of Malaysia. As a result, sixty-eight tourism impact items were complied and listed in the first round of determining the validity and clarity of the scale (see Appendix 1).

8.7.3 Expert Survey

In order to test the content validity of the items generated in the first stage, 10 experts in the field of tourism were identified and selected as judges. From the total of 68 items gained in the first stage of tourism impacts items generation, 18 items were eliminated from the scale, thus only 50 items remained in the pre-tested scale. Based on the survey, nine out of 10 experts agreed that eight items did not represent tourism impacts in the case of Malaysia. They believed that these items would be suitable to represent impact items in other destinations but, eventually, they found that these items were irrelevant in the context of Malaysia. In addition, another 10 items were perceived by the experts as items which were objectionable to the respondents. They had reached a consensus that the Malaysian community may not categorize these items as impacts of tourism development in the destination. All the 50 items remained were then brought forward to the pre-test study to confirm the level of each item as tourism impact items (see Appendix 2).

8.7.4 Scale Purification

Items surviving the assessment of the experts' surveys were then tested on the pre-test sample. The main purpose was to reduce the items into a more manageable number and to confirm the domains constituting the scale. The pre-test sample involved 220 respondents representing Malaysian community and was randomly selected among the UUM staffs. Data gained from the pre-test sample were factor analyzed using the principal components methods with varimax rotation (see Appendix 3). Seven factors with eigenvalues above 1 were derived from the analysis. However, only three factors were confirmed. They were named Factor 1: Amenity Services, Economic and Socio-cultural Impact, Factor 2: Negative Socio-cultural Impact and Factor 3: Financial Economic Impact. All the 50 items had factor loadings above .3 and loaded cleanly onto one factor. The factors were then analyzed for internal consistency using Cronbach's coefficient alpha and the results indicated alpha value ranged from .500 to .945.

Factor 1: Amenity Services, Economic and Socio-cultural Impact consisted of 39 items, with a cumulative variance of 29.087%. Factor 2: Negative Socio-cultural Impact consisted of five items, with a cumulative variance of 40.411%. Finally, Factor 3: Financial Economic Impact consisted of only two items, with a cumulative variance of 44.035%. Four items were found to be loaded onto one factor solution. These items, however, were included in the final analysis and revision of the scale based on the fact that they are considered as a statistical artifact.

8.7.5 Scale Verification

The final items in the scale were factor analyzed and the results indicated all the items loaded above .3 and cleanly onto one factor solution. The results also indicated that eight factors with eigenvalues above 1 derived from the scale (see Appendix 4). The results eventually enabled a more comprehensive number and range of items to be retained compared to the pre-test study. Thus, only one factor from the pre-test study was retained. Out of eight factors, only seven factors were confirmed, namely Factor 1: Amenity Services, Economic and Socio-cultural Impact, Factor 2: Negative Socio-cultural Impact, Factor 3: Financial and Socio-economic Impact, Factor 4: Historical and Cultural Impact, Factor 5: Socio-cultural and Community Impact, Factor 6: Service and Safety Impact, and Factor 7: Environmental Impact. Factor 8: Community Pride Impact was not included due to the fact that it consisted of only one item.

All the seven factors were further tested for internal consistent reliability. The results indicated a strong Cronbach's alpha value ranged from .479 to .904. Factor 1: Amenity Services, Economic and Socio-cultural Impact consisted of 16 items, with a cumulative variance of 14.001%. Factor 2: Negative Socio-cultural Impact consisted of 12 items, with a cumulative variance of 27.513%. Factor 3: Financial and Socio-economic Impact consisted of five items, with a cumulative variance of 34.074%. In addition, Factor 4: Historical and Cultural Impact consisted of five items, with a cumulative variance of 40.552%. Factor 5: Socio-cultural and Community Impact also consisted of five items, with a cumulative variance of 46.964%. Factor 6: Service and Safety Impact consisted of three items, with a cumulative variance of 52.213%. And finally, Factor 7: Environmental Impact consisted of two items, with a cumulative variance of 55.232%.

Both factors and items in the scale were further tested for reliability analysis. Factor 8: Community Pride Impact had no coefficient alpha value since it consisted only of one item. Thus, this item was eliminated from the scale which left only 49 items. The results indicated that 38 items had strong Cornbach's alpha value with strong levels of item-to-total correlations whilst 11 items had alpha value less than .5 (Table 8.1). Thus, all 11 items were

Table 8.1 Results of reliability analysis—Final test sample (n = 301)

Factors/Items	*Item-total correlation*	*Total items*	*Coefficient alpha*
Factor 1: Amenity Services, Economic and Socio-cultural Impact		16	.904
Demand for accommodation sector	.741		
Job opportunities in tourism sector	.723		
Demand for restaurants sector	.656		
Opportunities for businesses in the community' area	.653		
Opportunities to learn about other cultures	.644		
Opportunities to meet other tourists	.643		
Understanding of different cultures among community and tourists	.620		
Varieties of shopping facilities	.607		
Investment spending in the community's area	.596		
Opportunities for cultural exchange between communities and tourists	.582		
Revenue generated by the economy	.573		
Awareness of tourism image	.549		

Continued

Factors/Items	*Item-total correlation*	*Total items*	*Coefficient alpha*
Distribution of income to local businesses	.488		
Urbanization in the community's area	.403		
Improvement of public transportation	.310		
Better community's standard of living	.310		
FACTOR 2: Negative Socio-cultural Impact		12	.857
Changes in prices of goods	.660		
Adoption of unhealthy lifestyle among community	.651		
Materialistic values among the community	.637		
Drug abused in the community's area	.629		
Alcohol abused in the community's area	.625		
Prostitution in the community's area	.623		
Driving hazards by tourists	.615		
Crime in the community's area	.599		
Imitation of tourists' behaviour	.566		
Vandalism in the community's area	.312		
Destruction of the wildlife	.306		
Higher cost of living in the community's area	.264		
FACTOR 3: Financial and Socio-economic Impact		6	.781
Taxes collected for businesses run by community	.630		
Varieties of entertainment	.594		
Taxes collected for community's assets	.580		
Traffic congestion in the community's area	.566		
Size of crowds affected community's activities	.492		
The noise level in the community's area	.448		
FACTOR 4: Historical and Cultural Impact		5	.741
Demand for the historical activities	.644		
Demand for the cultural activities	.562		
Awareness of the local culture among community	.552		
Preservation of historical structures	.532		
Restoration of historical structure	524		
FACTOR 5: Socio-cultural and Community Impact		5	.742
Awareness of living in a society	.603		
Recognition of local culture	.597		
Varieties of cultural activities in the community's area	.523		
Community spirit among the local people	.416		
Awareness towards ethnic identity	.190		
FACTOR 6: Service and Safety Impact		3	.642
Quality of local services such as police, medical, etc.	.560		
Financial resources of local services such as police, medical, etc.	.496		
Awareness of safety in the community's area	.310		
FACTOR 7: Environmental Impact		2	.479
Preservation of the wildlife	.315		
Destroy of the natural environment	.315		

eliminated from the scale. In addition, one item had a very low alpha value of .190 and was also eliminated from the scale. Overall, the coefficient alpha for Factor 1: Amenity Services, Economic and Socio-cultural Impact was .904 with the highest item-to-total correlation of .741 and the lowest was .306. The coefficient alpha for Factor 2: Negative Socio-cultural Impact was .857 with the highest item-to-total correlation of .660 and the lowest was .310. In addition, Factor 3: Financial and Socio-economic Impact indicated a coefficient alpha of .741 with the highest item-to-total correlation of .644 and the lowest was .264. The coefficient alpha for Factor 4: Historical and Cultural Impact was .857, with the highest item-to-total correlation of .644 and the lowest was .524. The coefficient alpha for Factor 5: Socio-cultural and Community Impact was .857, with the highest item-to-total correlation of .603 and the lowest was .190. Furthermore, Factor 6: Service and Safety Impact indicated a coefficient alpha of .642, with the highest item-to-total correlation of .560 and the lowest was .310, Factor 7: Environmental Impact indicated a coefficient alpha of .479 with both items had item-to-total correlation of .315. The final scale, therefore, consisted of 36 items.

8.8 DISCUSSION OF FINDINGS

The main purpose of the study was to develop a standard scale for measuring Malaysian community's attitudes towards impact of tourism development. The scale was named MACTIAS, which stands for Malaysian Community Tourism Impact Attitude Scale. Table 8.2 depicts the summary of the stages in developing MACTIAS. Sixty-eight tourism impact items were generated from the literature search and interview session. Generally, most items identified were categorized into three major tourism impact factors, namely economic, environmental and socio-cultural. However, based on the interview session with individuals who had strong backgrounds in the tourism area, several new items were identified. Eleven items were actually specified under the context of tourism development in Malaysia such as *opportunities for education to the community, preservation of the community's cultural identity, understanding of the community's destination image, appearance of the community's area, peace of the community, homestay programme in the community's area, developing medical tourism product, demand for medical tourism accommodation, awareness of living in the society, awareness of safety in the community's area*, and *adoption of unhealthy lifestyle*.

Furthermore, the results of the expert survey indicated 18 items which were irrelevant in the context of tourism development in Malaysia. Thus, these items were eliminated from the scale. Eight items were: *creates vitality for the community's life, creates understanding of different people's cultures, increases the size of crowds which affect the enjoyment of community's activities, increases the physical activities of local services, creates a positive attitude by residents towards tourists, creates opportunities for education to the community, improves the appearance of the community's area*, and *disrupts the peace of the community.* In addition, another 10 items were perceived by the experts as items which were objectionable to the respondents. They had reached consensus that the Malaysian community may not categorize these items as impacts of tourism development in the destination. These items were: *creates a variety of cultural facilities, creates opportunities to meet other tourists, decrease the quality of natural environment, increases the amount of property taxes collected*

Table 8.2 Procedures in developing MACTIAS

Stage	*Procedures*	*Number of items*	*Factors named*	*Number of items*
1	Generation of item pool from literature and interviews session	68		
2	Assessment of content validity from a panel of tourism expert involving 10 judges	50		
3	Scale verification from pre-test sample (50 respondents)—factor analysis and reliability test: • Seven factors derived but only three were confirmed • Coefficient alpha value ranged from .500 to .945	50	Factor 1: *Amenity services, economic and socio-cultural impact*	39
			Factor 2: *Negative socio-cultural impact*	5
			Factor 3: *Financial and economic impact*	2
			Factor 4: *Positive environmental impact*	1
			Factor 5: *Negative environmental impact*	1
			Factor 6: *Community pride impact*	1
			Factor 7: *Community spirit impact*	1
4	Scale purification from sample respondents (301 respondents)—factor analysis and reliability test: • Eight factors derived but only seven were confirmed • Factor 8 was eliminated since it consisted of only one item, thus 49 items were retained • Coefficient alpha value ranged from .479 to .904. • 13 items were eliminated	49	Factor 1: *Amenity services, economic and socio-cultural impact*	16
			Factor 2: *Negative Socio-cultural impact*	12
			Factor 3: *Financial and socio-economic impact*	6
			Factor 4: *Historical and cultural impact*	5
			Factor 5: *Socio-cultural and community impact*	5
			Factor 6: *Service and safety impact*	3
			Factor 7: *Environmental impact*	2
5	Final scale—six factors were confirmed with coefficient alpha value ranged from .673 to .907	36	Factor 1: *Amenity services, economic and socio-cultural impact*	12
			Factor 2: *Negative socio-cultural impact*	9
			Factor 3: *Financial and socio-economic impact*	5
			Factor 4: *Historical and cultural impact*	5
			Factor 5: *Socio-cultural and community impact*	3
			Factor 6: *Service impact*	2

in the community's area, increases the amount of local sales taxes collected in the community's area, creates changes to the community's traditional culture, creates a Homestay program in the community's area, creates opportunities for developing medical tourism product, creates demand for medical tourism accommodation, and *creates demand for duty-free shop in the community's area*.

As for the results of factor analysis on the pre-test sample, it was found that seven factors derived but only three factors were confirmed from the 50 items. This was based on the fact that the four factors consisted of only one item. Two of the items which were expected to load saliently into the environmental impact did not, instead they loaded into two different factors, namely, Factor 4: Positive Environmental Impact and Factor 5: Negative Environmental Impact. The items were, 'preservation of the wildlife' and 'destruction of the natural environment'. The same goes with the other two items which were expected to load saliently into the community impact. These items loaded into two different factors, namely, Factor 6: Community Pride Impact and Factor 7: Community Spirit Impact. The items were: 'creates pride among the community' and 'community spirit among the local people'. The items, however, were brought forward to be tested for scale verification based on the fact that they represented the environmental impact and also the community impact which were not found in the other three factors.

Furthermore, the results also indicated that several economic and socio-cultural items loaded into one factor solution named as Factor 1: Amenity Services, Economic and Socio-cultural Impact. For instance, items such as 'demand for accommodation sector', 'job opportunities in tourism sector', 'demand for restaurants sector', 'opportunities for businesses in the community's area', 'changes in price of goods', 'taxes collected for businesses run by community', 'distribution of income to local businesses', 'investment spending in the community's area' and 'revenue generated by the economy' which were supposed to load into the economic impact did not. In addition, items which were expected to load saliently into the cultural impact also did not. These items were, 'understanding of different cultures among community and tourists', 'opportunities to meet other tourists', 'opportunities for cultural exchange between communities and tourists' and 'opportunities to learn about other cultures'.

Five items which loaded saliently into Factor 2 were named as Negative Socio-cultural Impact since all items represent negative impact to the community. However, one item which was expected to load into the environmental impact did not but instead it loaded into this factor. The item was 'destroy of the wildlife'. Factor 3 derived from the scale was named as Financial and Economic Impact since the two items loaded represent both the financial and economic aspects and not just totally economic. One of the items, 'financial resources of local services such as police, medical, etc.' can be seen clearly as a financial item. Since this is the only item which represents the financial aspect, it was not expected to load into other factors.

The results of factor analysis run for the final test sample indicated eight factors derived from the scale, but only seven were confirmed. One factor named as Factor 8: Community Pride Impact had only one item loaded and thus it was eliminated from the scale. It seems that this item had already appeared in the pre-test sample and once again reappeared in the final test. Eventually, it indicates that the item does not represent tourism impact for the community. Meaning the scale consisted of 49 items to be further tested. Out of these seven factors, two factors were retained as in the pre-test sample. They were Factor 1: Amenity

Services, Economic and Socio-cultural Impact and Factor 2: Negative Socio-cultural Impact. One factor was renamed as Factor 3: Financial and Socio-economic Impact. In addition, four new factors derived from the scale and were named as Factor 4: Historical and Cultural Impact, Factor 5: Socio-cultural and Community Impact, Factor 6: Service and Safety Impact and finally Factor 7: Environmental Impact.

Several items were still found to be loaded into different factors as they were not supposed to be. For instance, item 'destroy of the wildlife' was expected to load into Factor 7: Environmental Impact but it loaded into Factor 2: Negative Socio-cultural Impact. Two items which were expected to load into Factor 1: Amenity Services, Economic and Socio-cultural Impact also did not, but instead loaded into Factor 2: Negative Socio-cultural Impact. The items were 'prostitution in the community's area' and 'changes in price of goods'. This probably indicates that the Malaysian community has different point of views regarding the issue of prostitution in Malaysia. Some may perceive it as impact due to tourism development but in other circumstances, the issue may be perceived as positive economic impact caused by tourism development. The findings are in line with the study by Haralambopoulos and Pizam (1996) and previously by Rothman (1978). A similar perception can be seen with the item changes of price. As found in studies by Pizam (1978) and Var et al. (1985), for certain community, particularly the one who run businesses, increase in price may create positive economic impact whilst for others such as the local people it may be perceived as negative economic impact.

New factors derived from the scale named as Factor 4: Historical and Cultural Impact and Factor 5: Socio-cultural and Community Impact. The factors eventually would indicate community awareness and concerns towards the historical structure, cultural value and community spirit in the society. Thus, these items represent factors which they were expected to load into just as suggested by Akis et al. (1996), Belisle and Hoy (1980), Brougham and Butler (1981), Liu and Var (1986), and Liu et al. (1987). Verification of these new factors has probably led to the understanding that the Malaysian community has shared special value towards living in the society and they are really concerned about preservation and restoration of the historical and cultural value. Items 'demand for the historical activities' and 'demand for the cultural activities' consequently have significant impacts on the items 'preservation of historical structure' and 'restoration of historical structure'.

All the items were tested for reliability and the results indicated that 13 items had low coefficient alpha value less than .50. Thus, these items were eliminated from the scale. Four items were eliminated from Factor 1: Amenity Services, Economic and Socio-cultural Impact—'distribution of income to local businesses', 'urbanization in the community's area', 'improvement of public transportation' and 'better community's standard of living'. These items are probably perceived by the Malaysian community as less important impacts of tourism. The improvement of public transportation may not be because of tourism development but it may be due to the demand from the local people themselves to the authorities. Three items were eliminated from Factor 2: Negative Socio-cultural Impact—'vandalism in the community's area', 'destroy of the wildlife' and 'higher cost of living in the community's area'. Eventually the community probably perceives all these items as negative impacts but not because of tourism development. Vandalism may be caused by the local people themselves, particularly the youngsters, and destroy of wildlife has become a major issue to Malaysia due to other developments such as industrial and housing.

Furthermore, one item was eliminated from Factor 3: Financial and Socio-economic Impact—'the noise level in the community's area'. In fact, the item should not load into this factor in the first place. Noise level would be more relevant to load into the environmental impact or socio-cultural impact due to the fact that the impact has a strong effect on the community environment. The results also indicated that Factor 5: Socio-cultural and Community Impact had eliminated two items—'community spirit among the local people' and 'awareness towards ethnic identity'. Community probably perceives the item community spirit as tourism impact item which has low effect on them. The spirit may be shared due to other aspects particularly when they have to work together to achieve some benefits. Tourism development may be one of those aspects but not a strong significant impact. Item 'awareness of safety in the community's area' was the only item eliminated from Factor 6: Service and Safety Impact. The item was the only item representing safety, thus the factor was renamed as Factor 6: Service Impact. Finally, Factor 7: Environmental Impact eliminated both items—'preservation of the wildlife' and 'destroy of the natural environment'. These items may not be reliable probably because the community has different perceptions towards the level of impacts they affected the area. Moreover, the community probably perceives wildlife and natural environment as items which are not caused by tourism development. The findings significantly support the study by Edmonds and Leposky (2000). MACTIAS is presented in Table 8.3.

Table 8.3 Results of MACTIAS

Factors/Items	*Item-total correlation*	*Total items*	*Coefficient alpha*
FACTOR 1: Amenity Services, Economic and Socio-cultural Impact		12	.907
Demand for accommodation sector	.741		
Job opportunities in tourism sector	.723		
Demand for restaurants sector	.656		
Opportunities for businesses in the community' area	.653		
Opportunities to learn about other cultures	.644		
Opportunities to meet other tourists	.643		
Understanding of different cultures among community and tourists	.620		
Varieties of shopping facilities	.607		
Investment spending in the community's area	.596		
Opportunities for cultural exchange between communities and tourists	.582		
Revenue generated by the economy	.573		
Awareness of tourism image	.549		
FACTOR 2: Negative Socio-cultural Impact		9	.897
Changes in price of goods	.660		
Adoption of unhealthy lifestyle among community	.651		
Materialistic values among the community	.637		
Drug abused in the community's area	.629		

Continued

Factors/Items	*Item-total correlation*	*Total items*	*Coefficient alpha*
Alcohol abused in the community's area	.625		
Prostitution in the community's area	.623		
Driving hazards by tourists	.615		
Crime in the community's area	.599		
Imitation of tourists' behaviour	.566		
FACTOR 3: Financial and Socio-economic Impact		5	.805
Taxes collected for businesses run by community	.630		
Varieties of entertainment	.594		
Taxes collected for community's assets	.580		
Traffic congestion in the community's area	.566		
Size of crowds affected community's activities	.492		
FACTOR 4: Historical and Cultural Impact		5	.741
Demand for the historical activities	.644		
Demand for the cultural activities	.562		
Awareness of the local culture among community	.552		
Preservation of historical structures	.532		
Restoration of historical structure	524		
FACTOR 5: Socio-cultural and Community Impact		3	.673
Awareness of living in a society	.603		
Recognition of local culture	.597		
Varieties of cultural activities in the community's area	.523		
FACTOR 6: Service Impact		2	.731
Quality of local services such as police, medical, etc.	.560		
Financial resources of local services such as police, medical, etc.	.496		

8.9 IMPLICATIONS AND CONTRIBUTIONS

Theoretically, the study contributes towards the understanding of tourism impact items in the case of Malaysian tourism development. It also points out the most reliable item which represents tourism impact as perceived by the community. The results of the study also contribute to the body of knowledge generally in the field of tourism impact and specifically in the development of a standard measurement scale. As for the body of literature, the identification of new tourism impact items give indication of the measurement of community attitude. In other words, new tourism impact items should be taken into consideration when one intends to measure different community attitudes even in a similar tourism destination.

In addition, the study also contributes to a methodological and conceptual framework of developing a standard measurement tool for assessing community attitudes towards tourism impacts. The study majorly utilizes Churchill (1979) and DeVellis (1991) procedure of developing a standard measurement scale and the findings indicated significant restructuring of the stages involved. The procedures could be implemented by other researchers who intend to study the community attitude in other tourism destinations in Malaysia. New factors derived in the case of Malaysian community attitudes towards tourism impact represent actual and strong perspectives among the community, particularly towards tourism development. The factors such as economic, environmental and socio-cultural are no longer considered as major tourism impact factors in Malaysia. The combination of other tourism impact items in those factors eventually represents new dimensions for tourism development.

Most importantly, the study provides tourism planners, decision makers and marketers with greater confidence that it will effectively measure all aspects of the community's attitudes towards tourism impacts in Malaysia. Finally, the study could be utilized by the tourism marketers in providing tool of measurement which eventually can be used to segment the community support towards tourism development.

8.10 LIMITATIONS AND RECOMMENDATIONS FOR FUTURE STUDY

The study was conducted among UUM residences which represent the Malaysian community. Thus, the results may have limited generalization to other parts of tourism destination in Malaysia. Even though the respondents may have come from various destinations in the country, the issue of representativeness of the respondents may require further study using the whole community in Malaysia. Therefore, it is suggested that more comprehensive study should be carried out by taking into account several groups of communities in Malaysia. These communities may be categorized into region as well as specific tourism areas.

Furthermore, the study was also focused into three major tourism impacts, namely economic, environmental and socio-cultural. Any other impacts derived from the study would be considered as a new item of tourism impact in the case of Malaysia. In addition, the demographic characteristics of the respondents were not being analyzed since the main purpose of the study was only to develop the scale. Thus, the conse-quences of having significant relationships between the items derived and the demographic characteristics may indicate some impact towards their attitudes. It is recommended that for future study, these demographics variables should be studied in line with the items pool generation.

8.11 CONCLUSION

Even though the respondents specifically involved the Northern part of Malaysia, the findings generally represent significant items of tourism impacts for the whole country. In fact, it can be seen that all the items in the scale are consistent to other studies in other destinations. Overall, this explains that the Malaysian community has strong awareness towards tourism development. Moreover, they really have strong value towards historical and cultural aspects of their life. This is determined in the way they perceived the socio-cultural impacts of tourism. Such further study would encourage more awareness and understanding among the community towards impacts of tourism development. This consequently is expected to create positive impacts and bring more benefits to the local community in line with the growth of tourism development in Malaysia.

The study has achieved the purpose of developing a standard scale to measure community attitudes towards impact of tourism development in Malaysia. The scale has gone through several stages as suggested by Churchill (1979), DeVellis (1991), Lankford and Howard (1994) and Ap and Crompton (1998). In fact, the procedures have also taken into account the development of LATIAS by Shariff (2002). MACTIAS, which stands for Malaysian Community Tourism Impact Attitude Scale, consists of 36 tourism impact items within six factors, namely Factor 1: Amenity Services, Economic and Socio-cultural Impact, Factor 2: Negative Socio-cultural Impact, Factor 3: Financial and Socio-economic Impact, Factor 4: Historical and Cultural Impact, Factor 5: Socio-cultural and Community Impact and Factor 6: Service Impact. Even though these factors are named differently comparing to other studies, all items in the scale strongly represent the overall tourism impact items, particularly economic, environmental and socio-cultural.

The procedures of developing MACTIAS eventually involved five major stages. The first stage in generating the item pool ended with 68 tourism impact items derived from literature and interview session. The second stage involved testing for content validity of the scale. It was measured by a panel of experts in tourism. The results ended with 50 tourism impact items. The third stage was completed with testing for factor analysis and reliability of the scale using a pre-test sample. The results indicated seven factors derived, but only three factors were confirmed. All the 50 items were to be retained in the scale for being tested further. The next stage involved testing for factor analysis and reliability of the scale using Malaysian community as the main respondents. The results for factor analysis indicated eight factors derived but only seven factors were confirmed. Thus, the items to be further tested were only 49. Finally, the results for reliability test indicated 13 items had low coefficient alpha value and were eliminated from the scale. The process, therefore, ended with only 36 items to be retained in the scale. In conclusion, MACTIAS represents a standard measurement attitudinal scale which can be used for other destinations in Malaysia.

REFERENCES

Ahmad, H. and Jusoh, H. (2008). 'Langkawi sebagai Pulau Bebas Cukai: Impak Sosioekonomi Komuniti Setempat, In *Pelancongan Malaysia: Isu Pembangunan, Budaya, Komuniti dan Persetempatan*' (Eds.), Ibrahim, Y., Mohamad, S. and Ahmad, H., Universiti Utara Malaysia Press: Sintok, 231–246.

Akis, S., Peristianis, N. and Warner, J. (1996). Residents' Attitudes to Tourism Development. The Case of Cyprus. *Tourism Management*, 17: 481–494.

Allen, L.R., Long, P.T., Perdue, R.R. and Kieselbach, S. (1988). The Impact of Tourism Development on Resident's Perception of Community's Life. *Journal of Travel Research*, 27(1): 16–21.

Ap, J. (1990). Residents' Perceptions Research on the Social Impacts of Tourism. *Annals of Tourism Research*, 17: 610–616.

Ap, J. and Crompton, J.L. (1998). Developing and Testing a Tourism Impact Scale. *Journal of Travel Research*, 37: 120–130.

Andereck, K.L. and Vogt, C.A. (2000). The Relationship between Residents' Attitudes toward Tourism and Tourism Development Options. *Journal of Travel Research*, 39: 27–36.

Belisle, F. and Hoy, D. (1980). The Perceived Impact of Tourism by Residents. *Annals of Tourism Research*, 7(1): 83–101.

Brougham, J. and Butler, R. (1981). A Segmentation Analysis of Resident Attitudes to Social Impacts of Tourism. *Annals of Tourism Research*, 7(4): 569–590.

Butler, R.W. (1975). The Social Implications of Tourist Development. *Annals of Tourism Research*, 2: 100–111.

Bystrzanowski, J. (1989). *Tourism a Factor of Change: A Socio-cultural Study*. European Coordination Centre for Research and Documentation in Social Sciences: Vienna.

Churchill, G.A. (1979). A Paradigm for Developing Better Measures of Marketing Constructs. *Journal of Marketing Research*, 26(2): 64–73.

Cooke, K. (1982). Guidelines for Socially Appropriate Tourism Development in British Columbia. *Journal of Travel Research*, 21(1): 22–28.

Dalamere, T.A. (1998). Development of a Scale to Measure Local Resident Attitudes toward the Social Impact of Community Festivals. PhD Dissertation, University of Alberta, Canada.

DeVellis, R.F. (1991). *Scale Development: Theory and Application Applied Social Research Method Series*, 26, Newbury Park, CA: Sage.

Din, K.H. (1997). Tourism and Cultural Development in Malaysia: Issues for a New Agenda. In *Tourism and Cultural Development in Asia and Oceania* (Eds.), Yamashita, S., Din, K.H. and Eades, J.S., Universiti Kebangsaan Malaysia: Bangi, pp. 104–118. Economic Planning Unit (2011). Seventh Malaysia Plan 1996–2000. http://www.epu.gov.my/seventhmalaysiaplan

Edmonds, J. and Leposky, G. (2000). Ecotourism and Sustainable Tourism Development in Southeast Asia. In *Tourism in Southeast Asia: A New Direction* (Ed.), Chon, K.S., Haworth Hospitality Press: New York, pp. 39–45.

Harambopoulos, N. and Pizam, A. (1996). Perceived Impacts of Tourism: The Case of Samos. *Annals of Tourism Research*, 23(3): 503–523.

Hin, T.W. (2010). Issues and Challenges in Island Tourism Development: The Case of Pangkor Island. In *Tourism Research in Malaysia* (Eds.), Din, K. and Mapjabil, J. Universiti Utara Malaysia Press: Sintok, pp. 179–195.

Husbands, W. (1989). Social Status and Perception of Tourism in Zambia. *Annals of Tourism Research*, 16(2): 237–253.

Ibrahim, Y. (2010). Tourism Development and Community Perception towards Socio-cultural Change in Tioman Island. In *Tourism Research in Malaysia* (Eds.), Din, K. and Mapjabil, J. Universiti Utara Malaysia Press: Sintok, pp. 159–178.

Jalis, M.H., Zahari, M.S.M., Izzat, M. and Othman, Z. (2009). Western Tourists Perception of Malaysian Gastronomic Products. *Asian Social Sciences*, 5(1): 25–36.

Johnson, J.D., Snepenger, D.J. and Akis, S. (1994). Residents' Perceptions of Tourism Development. *Annals of Tourism Research*, 21: 629–642.

Jurowski, C., Uysal, M. and Willaims, D.R. (1997). A Theoretical Analysis of Host Community resident Reactions to Tourism. *Journal of Travel Research*, 36: 3–11.

Khalifah, Z. and Tahir, S. (1997). Malaysia: Tourism in Perspective, In *Tourism and Economic development in Asia and Australiasia* (Eds.), Go, F.M. and Jenkins, C.L., Cassell: London, pp. 176–196.

King, B., Pizam, A. and Milman, A. (1993). Social Impact of Tourism: Host Perceptions. *Annals of Tourism Research*, 20(4): 650–665.

Lankford, S.V. (1994). Attitudes and Perceptions toward Tourism and Rural Regional Development. *Journal of Travel Research*, (Winter): 35–48.

Lankford, S.V. and Howard, D.R. (1994). Developing a Tourism Impact Scale. *Annals of Tourism Research*, 21(1): 121–139.

Liu, J. and Var, T. (1986). Resident Attitudes toward Tourism Impacts in Hawaii. *Annals of Tourism Research*, 13(2): 193–214.

Liu, J., Sheldon, P. and Var, T. (1987). A Cross-National Approach to Determining Resident Perceptions of the Impact of Tourism on the Environment. *Annals of Tourism Research*, 14(1): 17–37.

Mapjabil, J. and Din, A.K. (2008). 'Komuniti Nelayan dalam Pembangunan Pelancongan di Pulau Mabul. In *Pelancongan Malaysia: Isu Pembangunan, Budaya, Komuniti dan Persetempatan* (Eds.), Ibrahim, Y., Mohamad, S. and Ahmad, H., Universiti Utara Malaysia Press: Sintok, 195–217.

Marzuki, A. (2011). Resident Attitudes towards Impacts from Tourism development in Langkawi Islands, Malaysia. *World Applied Sciences Journal (Issues of Tourism and Hospitality)*, 12: 25–34.

Mathieson, A. and Wall, G. (1993). *Tourism: Economic, Physical and Social Impacts*, Longman Group Limited: UK.

McCool, S.F. and Martin, S.R. (1994). Community Attachment and Attitudes toward Tourism Development. *Journal of Travel Research*, 33(3): 29–34.

Milman, A. and Pizam, A. (1988). Social Impacts of Tourism on Central Florida. *Annals of Tourism Research*, 15(2): 191–204.

Murphy, P.E. (1981). Community Attitudes to Tourism: A Comparative Analysis. *Tourism Management*, 2(3): 189–195.

Perdue, T.R. Long, P. and Allen, L. (1990). Rural Resident Tourism Perceptions and Attitudes. *Annals of Tourism Research*, 14(3): 420–429.

Pizam, A. (1978). Tourism Impacts: The Social Costs to the Destination Community as Perceived by Its Residents. *Journal of Travel Research*, 16 (Spring): 8–12.

Ross, G.F. (1992). Resident Perceptions of the Impact of Tourism on an Australian City. *Journal of Travel Research*, 30 (Winter): 13–17.

Rothman, R. (1978). Residents and Transients: Community Reaction to Seasonal Visitors. *Journal of Travel Research*, 16 (Winter): 8–13.

Sethna, R.J. and Richmond, B.O. (1978). US Virgin Islanders' Perceptions of Tourism. *Journal of Travel Research*, 17 (Summer): 30–31.

Shariff, M.N. (2002). Developing a Scale to Measure Resident Attitudes toward Impacts of Tourism in Langkawi, Malaysia. Unpublished PhD Dissertation, Glasgow: University of Strathclyde.

Shariff, M.N. and Tahir, S. (2003). Residents' Attitudes toward Impacts of Tourism: A Case Study of Langkawi, Malaysia. *Malaysian Management Journal*, 7(2): 13–24.

Singer, M. (1968). *The Concept of Culture.* In *International Encyclopedia of the Social Sciences* (Ed.), Sills, D., Macmillan: New York, Vol. 3, pp. 527–541.

Tinsley, H.O. and Tinsley, D. (1987). Uses of Factor Analysis in Counseling Psychology Research. *Journal of Counseling Psychology*, 34: 414–424.

Tourism Malaysia (2006). *Malaysian Tourism Key Performance Indicators*. Ministry of Tourism Malaysia: Planning and Research Division.

Tourism Malaysia Website (2010). Malaysia Tourism Statistics. http://www.tourism.gov.my

Var, T., Kendall, K. and Tarakcioglu, E. (1985). Resident Attitudes toward Tourists in a Turkish Resort Town. *Annals of Tourism Research*, 12(4): 652–658.

Wang, Chih-Yung and Miko, P.S. (1997). Environmental Impacts of Tourism on US National Parks. *Journal of Travel Research*, 35(4): 31–36.

APPENDIX 1

Tourism Impact Items Generated from Literature and Interview Session

1	Noise level in the community's area	35	Pride among the community
2	Demand for the cultural activities	36	Crime in the community's area
3	Demand for the historical activities	37	Community's standard of living
4	A variety of cultural facilities	38	Vandalism in the community's area
5	Opportunities to learn about other people's cultures	39	Changes to the community's traditional culture
6	Awareness of the local culture	40	Cost of living in the community's area
7	A variety of entertainments	41	Opportunities for cultural exchange
8	Restoration of historical structures	42	Opportunities for education
9	Opportunities to meet other tourists	43	Preservation of the cultural identity
10	Understanding of different people's cultures	44	Understanding of the community's destination image
11	Vitality for the community's life	45	Appearance of the community's area
12	Revenue generated in the economy	46	Trade for local businesses
13	Jobs to the community	47	Demand for accommodation
14	Community's personal income	48	Peace of the community
15	Income going to the local business	49	Prices of goods
16	A variety of shopping facilities	50	Homestay programme in the community's area
17	Investment spending	51	Developing medical tourism product
18	A variety of restaurants	52	Demand for medical tourism accommodation
19	Level of traffic congestion	53	Demand for duty-free shop
20	Size of crowds which restrict the community's activities	54	Awareness of living in a society
21	Size of crowds which affect the enjoyment. of the community's activities	55	Recognition of local culture
22	Driving hazards by tourists	56	Prostitution in the community's area
23	Natural environment	57	Materialistic values among the community
24	Wildlife	58	Imitation of tourists' behaviour
25	Quality of natural environment	59	Public transportation
26	Level of urbanization	60	Drug abused in the community's area
27	Physical ability of local services	61	Preservation of the wildlife
28	Quality of local services	62	Taxes collected for community's assets
29	Financial resources of local services	63	Demand for restaurant sector
30	Local taxes collected	64	Preservation of historical structures
31	Property taxes collected	65	Awareness of safety
32	Local sales taxes collected	66	Adoption of unhealthy lifestyle
33	Positive attitude by residents	67	Awareness towards ethnic identity
34	Community spirit	68	Alcohol abused in the community's area

Appendix 2
Tourism Impact Items Revised by the Experts

1	Increases the noise level
2	Demand for the cultural activities
3	Demand for the historical activities
4	Opportunities to learn about other people's cultures
5	Creates awareness of the local culture
6	Creates a variety of entertainments
7	Restoration of historical structures
8	Opportunities to meet other tourists
9	Increases the revenue generated
10	Increases the number of jobs
11	Increases the community's income
12	Increases the amount of income going to the local business
13	Creates a variety of shopping facilities
14	Investment spending area
15	Creates a variety of restaurants
16	Increases the level of traffic congestion
17	Increases the number of driving hazards
18	Destroys the natural environment
19	Destroys the wildlife
20	Increases the level of urbanization
21	Increases the quality of local services
22	Increases the financial resources of local services
23	Increases the amount of local taxes collected in the community's area
24	Community spirit among the community
25	Creates pride among the community
26	Increases the level of crime
27	Increases the community's standard of living
28	Increases the amount of vandalism in the community's area
29	Increases the cost of living
30	Creates opportunities for cultural exchange
31	Preservation of the community's cultural identity
32	Understanding of the community's destination image
33	Creates demand for accommodation
34	Increases the prices of goods
35	Creates awareness of living in a society
36	Recognition of local culture
37	Creates prostitution in the community's area
38	Materialistic values among the community
39	Imitation of tourists' behaviour
40	Improvement of public transportation
41	Drug abused in the community's area
42	Preservation of the wildlife
43	Increases the amount of taxes collected
44	Creates demand for restaurant sector
45	Preservation of historical structures
46	Creates awareness of safety in the community's area
47	Adoption of unhealthy lifestyle
48	Awareness towards ethnic identity
49	Alcohol abused in the community's area

APPENDIX 3
Factor Analysis Results with Varimax Rotation of Tourism Imact Items—Pre-test Sample (n = 220)

Items	1	2	3	4	5	6	7
FACTOR 1: Amenity Services, Economic and Socio-cultural Impact							
Demand for accommodation sector	.749						
Job opportunities in tourism sector	.717						
Urbanization in the community's area	.679						
Demand for restaurants sector	.672						
Opportunities for businesses in the community' area	.660						
Understanding of different cultures among community and tourists	.650						
Varieties of shopping facilities	.649						
Varieties of entertainment	.643						
Opportunities to meet other tourists	.642						
Changes in price of goods	.600						
Investment spending in the community's area	.598						
Imitation of tourists' behaviour	.589						
Opportunities for cultural exchange between communities and tourists	.584						
Varieties of cultural activities in the community's area	.582						
Opportunities to learn about other cultures	.582						
Adoption of unhealthy lifestyle among community	.576						
Taxes collected for businesses run by community	.575						
Recognition of local culture	.574						
Restoration of historical structure	.574						
Improvement of public transportation	.566						
Materialistic values among the community	.565						
Size of crowds affected community's activities	.565						
Revenue generated by the economy	.564						
Traffic congestion in the community's area	.562						
Higher cost of living in the community's area	.545						
Demand for the cultural activities	.538						
Preservation of historical structures	.536						
Awareness of tourism image	.531						
Better community's standard of living	.529						
Prostitution in the community's area	.528						
Awareness of the local culture among community	.516						
Demand for the historical activities	.510						

Continued

Items	1	2	3	4	5	6	7
Quality of local services such as police, medical etc.	.507						
Driving hazards by tourists	.482						
Awareness of living in a society	.475						
Distribution of income to local businesses	.464						
The noise level in the community's area	.463						
Awareness towards ethnic identity	.423						
Awareness of safety in the community's area	.382						
FACTOR 2: Negative Socio-cultural Impact							
Crime in the community's area		.641					
Vandalism in the community's area		.630					
Drug abused in the community's area		.536					
Alcohol abused in the community's area		.533					
Destroy of the wildlife		.494					
FACTOR 3: Financial and Socio-economic Impact							
Taxes collected for community's assets			.545				
Financial resources of local services such as police, medical, etc.			.535				
FACTOR 4: Positive Environmental Impact							
Preservation of the wildlife				.414			
FACTOR 5: Negative Environmental Impact							
Destroy of the natural environment					.404		
FACTOR 6: Community Pride Impact							
Creates pride among the community						.510	
FACTOR 7: Community Spirit Impact							
Community spirit among the local people							.510

Factor	**F1**	**F2**	**F3**	**F4**	**F5**	**F6**	**F7**
Eigenvalue	14.544	5.662	1.812				
% of Variance	29.087	11.324	3.623				
Cumulative Variance %	29.087	40.411	44.035				
Cronbach's Alpha	.945	.861	.500	–	–	–	–
Number of Items (50)	39	5	2	1	1	1	1

APPENDIX 4
Factor Analysis Results with Varimax Rotation of Tourism Imact Items—Final Test Sample (n = 301)

Items	1	2	3	4	5	6	7	8
FACTOR **1: Amenity Services, Economic and Socio-cultural Impact**								
Job opportunities in tourism sector	.746							
Opportunities for businesses in the community' area	.730							
Varieties of shopping facilities	.684							
Opportunities to meet other tourists	.654							
Demand for accommodation sector	.622							
Demand for restaurants sector	.599							
Awareness of tourism image	.547							
Understanding of different cultures among community and tourists	.547							
Improvement of public transportation	.546							
Distribution of income to local businesses	.515							
Better community's standard of living	.503							
Revenue generated by the economy	.445							
Opportunities to learn about other cultures	.441							
Opportunities for cultural exchange between communities and tourists	.441							
Investment spending in the community's area	.440							
Urbanization in the community's area	.409							
FACTOR **2: Negative Socio-cultural Impact**								
Drug abused in the community's area		.854						
Vandalism in the community's area		.854						
Crime in the community's area		.794						
Alcohol abused in the community's area		.750						
Prostitution in the community's area		.712						
Materialistic values among the community		.591						
Imitation of tourists' behaviour		.598						
Changes in price of goods		.590						
Adoption of unhealthy lifestyle among community		.586						
Higher cost of living in the community's area		.572						
Driving hazards by tourists		.570						
Destroy of the wildlife		.467						
FACTOR **3: Financial and Socio-economic Impact**								
Traffic congestion in the community's area			.566					
The noise level in the community's area			.548					

Continued

Items	1	2	3	4	5	6	7	8
Taxes collected for community's assets			.541					
Varieties of entertainment			.535					
Taxes collected for businesses run by community			.445					
Size of crowds affected community's activities			.429					
FACTOR 4: Historical and Cultural Impact								
Demand for the historical activities				.836				
Demand for the cultural activities				.687				
Preservation of historical structures				.583				
Awareness of the local culture among community				.562				
Restoration of historical structure				.505				
FACTOR 5: Socio-cultural and Community Impact								
Awareness of living in a society					.658			
Community spirit among the local people					.647			
Awareness towards ethnic identity					.599			
Recognition of local culture					.551			
Varieties of cultural activities in the community's area					.431			
FACTOR 6: Service and Safety Impact								
Quality of local services such as police, medical etc.						.713		
Financial resources of local services such as police, medical, etc.						.645		
Awareness of safety in the community's area						.409		
FACTOR 7: Environmental Impact								
Destroy of the natural environment							.901	
Preservation of the wildlife							.470	
FACTOR 8: Community Pride Impact								
Creates pride among the community								.987
Factor	**F1**	**F2**	**F3**	**F4**	**F5**	**F6**	**F7**	**F8**
Eigenvalue	7.000	6.756	3.280	3.239	3.206	2.625	1.510	–
% of Variance	14.001	13.513	6.561	6.478	6.412	5.249	3.020	–
Cumulative Variance %	14.001	27.513	34.074	40.552	46.964	52.213	55.232	–
Cronbach's Alpha	.904	.857	.781	.741	.742	.642	.479	–
Number of Items (50)	16	12	6	5	5	3	2	1

CHAPTER

9

COMMUNITY-BASED ECOTOURISM AND SUSTAINABLE DEVELOPMENT SUPPORTED BY CASE STUDY—KUMAON HIMALAYAS (Lake District of Uttarakhand)

—Bipin Chandra Pant

9.1 ABSTRACT

In recent years, mountain regions are drawing the attention of Indian tourists in general and foreign tourists in particular. The potential mountain resources for promoting green tourism are enormous in the form of natural and cultural heritage such as biosphere reserves, flora and fauna, lakes, rivers and traditional rural resources. In order to utilize tourism industry market, uncontrolled numbers of tourists and related haphazard infrastructural facilities in the vulnerable mountain regions pose serious environmental implications. The ecological pressures are threatening land, water and wild life resources through direct and indirect environmental impacts together with generation of solid and liquid wastes. So green tourism is emerging as an important task in order to develop new relationship between communities, government agencies and private sectors. The strategy focuses on ecological understanding, environmental protection and eco development. The major attributes of green tourism include environmental conservation and education and distribution of income to local people based on strong partnership. Various knowledge systems go a long way in achieving the goals of green tourism, which creates awareness about the value of environmental resources.

Mountains have ecological, recreational, educational and scientific values, which need to be utilized in a sustainable way. Various tourist activities and facilities need to be diversified in order to achieve multiple benefits including scientific field excursion, recreation in natural and cultural areas, community festivals and soft adventure tourisms. Green tourism considers tourism development as an integral part of national and regional development. The paper discusses the social, economic and environmental dimensions of green tourism with particular reference to village tourism development programme taking empirical evidences from the Himalaya. Such programme also minimizes biophysical and human vulnerability and risks in mountain regions. The environmental consciousness campaign and introduction of code through multi-purpose tourist resource centres are gaining currency in the above context.

KEYWORDS: mountain region; green tourism; development programme; sustainability.

9.2 INTRODUCTION

The concept of green tourism is entirely a new side of tourism industry. Green tourism has been developed to appreciate the natural beauty, culture and history of the environment without disturbing the ecosystem. It is, on the one hand, creating economic opportunities for conservation of natural resources and wildlife and, on the other, it is creating awareness among people to protect nature to maintain a balanced ecosystem. In India, green tourism is still at its nascent stage but due to increasing awareness among people, the concept is fast gaining popularity. India, being a land of such a diverse topography, offers a lot of opportunities for green tourism. This kind of initiative not only helps to preserve the nature's resources but also awakens the human responsibility towards Mother Nature. India has a multiple source of flora and fauna. So, declaration of various areas as National Park, sanctuaries has led to the growth of wildlife resources.

Among all the places in India, the Himalayan green tourism is the most visited destination. Various regions in the Himalayas are still unexplored by the people. Its varied topography is the reason for travel attraction and green tourism. The Himalayan region stretches from Jammu & Kashmir to the northeast end of Arunachal Pradesh. The region is rich in natural resources and showcases a variety of flora and fauna. It is also the home for various rare species. Different places in the Himalayan regions have unique characteristics. Places like Himachal Pradesh, Uttarakhand, Sikkim, Assam, West Bengal, and Arunachal Pradesh have its own features, which attract the tourist around the world because it is difficult to see such variations in one place. It is a combination of the green and the blue. On the one side, such lush green mountain valleys and on the other side such beautiful snow capped mountains attract the travellers.

Himalayas is the perfect destination for green tourism in India. Though Himalayas is rich in natural resources, still, due to unawareness of the people, the Himalayan region is facing a major crisis today as its natural resources have become limited. So, it is our duty to maintain the ecosystem for the betterment of mankind and environment. But now the scenario is quite different and people are realizing their responsibility towards nature, its preservation and growth. That is the reason green tourism has become so popular in India. Especially in the Himalayan region, it has gained so much of momentum. The travel operators who arrange the tour only provide booklets on ecotourism, which guide you what to do and what not to do. For example, springs and rivers should not be polluted with any harmful chemicals; you should not cut trees and plants; avoid littering of any sort, etc. The natural flora and fauna should be maintained. It is our duty to maintain law and order. Only then can we establish a balance between nature and man. So, to sustain the exotic beauty of the Himalayas, it is our responsibility to see that our behaviour does not cause any environmental hazards.

9.3 OBJECTIVES

The following are the objectives of the study:

- Determine how to reduce biophysical and human vulnerability in Himalayas.
- Find out potential benefits and costs of green tourism.
- National measures to encourage good environmental practice in tourism destinations.
- Discuss successful transition towards green sustainable tourism.
- Find out the problems and their solutions with recommendations.

9.4 METHODOLOGY

This research paper is based on primary research methods, i.e. field survey and interview with local people and NGOs, community surveys, focus group meetings and site survey. The data collection techniques have been straightforward and economically feasible in terms of the use of resources. My observation and innovative ideas for sustainable tourism in Himalayas by promoting various forms of tourism with different strategies, i.e. main city/town—mass tourism but natural areas, villages, parks—Green tourism, Wellness tourism. The model may be used for reducing vulnerability and promoting people for sustainable development of tourism in Himalayas.

9.4.1 Green Tourism Concerns

Principles

1. It entails a type of use that minimizes negative impacts on the environment and on local people.
2. It increases the awareness and understanding of an area's natural and cultural systems and the subsequent involvement of visitors in issues affecting those systems.
3. It contributes to the conservation and management of legally protected and natural areas.

4. It maximizes the early and long-term participation of local people in the decision making process that determines the kind and amount of tourism that should occur.
5. It directs economic and other benefits to local people that complement rather than overwhelm or replace traditional practices (farming, fishing, social systems, etc.)

Green tourism activities

1. Conservation NGOs working in partnership with private tour operators are ideally placed to provide the ecotourist technical guidelines which upgrade a nature tourism operation into a green tourism operation.
2. The inbound operators.
3. Local service providers.

Though the estimation of the growth of green tourism is rare due to definitional problems, most observers feel that green tourism has grown faster than tourism generally during the past several years. Based on a survey of few years, many are projecting higher growth in the coming years.

There are various explanations for green tourism's growth, including:

- Increasing environmental awareness and interest, including the desire to be perceived by others as environmentally sensitive.
- Increased media exposure to natural areas around the world.
- Related to the above two, a desire to see natural areas before they disappear.
- Increasing dissatisfaction with traditional tourism destinations and products, and a desire for more educative and challenging vacations.

Potential benefits and costs of green tourism

Green tourism is growing in many parts of the world, and is mostly on public lands. As the number of tourists grows, so does the interest in seeing new places and seeking new experiences, and some of these locations show how tourism can have negative impacts. Poorly planned and managed green tourism may damage the same wildlife, natural or cultural resources that draw the tourists. It is difficult to evaluate the benefits and costs of green tourism and these may vary over space and time.

However, the primary benefits are:

1. Increased funding for protected areas and local communities (Protected areas suffer from budget constraints, yet collect nominal entrance fees or none at all; but travellers are interested in helping the areas, as they become more environmentally conscious.)
2. Job creation for local residents (e.g., tour guides, park wardens, lodge owners, craft makers, etc.)
3. Environmental education for visitors (Increasing awareness can change behaviour, and use patterns, and create advocates for conservation.)

The primary costs are:

1. Environmental degradation (Related to visitor activities, management or behaviour.)
2. Economic instability and inequity (Any form of tourism may be an unstable income source, particularly due to external factors such as natural disasters, currency fluctuations, or political instability. The other problem is that financial leakage of tourist expenditures may occur, whether out of the region, or out of the country.)
3. Socio-cultural changes (While change may be both positive or negative, the negative is more usual when communities are not given the opportunities to decide if they want to become involved with tourism, and how.)

Reducing vulnerability

Vulnerability is generally defined as any condition of susceptibility to external shocks that could threaten people's lives and livelihoods, natural resources, properties and infrastructure, economic productivity, and a region's prosperity. In this context, a hazard is the probability that a natural or human induced phenomenon will occur. A disaster is the manifestation of vulnerability and the hazard with an impact that surpasses the coping mechanisms of the affected population.

There is no doubt that natural forces play an important role in the initiation of several disasters. However, it is no longer the case that they can be considered the main cause of such disasters. There seem to be three fundamental causes that dominate the disaster processes in the developing world, which is precisely where their incidence is the largest:

- Human vulnerability coming from poverty and inequality
- Environmental degradation caused by land abuse
- Fast demographic expansion, especially among poor people.

Social and environmental vulnerability to natural hazards can be explained by several factors. Recent trends in Himalayas that increase vulnerability to natural hazards are: population growth and density, rapid urbanization and unplanned human settlements, poor engineering of construction, lack of adequate infrastructure, inequities in social structure, poverty, and inadequate environmental practices.

Reducing social and economic vulnerability to natural hazards requires special attention at two levels:

- Analysis and characterization of hazards, which entails the assessment of the most vulnerable production areas, settlements and infrastructure, and adoption of risk reduction measures.
- An institutional framework for implementing risk reduction measures using development policy instruments, contingency plans and environmental management tools.

When undertaking risk reduction measures, it is also necessary to define the location of a potential hazard, its severity, return period and the probability of expected levels of loss. It is necessary to differentiate between very localized events and national, regional and global impacts. There are both sudden-onset events that can be predicted (e.g., volcanic eruptions, earthquakes or hurricanes in previously affected areas) and those which are more difficult to predict (e.g., earthquakes in previously not-affected areas). There are slow-onset events that are unpredictable (e.g., the creation of a hole in the atmospheric ozone layer), as well as slow-onset events that can be predicted (e.g., droughts and sea level rise due to climatic change).

Any effort to reduce vulnerability to natural disasters should focus on legal and instrumental aspects and on the institutional framework. Furthermore, vulnerability reduction forces us to consider stabilizing factors such as diversity and resilience—that is, the capacity of natural and social systems to absorb both exogenous and endogenous changes. For this purpose, it is not enough to focus on a set of policies and instruments, but also to understand the intimate relationship between natural and social factors.

National measures to encourage good environmental practices in tourism destinations

1. Design national and international investment, and development assistance programmes for local authorities and support locally relevant mechanisms to monitor and evaluate progress.
2. National governments should ensure implementation of Local Agenda 21 Plans through development of national action plans, and provision of resources and expertise. Establish Local Agenda 21 best practice networks to facilitate knowledge transfer across countries.
3. Use strategic environmental assessments and environmental impact assessments. These assessments should be made public for use by all stakeholders. Maintain the integrity of SEAs and EIAs through impartial and informed entities, such as research institutes and universities.
4. Land use planning and development control. The precautionary and polluter pays principles should be applied at local and regional levels.
5. Carrying capacity studies conducted in all tourist destinations prior to further expansion.
6. Promote tourism in natural and cultural heritage sites.

Management plans for each specific area should be given full attention by national governments, and adequate resources and expertise made available to develop competent plans. Projects combining preservation and promotion of cultural heritage sites should be supported, provided that proposals are of a high quality and are based on a sound visitor management plan.

Measures should be taken to support development of rural tourism as a key component of sustainable development in rural areas. Rural destinations should be encouraged to adopt the principles of Integrated Quality Management, involving local communities in measures to manage and develop rural products in line with market needs, plus maximizing the proportion of income retained in the community.

Loss of biodiversity and cultural heritage caused by tourism should be offset by resources at the regional level to mitigate habitat fragmentation and maintain and restore the regional landscape.

Ecotourism should be encouraged and regulated through use of eco-labels and certification schemes, to guarantee better environmental performance and progress towards sustainable development. If an activity is to be conducted in a designated protected area, then an Environmental Impact Assessment should be undertaken in advance by the responsible agency, and plans amended according to the outcomes of the assessment.

Sustainable tourism internet training should be developed for specific industry players.

Research the best ways for evolving product and service certification, through examination of which sectors to target, and of mandatory vs. voluntary certification. Use existing know-how and experience to achieve recognition and acceptance by the sector and consumers. High priority should be given to promoting the image of eco-labels, equating "environment friendly" with quality.

Set up a comprehensive enquiry into green taxes for the tourism industry, taking into account both the opportunity for punitive taxes via the polluter pays principle and tax breaks for certified good practice. Greater stakeholder consultation should be conducted to investigate how the industry can access suitable funding schemes. Monitoring of projects should focus on the sustainability criteria built into a project, and ensure compliance of commitment to sustainability.

Reinforce current increasing environmental awareness with greater stakeholder access to information, through improvements in government educational programmes and the refinement of the availability and content of information services.

9.5 PROBLEMS

- Excessive use of natural areas.
- Destruction of natural areas to accommodate tourism or other needs.
- Encroachment of buildings, facilities and roads close to the mountain areas.
- Pollution by waste, garbage, noise, traffic emission.
- Intersectional competition and conflict over space.
- Exclusion of local communities from any role of significance in decision-making.
- The loss of natural and architectural heritage in the face of rapid expansion.
- Stain on public utilities and facilities.
- Displacement of local population.
- Creation of restricted exclusive zones that are off-limits to the local people.
- Loss of business by local enterprises as all—inclusive resorts supplies all the needs of their guests.

9.6 SOLUTIONS

- Strict environmental standards for solid, liquid and gaseous waste emissions.
- Taking the integrity of mountain values and resources into account.

- Enhancement of public transport infrastructure.
- Locally adapted styles and maximum height/size limit for facilities.
- Setting of local/regional carrying capacities on a case-by-case basis.
- Limits to sale of property to outsiders for the construction (accommodation).
- Maintenance of public access to the mountain strip.
- Safeguarding cultural values and customary uses.
- Introducing environmental management (according to ISO 14000 or the European EMAS Initiative).
- Increasing cultural and natural awareness of tourists through interactions with local initiatives, guided nature walks, museums, etc.
- Integrating the local economy by giving priority to local produce.
- Increase the long-term success of tourism projects by involving key stakeholders in the development and implementation of tourism plans.
- Raise awareness of green sustainable tourism and its implementation by promoting exchange of information, between governments and stakeholders, on best practice for sustainable tourism, and establishing networks for dialogue on implementation of green sustainable tourism principles. Promote understanding and awareness to strengthen attitudes, values and actions compatible with sustainable development.
- Ensure effective implementation of green sustainable tourism, through capacity building programmes to develop and strengthen human resources and institutional capacities in government at national and local levels, and amongst local communities; and to integrate environmental and human ecological considerations at all levels.

9.7 FURTHER SUGGESTIONS

- Proper mapping and documentation of the region is required to identify the destinations, their distances, trekking routes, available bird species (more than 350 species available), available flora of Himalayan species (most of the Himalayan species are found in the region) and medicinal plant species found in the region.
- Destination could be promoted for soft adventure, meditation, yoga and ayurvedic treatments.
- Specialized guides training should be imparted to local youth in the areas of bird watching, flora related knowledge. (The destination has most of the Himalayan spp. and medicinal plants.)
- Pro-forest activities should be promoted in the region.
- Policy level intervention is required to stop selling of land.
- Trekking routes have already been identified. There is need to discuss the possibilities to explore such routes with forest officials.
- Proper training to villagers regarding hospitality services is required, besides promoting awareness about the tourism sector in rural villages.

- Information pertaining to various sites of Himalayan region should be made available to publicity section of Tourism Department for publication in various promotional materials (pamphlets/magazines/banners, etc).
- The destination needs to be promoted through tie-up with tour operators (start with city/town based tour-operators) by designing itinery that includes accommodation, logistics, food and various activities offered.
- Support private sector voluntary initiatives in conservation and provide opportunities for the private tourism sector to contribute to sustainable tourism management initiatives (community awareness and training, protected areas, etc.) through direct donations, in-kind services, and the establishment and maintenance of private reserves.
- Enforce existing laws and regulations to avoid inappropriate development of tourism in core conservation areas, and avoid perverse incentives for tourism development to be environmentally damaging (such as reduced land taxes for cleared land).
- Control the planning, sitting, design, and construction of tourism facilities and infrastructures according to biodiversity conservation principles and guidelines.
- Improve awareness and exchange of knowledge between those responsible for and affected by tourism and nature conservation at national, sub national, and local levels. Undertake carrying capacity and limits to acceptable change assessments for sensitive areas and implement visitor-management plans based on assessment results.
- Develop or adopt certification schemes, reflecting national and local priorities that include biodiversity criteria, and provide appropriate incentives for their adoption.
- Earmark adequate sources of funding for the management of natural areas.
- Develop management strategies, pilot projects, and mechanisms for sharing revenue from tourist visitation with the management authorities of protected areas, while keeping main management expenses covered by appropriate budgetary allotments.
- Promote and develop educational programmes to enhance awareness about nature conservation and sustainable use of biodiversity.
- Conduct market-assessment studies to avoid tourism facility construction in sensitive ecosystems that proves to be unfeasible and unnecessary.
- Tourism industry is characterized by a large number of small and medium-sized enterprises (SMEs). At the same time, a significant amount of control within the industry rests in the hands of a very few, increasingly vertically integrated, multinational corporations.
- A significant development in the last few years is the establishment of voluntary environmental initiatives by hotel chains, tour operators, and ground handlers, including green certification systems, conservation awards, and ecolabels. While some of these initiatives are supported by governments and NGOs, all voluntary performance standard-setting depends essentially on private sector commitment and consumer awareness.
- Initiatives such as the World Legacy Awards by Conservation International and National Geographic Society, British Airways' Tourism for Tomorrow Awards, the

Green Globe 21 certification system, Australia's National Ecotourism Accreditation Programme, Cooperative Research Centre's International Ecotourism Standard, and the International Hotels Environment Initiative's benchmarking tool all provide guidance and added incentives for corporate responsibility toward biodiversity conservation.

- Assembling the component parts of holidays and managing significant numbers of tourists, outbound tour operators play a significant role in making a destination successful. Their capacity to manage their supply chains, their ability to ensure steady flows of tourists, and their ability to influence consumer choices make them key players in tourism development and biodiversity conservation.
- Ground handlers often have a strong commitment to protect their destination because they are permanently based there, but their primary business concern is, responding to the demands of the outbound tour operators they service. Therefore, there is a vital role that international tour operators can play in encouraging their suppliers to adopt environmentally and socially responsible management practices.
- Hotels, resorts and other accommodation facilities are both the tourism industry's main job generators and the main resource users (water, energy, land) affecting biodiversity in hotspot destinations. They also require a significant amount of infrastructure, such as roads and facilities for water supply and treatment, which, if improperly developed, can cause significant harm to biodiversity. However, hoteliers are increasingly recognizing the importance of maintaining the ecological integrity of the areas in which they operate.
- Small, medium, and large-scale hoteliers, with their assets tied up in a particular site, have a strong stake in the long-term sustainability of the surrounding environment. For this reason, the accommodation sector is often proactive in terms of social and environmental corporate accountability and community outreach. However, the majority of environmental management programmes for hotels located in biodiversity hotspots are focused on procedures for internal resource conservation and their related cost-savings, such as washing towels every other day, water saving, recycling, switching off lights, and so on. Broader biodiversity considerations, such as maintaining natural habitats, avoiding land clearance, and setting aside property for species protection or as private nature reserves are yet to be integrated into such programmes. In addition, the many different forms of accommodation ownership increase the difficulties of disseminating information and practical tools on how and why to incorporate sustainability practices and principles into their management.
- Establish representative governance systems that allow local people to be accountable and assume responsibilities in tourism and conservation partnership, and take action to fulfil them within the duration of the partnership.
- Identify, prioritize, and manage critical conservation area networks with direct and indirect tourism use at the local level, using tools such as impact assessment, market studies, zoning, and sustainable use plans.
- Be actively involved in and benefit from community capacity-building efforts relating to local sustainable tourism and ecotourism initiatives, in accordance with the principles of prior informed consent.

- Support local tourism contributions, such as traditional building techniques and materials; modes of transport; traditional foods, medicines, and handicrafts; and respect access to cultural sites.
- Collaborate with visitor-awareness campaigns on biodiversity conservation, educating tourists on the significance of natural resources for the local culture and the economy.
- Respect local codes of conduct and visitor-management plans in sensitive areas.
- Ask tourism companies about their environmental and social standards and ensure they understand that your choice is determined by those standards.
- Actively support tourism businesses and NGOs that are biodiversity friendly and seek to benefit local people.
- Recognize the cultural and natural diversity associated with many natural areas, particularly regarding local and indigenous communities.
- Facilitate and mediate innovative, conservation-friendly tourism partnerships.
- Play a role in the capacity building, technology transfer, and training of local communities to participate in and benefit from sustainable tourism development.
- Monitor impacts of tourism developments related to all stakeholders, and report independently and openly on results.
- Work with governments to integrate sustainable tourism as a biodiversity conservation strategy in national biodiversity agendas.
- Required to promote them.
- Utilize Tourism Self-Employment Scheme for creating local village based enterprises (pro-poor linkages) in the field of hotels/restaurants/vehicle owners/tourist information centres/souvenir shops/tents, etc.
- The seven states of the North East with beautiful landscapes, lush green forests, exotic wildlife, unique forms of art and culture and affable tribal societies have hitherto remained backward due to various reasons including poor infrastructure. These states alone offer enormous potential for the development of ecotourism. At least, 10% of Plan funds of the Ministry should be used for the promotion of tourism in North East, apart from taking up special projects and schemes for the development of the area. Other Special Tourism areas such as Himalayan areas, Islands and coastal areas which are identified should also be developed.

9.8 RECOMMENDATIONS

- Work with the private sector to transform practices to more directly contribute to biodiversity conservation and benefit local and indigenous communities.
- Raise awareness among tourists as to the potential impacts—positive and negative of tourism activities.
- Encourage informed decision-making among all stakeholders regarding tourism development in or near local and indigenous communities.

- Fill research gaps on the dynamics of the relationship between tourism development and biodiversity conservation at both local and regional levels, and share best practices.
- Assess and monitor biodiversity impacts of tourism development (and their social and economic determinants)—from supply through production to consumption; this assessment should assist in identifying effective intervention areas.
- Develop pilot projects (and research existing ones) to establish guidelines to support development and implementation of conservation-friendly tourism policies by governments and local authorities. These policies should address how to balance conflicting economic, social, and environmental priorities.
- Encourage transparent reporting of conservation issues by tourism corporations, support the development of certification and accreditation programmes that consider conservation, and establish sector-specific sustainability reporting guidelines and performance indicators for biodiversity conservation.
- Work with key players and intermediaries to develop and implement customer awareness campaigns addressing conservation of biodiversity.
- Raise awareness of intermediaries on their key role in catalyzing change in the tourism supply chain, and build their capacity to improve conservation of biodiversity through networks and management tools (for example, screening indicators or environmentally sound technologies.)
- Incorporate biodiversity and socio-economic considerations into tourism master plans and other development strategies.
- Ensure widespread participation in tourism planning exercises, including biodiversity-focused stakeholders such as protected-area managers, NGOs, and traditional communities.

9.9 CONCLUSION

Over the past three decades, major losses of virtually every kind of natural habitat have occurred, and the decline and extinction of species has emerged as a leading environmental issue. Biodiversity is essential for the continued development of green tourism, yet this study indicates an apparent lack of awareness of the links, positive and negative, between tourism development and biodiversity conservation. Green tourism will require careful planning in the future to avoid having further negative impacts on biodiversity. Many of the factors associated with biodiversity loss, land conversion, climate change, pollution are also linked to tourism development.

Resources that are important for conserving biodiversity and supporting the livelihoods of local people, such as fresh water, are also affected by tourism development, and recognizing these links is important to managing tourism development into the future. At the same time, an increasing number of examples have shown that tourism development guided by the principles associated with green tourism—environmental sustainability, protection of nature, and supporting the well-being of local people can have a positive impact on biodiversity conservation. By creating private reserves, providing justification for existing and new national parks and protected areas, and building a local conservation constituency among the people who live closest to important biodiversity areas, tourism can have and has had a positive impact on biodiversity conservation. Properly managed tourism does have the potential to contribute to biodiversity conservation and to support poverty reduction.

However, the proximity of tourism development to high-biodiversity areas means that if it is not carefully managed, tourism could exacerbate the already rapid decline of biodiversity. It is increasingly clear that, where tourism development is not guided by principles that promote conservation of nature and contribute to the well-being of local people, both human welfare and biodiversity can seriously suffer as a consequence. The emphasis is on the need to increase the benefits from tourism for host communities, while enhancing the protection of natural heritage and ecologically sensitive areas.

Proper management of tourism to ensure both social and environmental benefits requires collaboration among the "sustainable development triad" of public agencies, the private sector, and local communities. Yet this study shows that the tourism industry and public authorities still appear to be largely unaware of the mutually supportive nature of the relationship between biodiversity conservation and tourism development and of the potential to use nature tourism as a way to contribute to biodiversity conservation efforts and poverty reduction. The recommendations developed through this study for the key players (government, private sector, development agencies, local authorities, residents, and tourists themselves) can apply to both tourism destination countries and to the main tourist originating countries. Acting on these recommendations will help to promote more responsible tourism activities and development that can positively affect both biodiversity and local economies.

During the past 10 years, and with the advent of green tourism principles and sustainable tourism guidelines, significant progress has been made among the key players, both in terms of strategies for tourism development and in terms of collaboration to form more effective partnerships that consider environmental and human factors in designing tourism development plans and policies. But as tourism continues to grow and expand into new natural areas, more concrete action needs to be put into place to safeguard the Earth's biodiversity, while promoting tangible economic benefits to local communities. It is our hope that the information contained in this study, by providing evidence of the overlaps and links between tourism, biodiversity, and local populations and the future implications of those overlaps, can contribute significantly to that effort.

REFERENCES

Akama, J.S. (1996). Western environmental values and nature-based tourism in Kenya. Tourism Management, 17(8): 567–574.

Bisht, D.S. (2006). *Poverty, Planning and Development—A Case Study of Uttaranchal State* (submitted to the Planning Commission), Central Himalayan Institute, Dehradun. Trishul Publications, Dehradun.

Bisht, S. (2005). Concerns and challenges. In M.L. Dewan and Jagdish Bahadur (Eds.), *Uttaranchal: Vision and Action Programme,* Concept Publishing Company, New Delhi, pp. 82–87.

Buckley, R.C. (2003). Case Studies in Ecotourism, CABI Publishing House, Wallingford, UK.

_____ (2002). Tourism and Biodiversity in North and South, *Tourism Recreation Research*, 27(1) pp. 43–51.

Cater, E. (1993). Ecotourism in the third world: problems for sustainable development. Tourism Management, 24: 85–90.

Chawla, R., *Tourism in the 21st Century*, Sonali Publications, New Delhi.

Datta, S.K. and Virgo, K.J. (1998). Towards sustainable watershed development through people's participation: Lessons from the Lesser Himalayas, Uttar Pradesh, India. *Mountain Research and Development*, 18(3), pp. 213–233.

Godwin, H. and Robson, S. (2004). "How can business in travel and tourism increase the contribution of the industry to local economic development and pro-poor growth?", *Tourism and local economic development*, The International Centre for Responsible Tourism, August, http://www.propoortourism.org.uk last viewed 01 Jan., 2011.

Elita, B. (2009). The Socio-Economic Impact of Tourism and Entrepreneurship in Vigan City, *E-International Scientific Research Journal* (EISRJ), 1(1), pp. 25–33

Jenkins, C.L. and Henry, B.M. (1982). Government Involvement in Tourism in Developing Countries, *Annals of Tourism Research*, 9(4), pp. 499–521.

Jodha, N.S. (1992). "Mountain Perspective and Sustainability: A Framework for Development Strategies", in N.S. Jodha, M. Banskota and T. Partap (Eds.), *Sustainable Mountain Agriculture*, Oxford and IBH, New Delhi, pp. 401–482.

Negi, J.S. (2007). *Rural Tourism and Economic Growth*, Cyber Tech Publications, New Delhi.

Singh, R. (2003), *National Ecotourism and Wildlife Tourism*, Kanishka Publishers, New Delhi.

Singh, S.P. (1999). *International Tourism and Sustainable Tourism*, Anmol Publications, New Delhi.

Sreedhar, R. (2005). Mountain tourism for local community development, in M.L. Dewan and Jagdish Bahadur (Eds.), *Uttaranchal: Vision and Action Programm*, Concept Publishing Company, New Delhi, pp. 285–296.

Tosun, C. (2006). Expected nature of community participation in tourism development, *Tourism Management*, 27(3), pp. 493–504.

Verma, L.R. and T. Partap (1992). "The Experiences of an Area-based Development Strategy in Himachal Pradesh, India", in N.S. Jodha, M. Banskota and T. Partap (Eds.), *Sustainable Mountain Agriculture*, Vol. 2, Oxford and IBH, New Delhi, pp. 609–636.

World Commission on Protected Areas (WCPA) (2000). Tourism and Biodiversity. Biodiversity Brief No. 9. Gland, Switzerland: Biodiversity in Development Project, IUCN, European Commission, and Department for International Development.

WWF International (2001). Guidelines for community-based ecotourism development.

Websites

http;//tourism.gov.in/survey/uttarakhand.pdf

http;//www.biodiv.org/programmes/cross-cutting/ecosystem/principles.asp.

http;//www.conservation.org

http;//www.nhm.ac.uk/science/projects/worldmap

http;//www.biodiv.org

http;//www.iclei.org

http;//www.ecotourism.org

http;//www.wri.org/wri/biodiv

http;//www.world-tourism.org

http://www.millenniumassessment.org/en/index.aspx

http://www.unep.org/biodiversity

SECTION III

CASE STUDIES AND PRACTICES ON TOURISM TRENDS

CHAPTER

10

TOURIST'S USE OF PUBLIC TRANSPORT INFORMATION A Case Study in Penang Island

—NG KOK MENG

10.1 ABSTRACT

The role of transportation in its operation is vital. It is largely due to the improvement of transportation that tourism has expanded. The advent of flight has shrunk the world, and the motor vehicle has made travel to anywhere possible (Sorupia, 2005). Public transport information plays a significant role in the overall tourist travel experience. The simplicity and accuracy of public transport information has been revealed to be the bottom line of public transport service quality for all users. However, it is a fact that the needs of tourists for public transport information, tourist interaction and satisfaction with public transport information have been the subject of attention in the transport literature.

This paper presents some results of a study of overseas' visitors' use of public transport in Penang Island by semi-structured interview method. The investigation of visitor use and perceptions of public transport information revealed that visitors had a greater requirement for information, particularly in the case of certain information items. In addition, some issues have been highlighted due to the overall experience in the island.

KEYWORDS: public transport information, tourist, Penang Island

10.2 INTRODUCTION

The recognition of the importance of tourism in Malaysia's major cities has remarkably increased since the late 1990s. Karen (2004) postulated that urban tourism acts as an important catalyst for the economic, social and physical regeneration of a city. Such "chemical reaction" indirectly creates benefits for the residents of a city, i.e. income and job creation as well as for industries located there. Moreover, tourism is perceived as an environment friendly yet labour intensive industry, which can benefit cities, particularly in the downhill of traditional economic activities (Law, 1993).

The significance of supply-driven tourism in historic cities has been powerfully demonstrated by deregulation of scheduled air services since the early twentieth century (especially recently opened at Melaka Airport), and the rapid growth of low-cost operators such as Airasia and Firefly that promote short distance travel to independents as well as family travellers with affordable low air fares. This has opened up heritage tourism to those travellers who have interests in heritage and culture. At the same time, the recognition by UNESCO to both Georgetown Penang and Melaka as world heritage sites had positive impacts on the number of visitors annually.

There are many arguments about the destination choice and visitor satisfaction which shall be determined by primary elements of the tourism product such as cultural and entertainment facilities and the socio-cultural characteristics of a destination (Karen, 2004). However, it is possible that the role of urban public transport in the visitor experience may have been unidentifiable and underestimated. Many international visitors are dependent on the available public transport while in Malaysia, they often arrive by airline without their own private vehicle. Therefore, there is a dire need for cities that receive visitors to focus attention on ensuring the availability of a user friendly public transport system, which would cater to the travel needs of visitor and ensure good internal accessibility to the tourist city. This paper focuses specifically on the information aspect of internal accessibility for the visitor. The use of information source as an element of both the tourism and transport products is emphasized and the existence of potential differences in the transport information requirements of international visitors and local residents is hypothesized. The results of the survey of overseas' visitors to Georgetown Penang are subsequently presented and appropriate implications for destination management are considered.

10.3 LITERATURE REVIEW

10.3.1 Penang as an International Destination

Penang, the Pearl of the Orient, is not only famous with its unbeatable delicious foods but also well-recognized of its enriched historical and cultural assets. Many different cultures and traditions are still put into practice by different ethnicity i.e. Chinese, Indian and Malay in inner city Georgetown. The architecture of George Town is seen as an eclectic mixture of the European classical style, mainly British, with Islamic, Malay, Indian, Chinese and later Art Deco motifs (Huang, 2002). However, the onset of nationwide industrial development since 70s has brought about the tremendous physical and social changes leaving us with a deterioration of cultural and tourist assets, traffic problems and standstill tourist arrivals.

Some researchers argued that the basic condition for a company to enter the market is to provide a high quality level of service. Thus, it is essentially important to consider how visitors reach a destination in both the marketing of places and also in the facilities or basic infrastructure that have to be provided, frequency with which a destination is served as well as appropriate routings where links and interpretation have to be developed. Considering the high dependence on cars and coaches, urban authorities must address the need for effective strategies to cope with large amounts of traffic and congestion, especially within the inner city (Orbasli and Shaw, 2004). There is, therefore, a strong argument for increasing the use of public transport for leisure journeys. However, it is also considerable that the available public transport supply must be able to cater for visitor needs if the uses of public transport are to be encouraged. The areas of the city which are best served by a public transport system designed for local users may not coincide with those foreign visitors who require to access. Moreover, there may be barriers to public transport use experienced by overseas visitors which are different to those identified for local users (Karen, 2004). In particular, the specific information requirements of foreign visitors can assist in the design of an integrated public transport system as part of a holistic destination management process.

10.3.2 Information Resources for Visitor in Penang Island

To encourage tourists, especially first-time visitors unfamiliar with the city to use local public transport systems and/or walk to reach historic city destinations, it is important to provide good links between the point of arrival and the destination area. This will not only be in frequent and reliable transport and attractive routes, but also the necessity for adequate sign posting in pictograms in a number of languages. For example, a Japanese visitor arriving with certain expectations of "historic" will not want to waste his/her precious time looking for direction or spend extra taxi fare to reach their destination.

Information plays a significant role in tourism development of a destination as it provides accurate and necessary details for visitors to reach their very own destinations. Moreover, the purpose for visitors to inquire information is for them to make a precise decision of how to get to the destination not even mention time and efforts factors that will influence visitors' experience for that particular place. Considering the vital role of information to the visitors of Penang, local authorities (MPPP) and industry players such as Rapid Penang co-operate to provide public transport information to foreign visitors, specifically to those first-timers to Penang. For instance, the placement of TV screens recently at Komtar bus terminal will eventually assist the bus passengers in knowing the bus arriving time. However, such information provision tends to be localized, geared more to necessary use by consumers to commute to work, travel to school, or for community leisure purposes, rather than use by visitors. Therefore, it is necessary to consider the accessibility of information by tourists. Meanwhile, information exists in different forms, i.e. brochure or fliers shall be placed at major tourist transit points so that tourists can access the information they need. Also, the interpretation of the information provided will determine how easily the information can be used to access the visitor's destination.

10.3.3 Significance of Information in Public Transport Service

The role of information in public transport service quality and modal choice has been great for local users. A study by Railtrack (1998) provides an indication of the importance of a range of attributes in determining modal choice (i.e., factors that would have to improve for bus usage to improve). Information listed sixth from the ten attributes, cited by 29% of respondents. Similarity, Quattro (1998) found that information was one of the service quality attributes most often included in the consumer evaluation surveys of European public transport operators. The results of the studies cited above provide evidence of the significance of public transport information as a factor in influencing perceptions of the quality of urban public transport but also future travel behaviour in terms of modal choice. However, information may play an even crucial role for overseas' visitors than it does for local users of an urban public transport service.[1]

10.3.4 Visitors' Use of Public Transport Information

Foreign visitors are expected to have particular characteristics and needs as public transport users in a foreign city. They are likely to be first time occasional users and may be wholly unfamiliar with the local public transport system and may require additional information to those generally available. In fact, studies on bus services had shown that there are significant differences in the types of information required by regular and occasional users, i.e. occasional users depend very much on friends or telephone enquiries for information (Blackledge, 1992). Balcombe and Vance (1998) further contend that there was a considerably higher percentage of bus users requiring information before and during the trip, particularly the first time visitors.[2]

On the other hand, van der Berg et al. (1995) highlighted that the public transport in urban tourist destinations is hardly accessible for foreign visitors because of the lack of public transport information in foreign languages. Foreign visitors may be unwilling to communicate with the local residents or person-on-duty due to lack of confidence in English language or vice-versa. Therefore, the usefulness and intelligibility of available information are also equally critical for the foreign visitor. At the international level, provision for comprehensive transport information for the tourist has been recognized and demonstrated. For example, ETC has recognized the potential to influence tourist travel through the provision of effective information (ETC, 2001). However, the significance of the use and usefulness of public transport information from a foreign visitor's perspective remains unexplored, particularly in the case of Penang Island. The study outlined below sought to address this gap in literature.

10.4 METHODOLOGY

A large-scale survey of foreign visitors to Penang Island was conducted in the peak visitation period, which fall from July to September 2010, and elicited 250 responses. The questionnaire was designed, inter alia, to investigate the relative importance of information in a scale of attributes which contribute to public transport performance. These attributes were drawn from

1. In a later study, security and cleanliness (labelled as 'design') was substantiated in relating to comfort (Friman et al., 2001).
2. 48% of passengers making a new journey require information on where to alight (Balcombe and Vance, 1998).

semi-structured interviews with a sample of foreign visitors to Penang Island as well as from a sample of domestic respondents, who were asked to convey their public transport experiences at an urban destination from which they had just returned. A 5-point Likert scale with 5 indicating the highest level of importance (1 symbolizes the least importance) was used in this particular study to measure the level of importance of the scale attributes. Eventually, the respondents were given a question to rate the usefulness of the public transport information sources available in Penang Island to foreign visitors. The respondents were measured on a three-point scale.

10.5 FINDINGS

Table 10.1 highlights the mean scores on the importance of attributes of public transport performance which included service quality and customer services. The results were calculated and presented in descending order of importance. Attributes of public transport performance of the first (highest mean scores) and second greatest importance to foreign visitors include information (5.68) and access to attractions at the destination (5.57). These results indicate the importance of good, accessible public transport information and the integration of the public transport system within the tourist city, as discussed in the literature review.

Table 10.1 Importance of attributes of system factors
(Attributes of Service Quality and Customer Service)

Importance variable	*Mean*	*Standard error*	*Standard deviation*
Information of public transport	5.68	.11	1.691
Easily accessible to attraction by public transport	5.57	.10	1.576
Personal safety	5.55	.10	1.667
Effective customer service	5.48	.11	1.765
Ticket cost	5.45	.12	1.921
Punctuality	5.40	.11	1.759
Helpful personnel	5.38	.10	1.749
Special public transport pass for tourists	5.32	.10	1.696
Cleanliness of vehicle/stops	5.25	.10	1.590
Easy ticketing system	5.06	.09	1.371
Driver attitude	4.42	.13	1.976
Speed	4.09	.13	1.935

As mentioned earlier, in order to investigate the use of information by foreign visitors to Penang, the respondents were questioned on the range of public transport information sources used in Penang Island and their respective usefulness. Table 10.2 shows the number and percentage of respondents who had used the various available information sources during their stays in Penang Island. It should be noted that the figures relate to all respondents which

Table 10.2 Public transport information sources used by foreign visitors to Penang Island during stay

Information source used during stay	*Number of respondents having used information source*	*Percentage of respondents having used information source*	*Number of respondents having used information source as a percentage of total responses*
Tourist information centre	217	96.4	18.3
Public transport information leaflets	195	86.7	16.5
Attraction leaflets	157	69.8	13.3
Electronic information—LCD screen at major bus stop	152	67.6	12.8
Reception at accommodation	133	59.1	11.2
Local people	126	56.0	10.6
Public transport information centre	122	54.2	10.3
Internet	48	21.3	4.0
Penang tourism website	35	15.6	3.0

included those who had used public transport, and therefore, the number of visitors who had used the information sources as a percentage of those who had used public transport may be higher. Again, the percentage may be lower as certain respondents may have sought public transport information but ended up against using public transport. Nonetheless, the high percentage of respondents having used the information indicates the extensive use of public transport information by foreign visitors to Penang Island. Respondents were most likely to have used one of Penang's Tourist Information Centres (TICs) to access the public transport information. This can be seen from the highest percentage of respondents who had approached TICs (96.4%), particularly for foreign visitors in Penang. Nonetheless, 54.2% of visitors claim to have used the public transport information centre. Indeed, given that in total 1,185 positive responses were recorded to this question, the indication is that many visitors had utilized more than one source of public transport information in Penang Island. The importance of leaflets in providing public transport information is confirmed by the fact that over three quarters of respondents said they had obtained public transport information from this source.

Interestingly, nearly half or 67.6% of the respondents were likely to obtain public transport information (public bus only) on the new launched electronic information provided by Rapid Penang. This confirms the importance of new technologies in the provision of transport information despite that the visitors may be accessing public transport information in advance of their trip by using internet (21.3%). The fact that the determinant variable "the electronic information from TV screen provides more accurate and useful information to passengers" has a mean rating of 5.26 on a seven-point Likert scale is further evidence for this phenomenon.

In order to gain a better picture of foreign visitors' satisfaction with the public transport information sources they have used, respondents were further asked to rate the information sources they had used on a three-point scale (not at all useful, quite useful, very useful) with a non-response option. Since the data was collected at the ordinal level, the mean ratings for the various information sources cannot meaningfully be compared. However, three of the variables have a mode rating of 3 (very useful): electronic information (TV-screen), local people, and public transport information centre. Thus, although TICs and information leaflets were used by a greater overall percentage of visitors, local people and public transport information centres were found more useful. This is not an unexpected result as the public transport information quality included in the attraction leaflets and public transport information leaflets are lacking in details with lots of nonrelevant information such as advertisements attached. Note that internet variable had a mode of one (not at all useful) which suggests dissatisfaction with public transport information sources, as most of the respondents asserted the public transport information provided in internet is not useful and information given were not up-to-date.

In addition, the questionnaire also measured the items of public transport information which foreign visitors would require to make a journey by public transport in a foreign city with the aim to investigating the use and usefulness of information sources. The information items employed for this part of questionnaire were borrowed from Balcombe and Vance (1998) to compare information requirements of local users and foreign visitors. Thus, Table 10.3 shows the comparison of responses from foreign visitors to the question of information requirements with data from Balcombe and Vance (1998), showing the percentage of local users who require the items of information to make a journey.

Table 10.3 Types of public transport information required to make journey: Comparison of foreign visitors and local users

Type of information required	Percentage of respondents requiring information	
	Local users	*Overseas visitors*
Departure time	78	95
Bus number	61	76
Boarding point	55	97
Bus route	53	79
Alighting point	47	88
Fares	45	66
Frequency	41	75
Arrival time	28	83
Journey length	15	77
Changing point	9	58

Significantly, the high percentage of foreign visitors requiring the items of information in the case of every item clearly indicates that foreign visitors have a greater requirement for information than local users when making public transport journeys. Notably, whilst a very high 97% of foreign visitors require information on where to board the public transport, only 55% of local users require this information. Such a big difference is likely to be due to the fact that foreign visitors are unfamiliar with public transport nodes at the destination. It is worth mentioning that information on journey length is required by considerably fewer respondents than all other items, potentially reflecting the use of public transport for leisure purposes. However, this variable was also relatively unimportant to local users.

10.6 CONCLUSION

There is very little integration of public transport information in Penang. It is beyond Penang tourist guide leaflets remit to provide information on travel times and frequencies, although it offers advice on general use of the public transport system to the foreign visitors. Since sources of public transport information are mainly designed for the use of residents (e.g. Electronic information-TV screen), visitors may tend to seek other sources of public transport information such as hotel reception and the TICs. Thus, public transport information is provided by an organization other than the public transport operator (bus driver) and hence the quality and accuracy of information provided may be out of the operator's control.

The findings have demonstrated that overseas' visitors use both different information sources to local users and same sources to different degrees. Moreover, a comparison of the items of information that foreign visitors make a journey to Penang Island with those of local residents illustrated that foreign visitors tend to have much greater need for information. There are certain types of information linked to local knowledge, for instance boarding points were highly sought by visitors than local users. In addition, the hypothesis that foreign visitors to Penang Island have different public transport information needs than local users is supported. An analysis of the public transport information sources that foreign visitors to Penang Island had used during their stay suggested that TICs and public transport information leaflets were used rather than the customary sources of public transport information used by local people (e.g., public transport operator).

10.7 RECOMMENDATIONS FOR PENANG'S GOVERNMENT AND LOCAL AUTHORITY

The availability, accuracy and reliability of public transport information is essential in providing exceptional value to tourist experience. As the quality of public transport information in Penang Island is largely out of the control of the public transport authority control, therefore, cooperation is expected between the public transport authority and other information providers, viz. travel agencies and hoteliers in order to ensure the accessibility of reliable public transport information to the foreign visitor.

Robin and David (2006) asserted that a sustainability city should reduce personal vehicle by promoting the usage of public transportation i.e. bus and metro to the local residents; however, in the case of Penang, it is more practical sound that a detail master plan of integrated transportation system to be formed by involving the local state government (MPPP) and public transport operator (Rapid Penang). As for the state ministry of transport, the authority should seek to help make public transport systems more attractive and efficient by providing:

- Support to stakeholders to anticipate and prepare for emerging challenges.
- An overview of the state-of-the-art knowledge and research.
- Specific guidelines and practical tools.

There is, therefore, a dire need for greater cooperation amongst the state government, local authority as well as other information providers in order to ensure the accessibility of reliable public transport information for the visitors, when and where they need it.

REFERENCES

Balcombe, R.J. and Vance, C.E. (1998). *Information for Bus Passengers: A Study of Needs and Priorities, Crowthorne*. Transport Research Laboratory.

Blackledge, D. (1992). *Some Recent Survey Results in a Medium Sized Town in a PTE Area*, Oxford: Transport and Travel Research.

ETC (2001). *Tourism and Transport: The Issues and the Solutions*, London: English Tourism Council.

Friman, M., Edvardsson, B. and Gärling, T. (1998). Perceived service quality attributes in public transport: inferences from complaints and negative critical incidents, *Journal of Public Transportation*, 2(1): 67–88.

Karen, T. (2004). *Tourists' Use of Public Transport Information: What They Need and What they Get*, Glasgow: Association for European Transport.

Law, C.M. (1993). *Urban Tourism: Attracting Visitors to Large Cities*, London: Mansell.

Orbasli, A. and Shaw, S. (2004). Transport and visitor in historic cities, in L. Lumsdon and S. Page (Eds.), *Progress in Tourism and Transport Research: Issues and Agendas for the New Millennium*, Oxford: Elsevier, pp. 93–104.

Penang Tourist Information Centre, Georgetown Penang (visited date: 20 July 2010).

Quattro (1998). *Quality Approach in Tendering Urban Public Transport Operations*, Final Report by QUATTRO Consortium on behalf of European Commision DGVII, Luxemberg: Office for Official Publication of the European Communities.

Rapid Penang, Penang Bus Terminal at Weld Quay, Georgetown Penang (visited date: 5 August 2010).

Railtrack (1998). *Public Attitudes to the Transport System in Britain*, A survey conducted by MORI for railtrack in association with the RAC, CPT, BAA, Sustrans and the Pedestrian' Association.

Shaw, S. (2003). Multicultural heritage and urban generation in London's city fringe. In *Conference Proceedings: Cultural Heritage Research: A Pan-European Challenge*. Cracow: European Commission and Polish Academy of Sciences.

Sorupia, E. (2005). Rethinking the Role of Transportation in Tourism. University of Melbourne.

van den Berg, L., van der Borg, J., and van der Meer, J. (1995). *Urban Tourism: Performance and Strategies in Eight European Cities*. Aldershot: Avebury.

CHAPTER

11

REBUILDING DESTINATION FUNCTIONALITY
A Strategic Framework Towards Crisis Communication

—Parikshat Singh Manhas and Zubair Ahmed Dada

11.1 ABSTRACT

While tourists have the freedom to skip destinations embedded with risk perception, the ramifications of catastrophic events on tourist destinations are unavoidable and can be intense. Violent events that target tourism can be viewed as a catastrophe for a destination and subsequent events can create a grave tourism crisis. This paper reviews the literature on destination crisis communication as a result of crisis events and to discern mechanisms by which crisis communications can be co-conspirators in crisis recovery and uses Jammu and Kashmir as a case study, directed towards understanding the stated research theme. Crises and disasters are inevitable and affect the hospitality and tourism industry with disproportionate frequency in the midst of the considerable economic impact this business generates. When a disaster strikes, we may be able to leverage crisis communication strategies to simultaneously enhance speedier disaster recovery and build stronger customer relationships. This paper primarily argues that tourist destinations—particularly those prone to politically induced violence—should induct crisis communication planning into their overall sustainable development and marketing/management strategies to protect and remodel their image of well-being/attractiveness, to re-establish confidence in prospective visitors about the security of the area, to restore the area's functionality/attractiveness, and to support local travel and tourism industry members in their economic recovery. The discussion, and therefore the conclusion, deliberates on having a crisis management framework in place, institutionalizing a tourism crisis management task force, building a crisis management manual, and collaborating with law enforcement agencies.

KEYWORDS: tourism crisis, crisis management, destination management and recovery.

11.2 INTRODUCTION

11.2.1 An Epistemological Approach towards Tourism Crisis Management

Crisis management relates to managing a critical event that may have major repercussions on the viability of a business. According to Regster and Larkin (2002), the core of crisis communication lies in the finding, cultivating and harvesting of the success that could potentially stem from a crisis. In broad terms, crisis management can be viewed simply (and easily remembered) as involving the '4 Rs' of a four-stage process of: reduction, readiness, response and recovery. DMOS, however, are faced with the reality of trying to implement this process and a broad literature has evolved relating to the processes involved in successfully managing crisis situations. The basic outline of a crisis communication operation is to recognize that a crisis is occurring, to take appropriate action and to make that action public, i.e. to be seen to be dealing with and attempting to rectify the situation. An effective crisis communication strategy allows an organization/destination to reduce the potential risk to its reputation presented by the crises or disaster situation. This is vital since poorly handled crisis and the resulting bad publicity can affect the public's perception of a company/destination for a much longer time period than the duration of the crisis itself.

Firstly, even though the popular press frequently uses the terms 'crisis' and 'disaster' interchangeably, it is necessary to distinguish between them as, in the context of tourism, their connotations differ. The word 'crisis', which is derived from the Latin word 'decision', is itself borrowed from the Greek word *krisis*, coming from *krinein*, to decide. As its Latin and Greek roots unequivocally show, deciding about something or someone is clearly at its core, either as a triggering event or as a way of resolving it or both. Defining a crisis as a crucial stage or turning point, especially in sequence of events or a disease, the Collins English Dictionary and Thesaurus further suggest that any such decision is to be made at a crucial stage or turning point. Moreover, by referring to it as an unstable period, especially one of extreme trouble or danger, the Thesaurus adds the notion of danger and instability to that of a critical decisional time. Two more quotes will further fine-tune the definition in the context of tourism: crises are periods of great uncertainty in which predictability and control are lost or severely diminished. They are also the possible but unexpected result of management failures that are concerned with the future course of events set in motion by human action or inaction, precipitating the events. These low probability and high impact situations (Pearson and Clair, 1998) are associated with critical changes and threats of destruction (Glaesser, 2003).

A disaster, on the other hand, whose name is derived from the Greek astro, a star, is defined in the Collins English Dictionary and Thesaurus, as an occurrence that causes great distress or destruction and as a situation where an external and unpredictable catastrophic change is associated with a low degree over the evolution of events. In short, whereas the origin of a crisis is predominantly internal, that of a disaster is essentially external. The fact is that in both cases, the final consequences depend on the pre-crisis or pre-disaster vulnerabilities. In the end, it all comes down to the level of awareness and preparedness of the destination. The less prepared a destination, the more vulnerable it will be to a crisis or a disaster, hence the need for crisis management.

It should be noted first that whilst some governments prepare for crises and disasters, others do not. Crises can thus be allowed to run their own courses (management by doing nothing) where resources such as medicine, health-care services, money, skilled people or equipment are scarce or locally unavailable. When people have to fend for themselves, delay in overcoming the crisis will extend the recovery time and increase the cost and may result in a crisis becoming a disaster. Moreover, during the extended recovery time, business as usual is impractical, adding an opportunity cost to the immediate loss. A recent tragic event in Myanmar, the early 2008 huge tidal surge in the wake of cyclone Nargis, provides a compelling case in point: Even though this Act of God wreaked havoc on many areas and caused heavy human losses, the government of Myanmar left its citizens to largely fend for themselves and, more regrettably, blocked international aid efforts to bring relief to its citizens. Some governments and private sector organizations, however, have begun to adopt a proactive approach to crisis management, i.e. they have started to anticipate both disasters and crises, prepare detection and warning systems, and establish recovery action-plans. They have also sequestered and mobilized resources so as to be in a position to manage disasters and crises when they occur.

In short, they have engaged in crisis management. It goes without saying that crisis management requires planning. Still, whether as a consequence of ignorance, internal resistance, community-based conflicts, and/or cost (Quarantelli, 1984) or political will (Hall and Sullivan, 1996), it appears that many tourist destinations have failed to establish an adequate level of disaster and crisis planning. In such destinations, most authorities and relevant stakeholders continue to lack crisis/disaster management capabilities, flexibility and confidence to deal effectively with unexpected, complex and critical situations (Faulkner, 2001; Santana, 2003). And, even in cases where some organizations may have put formal crisis management plans into place, the level of preparedness often still remains insufficient; such plans being generally reactive and designed to address limited professional objectives, rather than incorporating the priorities of the wider community. The most recent political crisis in Thailand fits into this category. Only after the crisis were the police shown undergoing advanced crowd control techniques, as employed abroad and viewable in any TV street protest coverage such as, for example, the London street protests during the recent prime ministerial meetings in the wake of the US-led financial crisis. Experience suggests that publicized images of incompetence, negligence, instability and inefficiency in times of adversity, can exacerbate and/or prolong crisis conditions.

Thus, preparedness will not only minimize human and material losses, it will also go a long way in limiting potential public relations damages. There are, of course, countries whose governments are well prepared for crisis or disasters. This is, for example, the case of Japan where preparedness to the irregular occurrence of earthquakes is monitored by various departments of the Japanese government that ensures that citizens of all ages and organizations are thoroughly prepared for these disasters. To that end, disaster plans are regularly practiced so that when a disaster occurs, every citizen will know instinctively how to respond and recovery time will be minimized, reducing thereby the likelihood of an ensuing crisis. Another such example, one closer to home, is that of Phuket where, two years after the tsunami had hit the island, an evacuation drill simulating that required of a tsunami was held. No preparedness drills, however, have since been publicized probably for fear of alarming tourists. In Phuket, as in some other tourist destinations, regular drills have proven to be successful in reducing the impact of disasters and mitigating ensuing crises. This is particularly true in the case of massive and devastating earthquakes such as that which occurred in Kobe on 17th January 1995. Basing his findings on the widely acknowledged work by Fink (1986), Keown-McMullan (1997) and Weiner and Kahn (1972), and further refining their crisis management theory, Faulkner (2001) identified the following key crisis management characteristics (Figure 11.1):

1. A triggering event, which is so significant that it challenges the existing structure, routine operations or survival of the destination.
2. The situation becomes characterized by fluid, unstable, dynamic situations (Fink, 1986).
3. The managerial environment is one of high threat, short decision time and includes elements of surprise and urgency.
4. There is an element of inability to cope among those directly affected.
5. A turning point when decisive changes, which may have both positive and negative connotations, are imminent (Prideaux, Laws and Faulkner, 2003).

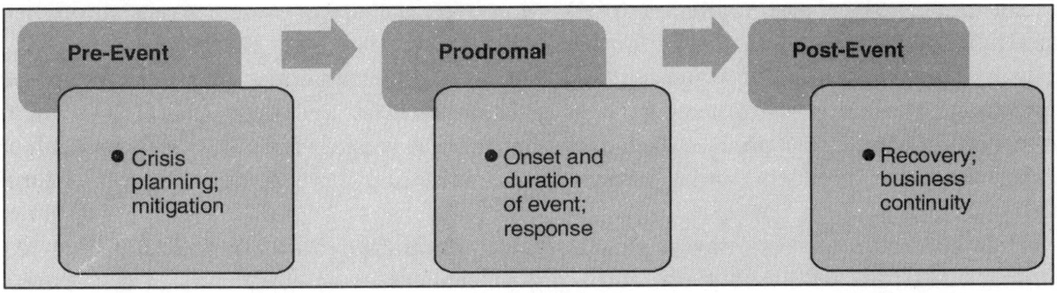

FIGURE 11.1 Stages of natural hazards or disaster management.

Source: Booth (1993), Faulkner (2001) and Mileti (1999).

In this list, two of the six elements of the Political, Economic, Sociological, Technological, Legal and Environmental model (PESTLE), a model often used in Strategic Management and useful to managers in organizations seeks to identify solutions to complex problems through identifying the multiple factors at play in a given situation and where resources fall short of requirements to address the problem at hand. Concomitant to the problem of the level of preparedness of a tourist destination to a crisis/disaster is that of its level of severity.

The World Tourism Organization (1998) has defined a tourism crisis as any unexpected event that affects traveller confidence in a destination and interferes with its ability to continue operating normally. Sonmez (1998) defined a tourism crisis as any occurrence which can threaten the normal operations and conduct of tourism related businesses, damage a tourist destination's overall reputation for safety, attractiveness and comfort by negatively affecting visitors perceptions of that destination and, interrupt the continuity of business operations for the local travel and tourism industry, by the reduction in tourist arrivals and expenditures. Beirman (2003) defined a destination crisis in the following terms: a crisis is a situation requiring radical management action in response to events beyond the internal control of the destination, necessitating urgent adaptation of marketing and operational practices to restore the confidence of employees, associated enterprises and consumers in the viability of the destination. Glaesser (2005) saw a crisis as an undesired, extraordinary, often unexpected and timely limited process with ambivalent development possibilities. It demands immediate decisions and countermeasures in order to influence the further development again positively for the organization/destination and to limit the negative consequences as much as possible. A crisis situation is determined by evaluating the seriousness of the occurring negative events, which threaten, weaken or destroy competitive advantages or important goals of an organization/a destination.

The concept of tourism destination is critical to understand the uniqueness of the process of building destination functionality. A tourism destination can be characterized in different ways. As first perspective on tourism destination is the understanding of it as a physical space in which tourism takes place. From this viewpoint, the tourist is an active participant in the production of tourism spaces and actively acts on them and interacts with them with the consequence that tourists' practices contribute to the ways in which places are constituted (Shaw and Williams, 2004). Moreover, a tourism system exists through the interactions of different elements. In this sense, a tourism destination can be recognized as an amalgam of products, facilities and services that all together comprise the travel experience. Thus, the destination is just a part of the tourist product (Middleton and Clarke, 2001) and is not to be considered as a product itself but simply as 'a geographical area within which any number of tourism products can be purchased and consumed (French, Colier and Crag-Smith, 2000).

Symbols and images play a fundamental role in the destination building process (Beriman, 2003; Pike, 2002) but also add a further element to the complexity of the definition of the destination. Physical space and physical attractions are just elements of the destination that the tourists interpret and combine in their mental world (Franzen and Bouwman, 2001). Along this way, bringing together the complexity of the various elements that build the destination, Bodlender et al. (1991) provide a definition of destination as a collection of physical and service features together with symbolic associations which are expected to fulfil the needs of the buyer. Tourism destinations are also spaces of leisure for the guests and space of work or home for the hosts (Methan, 2001). The different use of the tourist space and the co-existence between hosts and guests lead some authors to consider tourists as intruders in the space of the host community (McLaren, 1998). Others look at the amenities of a tourism destination as serving the residents and the working population on a permanent basis while also providing service to tourists (Burkart and Medlik, 1974).

Tourism and the vast travel industry that has grown up to facilitate it are particularly prone to external shocks beyond the control of its managers. Internal corporate shocks such as financial irregularities by contrast are also important to the industry. Arguably, however, these are not distinguishing characteristics of the industry, for as the events of Enron, Arthur Andersen, WorldCom and Parmalat have demonstrated they are prevalent in many industries where management have proved to be too ambitious, fraudulent or incompetent.

The travel industry, although not unique in its vulnerability, is nevertheless highly exposed to risks and prone to crises as the result of external events. Unlike internal events, which can be assessed and controlled by managers, external events are beyond their control and therefore inherently provide a greater degree of risk and uncertainty. Furthermore, the inherent characteristics of this service based industry (such as the perishability of the product and the interdependence of elements of the product) make the risks potentially very difficult to manage, because supply often cannot quickly be matched to rapid declines in demand (Evans et al., 2003).

External shocks, such as wars, hurricanes, terrorist attacks, pollution, adverse publicity and accidents, can have a dramatic and speedy effect upon levels of business in the travel industry. The external shocks can quickly develop into crises and indeed can be and should be viewed as a central concern of competent managers in the industry. Recent events such as the Bali bombing and '9/11' have clearly shown that terrorism in particular poses a major threat to the industry.

By their nature these events are unpredictable in relation to their geographical location, their timing and their scale and hence provide difficulties for industry managers in a number of ways. It is difficult to forecast such events in the first place and to foresee the full implications and the management steps that need to be taken can be complex at a strategic level but also in terms of effective implementation of management actions at an operational level. A brand, which may have been assiduously developed over many years, can be severely damaged or even destroyed by sudden events. For example, the Gulf War led to a severe downturn in travel and tourism in the early 1990s (which extended far beyond the Middle East location of the conflict), and the terrorist attacks in New York and Washington on 11 September 2001 had an immediate effect upon the industry.

Destination managers and tour operators, although not being able to plan directly for such events (because they are by definition not capable of being foreseen), nevertheless need to be able to assess the risks that the business is prone to and to have robust and clearly articulated contingency plans in place so that they are able to react quickly and effectively. One approach is to spread the risks so that one upset does not destroy the business entirely. Thus, a tour operator specializing in tours to only one country would be at risk if a war or environmental catastrophe were to occur there, but by operating to several countries the risks are spread and the overall risk is reduced. Such spreading of risks, however, is not always possible and may conflict with other commercial imperatives that require specialization and focus.

Crises within tourism and hospitality must be handled with particular care for a number of reasons: firstly, the majority of the industry relies on discretionary expenditure by the consumer. This means that tourism and hospitality organizations are particularly sensitive to ill-will, since the purchase of the product or service is not fundamentally important to the consumers and they can (relatively) easily go without. The marketing of tourism products and services depends largely on the perception the tourist holds about the destination and the degree of risk he/she is willing to bear. The higher the perceived risk, insecurity and uncertainty regarding a tourist destination, the lower the demand for it. Therefore, any element that contributes to an increase in the perceived risk in using a tourism product or service will negatively affect the consumer's purchasing behaviour. This consequence also applies to generic business crises (Gondlez-Hmero and Pratt, 1998).

Often, large numbers of people have a vested interest in the health of the local tourism industry. Stakeholders and the local economy depend on outsiders' perceptions of the community. For this reason, it is highly unfortunate that tourism crises receive wide publicity because tourism centres are, by definition, places with high visibility. Regardless of whether tourism crises are triggered by natural or human-caused disasters, travellers will shy away from afflicted areas. Consequently, the local tourism industry will suffer from a lag-effect, in which a negative image caused by the disaster may well outlive physical damages and the tourism community/industry will have to find ways to manage the disaster's after-effects. This, in turn, may cause an economic downturn that is as harmful to a destination's tourism sustainability as the initial disaster. Tourism crises triggered by terrorism are likely to be different from those caused by natural disasters. Although terrorism has been a political tool since early history, modern-day terrorism began in the later part of this century.

International terrorism increased rapidly during the late 1960s and the early 1970s. After a brief lull in activity, the 1980s began and ended with terrorist violence. By the end of the decade, terrorism had become commonplace (D'Amore and Anuza, 1986; Richter and Waugh, 1986). Fewer terrorist incidents in the United States have been recorded for the first half of the 1990s; however, their nature and magnitude are more severe than those of past years' events. Experts indicate that terrorism will continue to victimize "soft" targets; attacks will become more indiscriminate, terrorism will become institutionalized as a method of armed conflict, it will spread geographically, and the public will witness more terrorism than ever due to the media's improved ability to cover terrorist incidents (Atkinson, Sandler, and Tschirhart, 1987; Jenkins, 1988).

The tourism industry is highly vulnerable to natural (i.e., hurricanes, volcanic eruptions, torrential rains) and human-caused disasters—whether social or political (i.e., riots, insurgency, terrorism, crime, political upheaval, war, regional tensions). Regardless of their nature, disasters create difficult, often tragic, situations for the afflicted area and its residents. Over the years, media coverage of disasters has conveyed the resulting loss of life, human suffering, public and private property damage, and economic and social disruption. The ensuing negative publicity often characterizes the period after a disaster occurrence that lasts until full recovery is achieved and pre-disaster conditions resume. For a tourist destination, this period can represent a tourism crisis, which can threaten the normal operation and conduct of tourism-related businesses; damage a tourist destination's overall reputation for safety, attractiveness, and comfort by negatively affecting visitors' "perceptions of that destination; and, in turn, cause a downturn in the local travel and tourism economy, and interrupt the continuity of business operations for the local travel and tourism industry, by the reduction in tourist arrivals and expenditures (Sonmez, Backman, and Allen, 1994). Although the repercussions of a tourism crisis are likely to damage all destinations, the period of recovery can vary for each.

11.3 REVIEW OF LITERATURE

A crisis is a self-inflicted situation caused by inept management practices or an inability to adapt to a changing environment (Faulkner, 1999). A disaster, on the other hand, is a sudden catastrophic event over which the DMO has little or no control. In the emerging literature on destination disaster management, there have been a number of very useful cases about DMO responses to a wide range of disasters such as cyclones (Faulkner and Vikulov, 2001), Foot and Mouth disease (Frisby, 2002), bush fires (Christine, 1995), travel advisories (Beirman 2003), war (Mansfield, 1999), violence (Leslie, 1999) and terrorism (Hopper, 2002), while destinations in decline have also been mentioned in the literature, including Hamm (Buckley & Witt, 1985), Majorca (Morgan, 1991) and Canada (Go, 1987). However, little has been reported about attempts by a destination to recover from such a management crisis. A number of authors have concentrated their efforts on investigations which tend to focus on tourism, crisis management and recovery marketing. Gonzalez-Herrero, A. and Pratt, C., (1998) "Preventive marketing for crisis communications in tourism: Management strategies in the USA and Spain", conducted a comparative study of systematic sample of public relations, communication and marketing directors of tourism organizations in both the USA and Spain and have identified the types and the numbers of crisis that these organizations experienced from 1992 to 1994.

The study by Sonmez, S. and A.R. Graefe (1998) explores the relationship between selective sectors and several key stages of vacation tourism decision-making process. Another study by Sonmez, S., Apostolopoulos, Y. and P. Tarlow (1999) investigates the tourism crisis and explains how to manage the effects of terrorism. They argue that tourists destination—especially those vulnerable to political motivated violence—should incorporate crisis management planning into their overall sustainable development and marketing/ management to protect and rebuild their image of safety/attractiveness. Ioannides, D. and Apostolopoulos, Y. (1999) examine the divergent fortunes of the tourist industry on the divided island of Cyprus and discuss the prospects for crisis management and recovery. The study by David Beirman (2002) outlines the strategy for the Israeli tourism industry, and destination marketing management of a prolonged crisis is a core issue in this study. Lisa T. Fall (2004) examines the 11th September terrorist attacks on the USA that had greatly impacted the tourism industry, causing managers to restrategise their communication programmes. This national investigation illustrates the increasing role of public relations as a crisis management function. The study sought to determine if public relations activities are increasing and advertising activities are decreasing among tourism managers in the wake of 9/11. Gui Santana (2003) discusses the concept of crisis management and its relevance to tourism. It presents an overview of the general trends in tourism crises events of the last two decades, assesses the impacts of major man-made crises on the industry, and argues for the importance of crisis management in tourism management. The study also discusses the complex issue of crisis definition and its implications for organizations, and provides an operational definition of crisis management. Critical issues in crisis management, such as crisis anatomy, crisis incubation, risk perception in tourism and destination image, are discussed. Finally, the study explores and analyses, in the context of crisis anatomy, the public sector handling of a major resort pollution crisis in Southern Brazil. Once a destination experiences a political crisis, there is a tendency for a crisis mind-set to set in. Usually adaptive strategies are adopted which do not seek to change anything, but rather focus on the core of the tourism business, chart alternative action while the going is good and deck when the storm hits. In reality, a political crisis can denote two things: danger or an opportunity. It is prudent to adopt the later approach.

11.4 DISCUSSION

11.4.1 Framework for Crisis Management—A Case Study of Jammu and Kashmir

Crisis management in the contemporary geo-political environment is the competence of individuals and organizations to formulate such alternate options which meet the often conflicting and competing interest of the different stakeholders. This is expected to mitigate the catastrophic consequences of conflict and violence perpetuated by political and ideological sweep, being witnessed in Jammu and Kashmir. Recent events of turmoil and violence being witnessed in the state have resulted in civilian killings, abductions, rapes, forced migration, child and women trafficking, ethnic cleansing, armed insurgency, terrorism. In fact, human suffering, especially for women and children, has been cataclysmic. Consistent with the overall philosophy of managing a crisis with pragmatism is therefore the need of the hour. The situation is still alarming and sparks flames in South Asia geo-political heartland majorly because of reminiscent historical incidents.

The recent decades have proved challenging for classical destinations due to the emergence and escalation of a wide variety of violent conflicts around the globe. Regardless of the motives, violent conflicts prove disastrous in all aspects—political, socio-cultural and economic. Studies from conflict-affected areas show that the economic reconstruction contributes positively to long-term political harmony. Development process should continue even during the conflict situation and the pace of development can be increased with peace attempts bringing fruits. Necessity of this is basically due to four reasons: minimize the cost of the conflict; to provide means of survival to the people; to gradually defuse violent situations as, among many other things, poverty and under-development fuel violence in conflict situations; and to avoid the probability of a development vacuum in the post-conflict situation to minimize the chances of conflict revival. Increasing globalization, trans-border exchanges and popular acceptance of democratic means for conflict resolution are added fruitfully to this discourse. And Jammu and Kashmir is no exception to this. This emerging scenario appropriately fits into the discourse on Jammu and Kashmir conflict that is quite complex. This conflict is pronounced as one of the most complicated situations wherein on the one side two nuclear powers are involved and on the other side the people of the Jammu and Kashmir, developing constant alienation. The current scenario in Jammu and Kashmir, taking into account its recently gained peace capital, can be utilized to stimulate development in the region with the help of private investors, voluntary organizations and international donors. The ongoing peace process has created a space in which both peace moves and development activities can go simultaneously. The development of the region can act as a deterrent against violence since violence has not only affected development of the state but also has brought innumerable losses for both India and Pakistan and the people of Jammu and Kashmir. In the era of globalization when political issues are guided by the economic imperatives, it is necessary to bring the same realization into Jammu and Kashmir. This would likely steer the ongoing peace process further and help realize a peaceful solution of the crisis.

Tourism industry in Jammu and Kashmir underwent a colossal slow down as it had been badly affected by politically motivated violence especially during the last two decades. In spite of the fact, it being referred as "paradise on the earth" which has rich, interesting and a great wealth of geographical, anthropological, historical and cultural tourist attractions. In fact, Jammu and Kashmir is to Himalayas, what Switzerland is to Alps. "Kashmir only Kashmir" were the last words uttered by one of the most majestic Mughal Emperors—Jehangir. Its long and rich history includes a proud intellectual heritage, which is even admitted by Pt. Jawahar Lal Nehru, who said that Kashmir has been one of the biggest seats of Indian culture and learning throughout history. All these resources together make Jammu and Kashmir as an ideal tourist destination that has an inherent strength and huge potential to attract almost every type of tourist. Jammu and Kashmir, despite gaining popularity as a major tourist destination, the last two decades have hindered the smooth growth of tourism industry because of the spread of the militancy, which has discouraged travellers for visiting India's most beautiful tourist destination.

However, this paper specifically argues that tourist destinations—particularly those prone to politically induced violence—should induct crisis communication planning into their overall sustainable development and marketing/management strategies to protect and remodel their image of well-being/attractiveness, to re-establish confidence in prospective visitors of the security of the area, to restore the area's functionality/attractiveness, and to support local travel and tourism industry members in their economic recovery. This paper deliberates on having a crisis management framework in place, institutionalizing a tourism crisis management task force, building a crisis management manual and collaborating with law enforcement agencies in order to rebuild the destination functionality of Jammu and Kashmir.

Faulkner (2001) proposes a tourism destination framework (Figure 1.2) in response to the scant amount of research in tourism management regarding disasters and their impact and little theoretical grounding.

According to Sonmez, S., Apostolopoulos, Y., and P. Tarlow (1999), despite this growing body of research on disasters and crises, there is little published on destination recovery. Numerous disaster management frameworks and theories have been proposed (Faulkner, 2001; Faulkner & Vikulov, 2001; Murphy & Bayley, 1989; Pearson & Mitroff, 1993; Ritchie, 2004; Santana, 1999) but the attention devoted to the recovery phase is often limited. Most studies that have addressed recovery do so by considering short or medium term actions and no published research has been found that has considered the medium to long-term aspects of destination recovery. Similarly, there has been little research on building or testing destination recovery models although overall disaster management models and frameworks based on theory and/or real life have been developed.

Tourist destinations, especially those where economic viability depends mainly on tourism as holds true of Jammu and Kashmir where most of the population is directly or indirectly dependent on tourism, have little choice but to implement crisis management

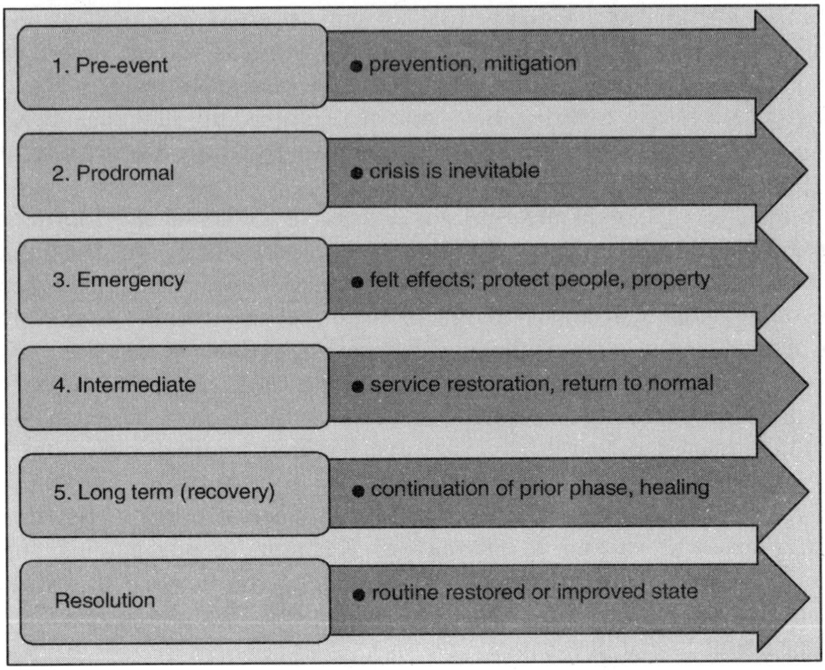

FIGURE 11.2 Tourism destination management framework (Faulkner, 2001).

strategies to deal with crisis especially political and social unrest at times being manifested as terroristic violence. Unless political terrorism is viewed as a crisis by the tourism industry in Jammu and Kashmir, energy and resources cannot be effectively channeled into its management. It is imperative for Jammu and Kashmir to augment its crisis management plans with marketing efforts, to recover lost tourism by rebuilding a positive image. There are surprisingly few sources for the tourism industry in Jammu and Kashmir to turn to for guidance on crisis management. Even more difficult is finding crisis management strategies tailored for political violence. Ideas can be gleaned from tourism crisis management manuals geared for natural disasters (Sonmez, Backman, and Allen, 1994). General suggestions begin with destinations having a task force, development of a crisis management plan and guidebook (Sonmez, Backman, and Allen, 1994), and partnering with law enforcement agencies (Tarlow, 1998).

Once a situation is identified as a crisis and the crisis mindset is in place, the gravity of the situation is likely to assure discipline and dedication from the initiation of crisis management activities until full recovery is achieved. The following recommendations are intended to guide the initial stages of crisis management in Jammu and Kashmir. The state should tailor these suggestions to fit its own needs.

11.4.2 The Crisis Management Taskforce

Being prepared for crisis management must include the timely (pre-crisis) organization of a taskforce as referred in Figure 11.3. It is recommended that this group be composed of local

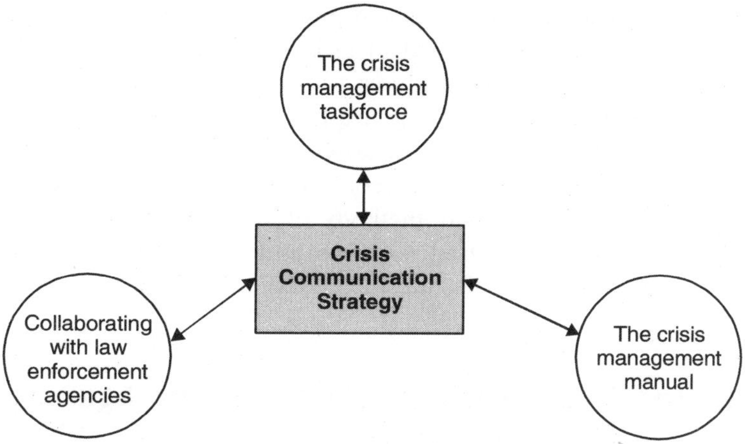

FIGURE 11.3 Framework for Crisis Management
Source: Sonmez, S., Apostolopoulos, Y. and P. Tarlow (1999)

government officials, local travel and tourism industry professionals, and community leaders in Jammu and Kashmir and be fully dedicated to achieving complete recovery. This crisis management taskforce can be developed as a special division of the primary tourism organization/agency in the state (i.e., tourism ministry/bureau, chamber of commerce, convention and visitors' bureau [CVB], industry association) and serve under a board of directors or executive committee with oversight authority. The group can be organized into teams according to delegated tasks, as follows: (1) a communication/public relations team headed by a qualified media spokesperson to represent the destination and local tourism industry to the media by providing a unified voice and conveying accurate information to prevent possible embellishment of the events by media members; (2) a marketing/promotion team to direct recovery marketing efforts including profiling the destination's past and potential visitors, tracking changes to destination image, developing appropriate messages to inform and attract visitors back to the destination; (3) an information coordination team to coordinate damage assessment activities and gather disaster-related information for accurate dissemination, to estimate the approximate period of recovery, and to convey recovery efforts to constituents; and (4) a finance/fund-raising team to track expenditures and conduct fund-raising activities to support crisis management efforts.

To ensure effectiveness and efficiency, the responsibility of heading each team should be delegated to individuals according to their areas of expertise and the entire group should be headed by a director to orchestrate all taskforce activities in Jammu and Kashmir.

11.4.3 The Crisis Management Manual

The development of a crisis management manual—also prior to any negative occurrences—detailing necessary actions is strongly recommended for Jammu and Kashmir. This document, which can serve as the only tangible guide at a time of distress and possible panic, can explain how to initiate taskforce activities, outline responsibilities for taskforce teams as well as team coordinators, suggest both pre-crisis and post-crisis actions in the form of a checklist, and detail various responsibilities delegated to taskforce members. Among other things, the plan should also detail by-laws of the taskforce to avoid confusion and disagreement among members, offer the proper use of terminology, explain how a tourism crisis differs from other crises, suggest how to orient law enforcement officials to tourism-specific crises, offer sample press kits/releases as well as a directory of contacts, suggest what to do or what to avoid during a press conference, recommend methods of developing and maintaining positive relationships with media members during no crisis times to ensure balance and accuracy of coverage during the crisis, and assist in identifying and communi-cating with various constituents.

11.4.4 Collaborating with Law Enforcement Agencies

Cooperation between the tourism industry and law enforcement is critical in Jammu and Kashmir. Although police departments are still struggling with issues of tourism policing, several destinations across the globe have started to create specific tourism policing divisions. Recently, police departments have begun to face the issue of tourism, crime, and security. Police officers receive training in how to interact with the tourism industry, how important tourism is to the local economy, and how necessary they are in aiding and protecting the industry (Tarlow, 1998). Tourism policing departments have been established in a number of destinations and a theory of tourism policing is slowly emerging. In being conditioned to consider tourists, police officers are trained to compare the needs of tourists to those of a popular form of policing, called community policing (CP). For example, part of CP is to know the community well in terms of its needs, customs, schedules, and social makeup. When CP is infused with tourism techniques, it means identifying the tourism markets/ segments, knowing tourism cycles/seasons, identifying needed services, and knowing the community's tourist attractions. Applying other CP principles to the tourism context also means communicating with tourists, understanding the importance of tourist perceptions, and accepting the role of tourism in the community's quality of life. The pivotal role law enforcement can play in managing crises and helping to restore public faith in the safety and normalcy of Jammu and Kashmir should not be underestimated.

The enormity of the task at hand necessitates cooperation from a variety of experts in developing pragmatic solutions for Jammu and Kashmir. It would be naive to believe that the suggestions made in this article could lead to a much needed crisis management model—one that would be applicable to Jammu and Kashmir in all the circumstances. For this reason, the authors challenge tourism scholars to search for truly effective solutions in dealing with tourism crises resulting from state and non-state terrorism and political turmoil in Jammu and Kashmir—possibly by organizing a national consortium to develop the needed model.

11.5 SUMMARY AND CONCLUSION

Although understanding the nature of crisis is important, understanding how to manage crisis is more critical. In particular, managing communication and perceptions through a crisis communication strategy can limit the negative media coverage and manage perceptions both during a crisis or disaster and at the recovery/resolution stage. Crisis communication and marketing is important to provide information to key publics and to help Jammu and Kashmir limit the impact of a crisis as well as help to recover from incidents by safeguarding its image and reputation which is of immense value to its competitiveness. The development of crisis communication and marketing strategies is therefore a critical competency for tourism managers in Jammu and Kashmir

Acknowledging the permanence of political terrorism and regional problems is a requisite to managing them. This is pertinent not only for Jammu and Kashmir government afflicted with political disturbances and tourist-generating nations but also for the international tourism industry. When the tourism industry experiences negative events caused by natural disasters, greater public and industry understanding and tolerance are invoked. But, human-caused events, especially those involving political violence, trigger public outrage or intimidation. Although the problem at hand is exceptionally complex, the hope for effective and applicable solutions lies in additional research and cooperative efforts of practitioners, government agencies, and academicians. It is high time for the academic community and tourism industry in Jammu and Kashmir to view these problems as crises in need of management rather than periodic problems. Clearly, a tourism crisis can begin after a disaster of some type (i.e., terrorist attack) occurs and can continue to escalate with negative media coverage and ruined image, as visitation and expenditures plummet—possibly destroying the profitability of a tourism community (Sonmez, Backman, and Allen, 1994; Tarlow, 1998;). If predictions hold true, political terrorism can be expected to continue, meaning that either tourism officials must develop a proactive stance or they will be forced to react on a piecemeal basis. Few nations around the world afflicted with political turmoil can afford to give up their tourism earnings. Instead, both governments and members of their tourism industries need to focus on the topic to assess risks to international travellers and strategize for effective crisis marketing (Hall and Sullivan, 1996).

Crisis management has its boundaries and is not intended to prevent actual disasters or focus on micromanagement (i.e., evacuation, rescue); having a plan in place can neither prevent random acts of violence nor aid in the capture of terrorists. Each crisis situation is unique and difficult to resolve with simple formulae; nevertheless, Jammu and Kashmir needs to be prepared with a plan of action. Having such a blueprint promises to save its valuable time, energy, and other resources. In light of societal and global complexities, no destination is immune to negative occurrences, thus adhering to an "it can't happen to us" philosophy can only be described as naive, if not reckless. It may be difficult, even impossible, to fully control political terrorism, but nations cannot ignore the problem either.

Greater research and understanding is required in the field of crisis communication and theory to help improve the understanding of such incidents. This understanding will hopefully aid the development of suitable crisis communication models for managers to implement which can be varied depending on the scale and type of crisis or disaster encountered. Faulkner's (2001) model is a useful start; however more research is needed into disaster phenomena and crisis communication in the tourism industry. The cost of developing a crisis management strategy would be far less than the cost of not having one and a key aspect to any crisis strategy is crisis communication. It is hoped this paper will contribute in some way to the field of crisis communication within the context of Jammu and Kashmir.

REFERENCES

Atkinson, S.E., Sandler, T. and Tschirhart, J. (1987). Terrorism in a Bargaining Framework. *Journal of Law and Economics*. 30(1):1–21.

Beirman, D. (2002). Marketing of Tourism Destinations during a Prolonged Crisis: Israel and the Middle East. *Journal of Vacation Marketing*, 8(2), 167–176.

_____ (2003). *Restoring Tourism Destinations in Crisis. A Strategic Marketing Approach*. Walligford. UK: CABI

Bodlender et al. (1991). *Developing Tourism Destinations. Policies and Perspectives*. Harlow, England: Longman.

Booth, S. (1993). *Crisis Management Strategy, Competition and Changes in Modern Enterprises*. London: Routledge.

Buckley, P.J. and Witt, S.F. (1985). Tourism in Difficult Areas: Case Studies of Bradford, Bristol, Glasgow and Hamm. *Tourism Management*. September: 205–213.

Burkart, A.J. and Medlik, S. (1974). *Tourism Past Present and Future*. London: Heinemann.

Christine, B. (1995). Disaster Management: Lessons Learned. *Risk Management*. October: 19–34.

D'Amore, L.J. and Anuza, T.E. (1986). International Terrorism, Implications and Challenge for Global Tourism. *Business Quarterly*. 4 (November) 20–29.

Evans et al. (2005). Models of Crisis Management: An Evaluation of their Value for Strategic Planning in the International Travel Industry. *International Journal of Tourism Research*, 7(3), 135–150.

Fall, L.T. (2004). The Increasing Role of Public Relations as a Crisis Management Function. An Empirical Examination of Communication Restrategising Efforts among Destination Organization Managers in the Wake of 11th September, 2001. *Journal of Vacation Marketing*, 10(3), 238–252.

Faulkner, B. (1999). *Tourism Disasters: Towards a Generic Model*. Gold Coast: CRC Sustainable Tourism.

_____ (2001). Towards a Framework for Tourism Disaster Management. *Tourism Management*. 22, 135–147.

Faulkner, B. and Vikulov, S. (2001). Katherine, Washed Out One Day, Back on Track the Next: A Post Mortem of a Tourism Disaster. *Tourism Management*, 22(4), 331–344.

Fink, S. (1986). Crisis Management: Planning for the Inevitable. *New York: American Association of Management*.

Franzen, G. and Bouwman, M. (2001). *The Mental World of Brands. Mind, Memory and Brand Success*. Henley-on-Thames: World Advertising Research Centre.

French, C.N., Collier, A. and Craig-Smith, S.J. (2000). *Principles of Tourism*. Sydney: Longman.

Frisby, E. (2002). Communicating in a Crisis: The British Tourist Authority's Responses to the Foot-and-Mouth. *Journal of Vacation Marketing*. 9(1): 89–100.

Glaesser, D. (2003). *Crisis Management in the Tourism Industry*. London: Butterworth Heinemann.

_____ (2005). *Crisis Management in the Tourism Industry*. Oxford Butterworth-Heinemann.

Go, F. (1987). Selling Canada. *Travel and Tourism Analyst*. Dec: 17–29.

Gondlez-Hmero, A. and Pratt, C. (1998). Communication Marketing Crises in Tourism. Strategies in the United States and Spain. *Public Relations Review*. 24(1), 83–97.

Hall, C.M. and Sullivan, V.O. (1996). Tourism, Political Stability and Violence. In *Tourism, Crime and International Security Issues*, edited by A. Pizam and Y. Mansfeld. New York. John Wiley, pp. 105–121.

Hopper, P. (2002). Marketing London in a Difficult Climate. *Journal of Vacation Marketing*. 9(1): 81–88.

Ioannides, D. and Apostolopoulos, Y. (1999). Political Instability, War, and Tourism in Cyprus: Effects, Management, and Prospects for Recovery. *Journal of Travel Research*, Vol. 38, No. 1, 51–56.

Jenkins, B.M. (1988). *Future Trends in International Terrorism*. In R.O. Slater, and M. Stohl (Eds.), *Current Perspectives on International Terrorism* (pp. 246–266). London: Macmillan.

Keown-Mcmullan, J. (1997). Crisis: When Does a Molehill become a Mountain? *Disaster Prevention and Management*. 6(1), 4–10.

Leslie, D. (1999). Terrorism and Tourism: The Northern Ireland Situation—A Look behind the Veil of Certainty. *Journal of Travel Research*. 38: 37–40.

Mansfield, Y. (1999). Cycles of War, Terror, and Peace: Determinants and Management of Crisis and Recovery of the Israeli Tourism Industry. *Journal of Travel Research*. 38: 30–36.

McLaren, D. (1998). *Rethinking Tourism and Ecotravel: The Paving of Paradise and What You can to stop it*. West Hartford, Conn. USA: Kumarian Press.

Meethan, K. (2001). *Tourism in Global Society. Place, Culture, Consumption*. Palgrave.

Middleton, V.T.C. and Clarke, J. (2001). *Marketing in Travel and Tourism* (3rd ed.). Oxford: Butterworth-Heinemann.

Morgan, M. (1991). Dressing Up to Survive-Marketing Majorca anew. *Tourism Management*. March: 15–20.

Murphy, P.E. and Bayley, R. (1989). Tourism and Disaster Planning. *Geographical Review*. 79(1), 36–46.

Pearson, C.M. and Clair, J.A. (1998). Reframing Crisis Management. *Academy of Management Review*, 23(1), 59–76.

Pearson, C.M. and Mitroff, I.I. (1993). *Crisis Management: A Diagnostic Guide for improving your Organization's Crisis-Preparedness*. San Francisco: Jossey-Bass.

Pike, S. (2002). *Positioning as a Source of Competitive Advantage—Benchmarking Rotorua's Position as a Domestic Short Break Holiday Destination*. University of Waikato.

Prideaux, B., Laws, E. and Faulkner, B. (2003). Events in Indonesia: Exploring the Limits to Formal Tourism Trends Forecasting Methods in Complex Crisis Situations. *Tourism Management*, 24, 475–487.

Quarantelli, E.L. (1984). Organisational Behaviour in Disasters and Implications for Disaster Planning , *Monographs of the National Emergency Training Centre*, Vol. 1, No. 2, 1–13.

Regester, M. and Larkin, J. (2002). Risk Issues and Crisis management: *A casebook*.

Ritchie, B.W. (2004). Chaos, Crises and Disasters: A Strategic Approach to Crisis Management in the Tourism Industry. *Tourism Management*, 25(6), 669–683.

Richter, L.K. and Waugh, Jr., W.L. (1986). *Terrorism and Tourism as Logical Companions.* Tourism Management, 7(4): 230–238.

Santana, G. (1999). Tourism: Towards A Model for Crisis Management. *Tourism Management,* 47(1), 4–12.

_____ (2003). Crisis Management and Tourism. Beyond the Rhetoric, *Journal of Travel and Tourism Marketing*, Vol. 15, pp. 299–321.

Shaw, G. and Williams, A.M. (2004). *Tourism and Tourism Spaces.* London. Thousand Oaks: SAGE.

Sonmez, S. (1998). Tourism, terrorism and political instability. *Annals of Tourism Research* 252: 416–445.

Sonmez, S., Apostolopoulos, Y. and Tarlow, P. (1999). Tourism in Crisis: Managing the Effects of Terrorism. *Journal of Travel Research.* 38(1) 13–18.

Sonmez, S. and Graefe, A.R. (1998). Influence of Terrorism Risk on Foreign Tourism Decisions. *Annals of Tourism Research,* 25, 112–144.

Sonmez, S.F., Backman, S.J. and Allen, L.R. (1994). *Managing Tourism Crises: A Guidebook.* Clemson, SC. Clemson University.

Tarlow, P. (1998). Keeping Tourists Safe, (Section 1) *Review Journal Las Vegas.* International Association of Community Police (IACP). *Tourism Recreation Research,* 15(2): 46–53.

Weiner, A.J. and Kahn, H. (1972). *Crisis and Arms Control in C.F. Hermann, International Crises: Insights from Behaviour Research.* New York, NY: The Free Press, p. 21.

World Tourism Organisation (1998). *Handbook on Natural Disaster Reduction in Tourist Areas.* Madrid: WTO.

CHAPTER

12

TRUST IN THE ONLINE HOTEL BOOKING DECISION

—PAULINE RATNASINGAM AND KULDEEP KUMAR

12.1 ABSTRACT

The focus of this chapter is to examine trust in the online hotel booking decision. We identify two entities in the trust dyad. First is the trusted party, the hotel whose role is that of a vendor and service provider and second is the trusting party, the customer or traveller who could be a potential guest staying at that hotel. We develop and present a simplified model for examining the role of the customer's trust relationship in the customer's online booking decision. The chapter addresses both the first or initial (pre-stay) booking decision and the subsequent repeat online booking decisions. We then identify the impact of three types of trust, namely, competence, predictability, and goodwill trust based on the customer's initial and subsequent booking decisions and factors that facilitate and are likely to change and impact the customer's online booking decision over time. We then develop a conceptual model to illustrate the impact of the customer's trust in the hotel that in turn impacts their online hotel booking decision. The model contributions to theory and provides insights for practical implications for the hotel industry, thereby promoting trust factors in order to attain their competitive and strategic advantages.

KEYWORDS: online hotel booking decisions, customer, competence trust, predictability trust, goodwill trust.

12.2 INTRODUCTION

Tourism is becoming a popular global leisure and business activity. The global hotels and motels industry revenue grew to $ 424.6 billion in 2009. In 2008, there were over 922 million international tourist arrivals, with a growth rate of 1.9% as compared to 2007. This was evidenced by the San Diego County which was among the markets riding a significant increase in hotel property sales transactions (Hirsch, 2010). Similarly, the US Bureau of Labour Statistics (BLS) has forecast strong employment growth in the American sector between 2004 and 2014. Further, according to the World Tourism Organization (UNWTO), international arrivals are expected to surpass 1.5 billion people by the year 2020.

The steady growth in tourism has not only increased the occupancy rate in hotels and resorts, as customers travel both inside the nation and internationally, but has also created intense competition in the hotel industry for ways to attract and retain customers. In today's internet era, tourists always compare different hotels for their rates, quality, services, facilities, reviews and information available on their website (Goodrich, 1997). The growth of the service industry has also switched from competition over quality of service to a competition creating memorable experiences for consumers. Online hotel reservations include reservations that are made by customers directly online, or are based upon customers accessing information online that is provided by the hotel or its agents (such as travel agents, travel portals or tour operators). Further, with a steady increase in customers using search engines, social media technology and independent travel blogs to obtain information about the hotel has encouraged and motivated customers to book their hotels to stay online. By examining the hotel's online (web) presence, the customer can now search for, select and book hotel stays online. Initially, before the first visit, the customer would make the first reservation decision without physically visiting the property. Consequently, the customer, in making his booking decision, has to rely on the information provided on the website and other information available from secondary or third party sources. Therefore, in such situations the customer is taking the risk and is vulnerable prior to confirming the payment as to whether he has made a correct choice. Hotels often display three-dimensional images of their hotel rooms and other facilities (such as the lobby, restaurants, shopping lots, gym, swimming pool, ballroom, etc.) even before the customer stays in his hotel. This motivates the customer to form an initial trust in the hotel, thereby facilitating the reservation decision online. Thus, it is important that customers trust the information presented to them by the hotel website. According to Morais and Lin (2010), hotel managers face challenges in convincing potential customers to choose their specific hotel over an increasing number of alternatives available either online or through other channels.

This chapter is limited to examining the customer's trust in the hotelier, as mediated through the hotel's website, online transactions, and later via actual stays at the hotel. The objective of this chapter is to develop and present a simplified model for examining the *role of trust* in the customer's *online hotel booking decisions*. By examining this objective, we aim to address the following research question: *How does the customer's trust in the hotel influence their online booking decision?*

The potential benefits of this study, both for the hotel industry executives and researchers in hospitality and tourism management, are discussed. The chapter addresses both the first or initial (pre-stay) booking decision and the subsequent repeat online booking decisions. The chapter starts out by first examining three parts of the customers' initial (pre-stay) hotel online booking decision, and subsequent online booking decisions that may be affected by the existence, confirmation, disconfirmation, or lack of trust. It then identifies the entities in a trusting relationship, followed by the three types of trust derived from the attributes that facilitate the customer's trust in the hotel, leading to a conceptual model and research hypotheses. Further, we discuss how these types of trust are likely to change and impact the customer's online booking decisions over time. It also provides a "learning" conceptualization of changes in trust levels as the customer's experiences with the particular hotel property increases over time. The chapter contributes to theory in the online hotel booking decision by incorporating the concept of trust the customer's has in the hotel that, in turn, influences their online hotel decisions. We believe that this study will provide insights for practical implications as it increases the awareness of hoteliers on the factors to increase their trustworthiness and in an effort to remain competitive by increasing and retaining their hotel's occupancy rate thereby meeting their strategic objectives.

12.2.1 Three Parts of the Online Booking Decision Making

The customer needs to trust the hotel during three parts of the online booking decision. First, the customer needs to rely on the information provided by the hotel's website and associated third-party information resources. Second, while making the reservation, the customer needs to have trust in the security of booking transaction. The customer needs to trust that the transaction information provided by the hotel and transmitted online to the hotel's reservation site will be secure during transmittal, especially with regard to the customer's personal information and credit card information, where the customer is vulnerable about his private personal information. Third, the customer has to trust that the reservation site has received and confirmed the booking, and the customer will receive some sort of acknowledgement or confirmation, thus further ensuring the hotel's promises to actually honour the reservation when the customer arrives at the hotel to claim the reservation. Thus, trust in the input, process and output activities impact the customer's trust in their hotel booking decisions. The actual honouring of the booking is not part of the booking decision but we believe that its anticipation would complete and conclude the customer's online booking decisions in a positive manner.

12.2.2 Entities in the Trusting Relationship

We identify two entities of trust in this chapter. First is the hotel whose role is that of a vendor and service provider. The hotel needs to present a trustworthy image on the web by providing accurate information, quality of services, such as functionality of the hotel's website, efficiently processing online bookings, reliably and promptly sending out acknowledgements, and subsequently providing services that are consistent with the website's promises, such as providing efficient check-ins, serving meals on time, providing a clean room, clean towels, etc. (Zeithaml 1998, p. 3) defined perceived service quality as *the consumer's subjective judgment about a product's overall excellence or superiority.* Quality is regarded as a key strategic component of competitive advantage and therefore the enhancement of service quality has been a matter of concern to hotels. Further, Dibb and Chen (2010) suggest the importance of the website's image and interface in influencing the customers' online behaviour. Website image and interface to quality features included features such as; web site usability (functionality), security and privacy assurance, quality of information, and speed of download. The promise that the hotelier will provide the above services may either be explicitly stated on the web, or implicitly in the website descriptions. Similarly, website usability included: ease of navigation and the various design features that customers experience when gathering information and proceeding with their online hotel booking decision. The customer then experiences the hotel's actual service once they arrive and stay at that hotel.

The second entity to the trusting relationship is the customer/traveler who is the guest at the hotel. The hotelier will need to trust the customer in that they will make their payment, keep the place clean, check in and check out according to the proper times, abide by the hotel's policy, and when satisfied will recommend the hotel to other customers. This chapter focuses on the unidirectional trust that is limited to examining the customer's trust in the hotel, as mediated through their website, online transactions, and later by the actual experience of the customer once they have completed their stay at the hotel. The hotel's trust in the customer will be the subject of a subsequent article.

12.2.3 Trust in the Hotel Industry

Lee and Back (2010) discussed the challenges customers had to face in the past when applying to traditional ways of booking a hotel. Researching about hotels and hotel selection by customers was a tedious process that relied almost exclusively on traditional channels including travel agents, word-of-mouth, broadcast media like television and printed media in the form of brochures and pamphlets. In addition, the potential customers had to telephone or write to the hotel or visit a physical travel agent in order to gather more information about the room availability and room rates. There were challenges in identifying hotels that were well-maintained and provided a comfortable environment to stay.

Alternatively, the growth of the Internet has provided many platforms for free exchanges of ideas and information, such as advertising content, and factual information about the hotels as well as feedback from past guests on forums and hotel review websites. The Traveller's Road to Decision study, conducted on behalf of Google, found that 41% of the customers surveyed made leisure travel plans and 50% made business travel plans. Further, social media networking sites promoted transparency, honesty and gave customers an opportunity to build trust. Thus, the online customers today are empowered to make informed decisions about hotel bookings. Customers can now place their booking directly on online reservation websites without much hassle, thus freeing them with more time to prepare for their trip. Further, they can enjoy cost savings by searching for, comparing different hotel websites, and identifying the best deals that will meet their requirements. However, despite the fact that the Internet provides information accessibility and availability, we posit that the customer's trust in the hotel's website is a key determining factor in their booking decisions. The input, process and outcome dimensions involved in the hotel booking tasks form the main basis of our conceptual model.

Trust is defined as *the willingness of a party to be vulnerable to the actions of another party based on the expectation that the other will perform a particular action important to the trustor, irrespective of the ability to monitor or control that other party* (Mayer, Davis and

Schoorman, 1995). Mishra (1996) defines trust as a party's willingness to be vulnerable to another party, based on the belief that the latter party is (a) competent, (b) open, (c) concerned, and (d) reliable. In the case of online hotel reservations, the customers are making themselves vulnerable to the actions (accommodations and service provision) of the hoteliers, based upon the expectation that the hotelier will provide the service as promised on the website. This expectation is based on the trust the customer has on the hotel's website, such as the functionality of the website, information accuracy, hotel rates, and services it claims to provide. Garbarion and Johnson (1999) define trust as customer confidence in the quantity and reliability of the services offered by the organization. Moorman, Zaltman and Deshpande (1993) define trust as the willingness to rely on an exchange partner with whom one has confidence. Therefore, trust has been viewed as (a) a belief, sentiment, or expectation; and as (b) a behavioural intention that reflects reliance on firms and involves vulnerability and uncertainty on the part of the trustor. We adapted the definitions of trust from previous research and define customer's trust in the online hotel booking decision as *the willingness of the customer to be vulnerable to the actions of the hotelier in their online hotel booking decision process, based on the expectations that the hotel will behave in certain agreeable ways, irrespective of the customer's ability to monitor or control the hotel.* We argue that trust is especially important under conditions of uncertainty and risks, which is relevant in the online hotel booking decision process.

12.2.4 Types of Trust

There are many sources of learning and in order to understand the pre-stay dimensions of the online hotel booking decision, we need to consider the creation of trust as a "learning" experience. Learning about the hotel can be derived from: documents and books; learning from others; transferring learning from one situation to another similar situation; and learning from personal experiences (Akhtar and Khan, 2011). Thus, the sources of customer's trust in the hotel can be derived from: learning about the hotel accommodations from documents (websites and travel guides); learning from others (customers' reviews and reputation of the hotel as expressed either through the social media technology or by word-of-mouth); and trust transference from stays at other hotels in the same chain (e.g. if one has stayed at a "Oberai" hotel in Thailand, he/she may transfer that expectation or experience to "Oberai Hotels" in New York); and learning from professional travel reviewers. Therefore, the initial booking decision depends on the following sources of knowledge, namely, the website content itself; reviews of the hotel property from travel guides (e.g. Trip Advisor, Fodors, Frommers, Lonely planet); finding out if the hotel is part of a chain, then confirming the customer's previous experience with other hotels in the chain; and finally the hotel's brand reputation. We add another source of information; the customer him/herself. After their first stay, the customer's experience with the hotel continues to increase with time, as each physical stay at the hotel adds to their experience of staying, and their knowledge about the hotel. Along with the time dimension (and customers' experience dimension), and the sources of information/ knowledge the customer's trust in the hotel is determined by these factors. Previous research on trust identified three attributes, namely: *ability, integrity and benevolence* (Mayer et al., 1995; and Lee and Turban, 2001). During the initial and subsequent interactions, the customer is able to experience the behaviour of the hotel's staff, and in the actual fulfillment of their promises. When expectations are not met, this affects the level of the customer's trust negatively. Thus, we conceptualize the trust-building process as a knowledge-acquisition or learning process.

Previous research on trust in e-commerce identified three types of trust: trust in their ability, competence of the supplier; trust in the reliability/integrity or predictability of the supplier; and trust in the goodwill of the supplier towards their customers (Ratnasingam, 2008). Previous research also examined the extent to which one supplier organization's products meet the quality needs of the buying organization, and the buying organization no longer inspects those products before accepting delivery, shows greater trust in the supplier organization's competence (Sako and Helper, 1998; Dyer and Chu, 2000). We adapt these three types of trust in the context of the customer's online booking decision and indicate the attributes that contribute to three types of trust as illustrated in Table 12.1.

Table 12.1 Three types of trust and its attributes

Types of trust	*Attributes of trust*	*Author*
Competence	Ability	Dyer and Chu (2000)
	Competence	Gabarro (1987)
	Reliable and accurate information	Mayer, Davis and Schoorman (1995)
		Mishra (1996)
		Sako and Helper (1998)
		Zucker (1986)
Predictability	Credibility	Dyer and Chu (2000)
	Consistency	Gabarro (1987)
	Integrity	Lewicki and Bunker (1996)
	Predictability	Mayer, Davis and Schoorman (1995)
	Judgment	McAllister (1995)
		Mishra (1996)
		Sako and Helper (1998)
		Zaheer et al. (1998)
		Zucker (1986)
Goodwill	Benevolence	Barney and Hansen (1994)
	Openness	Doney and Cannon (1997)
	Care	Dyer and Chu (2000)
	Concern	Lewicki and Bunker (1996)
	Commitment	Mayer, Davis and Schoorman (1995)
	Goodwill	
	Reputation	Mishra (1996)
	Motives/intentions	Sako and Helper (1998)
	Identification	Zucker (1986)

Based on the above discussions on the three types of trust, we developed a simplified conceptual model to illustrate the impact of the customer's trust on their online hotel booking decisions and discuss the research hypotheses. Figure 12.1, illustrates the model of trust and its impact on the customer's online hotel booking decision.

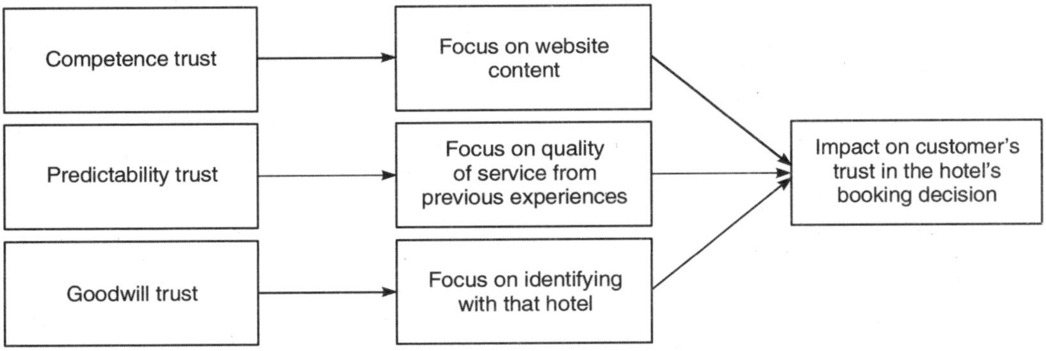

FIGURE 12.1 Model of trust and its impact on the customer's online hotel booking decision.

Competence trust is the trust the customer has in the hotel's ability to provide the necessary IT infrastructure web content, infrastructure, skills, knowledge, and competence of the hotel to provide the expected services to fulfil the customer's order in completing their online hotel booking process. Initially, the customer believes that the hotelier, through its infrastructure, staff and skills is competent and can be relied in providing the service promised by the hotelier. This trust is based upon two sources: first, the customer's examination of the quality of the hotel's website content, its functionality, transaction processing efficiency, and the reliability of the information about the hotel; second, customer's trust in third-party customer and travel-advisory reviews available on the web. The hotel's brand name and reputation can also add to the customer's trust in the hotel's competence in providing accurate and relevant information. Before the first visit, the customer will not have any personal prior experience with that particular hotel property. However, websites, provided both by the hotel, or by third parties such as *Tripadvisor* or travel guides such as *Frommers, Fodors,* or *Lonely Planet* may provide positive reviews of experiences by other customers. Therefore, customers evaluate their online booking experiences in terms of perceptions regarding hotel information, form of payment, hotel booking terms, services offered, risks involved, privacy, security, personalization, visual appeal, navigation, recreation and entertainment (Zeithaml et al., 1996).

Customers examine the quality of the hotel's website, that is: the website usability, ease of navigation, various design features, the brand name, image of the hotel, its functionality, transaction processing efficiency, and how accurate, relevant, reliable and current is the information displayed on the website. When the information displayed on the hotel's website seems reliable, the customer's competence trust in the hotel increases as the hotel's website exhibits clarity (as in giving clear directions and information on the process involved in undertaking an online booking), consistency, accuracy, and reliability in the information in their website. Further, information of the hotel's policies on booking a room online and security measures adapted by a hotel is provided. All of these features encourage the customer's confidence that their private personal information will not be misused, hacked or exposed. The customer who is booking the hotel online for the first time will rely on the information provided by the hotel's website, in addition to any reviews and recommendations by others (other previous guests, travel writers, etc.) that are linked to or available in the hotel's website. These positive reviews are similar to book or product reviews available on Amazon.com website. Competence trust, therefore, involves a formal, objective calculative process of business transactions. It focuses on the economic benefits derived from the hotel's ability and skills to provide accurate information about the hotel. There are benefits in savings of time and costs from the customer who decides to go ahead and reserve their hotel booking on an effective website. Therefore, we derive at research hypothesis 1 as:

Competence trust is positively associated with the customer's online booking decision.

Predictability trust is the trust in the customer's reliance upon their belief about the consistency of the quality of service provided by the hotel. After their first visit, and subsequent visits, competence trust is modified as the customer experiences the actual services provided by the hotel and compares them to their expectations. It implies that the hotel is dependable and can follow through promises; that in turn develops high levels of cooperation and reinforces trust (Mayer et al., 1995; Mishra, 1996). Korshak, (1995), suggests that hotel management should be involved in the process of engaging teams to identify solutions to workplace problems thereby building trust. After the customer's first visit, the customer's predictability trust based upon their actual experience of staying in the hotel would influence their expectations of the hotel's quality of service. Therefore, integrity beliefs reflect the customer's confidence that a hotel website adheres to a set of principles that guide their interactions. For example, a good website design can encourage customers to make inferences about the hotel's website interface, usability and functionality such as, ease of navigation, main menu options, hotel information, order fulfill-ment, and are therefore instrumental in generating beliefs about a website's ability to perform its stated function. Further, when customers obtain a confirmation number immediately after an online booking, this will enhance the customer's predictability trust based on the customer's perception of the hotel's competence.

The ability of the hotel to respond quickly indicates that the hotel has the necessary IT skills and competencies for the customer to complete their hotel online booking. Thus, hotels who respond quickly to their customers via email acknowledgements not only increase predictability trust of their customers, but also facilitate and hasten the process in completing their online booking. Then, when the hotel fulfills the services it promised to the customer, it enhances the customer's predictability trust in the hotel. Thus, customers' predictability trust depends on the hotel's ability to perform the promised services promptly and correctly. In the context of online booking environment, it is common for customers to frequently book online due to past experiences, word of mouth that in turn impacts their predictability trust. If the hotel is part of the chain, the customer's experience in staying in that hotel elsewhere also enhances predictability trust. Elliot and Fowell, (2000), discussed customers' experiences and comfort with the Internet in turn increases the growth of online hotel bookings. Similarly,

Shim and Drake (1990) argue that customers with strong online booking intention usually have prior hotel booking experiences that assist in reducing their uncertainties. In addition, customers who had prior online hotel booking experiences will be more likely to book their hotel online than those who lacked such experience.

Predictability trust in the hotel encourages repeat customers when services provided by the hotel meets the customer's expectations. Predictability trust is an extension of competence based trust (i.e., a series of positive, consistent and reliable behaviours) that makes the hotel predictable and therefore trustworthy (Lewicki and Bunker, 1996). In addition, the consistent behaviours of the hotel lead to a foundation of familiarity for the customers based on their prior experiences with the hotel. Predictability trust, thus, allows customers to make predictions and develop expectations of the hotel based on their prior experiences. Therefore, we derive at research hypothesis 2 as:

Predictability trust is positively associated with the customer's online booking decision.

Goodwill trust or relationship trust is the customer's reliance upon the care, concern, honesty, and benevolence shown by the hotel's staff. The customer believes that the hotel's staff will not only act in a competent and reliable manner, but will also have the well-being and interests of the customer at heart when making service decisions and providing service. Goodwill trust examines the hotel's staff honesty, care, and concern given to their customers, and is dependent on competence, and predictability trust. For the first time online booking decision, the customer will need to rely on the branding and reputation of the hotel, as well as word of mouth from others who have stayed in that hotel before and/or reading the positive recommendations and reviews about the hotel on their website. However, after the first and subsequent visits, the customer would have already interacted with the hotel staff and have experienced personally the service provided by the staff.

A brand is defined as a name or symbol, trademark and package design that uniquely identifies the products or services of a retailer or hotels, and differentiates them from those of its competitors (Aaker, 1991). Likewise, Lee and Back (2010) suggests that customers often make decisions about hotels based on their perception of specific hotel's brand name. Customers look at the brand name of the hotel. Oliver (1999, p. 392) defined brand loyalty as *a deeply held commitment to repurchase or patronize a preferred product or service consistently in the future, despite situational influences and marketing efforts having the potential to cause switching behaviour.* Thus, loyalty is a willingness to revisit a hotel with a disposition to treat the relationship as a partnership thereby creating goodwill trust. Likewise Aaker (1997, p. 347) defined brand personality as *the set of human characteristics associated with a brand.* We suggest that the impact of the customer's goodwill trust in the hotel can also be determined by the mediating effects and the relationship between brand personality and loyalty. Kam et al. (2010) discussed the benefits of a strong hotel brand name as it motivates the customer to identify the hotel and differentiate it with other hotels, thereby increasing their trust in the hotel. Co-branding, which is combining two or more brands to create a single unique product or service, is used by hotels to attract customers (Cornelis, 2010; Grossman, 1997). Therefore, the customer would be able to make a first-hand assessment of the goodwill trust.

Goodwill trust implies the hotel's ability to commit and deliver high quality services to the customer's, thereby leading to satisfied customers (Yilmaz, 2010). Customers experience loyalty which constitutes behavioural and attitudinal aspects of the hotel's staff. Oliver (1999) suggests that website loyalty encourages revisit and stickiness (or commitment). Website loyalty is defined as a deeply held willingness and commitment to revisit the website each time, thereby causing repetitive visits. Likewise, benevolence beliefs reflect the customer's confidence in having a positive orientation towards the hotel. Due to the competition in the online hotel booking industry, hotels attempt to positively influence public opinion by participating in web blogs, publishing guest posts on hotel related websites, and becoming a regular contributor to blogs and forums in the hotel industry. These measures build the reputation of the hotel as customers perceive the hotel to communicate openly, share information and commit to the goodwill trust.

Moreover, experience with cases where the hotel was asked to rectify some shortcomings or solve problems, and the hotel staff's prompt response to the issue will also provide the customer with a way of assessing and changing their levels of goodwill trust and loyalty they have in that hotel. Gupta and Setan (2010) examined the trust-loyalty relationship on a website and based it on the customers' motives towards meeting their goals and experiences. When expectations of reliability and dependability are met, trust moves to affective foundations that include emotional bonds, such as, care, concern and benevolence to further invest in the relationship with the hotel thereby enhancing their reputation. We argue that these factors enhance the customer's goodwill trust based on the loyalty they have towards the hotel. Therefore, we derive at research hypothesis 3 as:

Goodwill trust is positively associated with the customer's online booking decision.

We conclude the chapter with theoretical and practical implications of this study and directions for future research in the next section.

12.3 CONCLUSION

In this chapter we discussed the impact of the customer's trust in the hotel and how it influences their online hotel booking decisions. We adapted three types of trust, namely, competence, predictability and goodwill trust from previous research into the context of the customer's trust in their online hotel booking decision. The focus of competence trust was on the hotel's website interface, usability, functionality, and other secondary sources of information derived from documents and reviews of the hotel. Then once the customer has stayed in that hotel, or another hotel that is part of the hotel chain, the customer gained their own experience about that hotel thereby leading to predictability trust whose focus was based on prior experiences. Finally, the customer's trust evolves to goodwill trust creating a win-win relationship with the hotel, its reputation and brand name as their expectations are met and they are satisfied with that hotel.

The conceptual model of customer's trust in the online hotel booking decision developed in this study, illustrates the impact of three types of customer's trust on their online hotel booking decisions. This is useful for academic researchers in hospitality and tourism as well as hotel industry executives and decision-makers as it contributes to theory by incorporating the concept of trust. Future research aims to test the model with factors/indicators under each type of trust via online surveys, thereby contributing to new knowledge and providing answers to the impact of customer's trust in their online hotel booking decisions. We are certain that the findings will contribute and increase the hotel's awareness to incorporate the trust attributes in their website, day-to-day operations, benchmarking standards, quality checklists and other policies enforced by the hotel.

REFERENCES

Aaker, D.A. (1991). *Managing Brand Equity*, The Free Press, New York.

Aaker, J.L. (1997). Dimensions of brand personality, *Journal of Marketing Research*, 34(3), pp. 347–356.

Akhtar, N. and Khan, R.A. (Jan. 2011). Exploring the Paradox of Organizational Learning and Learning Organization. *Interdisciplinary Journal of Contemporary Research in Business*, 2(9), pp. 257–270

Cornelis, C.M. (2010). Effects of Co-Branding in the Theme Park Industry: A Preliminary Study. *International Journal of Contemporary Hospitality Management*, 22(6), pp. 775–796.

Dibb, S. and Chen, J. (2010). Consumer Trust in the Online Retail Context: Exploring the Antecedents and Consequences, *Psychology and Marketing*, 27(4), pp. 323–346.

Dyer, J.H. and Chu, W.C. (2000). The determinants of trust in supplier auto-maker relationships in the U.S., Japan and Korea. *Journal of International Business Studies*, (31)2, pp. 185–259.

Elliot, S. and Fowell, S. (2000). Expectation versus reality: A snap shot of consumer experiences with Internet Retailing. *International Journal of Information Management*, 20(5), pp. 323–336.

Gabarro, J. (1987). *The Dynamics of Taking Charge*, Harvard Business School Press. Boston.

Garbarion, E. and Johnson, M.S. (1999). The different role of satisfaction, trust, and commitment in customer relationships. *Journal of Marketing,* 63(2), pp. 70–87.

Goodrich, J.N. (1997). A New Approach to Image Analysis through Multi-Dimensional Scaling, *Journal of Travel Research*, 16(2), pp. 3–7.

Grossman, R.P. (1997). Co-branding in advertising: developing effective associations. *Journal of Product and Brand Management*, 6(3), pp. 191–201.

Gupta, R. and Setan, K. (2010). The Relationship Between Trusting Beliefs and Web Site Loyalty: The Moderating Role of Consumer Motives and Flow, *Psychology and Marketing*, 27(2), pp. 166–185.

Hirsch, L. (Aug. 23rd 2010). As Hotel Industry Improves, Buyer Interest Rises. *San Diego Business Journal*, 31(34), p. 3.

Kam, K.S., Fung and King, C. (2010). When Experience Matters: Building and Measuring Hotel Brand Equity, *International Journal of Contemporary Hospitality Management*, 22(5), pp. 589–608.

Korshak, S.R. (1995). Negotiating Trust in the San Francisco Hotel Industry. *California Management Review*, 38(1).

Lee, J.S. and Back, K.J. (2010). Examining Antecedents and Consequences of Brand Personality in the Upper—Upscale Business Hotel Segment. *Journal of Travel and Tourism Marketing*, 27(2), pp. 132–145.

Lee, Matthew K.O. and Turban, E. (2001). A Trust Model for Consumer Internet Shopping, *International Journal of Electronic Commerce*, 6(1), pp. 75–91.

Lewicki, R.J. and Bunker, B.B. (1996). Developing and Maintaining Trust in Work Relationships, in Kramer, R.M. and Tyler, T.R. (Eds.), *Trust in Organizations: Frontiers of Theory and Research*, Sage, Thousand Oaks, CA, pp. 114–139.

Mayer, R.C., Davis, J.H. and Schoorman, F.D. (1995). An integrative model of organizational trust. *Academy of Management Review*, (20)31, pp. 709–734.

Mishra, A.K. (1996). Organizational responses to crisis—the centrality of trust, in Kramer, R.M. and Tyler (Eds.), *Trust in Organizations: Frontiers of Theory and Research*, Sage, Thousand Oaks, CA, pp. 261–287.

Moorman, R., Zaltman, G. and Deshpande, R. (Ja. 1993). Factors affecting trust in market research relationships. *Journal of Marketing,* 57, pp. 81–101.

Morais, B.M. and Lin, C.H. (2010). Why Do First Time and Repeat Visitors Patronize a Destination? *Journal of Travel and Tourism Marketing*, 27(2), pp. 193–210.

Oliver, R.L. (1999). Whence customer loyalty? *Journal of Marketing*, 63(4), pp. 33–44.

Ratnasingam, P. (2008). The Impact of E-Commerce Relationships in Business to Consumer E-Commerce. *Journal of Electronic Commerce in Organizations*, 6(4), pp. 30–46.

Sako, M. and Helper, S. (1998). Determinants of trust in supplier relations: Evidence from the automotive industry in Japan and the United States. *Journal of Economic Behavior and Organization,* 34, pp. 387–417.

Shim, S. and Drake, M.F. (1990). Consumer intention to utilize electronic shopping. *Journal of Direct Marketing*, 4(2), pp. 22–33.

Yilmaz, I. (2010). Do Hotel Customers use a multi-expectation framework in the evaluation of services? A Study in Cappadocia, Turkey. *Journal of Tourism and Hospitality Research,* 10(1), pp. 59–69.

Zaheer, A., McEvily, B. and Perrone, V. (1998). Does trust matter? Exploring the effects of interorganizational and interpersonal trust on performance. *Organization Science*, 9(2), pp. 141–159.

Zeithaml, V.A., Berry, L.L. and Parasuraman, A. (1996). The behavioural consequences of service quality. *Journal of Marketing*, 60(2), pp. 31–46.

Zucker, L.G. (1986). Production of trust: Institutional sources of economic structure: 1840–1920. In B. Staw and L. Cummings (Eds.), *Research in Organizational Behaviour*, (8), pp. 53–111.

CHAPTER

13

ENDOGENOUS PROJECT ON RURAL TOURISM
A Case Study of Kalamkari

—P. SIVA SANKARA REDDY

13.1 ABSTRACT

Rural Andhra Pradesh has a rich tradition of art, craft and culture, which not only enriched the milieu but also kept the traditions alive through the ages. Rural tourism is, therefore, seen as a major avenue for this endeavour and the Government of India has given priority to tourism in the 10th plan as it has great potential, particularly in rural areas, to create jobs and to ensure 'sustainable livelihood.' The Ministry of Tourism, Government of India has launched the Scheme for Rural Tourism in the 10th Five-year Plan period in order to promote village tourism as primary tourism product to spread tourism and its socio-economic benefits to the artisans in particular and the people of the area in general. The project seeks to promote local culture and craft based tourism for sustainable livelihoods and integrated rural development. The aim of the paper is to study the Kalamkari industry and how the endogenous project helps in the improvement of social and economic well-being of artisan households through the development of rural tourism. Kalamkari art in Srikalahasti in Chittoor district is a rare art of drawing on cloth with the help of pen. The outstanding feature of Kalamkari is the extensive use of vegetable dyes. Srikalahasti craftsmen used only a quill to draw designs and depict scenes from the epics, which are later coloured with vegetable-extracted dyes. Kalamkari handicraft is promoted by the Department of Tourism through UNDP endogenous project. The project is to equip the artisans to produce the artistic products with good quality and encourage product diversification and provision of market linkages as well as credit facilities, thereby increasing the sales of the local art and craft forms.

Keywords: rural tourism, handicrafts, artisans, sustainable, kalamkari.

13.2 INTRODUCTION

Kalamkari is the craft of painted and printed fabrics. It derives its name from *kalam* (pen) with which the patterns are traced. It is an art form that developed both for decoration and religious ornamentation. The two towns in Andhra Pradesh which are the major centres of the *Kalamkari Art* are Machilipatnam and Srikalahasti. The Kalahasti tradition, which developed in the temple region, mostly concentrated on themes from Hindu mythology, epics (Ramayana, Mahabharata), images of Gods and heroes. The art practiced in Machilipatnam is influenced by the Persian and British patterns.

In Srikalahasti, temples were a major inspiration. The art flourished under the patronage of the temples with their demands for hangings with strong figurative and narrative components. This specialization in figurative work continues till today. Richly displayed episodes from the Puranas and other mythological material form the themes. Masulipatnam style is more famous for home furnishings, bed covers and curtains, but the traditional Kalahasti style is more prominently seen in wall hangings and dress materials. The basic technique for both the forms is same except that Kalahasti style uses only *kalam,* i.e. the pen and Masulipatnam uses hand blocks and pen both.

Kalamkari is a traditional art form that took root in India in the temple town of Srikalahasthi in Andhra Pradesh in the thirteenth century. Kalamkari grew to be very popular and was predominantly used in temples to depict stories in the form of narrative panels. These exquisite paintings echo the effervescent look towards life prevalent 750 years ago, when the art flourished under the patronage of King Krishnadevaraya. Derived from the words *kalam* meaning pen and *kari* meaning work, the art of Kalamkari is painted using combinations of plant materials as natural vegetable dyes on fabric. Kalamkari refers to a method of painting natural dyes onto cotton or silk fabric with a bamboo pen. The name *Kalamkari* translates as pen (*kalam*) work (*kari*) in Hindi/Urdu, and was most likely derived from the trade relationships between Persian and Indian merchants as early as the 10th century A.D. European merchants also had names for this type of fabric decoration: the Portuguese called it *pintado*, the Dutch used the name *sitz*, and the British preferred *chintz*. The name *Kalamkari* is used prominently today, and is synonymous with both painted and hand block printed textiles that incorporate natural vegetable/organically-derived dye stuffs. While there are many forms of *Kalamkari* throughout India and the world, the *Kalamkari* practice in Srikalahasti, in Andhra Pradesh, is famous in South India.

The exact nascence of *Kalamkari* in Srikalahasti is unknown; however, textual resources indicate that the art form flourished throughout the Deccan plateau in the 13th and 19th centuries A.D. due to extensive textile trading that occurred along the Coromandel Coast. Srikalahasti was most likely established as a *Kalamkari* centre due to its close proximity to a constant supply of clean, flowing water (a necessary component to *Kalamkari* production), found in the River Swarnamurki that runs through the town. It is possible that Srikalahasti also enjoyed local patronage from the Srikalahasteewara temple, a prominent Shiva temple that draws pilgrims from all over India each year. Other local patrons may have included nearby landowners and *zamindars*, and possibly the Vijayanagara rulers during the 13th to

16th centuries A.D. *Kalamkari* from Srikalahasti reflects a predominately Hindu patronage, and artists in the area continue that tradition through the painting of a variety of Hindu narrative themes, including the *Ramayana*, the *Mahabharata*, and the *Shiva Puranas*. The main artist families involved in *Kalamkari* during the 19th century were members of the *Balaji jati,* a community traditionally involved in agricultural work and small industry. Today, there are over 800 individuals in and around Srikalahasti involved in some aspect of *Kalamkari* art work, from preparing cloth and dyes, to design motifs and format layout, to final painting and execution. As a result it fetches them an annual turnover of five crores.

Around the middle of the 20th century, the popularity of *Kalamkari* in Srikalahasti waned to the point of near disappearance, with most artists focusing on agricultural work and other local occupations. At this point, around the late 1950s, *Kalamkari* received government attention and sponsorship, through the intervention of art activist, Kamaladevi Chattopadyaya. The material for robes and jackets was sent to East Asia. In 1957, Kamaladevi Chattopadyaya helped to establish a government-run *Kalamkari* training centre that focused on teaching a new generation of artists the techniques and stylistic vocabulary of *Kalamkari*. The ebb and flow of *Kalamkari* popularity continues to plague the artistic community at Srikalahasti. However, at the moment there is an upsurge in interest in the art form by designers, NGOs and entrepreneurs living and working in nearby cities. DWARAKA (Development of Weavers and Rural Artisans in Kalamkari Art) has brought about a revival of the Kalamkari Art, which would have otherwise faded and perished due to the poverty that these village artisans faced. The products made at DWARAKA by the Kalamkari artisans of Srikalahasti range from apparel, stoles, scarves and ties, bags, paintings and art for wall decor, home décor and corporate items.

A range of products are now created using *Kalamkari* cloth and are available for sale at craft exhibitions, small boutiques and from the artists directly. In addition to the traditional style narrative wall hangings, artists also create hand painted *saris*, *dupattas*, personal items and home accessories. It has been responsible for re-establishing artisans in and around the villages of Srikalahasti, nurturing their innate talent and potential, and making communities empowered, self-reliant and sustainable. Hand painted Kalamkari art is done on fabric using natural vegetable dyes. It involves kneading fabric in a large pot of milk and then painting on the dried fabric using burnt tamarind, mango or bamboo twigs. These twigs are sharpened into "kalams" or quill like pens.

The range of natural colours comes from natural ingredients including pomegranate seed, mango bark, indigo, and myrobolan fruit. The end result of this process is a stunningly beautiful art form and paintings that come alive in a myriad of hues. The artisans use their imagination and skill to depict the culture of ancient India, making each hand painted Kalamkari work on cloth a unique one. The end result is always a piece of art by itself. Hand painted Kalamkari is an exclusive art historically and traditional kept going only at Srikalahasti. DWARAKA is the only co-operative effort and platform keeping this traditional art alive.

With the support of DWARAKA, the artisans of Kalahasti are doing Kalamkari on almost all kinds of fabrics including natural silks, crepes, tussores, organza, cotton and linen. The League of Artisans markets a range of DWARAKA's products, from Kalamkari journals to silk crepe scarves to cosmetics bags.

13.3 CONCEPT OF RURAL TOURISM

The objective of rural tourism is to showcase rural life, art, culture and heritage at rural stations and in villages, which have core competence in art and craft, handlooms and textiles as also an asset base in the natural environment. The intention is to benefit the local community economically and socially as well as to enable interaction between tourists and local population for a mutually enriching experience. Under the scheme, the thrust is to promote village tourism as the primary tourism product to spread tourism and its socio-economic benefits to rural and its new geographic regions, thereby stopping the exodus from rural to urban areas. The village level council is the interactive forum for local community participation in work plan implementation, further supported by other community level institutions. For the visitor, whose expenditure creates revenue for host community service providers, rural tourism adds value through packaged programmes in art and craft imparted by skilled local artisans. Village entertainment groups unveil local history and culture, natural and oral treasures. The visitor thus comes face to face with India's rural traditions.

The development of a strong platform around the concept of rural tourism is useful for a country like India, where 74% of the population resides in seven million villages. Rural tourism is one of the few activities which can provide solution to problems like falling income levels and lesser job opportunities. The potential of rural tourism has been harnessed as a strategy for rural development. Besides, increasing level of awareness, growing interest in heritage and culture and environmental consciousness is enabled by rural tourism. The 10th Five-year Plan has identified tourism as one of the major sources of generating sustainable livelihoods and employment in India. Rural India has a rich tradition of art, craft and culture. Rural tourism is, therefore, seen as a major avenue for this endeavour and the Government of India has given priority to tourism in this plan as it has great potential, particularly in rural areas, to create jobs and to ensure 'sustainable livelihood.'

The Ministry of Tourism, Government of India has launched the Scheme for Rural Tourism in the 10th Five-year Plan period in order to promote village tourism as primary tourism product to spread tourism and its socio-economic benefits in various geographical regions all over India. Under this scheme, substantial funds have also been given to State Governments. The Rural Tourism project has also been taken up with the United Nations Development Programme (UNDP) support under the Ministry's Endogenous Tourism Project with the local involvement of grass-roots workers and village Panchayat. So far, 158 rural tourism sites in 28 States/Union territories have been sanctioned by the Ministry of Tourism including 36 rural sites where UNDP has supported for carrying building. Six rural tourism sites have been identified in Andhra Pradesh and they are Endogenous Projects of Pochampalli Ikaat Tie and Dye and Kalamkari art work at Srikalahasti and centrally sponsored projects of Nirmal toys, Dharmavaram Silk Sarees, Kuchipudi Dance art form and Etikoppaka Toys. The Endogenous Projects at Pochampalli and Srikalahasti are completed and are now maintained by the local community. The scheme identified key villages with core competency in heritage, culture, handlooms and handicrafts, aiming to build unique experiences with infrastructure components of ₹ 50 lakh per village. The more significant aspect was the community participation, component of additional ₹ 20 lakh in each village to enhance the host community's tourism awareness, art, and skill development, training in visitor handling and gender sensitization. The projects are being implemented through local Non-Governmental Organizations (NGOs) whose role is critical and significant. The implementation of this scheme has provided an opportunity to position the Indian rural tourism project as a unique tourism visitor experience in a low-impact setting. The primary target has been the low volume but high yielding visitor community experience.

13.3.1 Enhancement of Artisan Skills

Craftsmanship of any kind has always been a basic activity in human society, which depicts the age-old tradition and cultural heritage, living style in more expressive way than the language itself. Lack of market intelligence compelled many of them to give up this profession and migrate to towns to earn their bread. The rural tourism programme aims to revive and sustain the artistic forms as the artistic value of these products has no alternative. Besides, the master craftsmen are very few and the migration of the younger artisans is very high. Under the Rural Tourism Scheme, various types of artisans have been identified and their capacity has been built. The strength, weakness, opportunity and threat analysis of the rural art and handicraft was done along with the participatory rural appraisal and necessary tasks being put forward for the livelihood promotion of the people. The prime motive of the Rural Tourism Project is to enhance the capacity of local artisans. As a result of the UNDP and other schemes, the implementing agency has conducted different workshops, seminars to provide value addition to existing artisan's skills. This has helped in exposing the arts and crafts and in generating income to the artisans and overall revival of the rich heritage of the village.

The Gurukul process is an important element of the rural tourism programme which imparts knowledge among the youth or the new learners about the traditional history, art, culture and craft of the place. The rural tourism model seeks to revive those art forms, where the master craftsmen are few and the migration of the younger artisans is high. The knowledge is imparted by a guru or a number of gurus in the rural setting itself, where learners stay and learn about art and culture. The concept behind such a process is to enable the young people to have awareness and pride for their culture. Design-cum-training workshops have also been conducted for more participation of the youths. It helps them to give up the obsolete methods and designs and adapt to the new designs suitable to the market needs. Various training programmes covering technical and marketing aspects also were given to artisans and entrepreneurs with an objective to encourage entrepreneurial skills to the newcomers to start their activity by sharing information. Participation in national and international events such as exhibitions, *melas* provides the required exposure to the artisans and instills a sense of competition. The artisans meet people from other parts of the country specializing in the same trade domain and learn the worth of their product. Events like the one organized at Delhi Haat, gave the requisite exposure to the rural people. The project site also gets marketed and the awareness spreads through the word of mouth. The sale of handicrafts to the tourists in local *melas* will generate money. The artisans have been provided the facility to showcase their products in the craft centre in the village. Eighty families are taking an active participation in the preparation of Kalamkari work at Srikalahasti Rural Tourism Project and the turnover is ₹ 5 crore.

13.4 CREATION OF TOURISM INFRASTRUCTURE

The creation of common facilities has been given importance in the rural tourism scheme as it provides the local people a quality life and also helps in providing the satisfaction to the tourists. Creation of facilities such as rest houses, parking space, drinking water, restaurant and improvement of pathways and landscaping has improved the surroundings of the villages. With creation of common facilities, the environment in the rural tourism sites has become clean and beautiful. The development and improvement of infrastructure has benefitted the village communities in projecting a good image of the rural areas and also enhancing the chances of providing the good infrastructure support to the tourists. Tourism is leading to assets creation and public amenities in rural villages and is benefitting the local residents. The scope of tourism at Srikalahasti is tremendous, but the facilities were not sufficient to meet the requirements and a need was felt to create decent restaurant and accommodation by Andhra Pradesh Tourism Development Corporation (APTDC) as it is nearer to Tirumala. It is planning to construct tourism complex at Srikalahasti to showcase the rich art and culture of Rayalseema region.

A craft museum serves to showcase the traditional materials created especially for the tourism development. These facilities are well maintained by the local population enabling ownership at workplace. Many of the treasures used by the people have been lost over the period of time and their manning could be seen in these museums. The craft museums serve the purpose of displaying the rare art, craft and artefacts of the region. The visitors obtain a wealth of information about all these products, thereby enriching their knowledge about the site. A building to house the exhibition on traditional weaving has been constructed in Srikalahasti village of Chittor district.

13.5 AWARENESS OF LOCAL COMMUNITY

Systematic tourism development in rural sites through public participation has contributed towards the socio-economic development of the areas. Tourism has ensured that heritage, history and culture, both tangible and intangible, is conserved in its right context and at the same time generates livelihood opportunities for the villagers. To achieve this output, creation of awareness about the importance of rural tourism among the local community has been one of the most important tasks carried out in the villages. Villagers migrate to towns and cities looking for opportunities leaving behind traditions and cultures which are subsequently lost, while the younger generation loses pride in its culture and adopts urban ways of the cities. To address these issues, awareness was created among the younger generation, so that they start afresh on the work of their forefathers and infuse it with new designs and ideas. Alternative employment avenues as guides and cooks in the tourism sites have been adopted by the youth as alternative livelihood opportunities while continuing to practice their inherited crafts. Awareness has also been created in the community by village level consultation meetings, door to door visits, street plays, community workshops, etc. to educate the community to understand the role of community in preserving the environment and enriching it further through maintaining hygiene and adopting waste disposal measures. The Gram Panchayat and the community level implementing partners like the men and women of Srikalahasti Self Help Groups (SGH) and their federations, Kalanetha Committee and cooperatives are working together for developing the weavers' cause. More importantly, the Kalanetha Committee with support from the NGO organizations has helped in improving the level of participation of the weaker sections of the people, specially women. With 138 SHGs in the village and various training programmes being conducted, the situation has improved a lot.

13.5.1 Direct Revenue and Employment Generation

The overall goal of rural tourism is to create a community managed rural tourism model by strengthening sustainable livelihoods of the local communities for the preservation and development of local heritage of the villages. Due to the government initiative to promote rural tourism, a number of avenues for the employment of local population have opened. Tourism supports direct or indirect employment opportunities in rural areas without adversely affecting agricultural workforce. Overall, its contribution to the rural economy is considered to be substantial. It has helped in reducing the migration by providing employment opportunities in the villages by restructuring rural entrepreneurial system. It has been observed that rural tourism has become a source of income for rural communities.

Regular wages for those with jobs: It has been reported that the income from tourism activities in the villages is not regular, but a spurt in cash during some season to rural families has lifted their status socio-economically. These earnings, in turn, are partially recycled within the local economy creating a multiplier effect.

Casual earning opportunities from selling food, handicraft products, etc.: The artisans, casual labourers and others sell their products to tourists. They earn smaller amounts from casual sales than is earned by those in waged employment.

New business opportunities: Tourism generates new opportunities for the local community. Even those rural businesses not directly involved in tourism can benefit from tourist activity through developing close relationships with tourist facilities where local food can be used as part of the tourism offering in a locality. Rural tourism facilitates the expansion of complimentary businesses such as service stations, and new businesses are created to cater to tourist needs for hospitality services, recreational activities and arts and crafts.

New development and enterprises: Diversification into rural tourism tends to stimulate new development and enterprises within a rural community that enables locations in decline to take control of their economic destiny. Rural tourism development eventually diversifies the resident population of a community along with the product offerings of the region. These offerings include changed agricultural activity and changed mix of goods and services. If the services like guides, managers, administrators, cooks, etc. were to be offered from the members outside the village, it could have led to a loss in interest of the community in sustaining and promoting rural tourism. To avoid this, community members were encouraged to take active part in the training process. A whole range of capacity building exercises have been formulated by the community to enhance the capacity of the villagers so that they can undertake the administration and management of tourist facilities. For instance, NGOs have facilitated the training of women in the preparation of cuisine.

Enhanced quality life: It is important to note that rural tourism has enhanced the local quality of life and also supported local culture in rural areas by encouraging restoration of historic sites. The local youths in the village are quite eager to take up Tour Guide as a profession. Andhra Pradesh Tourism Development Corporation has provided guide training programme to 25 local people. The content of training harped on hospitality management, language skills and information management. The period of training was between 3 and 6 months.

Gender perspective: Integration of gender perspectives with tourism industry has also evolved as an important concept through the rural tourism, as it is the major employer of women and offers various opportunities for independent income generating activities for them. The SHGs provided all sort of financial and marketing linkages, helping them to increase their income. In many cases, bank linkages have also been provided.

Host family: The concept of host family in the rural villages is an interesting one which serves the dual purpose of increasing livelihood opportunities as well as resolving the accommodation problem for the visitors. Host families have been identified in most of the sites and in Pochampall and Etikoppaka, they are already functional. These families have traditional accommodation facilities and have converted one or two of their rooms for home stay purpose. The services in the home stays include room, food, toilets, drinking water, and information about the life in village. Suitable technical know-how on the specifications for such accommodation and modalities for keeping paying guests has already been provided to the host families. Most of these home stays are equipped with the facilities like personnel to attend the tourists, products of good quality, services of high standard, environment which is clean and comfortable, family members for interaction and opportunity for the tourist to engage in household chores and activities. The rationale is developing the visitor's love to stay in the rural atmosphere and want to be part of the community. This is only possible when they stay with the native families, eat food with them and enrich their experience about the history and culture by conversing with them. On the other hand, this type of accommodation also ensures immediate economic benefits to the host families. It was observed that many host families have entered with the assumption that making use of their property will reap financial reward as a form of supplementary income. Although these ventures may be financially relatively unrewarding, a great number of stakeholders reported that the social benefits such as making friendships outweigh the lack of financial return. It contributed to the sustainability of rural communities.

13.5.2 Contribution of the Local Community

One of the preconditions of sustainable tourism development is the consideration of long-term interests of local residents. Rural tourism cannot succeed without the participation of rural society. Under the rural tourism scheme, rural tourism had the multiplier effect on rural society. It has developed the rural economy by improving the rural income by providing employment for people in the village, and supporting small businesses such as restaurants and art shops. A less obvious impact, but important over the long-term is the change in attitude towards sustainable tourism and its delivery by a large number of stakeholders who participated in consultative meetings and training. The participants achieved a substantive shift in their attitudes to rural tourism. The aim of rural tourism is to increase the net benefits to rural communities from tourism, and increase their participation in managing the tourism product. If more tourism can be developed in rural areas, particularly in a way that involves huge local participation in decisions and enterprises, then poverty impacts are likely to be enhanced. In a broader context, tourism has brought a range of other benefits to rural areas, such as infrastructural development and spin-off enterprise opportunities. The project focused on creating community institutions, not just supporting individual entrepreneurs. Community associations are seen as the guardians of culture, the developers of the tourism resource, and the agents for community benefit. This is more in line with a development approach in rural areas than a typical small business approach. The project has focused on institution building of local communities as much as developing entrepreneurship, and it is still very early to make judgement with regard to acquisition of skills. The quality of micro-enterprises inevitably varies across the artisans depending on their capacity, as does their potential to diversify service provision. One of the most common features of rural tourism, as offered to local communities, is an incentive to consider starting a tourism business, its ability to generate an alternative income stream. This income can come at times that supplements income during seasonal fluctuations, but local communities are looking for alternative income that does not impact or interfere with their 'real' business. The actual level of income is not as important as the fact that they have an alternative source of income. Factors affecting income were room capacity, visitor numbers and price. It has been reported that low revenues from rural tourism will result in low room numbers and so many rural tourism activities may have difficulty securing sufficient tourist numbers to be financially self-sufficient. The employment theme is extended to include specific opportunities for young people within rural communities in the hope that tourism may provide an incentive for them to remain. The rural tourism has promoted an exciting and growing industry suited to the energies and enthusiasm of young rural people. Career options are enhanced with the opportunities for training and direct involvement in running tourism business.

13.5.3 Impediments in Implementation

During the interaction with various stakeholders, it was found that there were project constraints during the implementation of the rural tourism scheme. These include:

1. The initial common understanding developed among all the stakeholders gets diluted with the frequent transfer of local personnel, like the District Collector (DC) Joint Collector and Mandal Revenue Officer.
2. At the sites which did not have a software component, there was a lack of awareness among the people about the scheme.
3. There has been no direct synergy between the hardware activities and the software activities under Rural Tourism Scheme. In a few sites, hardware activities have been

preceded the software activities. Whenever there is a lack of software activities, i.e. community awareness and understanding of the scheme, then the participation and ownership of the local community in the project declines.

4. The community participation and ownership can be achieved only when the local governing institutes like Gram Panchayats cooperate with the NGO. Unfortunately, in some cases, due to vested interests, there seems to be lack of coordination between the Gram Panchayats and the local NGOs.
5. There are many stakeholders like the Rural Department, the Ministry of Environment, Archaeological Survey of India, PWD, and Water Department, etc. in the implementation of the scheme. Due to the involvement of different stakeholders in the scheme, sometimes there is a problem in executing the project.
6. The size and population of the village also needs to be taken into consideration before deciding the duration of software activities. The formation of the community groups, product development and marketing is expected to take longer time to reach a reasonable standard for foreign and domestic tourism markets.
7. The challenges in rural tourism have been compounded by institutional obstacles, i.e. the administrative complexity. During the field visit, it was reported that in some cases the software implementing partner cannot continue with their efforts, due to delay in the release of the funds.
8. Another major constraint in the rural tourism scheme has been the lack of statistics about the site. For instance, in many cases, the correct data of tourist inflow to a particular site was impossible to obtain. No one had ever maintained the records.
9. It has been reported that the interest of tourists looking for authentic rural experiences very often conflict with the interest of locals looking for urban comfort.

13.6 CONCLUSION

The rural tourism scheme is based on the principles of sustainable development and the aim is to promote tourism sites in India. The scheme emphasizes entrepreneurship and active community participation in development and policy-making in rural tourism.'To conclude, rural tourism is not the end, but the means to stimulate economic growth, to increase the viability of underdeveloped location, and to improve the living standards of local population. Rural tourism scheme has been a valuable vehicle to bring the ultimate rural stakeholders in touch with the tourism sector to increase employment. In order to make the scheme more meaningful, it is very important that the sustenance issues be discussed with the community before the start of the project and software programmes should precede the hardware activities at least six months before and also aggressive marketing of the destinations be taken up with the local and international tour operators.

REFERENCES

Aneeta, H.R., Census; Handicraft artisans 1995–1996 in *Seminar*, Vol. 523; March 2003, pp. 73–75.

Annual Report of Ministry of Tourism 2009–2010, Ministry of Tourism, Govt. of India, New Delhi, 2010.

"Arts and Crafts of Andhra Pradesh: Lepakshi," Andhra Pradesh Handicrafts Development Corporation, Hyderabad, 2009.

"Community Based Rural Tourism in Andhra Pradesh", Ministry of Tourism, Government of Andhra Pradesh, Hyderabad, 2010.

Compendium of Handicrafts Schemes for 11th Five Year Plan, Ministry of Textiles, Govt. of India, New Delhi, 2008.

Coomaraswamy, A.K., *The Arts and Crafts of India and Ceylone*, Today and Tomorrow Publishers, New Delhi, 1913.

Crafts and Craftsmen in Traditional India, Konark Publishers, New Delhi, 1978.

"Hall Mark Handicrafts: Arts and Crafts of Andhra Pradesh", A.P. Handicrafts Development Corporation, Hyderabad, 2008.

"Heritage and Rural Tourism" in *Today's Traveller*, October 15–November 15, 2002. Indian Folklife S. No. 29, June 2008, Paper on "Toy making A popular craft", pp. 14–16.

"Lepakshi 25 years: Nurturing Artisans 1982–2007," A.P. Handicrafts Development Corporation, Hyderabad, 2009.

Mehta, R.J., *The Handicrafts and Industrial Arts of India*, Taraporewala Treasure House of Books, Bombay.

Pruthi, R.K., *Rural Tourism: Challenges and Paradoxes*, Rajat Publications, New Delhi, 2006.

Ranjan, A. and M.P. Ranjan (Eds.), *Crafts of India: Handmade in India*, Mapin Publishing, Ahmedabad, 2010.

Rao, R.V., *Indian Handicrafts*, Book Lovers, Hyderabad, 1967, Rural Tourism Project, Srikalahasthi (APTDC Report) 2011.

Report of National Productivity Council, New Delhi, on "Guru-Shishya Parampara", 2010.

Report of National Productivity Council, New Delhi, on "Bhima Yojana for Handicraft Artisans, 2011."

Report of the Task Force on Handicrafts for the VIII Five Year Plan, "Explore Rural India", Booklet prepared by Ministry of Tourism, Govt. of India, New Delhi, 2004.

Report on State Level Marketing Workshop on "Handicrafts of Andhra Pradesh", Vijayawada, 27th October, 2009.

Saraf, D.N., *Craft Development 1941–1991*, Sampark, New Delhi, 1991.

_____, *Indian Crafts; Development and Potential*, Vikas Publishers, Delhi, 1982.

Sethna, Nelly H., *Living Traditions of Kalamkari*, Mapin International, Ahmedabad, 1985.

Upadhyay, M.N., *Economics of Handicrafts Industry*, S. Chand Co., Delhi, 1973. Jena, P.K., Global Culture and Local Goods; Indian Handicrafts in the Age of Globalisation, *South Asia Politics*, Vol. 6, October 2007, pp. 40–42.

_____, *Handicrafts* (India), Andhra Pradesh Book Distributors, Secunderabad, 1976.

Vanninae, E., *Urban Crafts and Craftsman in Medieval India*, Munshiram Manoharlal Publishers, New Dlehi, 2004.

CHAPTER

14

CAUSALITY BETWEEN TOURISM AND EDUCATION

—G.S. Prema Kumara and Riyaz Ahmad

14.1 ABSTRACT

Tourism activities are determined by various aspects such as location, development, availability of infrastructure as well as knowledge and communication skills of the people. Education is one of the important factors which highly influence the communicative skills and knowledge of the people and thereby the people of the particular location can interact with and explain to the tourists about the special features of the location, and make their visit comfortable. In this sense, education plays a predominant role and has considerable impact on the development of tourism. In this paper, an attempt has been made to analyze the causality between tourism and education. For empirical estimation and analysis, numbers of tourist arrival and literacy rate have been considered as proxy to tourism and education, respectively. Tourists visit Jammu and Kashmir for several reasons, like philanthropical, aesthetic, etc. But the number of tourists visiting the state is not distributed evenly among the different regions of Jammu and Kashmir. It is found from the analysis that there is an increase in tourist arrivals on the one side and, on the other, the literacy rate has also increased. The findings reveal that an increase in the number of tourist arrivals has resulted in the increase in the literacy rate of all three divisions or regions of Jammu and Kashmir. Interestingly, the tourist arrival has increased by three times to Jammu region, sixty eight times to Kashmir region, and ten times to Ladakh region. The literacy rates have almost doubled in Jammu and Kashmir region, and three times in Ladakh region, in the same period (1990–2008). Therefore, there is a positive correlation between tourism and education.

Keywords: education, tourism, regions, development, causality, enrolment, tourist arrival.

14.2 INTRODUCTION

Tourism is one of the prospering economic activity plays important role in terms of providing employment and thereby generate considerable income to the service provider as well as parties involved in this. Tourism has become a prominent activity after the globalization, both domestically and internationally. The number of travellers is increasing significantly over the period of time. The magnitude of tourism is determined by a number of variables, and one such variable is education. In contradiction, tourism also determines a number of activities and one such is education. (The Granger causality test conducted in this paper clearly reveals that tourism is cause for education.) Jammu and Kashmir being one of the most important geographical region, most of the domestic and foreign travellers do visit for unique reasons. The majority of J&K people are depending on tourism for source of income their. Invariably, the spending activities of these people also depend on the tourism, since it is one of the main sources of their income. Accordingly, the spending activities on education will also depend on the arrival of tourists to J&K. Therefore, there is a positive relationship between tourist arrival and educational development. (The study uses school enrolment as proxy of educational development.) More appropriately, tourism has positive impact on educational development of J&K. The present paper analyses the trends in tourists' arrival and trends in school enrolment. The study also examines the impact of tourism on education.

14.3 LITERATURE REVIEW

Tourism is travel for recreational, leisure or educational or business or other purposes. The World Tourism Organization defines tourists as the people who "travel to and stay in places outside their usual environment for more than twenty-four (24) hours and not more than one consecutive year for leisure, business and other purposes not related to the exercise of an activity remunerated from within the places visited" (UNWTO, 1995).

Tourism is a significant service in the economy. Tourism industry provides various segments, which provide a wide range of services to the tourist. On the one hand, it enables tourists to enjoy the stay and, on the other, it provides employment opportunities to the people who are directly and indirectly involved in tourism activities (Ramona, 2007 and Tigu, Andreeva and Nica, 2010). This increases their income and hence improves their standard of living in general and their socio-economic condition in particular. Therefore, it contributes to the growth of GDP to the host country (Eugenio-Marten et al., 2004 and Novelli and Burns, 2010). Tourism can not only be helpful to overcome the serious problems of unemployment but also enables the people who are involved in tourism industry to expand their business and also involve others in their business. This study made by Reeder and Brown (2005) analyzes the effect of leisure activities and tourism development on socio-economic position in rural recreational countries. The findings show that the development of tourism highly contributes towards the socio-economic welfare of rural people. It also concludes that tourism results in increasing employment and improvement in health and education (Reeder and Brown, 2005). There are a good number of studies which explain and examine the relationship between education and tourism and impacts of tourism in terms of employment, income generation and socio-economic development as well as need of infrastructural development for sustainable tourism (Blank et al., 1983; Liberto, 2010; Rivera and Leon, 2005; Yildirim, 2009; and Valerian DRAGU and Ema CORODESCU, 2010). Dorothea and Medalla (2004) analyze the use of English language for the development of tourism industry. It can be concluded from these reviews that tourism significantly influences the economy in general and education in particular.

14.4 METHODOLOGY

The study uses secondary data for analysis. It has used various annual reports published by the Directorate of Tourism, Government of Jammu and Kashmir, Srinagar, for the various years from 1990–1991 to 2007–2008. Data has also been collected from Digest of Statistics, Directorate of Economics and Statistics, Government of Jammu and Kashmir, Srinagar, for the various years from 1990–1991 to 2007–2008 related to the tourists' arrival to all the three regions of Jammu and Kashmir, i.e., Jammu, Kashmir and Ladakh regions. The researcher has also used total enrolment at primary, middle and high/higher secondary level as proxy of education.

This paper has also developed appropriate models and statistical techniques to make the study scientific and realistic. The statistical techniques and models used in this paper are Granger Causality Model to estimation of causality between education and tourism, GLS regression model to estimate the impact of tourism on education, Breush-Godfrey, Prais-Winsten regression, correlation models and models to calculate trend values, and also used formulas to calculate AAGR, and others.

Model for trend analysis:

$$Y^t = [(Y^t - Y^{t-1})/(Y^{t-1})]*100$$

Granger causality model:

$$T_t = \Sigma\alpha i E_{t-I} + \Sigma\beta j T_{t-j} + u_{1t}$$

$$E_t = \Sigma\alpha i E_{t-I} + \Sigma\beta j T_{t-j} + u_{2t}$$

Prais–Winsten GLS regression iterated estimates model:

$$T_t = \alpha + \beta E_t + u_t$$

where

T = Tourists arrival

E = Enrollment

14.4.1 Trend Analysis

Tables 14.1 and 14.2 present trend and absolute values for tourists' arrival and enrollment in education.

Table 14.1 Tourists trend in J&K

(Numbers in lakhs and percentage)

Year	*Tourist arrival*	*AGR*	*Kashmir*	*AGR*	*Jammu*	*AGR*	*Ladakh*	*AGR*
1990–1991	2,191,486		15,546		2,169,202		6,738	
1991–1992	3,182,251	45.21	21,886	40.78	3,151,310	45.28	9,055	34.39
1992–1993	3,608,269	13.39	64,962	196.82	3,527,289	11.93	16,018	76.90
1993–1994	3,447,162	–4.46	64,026	–1.44	3,368,735	–4.50	14,401	–10.09
1994–1995	3,768,408	9.32	46,814	–26.88	3,705,945	10.01	15,649	8.67
1995–1996	4,118,632	9.29	68,520	46.37	4,032,127	8.80	17,985	14.93
1996–1997	4,482,072	8.82	129,967	89.68	4,335,532	7.52	16,573	–7.85
1997–1998	4,546,207	1.43	95,173	–26.77	4,434,233	2.28	16,801	1.38
1998–1999	4,903,925	7.87	259,803	172.98	4,622,092	4.24	22,030	31.12
1999–2000	5,011,572	2.20	331,658	27.66	4,668,340	1.00	11,574	–47.46
2000–2001	5,412,863	8.01	285,246	–13.99	5,109,575	9.45	18,042	55.88
2001–2002	5,268,246	–2.67	191,628	–32.82	5,056,919	–1.03	19,699	9.18
2002–2003	4,578,404	–13.09	138,149	–27.91	4,432,176	–12.35	8,079	–58.99
2003–2004	5,773,176	26.10	344,478	149.35	5,400,296	21.84	28,402	251.55
2004–2005	6,921,915	19.90	776,729	125.48	6,109,895	13.14	35,291	24.26
2005–2006	7,283,826	5.23	993,382	27.89	6,251,998	2.33	38,446	8.94
2006–2007	7,692,361	5.61	697,888	–29.75	6,950,573	11.17	43,900	14.19
2007–2008	7,968,025	3.58	655,840	–6.03	7,262,000	4.48	50,185	14.32
Average	5,008,822	8.57	287,871.9	41.85	4,699,347	7.98	21,603.78	24.78

Table 14.2 Trends in school enrolment

(Numbers in lakhs and percentage)

Year	*Primary*	*AGR*	*Middle*	*AGR*	*Secondary/ Hr. Secondary*	*AGR*	*Total*	*AGR*
1990–1991	4.34		3.96		4.2		12.5	
1991–1992	4.54	4.61	4.19	5.81	4.38	4.29	13.11	4.88
1992–1993	4.7	3.52	4.29	2.39	4.54	3.65	13.53	3.20
1993–1994	5.84	24.26	4.5	4.90	3.41	–24.89	13.75	1.63
1994–1995	6.25	7.02	4.86	8.00	3.78	10.85	14.89	8.29
1995–1996	6.31	0.96	3.72	–23.46	2.45	–35.19	12.48	–16.19
1996–1997	6.31	0.00	4.85	30.38	4.03	64.49	15.19	21.71
1997–1998	10.11	60.22	4.05	–16.49	2.93	–27.30	17.09	12.51
1998–1999	11.47	13.45	4.31	6.42	3.05	4.10	18.83	10.18
1999–2000	11.05	–3.66	4.24	–1.62	3.05	0.00	18.34	–2.60
2000–2001	11.19	1.27	4.6	8.49	3.51	15.08	19.3	5.23
2001–2002	9.68	–13.49	5.35	16.30	4.41	25.64	19.44	0.73
2002–2003	6.65	–31.30	3.41	–36.26	3.26	–26.08	13.32	–31.48
2003–2004	7.43	11.73	3.52	3.23	3.04	–6.75	13.99	5.03
2004–2005	10.73	44.41	4.57	29.83	3.55	16.78	18.85	34.74
2005–2006	12.36	15.19	4.77	4.38	3.6	1.41	20.73	9.97
2006–2007	9.25	–25.16	4.64	–2.73	3.04	–15.56	16.93	–18.33
2007–2008	11.36	22.81	7.26	56.47	4.97	63.49	23.59	39.34
Average	8.31	7.99	4.51	5.65	3.62	4.35	16.44	5.23

Table 14.1 reveals that the tourist arrival to J&K increased in the reference period. On an average, 5,008,822 tourists arrived to J&K during the reference period. And it varies among the different regions. According to the information, more number of tourists visited to Jammu region and less number of tourists visited to Ladakh region, and tourists visited to Kashmir moderately. The growth of tourists to J&K varies during the reference period as well as among the regions. The average growth of tourists to J&K was 8.57% and it varies among the regions. Kashmir registered 41.85% of Average Annual Growth Rate (AAGR), Ladakh registered 24.78% of AAGR and for Jammu it is 7.98%. Even though the number of tourists to Kashmir and Ladakh region is comparatively less, over the period, it is rapidly increasing.

Table 14.2 presents the information about the enrollment to school education in J&K. Enrolment to school education increased in the reference period, but it varies at different levels of schooling. The AAGR of total enrollment increased at 5.23, 7.99, 5.65 and 4.35% at primary, higher primary and high school level

From Tables 14.1 and 14.2, it is found that both education in terms of enrollment and tourism in terms of tourists' arrival have shown positive trends and both have increased significantly. It provides the scope to analyze the impact of one another or, in other words, causality between education and tourism.

14.4.2 Causality Analysis

The following results from Granger Causality test explain cause and effect between education and tourism:

Sample: 1991–2008

Lags: 2

Null Hypothesis:	Obs	F-Statistic	Prob.
TOTAL (does not Granger Cause TA)	16	3.38820	0.0714
TA (does not Granger Cause TOTAL)		4.46540	0.0380

The Granger Causality test had run for total enrolment and total tourist arrival. It is found that total enrollment does not cause total arrival significantly at 5%, whereas tourists' arrival significantly causes total enrollment. Therefore, total tourist arrival cause as total enrollment. Based on this, total tourist arrival is considered as the predictor of total enrollment. Hence, in the next model tourist arrival is treated as the independent variable and total enrolment is treated as the dependent variable.

14.4.3 Impact of Tourism on Education

Tourism is one of the contributors to the development of education in J&K. The following regression results explain the impact of tourism on education:

Prais–Winsten GLS regression–iterated estimates

Number of jobs = 18
F (1, 16) = 17.05
Prob > F = 0.0008
R-squared = 0.5159
Adj R-squared = 0.4857
Root MSE = 2.0945

Enrolment Coefficient		Std. Err.	t	P > t
Tourists arrival	1.61	3.59e-07	4.50	0.000
Constant	8.382117	1.891598	4.43	0.000

Durbin–Watson statistic (original) 1.622941
Durbin–Watson statistic (transformed) 1.837455

Prais–Winsten GLS regression model is fairly good fitted with 0.52 r^2 value. The constants are acceptable, and there is no autocorrelation since DW statistic is 1.84, which is very close to 2. According to the results, tourism has positive impact on education. If tourists' arrival increases, the enrolment in J&K also increases.

14.5 CONCLUSION

In Jammu and Kashmir, tourism and education have shown positive trends during the period 1992–2008. It is found that tourism in J&K significantly influences the educational activities. In J&K tourism is one of the major economic activities and it provides considerable income to people engaging in it. Therefore, there is a dire need of development of tourism infrastructure in order to attract more number of visitors and thereby develop the education system in general and increase the enrolment in particular. To summarize, tourism is one of the important determinants of education and it also leads to human development of J&K.

REFERENCES

Adrian Di Liberto (2010). High skills, high growth: is tourism an exception? Working papers CRENoS from Centre for North South Economic Research Centre, University of Cagliariand Sassari, Sardinia.

Atay, Lutfi and and Yildirim, Haci Mehmet (2009). Determining Factors that Affect satisfaction of Students in Undergraduate tourism education, *An International Multidisciplinary Journal of Tourism,* No. 1.5, pp. 73–87.

Dorothea C. and Lazaro Medalla M.Author (2004). English as the Language of Trade, Finance and Technology in APEC: An East Asia Perspective, Discussion Papers from Philippine Institute for Development Studies, No. DP 2004.

Gabriela Tigu, Maria Andreeva and Ana-Maria Nica (2010). Education and Training Need in the Field of Visitors Receiving Structures and Tourism Services in the Lower. Danube Region, *The Amfiteatru Economic Journal*, 2010, Vol. 12, Issue Spl. No. 4, pp. 735–760.

Gruescu Ramona (2007). Tendencies Regarding the Training and the Education in Tourism, *Revista Tinerilor Economisti* (The Young Economists Journal), Vol. 1, No. 7, pp. 71–82.

Jorge Rivera and Peter Leon (2005). Chief executive officers and voluntary environmental performance: Costa Rica's certification for sustainable tourism, Policy Sciences, 2005, Vol. 38, Issue 2, pp. 107–127.

Juan Luis Eugenio-Marten, Noelia Marten Morales and Riccardo Scarpa (2004). Tourism and Economic Growth in Latin American Countries: A Panel Data Approach, Working Papers from Fondazione Eni Enrico Mattei, No. 2004–26.

Maina Novelli and Peter Burns (2010). Peer-to-peer capacity-building in tourism: Values and experiences of field-based education, *Development Southern Africa*, Vol. 27, No. 5, pp. 741–756.

Richard J. Reeder and Dennis M. Brown (2005). Recreation, Tourism, and Rural Well-Being, Economic Research Report from United States Department of Agriculture, Economic Research Service.

Uel Blank, Lawrence Simonson, Gary Ballman, James Burke, Richard Korte and Arnie Heikkila (1983). Contributing to Tourism Industry Vitality of Natural Resource Based Region Through Educational/Technical Assistance, Staff papers from University of Minnesota, Department of Applied Economics, No. 13528.

UNWTO technical manual (1995). Collection of Tourism Expenditure Statistics. World Tourism Organization, p. 14.

Valerian DRAGU and Ema CORODESCU (2010). The Perspectives of a Sustainable Tourism Development in Barnova Village, *Buletin Scintific*, Vol. 19, pp. 135–140.

CHAPTER

15

GREENING THE MARIKINA CITY
Cycling as an Alternative Transportation

—Joy Sheelah Baraero Era and Evangeline E. Timbang

15.1 INTRODUCTION

> Let every individual and institution now think and act as a responsible trustee of Earth, seeking choices in ecology, economics and ethics that will provide a sustainable future, eliminate pollution, poverty and violence, awaken the wonder of life and foster peaceful progress in the human adventure.
>
> — John McConnell, Founder of International Earth Day

Global warming is not a threat to the existence of our environment; it is a threat to the existence of mankind. Environment will survive but shall we survive the kind of environment that we will have in the future? "Global warming" refers to the rise in the earth's temperature resulting from an increase in heat-trapping gases in the atmosphere. Studies conducted by the United Nations Programme (UNP) and the World Meteorological Organization (WMO) through the Inter-governmental Panel on Climate Change (IPCC) in its Third Assessment Report concluded that global warming is happening. To quote: "An increasing body of observations gives a collective picture of a warming world and other changes in the climate system."

The Philippines have started to experience the effects of this phenomena with the massive flooding in the Philippines like Metro Manila, Pangasinan province and other places brought by typhoons "Ondoy" and "Pepeng", which caused the loss of lives and properties. In India, flooding brought by heavy rainfall left 250 dead and 2.5 million people homeless, 5 million people in need of food (as posted in online news hour October, 2009). On the other hand, Indonesia was hit by a deep-sea earthquake and tsunami which left 169 people dead.

With these natural disasters happening in different parts of the world, the stakeholders of the tourism and hospitality industry, which largely depend on natural and cultural resources, were once more challenged to undertake measures to help address environmental concerns. Thus, the need for tourism and hospitality industry to further engage in environment related studies and projects remains imperative.

Business enterprises around the world have made statements on how their operations impact the environment in various areas over time. This awareness heightened the tourism and hospitality industry as food and lodging companies investigate and initiate green projects that promote energy efficiency and sustainable business practices.

They are designed to sustain natural capital, minimize pollution and waste, and create healthy, productive environments. Green initiatives also are fast becoming a requirement for conducting business with global enterprise customers along the entire supply chain.

Furthermore, due to technological advancements, more and more people can travel at an easier and faster rate by air (Gossling and Hall, 2006). Due to the development of transportation and infrastructure, long haul travel (defined as travel between continents or from 1,000 miles) will be more possible. To date, there are very few studies that explore the environmental impacts of travel and tourism in the transportation sector in the destination region. As the demand for more popular mode of transport in travelling to other countries/continents improves, the need to conduct further studies on how to address mitigating factors on the impact of air and land travel likewise increases.

As a point of departure, this paper focused on cycling as an alternative form of transportation upon arriving in the destination with the Marikina City Bikeways Programme in the Philippines as the main subject of the study.

15.2 BACKGROUND OF THE STUDY

Marikina City is known as the Shoe Capital of the Philippines and currently holds the Guiness Book of Records as the city with the Largest Shoe. It used to be part of Morong Rizal before it became one of the four cities and thirteen towns of Metro Manila in 1975 through Presidential Decree (PD) no. 824. It is a vibrant growing city, with a land area of 2,150 hectares, 2 districts, 16 Barangays (local government unit) and with approximately a population of 490,612.

The researchers chose the city of Marikina because it is the only city in Manila which has established an innovative programme in promoting cycling through the Marikina Bikeways Project. A paper presented in the national conference on Environmentally Sustainable Transport in 2007 pointed that Marikina is an excellent site because the city's transport congestion has not yet reached intolerable levels. Based on 1996 MMUTIS, about 10,500 daily trips (2.9% of all trips) are still made by bicycle in Marikina in comparison to 160,200 trips (1.7%) approximately made by bicycles in Metro Manila.

15.3 STATEMENT OF THE PROBLEM

This study aimed to be the basis for further studies in order to achieve more concrete actions in developing cycling or cycle tourism in the Philippines as an alternative form of transportation.

The central question it sought to answer was: "How can we develop and promote cycling as an alternative means of transportation both for locals and tourists in Marikina City?" To answer this, the researchers made a study on the ACCESS and Bikeways Programme of Marikina City and provided recommendations for future actions.

15.4 REVIEW OF RELATED LITERATURE AND STUDIES

15.4.1 Tourism and Sustainability

The tourism industry is the world's largest service industry and undoubtedly contributes to the economic growth and development of the country. It can also pave the way for the industrialization of rural areas which will benefit the local communities in terms of employment, income and better living conditions. Nonetheless, it is important to seriously consider the economic, socio-cultural and environmental costs of tourism activities in the local, national and global scale.

To quote, "If our economies are to flourish, if global poverty is to be banished, and if the wellbeing of the world's people (is to be) enhanced—not just in this generation but in succeeding generations—we must make sure that we must take care of the natural environment and resources on which our economic activity depends." (Brown, 2005).

Tourism must be recognized as a long-term renewable resource. The Brundtland Commission defined sustainable tourism as "meeting the needs of the present without compromising the ability of future generations to meet their own needs." Narasalah (2004) questioned if the concept of sustainable tourism is an illusion or a realistic alternative.

To attain sustainability, Narasaiah advocates for "responsible" tourism where the government is an important agent to regulate and control the tourism industry in order to strike a balance between economic benefits and environmental protection. The term "responsible" tourism refers to ecotourism which is defined by The International Ecotourism Society (TIES) as "responsible travel to natural areas that conserves the environment and improves the well being of local people" (Gorham and Rice, 2008:38). Ecotourism and sustainable tourism development promote tourism as being environment-friendly and contribute in the preservation and conservation of the environment.

15.4.2 Tourism Policy

Sustainable tourism development can be sustained through formulation of tourism policies. Tourism policy is defined as a set of regulations, rules, guidelines, directives, development/promotion objectives and strategies that provide a framework for an organization's or individual's decisions both on a daily and long-term basis (Goeldner and Ritchie, 2006). Policy-making is a continuous process which is applicable to the way tourism issues are considered by government bodies (Page and Connell, 2008). These policies are formed based on the destination's vision. As pointed by Goeldner and Ritchie, the destination vision sets out all the over-all nature of tourism in a destination. The elements of a destination's vision are the government's values and principles. In this case, that of the Marikina City government.

15.4.3 Tourism and Transportation

The World Tourism Organization (WTO) predicts that tourist arrivals will reach 1 billion in 2010 and by 2020, international arrivals will reach a 1.6 billion mark. While globalization increases the mobility of people and will subsequently increase tourist arrivals and tourism receipts in a destination region like the Philippines, it inadvertently causes pollution of the atmosphere due to road and air traffic.

Gossling and Hall (2006) contended that the farther one travels, the greater will be the environmental impact of tourism away from the destination. They further observed that most studies on environmental impact of tourism in the destination region were focused on the grave effects of travel transporting the tourists to and from the origin to the destination region.

To quote: "From a global perspective, transport produces approximately 20% of carbon emissions and smaller shares of the other five greenhouse gases covered under the Kyoto Protocol. According to International Energy Agency Statistics, the transport sector's share of world greenhouse gas (GHG) emissions increased from about 19% in 1971 to 23% in 1997 (PIPCC, 2001), with CO_2 from combustion of fossil fuels, the predominant GHG produced by transport, accounting for over 95% of the annual global warming potential produced by the sector (IPCC, 2001). The transport dimension is clearly critical in understanding the impacts of tourism because, although transport is responsible for about one-fifth of worldwide energy consumption, approximately two-third of transport energy demand in OECD is from passenger travel." (Gossling and Hall 2006:306)

The increase in air traffic also increases the use of nonrenewable resources such as oil and gasoline. It is ironic that with the rising cost of fuel due to the scarcity of resources, there is an emergence of low cost carriers that are budget, no-frills airlines that reinforce the notion that travelling by air is cheap. It is also paradoxical that the impact of tourism mobility also becomes the factor that "leads to irreversible environmental change", as noted by Gossling and Hall (2006).

On the other side of the spectrum are studies on urban greening advocate activities which promote green spaces, ecotours, organic food stores and sustainable transportation options (Dodds and Jopp, 2001). Sustainable development should not only focus on the destination but also on the act of transporting tourists predominantly by air travel which continue to contribute to environmental degradation.

Moreover, modal shifts caused by travel friendly initiatives may lead to significant effects on the consumption of energy and greenhouse gas emissions associated with land-based visitor travel. Research findings contribute to the growing theoretical and applied strategies needed to create more sustainable forms of tourism-destination development (Kelly, Haider and Williams, 2007).

15.4.4 Cycling as an Alternative Transportation

A study by Cornwell entitled, "Bikes and the Environment, facts on the benefits of biking" (2009) presented how biking helps to reduce the use of fossil fuel. Bicycling as transportation is recommended by the Union of Concerned Scientists as a personal way to stop global climate change. Figure 15.1 shows the increase of carbon dioxide emissions of cars from 1960 to 2000 while biking adds no harmful gases at all.

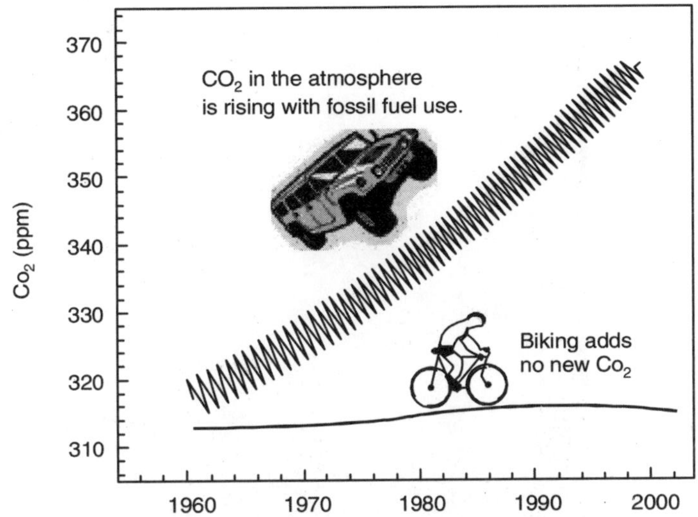

FIGURE 15.1 Increase of carbon dioxide emissions of cars from 1960 to 2000 while biking adds no harmful gases at all.

Motorized deriving emits gases such as carbon monoxide, volitle organic compounds, nitrogen oxides and carbon dioxide which cause air pollution harmful to the environment. All these things are bad for human health, for ecosystems, and eventually for future generations. People are working on technology to make driving more efficient, but despite technological improve-ments, the main problem is that people are driving more than ever before.

There are 4.2 pounds of carbon monoxide, 0.3 pounds of hydrocarbons, 0.4 pounds of nitrogen oxides and 94 pounds of carbon dioxide that a single car can produce for every 100 miles it travels. In contrast to motorized modes of transport, the bicycle is one of the most environment-friendly means of transport. Unlike carbon monoxide and hydrocarbons which contribute significantly to the global warming phenomenon, bicycle produces no harmful elements to the environment. Biking does not require heavy fuel sources and it helps in preserving the planet's diminishing natural resources. Moreover, the noise created by a bicycle is negligible that it does not add to noise pollution.

Cycling is said to be the most sustainable form of tourist transport (Lumsdon and Tolley, 2004; Page and Connell, 2008) one can use because being non-motorized, it does not require fuel and does not always have a major impact on the built and physical environment. Aside from walking, cycling has minimal environmental impact, limited infrastructure requirements and is a good form of physical exercise. As discussed in the study by Lumsdon and Tolley (2004), cycling is already a popular form of transport in European countries such as Denmark, Germany and the Netherlands. In addition, Page and Connell (2008) cited that New Zealand has distinct patterns of cycle tourism.

In the Philippines, the promotion of cycling and improved pedestrian access has resurfaced in Metro Manila. The Metropolitan Manila Development Authority (MMDA) has

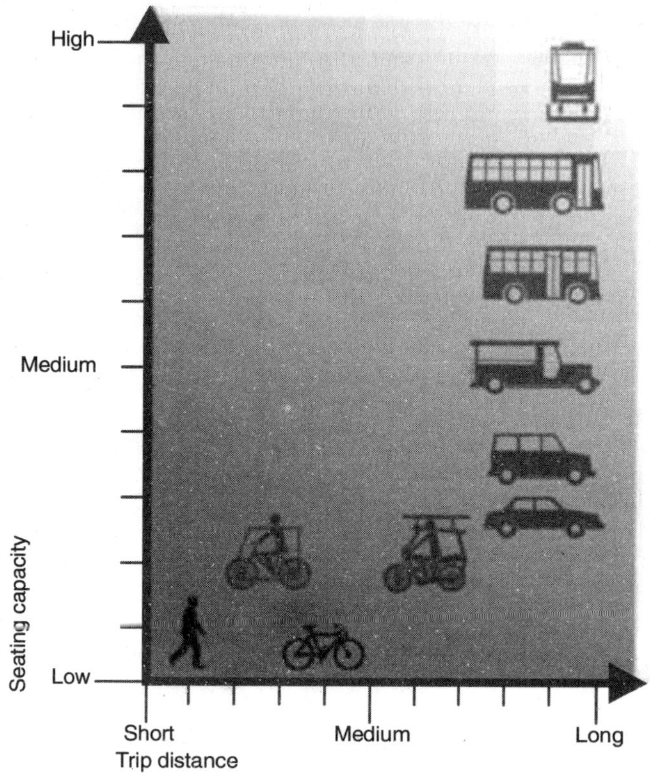

Figure 15.2 Hierarchy of transport modes in the Philippines.

in the blue print the creation of a network of bikeways and footpaths in the metropolis. It is expected that improving bike and walk ways will result in a reduction of private car use and attract private car users to shift to public transport. When the use of private cars is reduced and public transport patronage is increased, problems on fuel consumption, traffic congestion, and air quality will be addressed properly.

15.5 CONCEPTUAL FRAMEWORK

The World Travel and Tourism Council (WTTC) advocates for a sustainable development approach in economic and tourism development. This concept is not new and works on the premise that it is interdependent, multidisciplinary, with underlying politics and powers involved.

In order to promote and develop cycling as an alternative transportation to both tourists and locals in Marikina city, this paper uses the Destination vision framework developed by (Goeldner and Ritchie, 2006) on Tourism policy, structure, content and process (Figure 15.3).

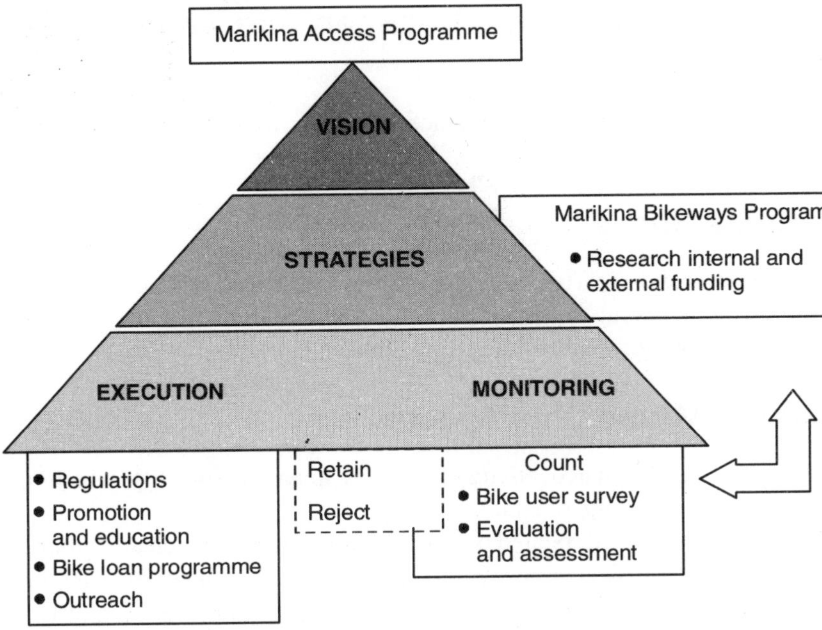

FIGURE 15.3 Conceptual framework on the Marikina Bikeways Programme.

According to Goeldner and Ritchie (2006), a vision or destination vision provides the more functional and more inspirational portrait of the ideal future that the destination hopes to bring about in some defined future. Marikina city, therefore, started with a vision on what they want their city to be.

On strategies, one of their strategy to attain their vision is the Marikina Bikeways programme, which was developed through research and government's support. The execution of the said programme, was made through the development of the following: facilities, regulations, education and promotion, financial assistance and outreach projects. Monitoring and evaluation was conducted through annual bicycle traffic counts, surveys and discussions with the stakeholders such as schools, local communities as the bases for evaluation and assessment. In order to make this programme sustainable, continuous evaluation and monitoring should be done in order to assess whether to modify, retain or reject projects/activities that were done.

15.6 FINDINGS OF THE STUDY

15.6.1 Destination's Vision

Marikina city's official website states that, Marikina envisions itself as a city that will transform itself as a "little Singapore" alleviating the residents through poverty reduction. To achieve this, the government will develop the following basic elements.

15.6.2 Ensuring Good Access between and among Different Areas of the City

It is said that the key word in urban governance is access to work, residence, transportation system, recreation centres and others.

15.6.3 Defining Space

Land uses are reasonable and clearly defined to allow judicious, practical and maximum use of the city's limited land resource. This has been addressed in the city's newly approved Zoning Ordinance and Comprehensive Land Use Plan.

15.6.4 Making Memorable Spaces

There are areas identified, designated or maintained as **areas of identity** which shall include cultural and historical zone among others.

Among other efforts exerted related to making the city more clean, green and livable were: discard of the two-stroke motorcycles, proper maintenance of car, factories and industrial machineries, anti-smoke belching measures, strict monitoring of industrial emissions and planting of trees. With almost 650,000 trees planted all over the city, Marikina city has become one of the most breathable areas in Metro Manila.

15.6.5 Marikina Bikeways Programme

Aside from greening the city by planting 10,000 trees every day, the Marikina Bikeways Programme was created to provide more access and mobility that are also environment-friendly. This programme envisions for a great number of commuting public to move around the city on bicycles. The city government created a Bikeways Project Office, headed by the city mayor herself. Two strategies were identified in the development of the said programme: through research and funding. Researches and benchmarking were done on the design of bicycle facilities, bicycle lanes, routes, signage based on international best practices in Cycle Notes prints (May 1999–2005) based in Australia and Collection of Cycle Concepts in Denmark (2000) and other cycling programmes abroad. The city also received a total of US $ 1.43 million grant from the Global Environment Facility of World Bank to develop 19 kilometres of the 52 kilometres of bikeways while Marikina's total investment in the bikeways infrastructure was more than US $ 20 million.

The implementation of the plan is seen through the development of bike facilities such as bike lanes, bicycle pathways, road signs and signage. Regulations on bicycle use and safety were also developed such as the inclusion of salient provisions regarding bicycle operations in the 2006 Traffic Management Code.

15.6.6 Changing Mindset

The Marikina City Bikeways Programme was envisioned to make the Marikina city a bicycle-friendly destination. The project was also designed not only to ease the traffic, increase mobility and provide low cost of transportation but to guarantee a healthier lifestyle to the constituents. To increase acceptance of bicycle as the preferred non-motorized transport (NMT) mode for inter city trips was among the objectives set. It was not easy for the city officials to make the community accept the sharing of the roads concept with bicycles. As of 2008, data compiled by the Marikina City Bikeways Office showed that the number of bicycle users had grown to about 8.9% of all traffic in the city. This compares to 4.25% in 1999 when the bike lanes programme was still being studied and to 5.36% in 2002 when the bike lanes started to become available to riders.

About half of the total 101,782 households report regular use of the bicycle lanes, which also implies that 1 in 2 families in the city own a bicycle. A recent survey indicated that for the residents of Marikina, the bicycle is not just for recreational use but also for utilitarian, everyday use, such as going to places of work. An ongoing survey on bicycle ownership and use conducted this year in coordination with the city government showed that 9 out of 20 respondents own a bicycle and use it for leisure, sports and going to work.

15.6.7 Bikeways Facilities

The city government did not only build bike lanes but also bike parking areas near mass transport stations like the monorail transit system (MRT). It is made of 49.7 kilometres of segregated bikeways on existing roads and 16.6 kilometres of bikeways along the Marikina river. The project featured bikeways which were found to be safe, well-paved and well-lighted with appropriate signages, informative directions and parking facilities connecting strategic areas in the city to major transport terminals and urban facilities. The Master Plan for Bikeways included the links and access to the Light Rail Transit (LRT), hotels, hospitals, markets, schools, commercial establishments and places of work.

Furthermore, a cycling track was constructed at the city's main sports park in support of the cycling enthusiasts. Rules and regulations on the use of non-motorized transport were included in the city Traffic Management Code.

15.6.8 Education and Promotion Campaign

Carlota Contreras, Officer in Charge, Marikina Bikeways Programme, said: "Bike use is almost seven to ten percent of total traffic. There is increased acceptance of bike use in Marikina because it is both practical and inexpensive." By conducting regular awareness campaign, the city government reminded the public about the benefits of biking. Among the prime activities cited were car-less days in a year and the conduct of a bike festival.

15.6.9 Kapihan

For the promotion and protection of the bikers, a road side coffee shop ("Kapihan") was established to serve as the venue for biking programme officials and enthusiasts to meet and discuss issues and concerns related to the project on Sundays. Partnering with the peacekeeping bodies was found to be an efficient strategy to ensure safety of the bikeways. Thursday nights found bike riders with cycling enforcers, with women bikers on Friday evenings at the Oval area of the city.

15.6.10 Bike to School Programme

Back to back with this project was the "bike to school programme" featuring the following: (a) Saturday bicycle clinic for the elementary pupils, (b) "lend a bike" for the secondary students and (c) the integration of the bicycle promotion to the National Service Training Programme (NSTP) for tertiary students. The cycling clinic provided awareness on the environment, and safe cycling education from bike anatomy to group biking rules. It included practical cycling component of the course and bike maintenance as well. The city government statistics showed that 49% of the youth sector surveyed did not know how to use the bicycle.

Furthermore, their records revealed the mode of travel taken by the students going to school were as follows: 22% tricycle, 20% jeepneys, 6% school service, 42% walking, 5% owned bike and 5% borrowed bike. The city government identified the safe routes to school, sought assistance from the volunteers, NGOs and traffic aides among others in providing assistance to children when biking to school. They consulted parents on safety and protection of both the child and the bicycle and contributed in the evaluation of the Bikeways programme.

Economically, the bike to school programme offered an alternative way for the students to save money in travelling around the city and in going to the school. Many trips in the city were found to be short and internal trips were of cycling distance.

15.6.11 Bicycle Safety Education Classes

The Bikeways Office also regularly conducts Bicycle Safety Education classes in the city's schools and Cycling Clinics every Saturday for children and women who want to learn to use the two-wheel transport device. Another bicycle safety project conducted in 2007 was the launching of the Bicycle Comics intended to educate the youth and children. In the same year, the city government also sponsored a poster-making contest with the theme, "The Role of Children in Bicycle Safety", wherein 28 public schools participated.

15.7 LOW COST FACTOR

15.7.1 Bike Loan Programme (Bicycle Loan Project, City Ordinance 92 Series of 2004)

The city aimed to promote biking as a better alternative to minimize transport cost while preventing pollution. The local government introduced a bike loan programme to: (a) further encourage the community to use the bike as a mode of transportation within the city, (b) offer a no interest purchase of bike and (c) increase a fitness level programme through the bike-to-work scheme. Bicycle Ownership Survey showed that 55% of families in Marikina owned or has access to a bicycle, majority of which (or 22%) is used for work purposes. To date, Marikina City has a total of 23 bicycle shops. One of the bicycle shops that benefitted from this programme was John-Wilky, a bicycle shop in Marikina since 1978. To date, this shop has loaned more than 200 mountain bikes and BMX bikes to the locals.

15.7.2 Recognition

In 2005, the Marikina Bikeways project garnered recognition and awards as the "Outstanding Programme in Local Governance" by the Gawad Gallng Pook, "Cleanest City in Metro Manila" award and "Model City" award. In addition, the World Bank gave a citation to the city as one of the "Model Cities in the World" during the World Bank's Annual Bank Conference on Development Economics in June 2006, Tokyo, Japan.

15.8 SUMMARY AND CONCLUSION

Government and industry policy should focus not only on developing tourism for its economic (monetary) benefits but also in creating and effectively implementing socio-cultural and environmental regulatory frameworks that will both maintain and sustain the tourism industry in the long run and will in turn benefit not only the tourists but also the local/host communities. Marikina City has found an effective and cost efficient alternative mode of transportation with cycling for the community. Being a tourist destination known for the shoe industry, highly disciplined constituents and a clean and green city mark, the government launched another green project to minimize and control air and noise pollution through the introduction and implementation of Bikeways programme using a non-motorized transport, the bicycle. The community based green tourism oriented programme has likewise addressed the ACCESS programme of the city government for greater and much improved citywide mobility and accessibility.

It were political will and development funding that served as the key drivers to the Marikina Bikeways project. By maintaining the physical condition of the bikeways, the city government was able to achieve what they perceived before only as a dream. The city was able to reduce pollution concerns of the community. The project has made Marikina not only a tourist destination because of its famous quality footwear but as an innovative, safe to live city promoting a healthy lifestyle though biking.

The city continues to strengthen the project awareness through the following undertakings: conduct of continuous, safe cycling education and biking clinics, permanent biking training camp and playground, creation of a bicycle museum, legislation of the bicycle code of Marikina, and the conduct of bikeways experiences among the stakeholders.

Finally, though green initiatives like the introduction of bikeways may require investment as new policies and programmes are designed and implemented, these investments are returned over the long-term in the form of healthier communities to work and live.

15.9 RECOMMENDATION AND FUTURE DIRECTION

Based on the GEF Country Portfolio Evaluation in March 2008, the Marikina pilot project will only marginally contribute to the overall project target of annual reduction of about 20,000 of CO_2 equivalent, which means that it will have minor or no effect on addressing climate change.

However, as an alternative non-motorized transport, their evaluation was that the Marikina Bikeways was moderately successful in introducing a new approach to transport for replication elsewhere in the country. The project demonstrated that NMT networks are a low-cost and acceptable alternative method of city transportation over short-to-moderate distances.

With the implementation of the Bikeways programme in Marikina city, it becomes necessary to conduct a review of the Philippine Traffic Law to ensure safety and protection provisions for the cyclists should the programme be adopted as a model on a wider scale in the metropolis. Ordinances on bikeways would need to be pursued to guarantee order and safety in the communities.

However, a continuous assessment and evaluation of the Bikeways programme is necessary to further strengthen and improve the project. Furthermore, it is highly recommended to market the cycling as a mode of transportation also to the upper and middle class groups since they mostly own vehicles that cause the traffic congestion in the city.

With the local and global recognitions received, the Biking programme success is not only worth sustaining but also replicating. The sustainability of the Biking project remained one of the great challenges to the government and the community of the city of Marikina taking into consideration the new administration both at the national and local levels.

Note: The major source of all materials is from the Marikina City Government e.g., pictures, PDF files from the Office of Ms. Carlota Contreras from 2009–2010.

REFERENCES

Cruz, Reil (2000). *Principles of Tourism.* Quezon City.

Gorham, Ginger and Rice, Susan (2008). *Travel Perspectives.* Delmar/Thomson, Singapore.

Hall, Michael (2000). *Tourism Planning, Policies, Processes and Relationships.* Pearson, NY.

Hall, Michael and Gossling, Stefan (2006). *Tourism and Global Environmental Change: Ecological, Social, Economic and Political Interrelationships.* Routledge, London and NY.

Kamra, Krishan (2004). *Economics of Tourism.* Kanishka Publishers, New Delhi.

Kellly Joe, Haider Wolfgang and Williams, Peter (2007). *A Behavioral Assessment of Tourism Transportation Options for Reducing Energy Consumption and Greenhouse Gases.* Journal of Travel Research, Vol. 45, No. 3, 297–309.

Marikina City Bikeways Office (MCBO). (2006). *Accomplishment Report (*March 2006). City Government of Marikina.

Narasaiah, M.L. (2004*). Globalization and Sustainable Tourism Development.* Discovery Publishing House, New Delhi.

Page, Stephen and Connel, Joanne (2008). *Tourism: A Modern Synthesis.* Thomson Learning, Singapore.

Rachel Dodds and Marion Joppe (2001). Promoting Urban Green Tourism: The development of the other map of Toronto. *Journal of Vacation Marketing,* 2001; 7; 261.

Villegas, Bernardo and Abola, Victor (2001). *Economics: An Introduction.* 5th ed., UAAP. Manila.

Weaver, David (2004). *Tourism Management.* Singapore.

WEBSITES

http://www.marikina.gov.ph/citygov.dept.home.do. [Accessed January 17, 2007]

Cycle Notes, 1999-2005 Australia

Concepts on Cycling, 2000 Denmark

Marikina Bikeways Program, 2008

Marikina Bikeways User Guide, 2007

All materials from the Marikina City Government e.g., pictures, PDF files from the Office of Ms. Carlota Contreras from 2009–2010

Marikina City government's presentation on the MMURTRIP SUPERVISION MISSION, March 16, 2010 Marikina City.

CHAPTER

16

THE STUDY OF RELATIONSHIP BETWEEN CLIMATE AND ANNUAL TOURISM TRENDS CONDITION

Case of Tabriz, Iran

—Banafsneh M. Farahani and Jafar Mosivand

16.1 ABSTRACT

Tourism plays an important economical role for many countries. Different tourists by having various demographic profiles, travel to different destinations every day. There are a number of attributes which influence their decision making to travel to the destination in certain time and for specific purpose. Climate and weather are one of the most important attributes which affect tourists' decision making. The importance of climate in tourism is ignorable and lots of studies have been done by different perspectives in this area. This paper intends to find the influence of climate on annual tourism trends condition in the city of Tabriz, Iran which faces different climate conditions throughout the year. The study assessed the climate condition for tourism by using Tourism Climatic Index (TCI). To investigate the relationship between the climate and tourism in the city of Tabriz, inbound tourists statistics in 2010 (domestic and foreign) have been used. The result shows that due to the climate characteristics of the station of Tabriz, the highest rated rainfall is in the month of April (52.7 mm) and the lowest is in the month of August (3.2 mm). The maximum relative humidity is 57% in the month of January and the minimum is 23% in the month of June. The highest temperature can be seen in the month of July (32.7) and the lowest in the month of January (2.3). Two months of May and October have the best condition by scoring the highest CID, daily comfort index. In this regard, the best comfort index boarding is during summer time and the weather is pleasant for tourism activities.

KEYWORDS: climate, annual tourism trends, TCI index, tourism activity and Tabriz.

16.2 INTRODUCTION

Tourism is known as one of the fastest growing industries in the world, which turned out to be one of the biggest foreign incomes for lots of countries. Tourism by its variety of subset is the economical target for those areas which have something to present in this industry. With reference to its potentiality in economic development, its sensibility towards climate could not be ignored. This sensibility is more in some places while in other, it is not so obvious. In this regard, seasonality of some tourism activities required more elaboration in tourism studies. Although alternation of climate is not something which the destination can do anything about by itself, policy makers can develop their programme in a seasonal base. Even though the relation between climate and tourism has been absorbed some researchers, still lack of research in this area is obvious. Considering economical and commercial influence of climate in tourism is the part which needs to be more concerned.

De Freitas (2001, p. 3) believes that "Thus far, much of the research, specifically on climate and tourism, reported in the journal's literature, have been superficial, in that relationships between climate and tourism are assumed rather than observed and seldom objectively tested." The main aim of this paper is to uncover the influence of climate on annual tourism trends condition in the city of Tabriz, Iran since it has different climate condition during the year in order to locate the months with the best and most comfortable climate for tourists to visit the city.

16.2.1 Importance of Climate in Tourism

Regarding tourism sources, De Freitas (2001, p. 4) presents his idea as "together with geographical location, topography, landscape, flora and fauna, weather and climate constitute the natural resource-base of a place for recreation and tourism. The concept of tourism climate recognizes a climatically controlled resource, which along with weather". Hibbs (1966) in De Freitas (2001) asserts that weather in different tourism destinations varies from favourable to unfavourable. He refers to climate which can be measured and considered as an economic benefit for tourism. He believes that there are several problems while measuring the climate. "One major problem is the selection of meteorological or climatological criteria. For example, what exactly are the criteria for ideal, suitable, acceptable, or unacceptable conditions? Only after appropriate climatological criteria have been clearly identified can the key questions be answered. When is the best time to visit? What clothing equipment is needed? What are the weather hazards or climate extremes likely to be? (De Freitas, 2001, p. 5).

Becken (2010) believes that climate and weather are fundamental factors in tourists' decision making process in their pre-trip behaviour. She also refers to another importance of climate for a better operation in tourism industry. She adds: "More specifically, climate is defined as the prevailing condition observed as a long term average in a location. In contrast, weather is the manifestation of climate at a specific point in time and place." (Becken, 2010, p. 2).

Economical variables were the focus of most researches done in the area of tourism demand (Crouch, 1994; Lim et al., 2008), but climate was the destination key attribute in tourism demand (Hu and Ritchie, 1993). Moreover, climate is recognized as the major tourism resource in specific destinations like beaches (Kozak et al., 2008) or as the facilitator in other destination in the way to help tourism activities to be possible and pleasing (Gómez Martin, 2005). Gómez Martín (2005) also finds the significance of climate attributes on tourism marketing and advertisement. He asserts that while some destinations sell good weather with a "money back guarantee", other places are not receiving any request regarding their unreliable weather.

Regarding the tourist motivation, a number of studies have been done and they show the importance of destination weather on tourist motivation to visit the place (Lohmann and Kaim, 1999; Scott and Lemieux, 2009). The results of the studies done in Germany, the UK and Canada show that although destination choice is important in the timing of travel, climate is also an important factor in this matter (Lohmann and Kaim, 1999; Hamilton and Lau, 2005). This issue causes the challenges of seasonability for some tourism destination. Butler (2001) believes that climate is just one of the reasons of destination seasonability, and some other factors in tourist home countries such as school holiday influence the seasonability of the tourism activities.

In order to measure the climate suitability for tourism activities, Mieczkowski (1985) developed the Tourism Climate Index (TCI). Seven applicable climate parameters in tourism were combined in his model. The theory was used again and again by different researchers and diverse perspective. Beach tourism (Morgan, 2000 in De Freitas', 2001), climate change and global flows (Amelung et al., 2007), North American cities climate ranking and (Scott and McBoyle, 2001) are different examples of mentioned researches.

De Freitas et al. (2001) came up with the new Climate Index for Tourism (CTI). They include thermal, aesthetic and physical aspects of weather regarding beach tourism. Becken and Hay (2007), by reviewing De Freitas' (2001) classification of tourism climate facet, divided it into aesthetic, physical and thermal (Table 16.1).

Table 16.1 Facets of climate and impact on tourists

Facet of climate	*Impact on tourists*
Aesthetic	
Sunshine/cloudiness	Enjoyment, attractiveness of site
Visibility	Enjoyment, attractiveness of site
Day length	Hours of daylight available
Physical	
Wind	Blown belongings, sand, dust, etc.
Rain	Wetting, reduced visibility
Snow	Participation in activities
Ice	Personal injury, damage to property
Air quality	Health, physical well-being, allergies
Ultraviolet radiation	Health, suntan, sunburn
Thermal	
Integrated effects of air temperature wind, solar radiation, humidity, long-wave radiation, metabolic rate	Environmental stress, heat stress Physiological strain, Hypothermia Potential for therapeutic recuperation

Source: Becken and Hay (2007) after De Freitas (2001).

"The thermal component describes how comfortable the tourist feels. The physical dimension relates to non-temperature climatic conditions such as wind and rain and is important to assess whether a certain activity is possible or not. The aesthetic aspect describes a psychological perspective as the tourist enjoys certain climatic conditions, for example the light or formation of clouds" (Becken, 2010, p. 5).

16.2.2 Tourism Climate Index (TCI)

The theory of tourism climate index (TCI) was formerly brought up by Mieczkowski (1985) "as a composite measure that would systematically assess the climatic elements most relevant to the quality of the tourism experience for the 'average' tourist (i.e., the most common tourism activity of sight-seeing and shopping)" (Scott and McBoyle, 2002, p. 70). Scott and McBoyle (2002) believe that Mieczkowski (1985) build up the theory of TCI based on studies done in the area of human comfort especially in tourism activities (Burnet, 1963; Dammann, 1964; Hofer, 1967; Heurtier, 1968; Danilova, 1973; and Kandror et al., 1974 in Scott and McBoyle, 2002) and climate classification for tourism and recreation (Heurtier, 1968; Crowe, 1976).

The image of a tourism destination is an important factor both for host and guest and it absorbs lots of researchers' attention towards it. The role of climate in destination image cannot be ignored as some areas are famous for having tropical weather and the other has cold and snowy weather, which is suitable for skiing and alike tourism sports activities.

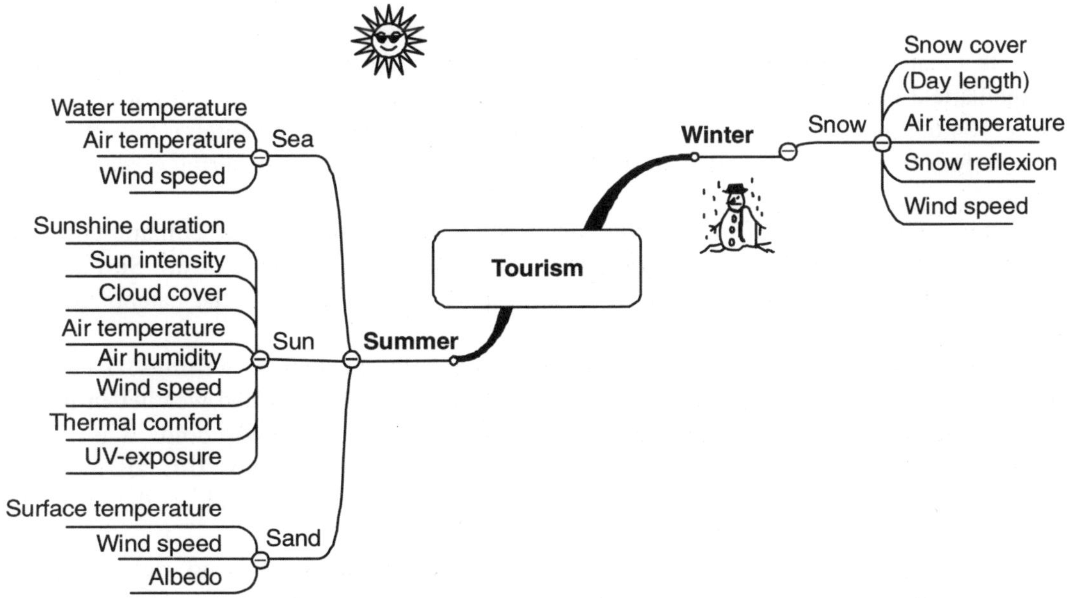

Source: Matzarakis (2006).

FIGURE 16.1 Relations between climate and tourism.

Gallarza et al. (2002) had a research about the influence of climate in destination image considering climate attributes.

What role does climate play in destination image? Not all studies of destination image include climate as an image defining attribute, as can be seen in the extensive review of destination image studies by Gallarza et al. (2002). Hamilton and Lau (2005) reviewed 25 destination image researches which climate consider as an attribute in 12 of them. They found that among 20 attributes used in those studies, climate was the 7th common attribute. Those studies which used climate and weather as one of the attributes notice that climate is one of the most significant attributes among others. Considering different tourists and different destinations the results were the same (Hu and Ritchie, 1993; Shoemaker, 1994; Kozak, 2002; and Beerli and Martin, 2004).

In the same way, Pike (2002) reviewed 142 studies related to destination image, but unfortunately just one of them specifically focused on climate as the main attribute. The study was done by Lohmann and Kaim (1999) through a survey from German citizens. They asked about essential destination characteristics and found landscape as the most fundamental attribute before price consideration. Surprisingly they found weather and bioclimate as the third and eighth important attributes, respectively.

The other study was done by Gössling et al. (2005) by conducting a survey from tourists in Zanzibar. In their result, they found that more than half of the respondents considered weather as an important factor in their decision making.

16.3 CASE STUDY

Tabriz is located in northwestern part of Iran, in East Azerbaijan province. This area has a mathematical position of 38 degrees, 12 minutes and 9 seconds in north latitude. In 2010, a total of 104,689 people have visited this city and 11,402 of them were foreign tourists. Ahour (2011) refers to traditional and historical bazaar in Tabriz as world heritage registered by UNESCO.

Tabriz area, in terms of topography and location of mountain ranges, climatic conditions and significant precipitation, has several permanent and seasonal surface flows. Surface water drainage is done by Oroomiyeh Lake, a so large part of the area is in the catchment of the lake.

Tabriz has a pleasant climate and tends to be cold. In ancient writings, Tabriz was described as having very cold climate. Even some foreign scholars put the weather in this city in the E category of the classification of coupon, which is the snowy cold. It is like the climate in cold Polar Regions, which have average temperatures below 0°C all months of the year and there are permanent glaciers in the mountains surrounding the city (Iran Meteorological Organization, 2011).

Tabriz has the constant wind, which is related to the local wind rather than the continental flows. But sometimes, it flows from Siberia and after passing the Caspian Sea shores, reaches Tabriz area and causes severe cold weather in winter and blizzards as well as general blockade. Tabriz faces early winter, which starts soon and ends late. In November, cold winter begins and continues until late April (Iran Meteorological Organization, 2011).

Tabriz has a clean and pleasant air. It has mild climate, although it was thought to be cold. In this regard, the establishment of fruit garden, vineyard and recreational area has been done since centuries ago. Due to its mild climate, it is suitable for nurturing the silkworm in the area from Tabriz to Marand.

Tabriz in present time is in row Klima C s (b), which is the classification of the Mediterranean type of coupon or summer cooling. Coupon is for the areas that have this kind of weather. The annual temperature is between 12 and 18°C with lowest temperature of –3°C up to 18°C during the year. The average of warm months of the year is between 6 and 22 and considered as dry Klima.

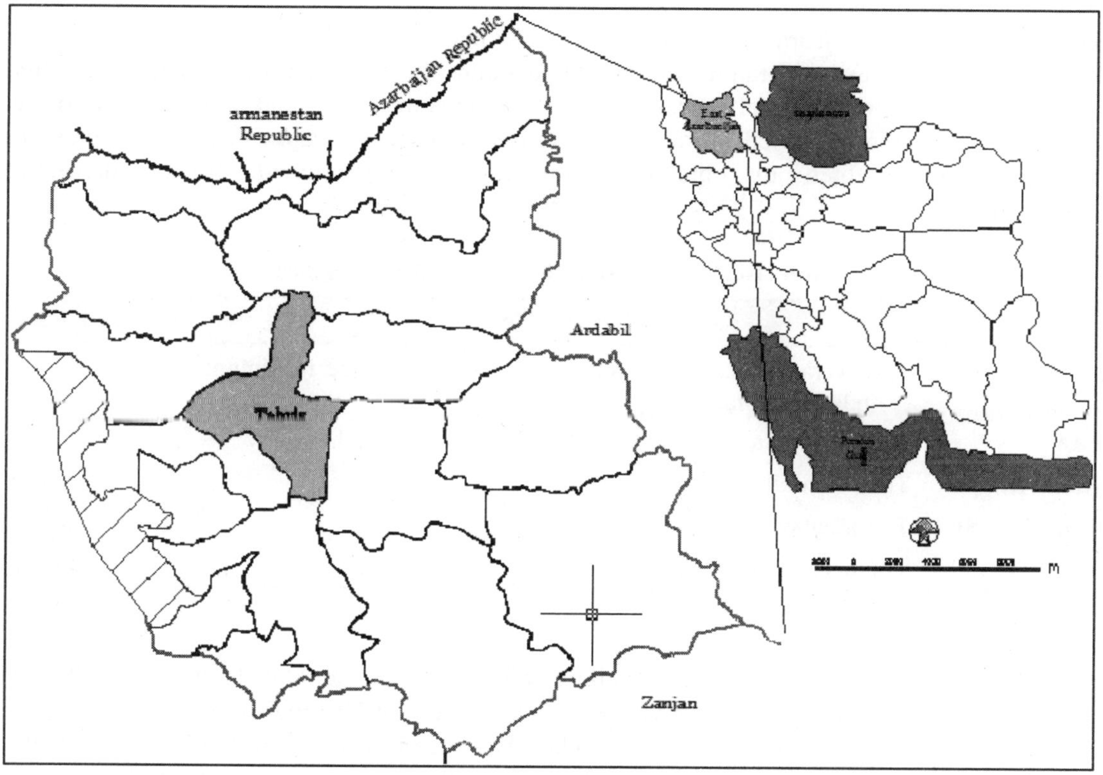

Source: Iran Statistical Centre (2011).

FIGURE 16.2 East Azerbaijan Map.

16.4 METHODOLOGY

This study aimed to evaluate the climate of the city of Tabriz. The data was used from Tabriz synoptic stations of meteorological in a 23-year period (1987–2010) as monthly average. This study assessed the climate condition for tourism by using Tourism Climatic Index (TCI). To investigate the relationship between the climate and tourism in the city of Tabriz, inbound tourists statistics in 2010 (domestic and foreign) have been used.

Daytime Comfort Index (CID) is obtained by intersection of two elements, the maximum temperature and minimum relative humidity.

Daily Comfort Index (CIA) is obtained by intersection average temperature and relative humidity.

16.4.1 TCI Index

This index is obtained from the combination of 7 indicators of climate parameters including the average maximum temperature, average temperature, average minimum relative humidity, average relative humidity, total perception, average sunshine hours and average wind speed. All these parameters are used as monthly average in these indicators. TCI index includes 5 sub indicators which are obtained from the above mentioned climate parameters (Table 16.2).

Table 16.2 TCI sub indicators and their scores

Index	*Climate variables*	*TCI score*
CID	The average maximum temperature and the average maximum relative humidity	40
CIA	The average temperature and the average relative humidity	10
Rain (R)	Total rainfall	20
Sunshine (S)	The number of sunshine hours	20
Wind (W)	The average wind speed	10

Source: Mieczkowski (1985)

CID and CIA are considered as welfare indicators that their levels are obtained from psychometrics diagram which ASHRAE (American Society of Heating, Refrigerating and Air-conditioning Engineers) thermal comfort standard has been drawn. According to the definition of ASHRAE, thermal comfort is the mental condition that can be expressed satisfaction with the environment. The person in thermal comfort condition does not prefer warmer or colder weather (Ranjbar et al., 2009). Tourism climate index (TCI) is obtained from the following formula:

$$TCI = 2[(4 \times CID) + CIA + (2 \times P) + (2 \times S) + W]$$

All indices used in TCI range from 5 (ideal) to 3 (extremely unpleasant) in which 5 is the most desirable rating in TCI formula. At the last stage, after the calculation of TCI for every month in a year, the index values obtained the range from 30 to 100. In this calculation, 100 is rated as an ideal condition and 30 is considered as an impossible situation for tourism activities.

16.5 ANALYSIS AND RESULT

Due to the climate characteristics of the station of Tabriz, the highest rated rainfall is in the month of April (52.7 mm) and the lowest is in the month of August (3.2 mm). The maximum relative humidity is 57% in the month of January and the minimum is 23% in the month of June. The highest temperature can be seen in the month of July (32.7) and the lowest in the month of January (2.3). Table 16.3. shows the climate index of each month separately. CID, CIA, rainfall, sunshine and wind are separately scored for the whole year.

Table 16.3 Tabriz monthly climate index

Index	*Jan.*	*Feb.*	*Mar.*	*Apr.*	*May*	*June*	*July*	*Aug.*	*Sep.*	*Oct.*	*Nov.*	*Dec.*
CID	1.1	1.75	2.5	3.1	4.7	1.1	0.1	0.1	2	4.5	2.2	1.75
CIA	0.5	1.1	1.8	2.3	3.1	5	4	4	4.5	2.5	1.8	1.2
Rain (R)	4.5	4.5	4	3.5	4	4.5	4.5	5	5	4.5	4.5	4.5
Sunshine (S)	2	2	2.5	3	4	5	5	5	5	3.5	2.5	2
Wind (W)	4.5	3.5	3	3	3	3	3	3	3	3.5	4	4

Source: Iran Meteorological Organization (2011).

It should be noted that the daily comfort index (CID) is the time tourists have the most active time. Accordingly, Table 16.3 shows that just two months of May and October have the best condition.

Tourism climate index (TCI): Since the primary factors of all indicators have been calculated, they just needed to be inserted in the final formula:

Jan. = 2[(4*CID) + CIA + (2*R) + (2*S) + W]

Jan. = 2[(4*1.1) + 0.5 + (2*4.5) + (2*2) + 4.5] = **TCI** = 2[4.4 + 0.5 + 9 + 4 + 4.5] = 44.8

Feb. = 2[(4*1.75) + 1.1 + (2*4.5) + (2*2) + 3.5] = **TCI** = 2[7 + 1.1 + 9 + 4 + 3.5] = 49.2

Mar. = 2[(4*2.5) + 1.8 + (2*4) + (2*2.5) + 3] = **TCI** = 2[10 + 1.8 + 8 + 5 + 3] = 55.6

Apr. = 2[(4*3.1) + 2.3 + (2*3.5) + (2*3) + 3] = **TCI** = 2[12.4 + 2.3 + 7 + 6 + 3] = 61.4

May = 2[(4*4.7) + 3.1 + (2*4) + (2*4) + 3] = **TCI** = 2[18.8 + 3.1 + 8 + 8 + 3] = 81.8

June = 2[(4*1.1) + 5 + (2*4.5) + (2*5) + 3] = **TCI** = 2[4.4 + 5 + 9 + 10 + 3] = 62.8

July = 2[(4*0.1) + 4 + (2*4.5) + (2*5) + 3] = **TCI** = 2[0.4 + 4 + 9 + 10 + 3] = 52.8

Aug. = 2[(4*0.1) + 4 + (2*5) + (2*5) + 3] = **TCI** = 2[0.4 + 4 + 10 + 10 + 3] = 54.8

Sep. = 2[(4*2) + 4.5 + (2*5) + (2*5) + 3] = **TCI** = 2[8 + 4.5 + 10 + 10 + 3] = 71

Oct. = 2[(4*4.5) + 2.5 + (2*4.5) + (2*3.5) + 3.5] = **TCI** = 2[9 + 2.5 + 9 + 7 + 3.5] = 46

Nov. = 2[(4*2.2) + 1.8 + (2*4.5) + (2*2.5) + 4] = **TCI** = 2[4.4 + 1.8 + 9 + 5 + 4] = 48.4

Dec. = 2[(4*1.75) + 1.2 + (2*4.5) + (2*2) + 4] = **TCI** = 2[7 + 1.2 + 9 + 4 + 4] = 50.4

According to the calculations above and the tables below, the best month for tourism in the city of Tabriz is May with excellent quality value. September with very good quality value is the second month. Finally, two months of April and June are good in terms of tourism climate comfort.

Table 16.4 TCI scores and values

TCI score	*TCI descriptive value*
90–100	Ideal
80–89	Excellent
70–79	Very good
60–69	Good
50–59	Acceptable
40–49	Poor
30–39	Unfavourable
20–29	Very unfavourable
10–19	Extremely unfavourable
00–09	Other

Source: Ranjbar et al. (2010)

Table 16.5 Monthly result of climate condition

	Jan.	*Feb.*	*Mar.*	*Apr.*	*May*	*June*	*July*	*Aug.*	*Sep.*	*Oct.*	*Nov.*	*Dec.*
Condition	Poor	Poor	Acceptable	Good	Excellent	Good	Acceptable	Acceptable	Very good	Poor	Poor	Acceptable

As far as the best time for tourism regarding to climate has been clarified, the relationship between climate and tourists should be measured. In this regard, the Pearson correlation coefficient is used, which was equal to 0.422%. The correlation coefficient is insignificant and the lack of consistency between climate and tourism in the city of Tabriz is because of the winter sports, since the cold season in each year attracts many sport tourists. Figure 16.3 shows the changes of climate index and tourist arrivals.

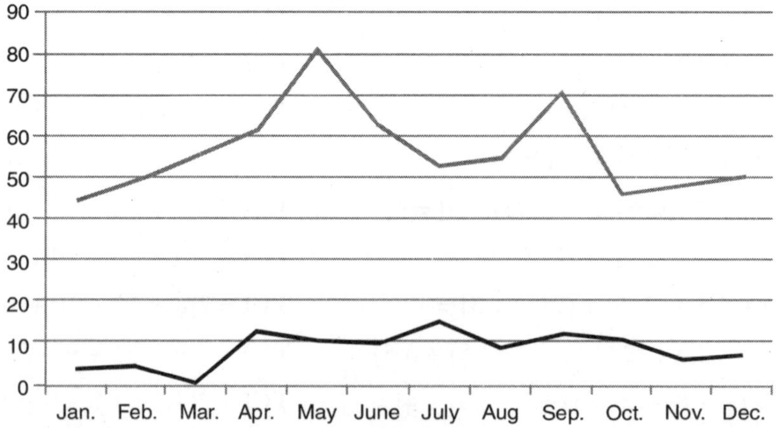

FIGURE 16.3 Tabriz climate index and tourist arrival.

Table 16.6 Tabriz tourist arrival

	Tourists arrival to Tabriz 2010		
Months	*Foreign*	*Iranian*	*Total*
April	1,338	11,898	13,236
May	2,061	8,917	10,978
June	1,171	9,377	10,548
July	1,175	14,402	15,577
August	541	8,589	9,130
September	957	11,766	12,723
October	1,292	9,791	11,083
November	748	4,998	5,746
December	1,010	6,281	7,291
January	382	2,999	3,381
February	636	3,963	4,599
March	91	306	397
Total	11,402	93,287	104,689

Source: East Azarbaijan Cultural Heritage Handicraft and Tourism Organization (2010).

16.7 CONCLUSION AND RECOMMENDATION

The results of lots of studies show that climate and weather are deeply connected with tourism and recreational activities. In this regard, tour operators, travel agencies, tourism planners, stakeholders and other related organizations should plan their programme according to tourism climate index of their destination. Cancellation of any tours due to bad weather causes tourists unsatisfaction and if the organizer is concerned about probable changes in the climate, such cancellations can never happen. Moreover, cities like Tabriz cannot accommodate tourists in every month of the year with the same tourist activities. The result of this study shows that Tabriz has variety of climate throughout the year. This climate distinctiveness of cities like Tabriz can attract unsimilar tourists in different months by dissimilar weather. In this regard, more tourism activities are needed to be provided for dissimilar tourists, concerning the suitable climate for that particular activity. Additionally, the result gained through the analysis of this study shows that among 12 months of the year, May is the best time for tourism activities (TCI = 81.8, Excellent) and January in improper time for the mentioned activities (TCI = 44.8, Poor).

REFERENCES

Ahour, I. (April 2011). The qualities of Tabriz historical bazaar in urban planning and the integration of its potentials into megamalls. *Journal of Geography and Regional Planning*, Vol. 4(4), pp. 199–215, April 2011.

Amelung, B., Nicholls, S. and Viner, D. (2007). Implications of Global Climate Change for Tourism Flows and Seasonality. *Journal of Travel Research*, Vol. 45, pp. 285–296.

Becken, S. and Hay, J. (2007). *Tourism and Climate Change—risks and opportunities*. Clevedon: Channel View Publications.

Becken, Susanne (2010). The Importance of Climate and Weather for Tourism. LEaP. February, 2010.

Beerli, A. and Martin, J.D. (2004). Tourists' characteristics and the perceived image of tourist destinations: A quantitive analysis—A case study of Lanzarote, Spain. *Tourism Management*, Vol. 25(5), 623–626.

Burnet, L. (1963). Villégiature et tourism sur les Côtes de France. Librairie Hachette, Paris, France.

Butler, R. (2001). Seasonality in tourism: Issues and implications, pp. 5–22. In T. Baum and S. Lundtorp (Eds.), *Seasonality in Tourism*. London: Pergamon.

Crouch, G.I. (1994). The Study of International Tourism Demand: a Survey of Practice, *Journal of Travel Research*, Vol. 32(4), 41–55.

Crowe, R.B. (1976). A climatic classification of the Northwest Territories for recreation and tourism. Environment Canada, Toronto, Canada.

Dammann, W. (1964) Die Schwule als Klimfaktor. Beriche zur Deutschen Landeskunde, Vol. 32(1): pp. 100–109.

Daniel, Scott and Geoff, McBoyle (2002). Using a 'tourism climate index' to examine the implications of climate change for climate as a tourism resource. Adaptation and Impacts Research Group, Environment Canada, at the Faculty of Environmental Studies, University of Waterloo, Waterloo, Ontario, Canada, N2L 3G1.

Danilova, N.A. (1973). Klimat pribaltiki i prodolzhitelnost perioda blagopriyatnogo dia turizma. In Kolalev, J.A. (Ed.) Geografia i turism. Voprosy geografii, Vol. 93: pp. 164–176.

De Freitas, Chris. R. (Dec. 2001). Theory, Concepts and Methods in Tourism Climate Research. Proceedings of the First International Workshop on Climate, Tourism and Recreation.

East Azarbayjan Cultural Heritage Handicraft and Tourism Organization (2010), retrieved from http://www.eachto.ir in June 2011.

Gallarza, M.G., I.G. Saura and H.C. Garcia (2002). Destination image: towards a conceptual framework. *Annals of Tourism Research*, Vol. 29(1), pp. 56–78.

Gómez Martín, Ma. (2005). Weather, Climate and Tourism. A Geographical Perspective. *Annals of Tourism Research*, Vol. 32(3), pp. 571–591.

Gössling, S., M. Bredberg, A. Randow, P. Svensson and E. Swedlin (2005). Tourist perceptions of climate change: A study of international tourists in Zanzibar. Climatic Change, submitted.

Hall (Ed.). *Tourism and Global Environmental Change*. London: Routledge.

Hamilton, J.M. and Lau, M. (2005). The Role of Climate Information in Tourist Destination Choice Decision-Making, pp. 229–250. In Gössling, S. and C.M. Hall (Eds.), Tourism and Global Environmental Changes. London: Roufledge).

Heurtier, R. (1968). Essaie de climatologie touristique synoptique de L'Europe occidentale et Mediterranéene pendant la saison d'été. La Météorologie, 7: 71–107 and 8: 519–566.

Hofer, K. (1967). Klimabehaglichkeit und Kurort. Wiener Medizinische Wochenschrift, 16: 444–446.

Hu, Y. and Ritchie, J. (1993). Measuring destination attractiveness: a contextual approach. *Journal of Travel Research*, Vol. 32(20), pp. 25–34.

Iran Meteorological Organization (2011). Retrieved from http://www.irimo.ir/farsi/amar/map/province/Azar-sharghi.asp in June 2010.

Iran statistical centre. Retrieved from www.amar.org.ir in May 2011.

Kandror, I.D., Demina, D.M. and Ratner, Y.M. (1974). Fiziologicheskye principy sanitarno—Klimatologicheskogo rayonirovanya territoriè SSSR. Moskva: Meditsina.

Kozak, N., Uysal, M. and Birkan, I. (2008). An analysis of cities based on tourism supply and climatic conditions in Turkey. *Tourism Geographies*, Vol. 10(1), pp. 81–97.

Lim, C., Min, J.C.H. and McAleer, M. (2008). Modelling income effects on long and short haul international travel from Japan. *Tourism Management*, Vol. 29(6), pp. 1099–1109.

Lohmann, M. and Kaim, E. (1999). Weather and holiday preference—image, attitude and experience. *Revue de Tourisme*, Vol. 2, pp. 54–64.

Mieczkowski, Z. (1985). The tourism climatic index: a method of evaluating world climates for tourism. *The Canadian Geographer*, Vol. 29: pp. 220–233.

Pike, S. (2002). Destination image analysis—a review of 142 papers from 1973 to 2000. *Tourism Management*, Vol. 23, pp. 541–549.

Ranjbar. F. (2009). Evaluation of climate conditions for tourism development by using TCI: case of Fars Province. MS Thesis. Department of Geopraphy. University of Tehran.

Ranjbar, F., Moghbel, F., and Arsalani, M. (Spring 2010). The study of relationship between climate conditions and tourist arrival in Marvdasht. *Journal of Natural Geography*. 3rd year. No. 7.

Scott, D. and Lemieux, C. (2009). Weather and Climate Information for Tourism. White Paper, commissioned by the World Meteorological Organisation.

Scott, D. and McBoyle, G. (Spring 2001). Using a 'tourism climate index' to examine the implications of climate change for climate as a natural resource for tourism. A. Matzarakis and C. de Freitas (Eds.). Proceedings of the First International Workshop on Climate, Tourism and Recreation. 5–10 October 2001: International Society of Biometeorology, Commission on Climate, Tourism and Recreation, Greece.

Shoemaker, S. (1994). Segmenting the U.S. travel market according to benefits realized. *Journal of Travel Research*, Vol. 32(3), pp. 8–21.

INDEX

Adventure tour, 55
Adverse publicity, 185
Agri-tourism, 45
    advantages of, 45
    scope of, 45
    principles of, 46
Amenity forest, 33
Andhra Pradesh Tourism Development Corporation (APTDC), 215
Areas of identity, 234
Artisan, 209, 214

Bicycle comics, 236
Biking programme, 238
Biodiversity, 163, 164, 166
Border tourism, 11
Brand, 205
    personality, 205

Case study approach, 91
Casuality analysis, 224
Centre for Rural Tourism (CRT), 42
CESTUR, 5
CIA, 246
CID, 246
Cleaning methods, 100
Climate, 241, 245, 248
    change, 165
    condition, 240
    in destination image, 243
    parameters, 246
Cob architecture, 17
Co-branding, 205
Cold weather, 244
Comfort Index (CID), 247
Community, 127
    assistance, 30
    attitudes, 130, 132
    impact, 138
    participation, 7
    wildlife management, 75
Competence trust, 203, 204
Conflict, 74
Conjoint analysis, 109, 112
Conservation development paradigm, 76
Consultation meetings, 214
Coromandel coast, 211
Corporate Social Responsibility (CSR), 70, 90
Cost
    benefits, 86
    factors, 35
Creative cities, 7
Creativity, 110
Crisis, 180, 181, 187, 190, 193
    anatomy, 188
    communication, 180
    incubation, 187
    management manual, 191
    management taskforce, 190
Critical competency, 193
    shortages (of resources), 22
Cultural
    attractions, 5
    dimension, 117
    heritage, 20
    and heritage tourism, 7, 45
    tourism, 3, 45
    tourist, 5
Cycle tourism, 228
Cycling, 228

Dependent variable, 224
Design-cum-training workshops, 213
Destination, 27
    seasonability, 242
    vision, 230, 233
Development funding, 237
Disaster, 158, 181, 182, 193
Documentation, 92, 97

E-commerce, 202
Ecology, 31
Economic
    coalescence, 109
    opportunities, 76
    recovery strategy, 75
    and socio-cultural items, 139
    stability, 49
    viability, 189
Ecotourism, 45, 57
Education and tourism, 224
Educational development, 221
Endogenous tourism project, 213
Energy management, 104
Entrepreneurial opportunities, 128
Entrepreneurship, 217, 218
Environmental
    change, 231
    check list, 97
    conservation, 86
    costs, 87
    plan, 97
Exploratory study, 4

Factor analysis, 133
    rotation, 133
Factorial design, 113
Farm tourism, 44
Forestry museum, 33
Fossil fuel, 230
FSIAS, 131

Global warming, 227
Granger causality model, 222
Green tourism, 155
Growing city, 228

Human resources, 20

Impact generation, 74
Independent variable, 224
Indicator, 32
Inductive approach, 36
Information, 173
International terrorism, 186
International Union for the Conservation of Nature, 26
Interviews, 92
Item generation, 133

Kalamkari, 210
Kapihan, 235

LATIAS, 131
Liquid wastes, 154
Living culture, 13
Local
    economy, 192
    knowledge, 178
Luxury-tented camp, 72

Macro environment, 8
MACTIAS, 141
Main suppliers, 99
Man-made resources, 31
Marikina, 228
Marketing Malaysia, 129
Millennium Development Goals (MDGs), 76
Mitigation strategies, 75
Models, 189
Motivational factor (for tourists), 62
Mountain regions, 154
Multiplier effect, 43, 216

National Institute of Anthropology and History (NIAH), 12
Natural disasters, 193
Non-motorized transport, 235
Normative model, 3, 6, 8

Observation, 93
Online booking, 197
    decisions, 198

Peneda-Gerês National Park (PNPG), 116
Perverse incentives, 162
Pilgrim sites, 43
Pilgrimage tourism, 58
Political crisis, 188
Prais–Winsten GLS regression model, 225

Predictability trust, 202
Profile, 112
Project awareness, 237
Protected areas, 162
Public transport information, 174

Qualmark
- assessments, 105
- rating, 99, 103

Questionnaire, 92

Random and purposeful sampling, 77
Random sample, 35
Recreation, 31
Relationship trust, 205
Reliability test, 133
Reputation, 182
Research instrument, 37
Resource sharing, 82
Responsible tourism, 30, 230
Risk perception, 187
Rural tourism, 42, 159, 212, 215

Satisfactory level, 38
Scale, 134
Scandic, 89
Service provider, 221
Socio-cultural impact, 134
Socio-economic
- benefits, 209
- condition, 221
- viability, 43
- welfare, 221

Staff training, 103
Standard of living, 29
Stated preferences, 108
Statistical artifact, 134
Strategic
- guidance, 16
- level, 185

Structured questionnaires, 58
Sustainable
- cultural and heritage development, 21
- development, 27
- development approach, 232
- indicators, 26, 32
- tourism, 27, 222

Sustainability, 85
- committee, 104

Symbolic capital, 117

Tasks, 200
Therapeutic recuperation, 242
Tourism, 181
- activities 241, 242
- climate index, 243
- community, 186
- crisis, 184, 186
- destination management framework, 190
- destinations, 110, 184
- impact attitude scale, 131
- industry, 194
- information centres, 22
- managers, 187
- markets/segments, 192
- planning exercises, 165
- product, 30, 212
- resource potential, 58
- resources, 115
- stakeholders, 21

Tourist arrival, 221
Traditional practices, 157
Training, 217
Transit
- points, 173
- system, 235

Transport information, 171
Tripadvisor, 203
Trust, 201
- and its attributes, 202

Trust-loyalty relationship, 206

Urbanization, 140

Vandalism, 140
Varimax rotation, 133
Voluntary certification, 160
Vulnerability, 158

Water sources, 72
Welfare indicators, 246
Wildlife security, 76
Word-of-mouth communication, 58
World heritage, 244
WTTC, 232

Zero-tolerant tourism, 43

